MORE PRAISE FOR AMERICA INVADES

"Simultaneously readable and reference material, destined to become the go-to for those who want to understand America's place—literally anywhere—in the world."

William Bernstein
The Birth of Plenty and *A Splendid Exchange*

"The writing is brisk and chatty, the history is fascinating, and the message is arresting, no matter where you are on the political spectrum. This should be required reading by American presidents."

William Dietrich
The Three Emperors: An Ethan Gage Adventure

"I would have lost the bet. I had no idea that the United States over its history has invaded almost HALF the countries on the globe. That's an astounding amount of K-rations and munitions and mayhem, however well-intentioned. Authors Laycock and Kelly, with breezy wit and a dogged pursuit of neutrality, deliver a country-by-country compendium of U.S. intervention. Use it as reference; or, read it cover to cover, sea to shining sea, for the adventures and misadventures of American attacks on foreign soil. An eye-opener! A mind-expander! Can an attack of Bhutan or Lichtenstein be far off? One important final note: this book is written with respect for the men and women of the U.S. armed forces."

Richard Zacks
The Pirate Coast: Thomas Jefferson, the First Marines and the Secret Mission of 1805 and *An Underground Education*

AMERICA INVADES

HOW WE'VE INVADED
OR BEEN MILITARILY INVOLVED
WITH ALMOST EVERY COUNTRY ON EARTH

Christopher Kelly and Stuart Laycock

BOOK PUBLISHERS NETWORK
Changing the World One Book at a Time

Book Publishers Network
P.O. Box 2256
Bothell • WA • 98041
Ph • 425-483-3040
www.bookpublishersnetwork.com

Five percent of all sales from America Invades will be donated to military charities.

10 9 8 7 6 5 4 3 2 1

Printed in the United States of America

LCCN   2014946383
ISBN   978-1-940598-42-0

Kelly, Christopher (Christopher Robert), 1959-

America invades : how we've invaded or been militarily involved with almost every country on earth / Christopher Kelly and Stuart Laycock. -- Bothell WA : Book Publishers Network, [2014]

  pages ; cm.

  ISBN: 978-1-940598-42-0
  Includes glossary and index.
  Summary: America has invaded 43% of the countries in the world, and it has been militarily involved with nearly all the rest. This book offers a global tour of America's military activity, arranged by country, relating a history of gallantry and sacrifice as America has spread its power and influence worldwide.--Publisher.

Editor: Julie Scandora
Cover Designer: Blaine Donnelson
Book Designer: Melissa Vail Coffman
Production: Scott Book
Indexer: Carolyn Acheson

Photo permission asked for but not received from USS *Constitution*.

Dedicated to Robert E. Kelly, PFC US Army, 1929-2008

TABLE OF CONTENTS

ACKNOWLEDGMENTS

WE WOULD LIKE TO THANK OUR MANY FRIENDS whose assistance made this book possible. I (Chris Kelly) would like to thank my late grandmother Georgina Van Rensselaer for encouraging my interest in history. John Broskie was very helpful with selecting our title. James Hooper guided me through Texas and provided some excellent suggestions on Scandinavian countries. Steve Bilbrey toured the United States Military Academy with me at West Point. Interviews with Captain William Funk (USMC ret.) and Major Jack Coughlin (USAF ret.) were invaluable in addressing the US involvement in Vietnam and Southeast Asia. I am grateful to Gerard Richardson MBE for extending me every courtesy on my recent trip to Whitehaven England, the site of John Paul Jones's 1778 raid. Particular thanks also go to Sir Paul McCartney who suggested I research Cole Porter's songwriting during World War I. Many friends, such as Algis Pabarcis, Hassan El Masry, Claudio Buccieri and Ken Carter, reviewed chapters in the book. Other friends, including Chris Moran, Jeff Dody, Paige Jernigan, Bernie Podurgiel, and Vincent Driano, assisted in acquiring photography for the book. Karim Merie provided professional photography and videography (see our website, www.AmericaInvades.com) in the UK. Thanks to Blaine Donnelson for building our website. Thanks to Julie Scandora for her meticulous editing of our efforts. Thanks also to Piranha Productions for their efforts in editing the America Invades videos. Special thanks also go to many institutions that have aided us along the way, particularly the IWM Duxford, the RAF Museum Hendon, the Cambridge-American Cemetery, the American embassy in London, the Battleship *Texas*, the USS *Pampanito*, the West Point Museum, the Maryhill Museum of Art, Visit Spokane, and the Whitehaven Archive in Cumbria. The flaws you will find herein are entirely our own.

INTRODUCTION BY CHRISTOPHER KELLY

AS AN AMERICAN, I've long been curious about exactly how many countries my own country has invaded and been involved with militarily around the world.

How many countries do you think the United States invaded over our history? Thirty? Forty? How many countries do you think we've been involved with militarily. Ninety? A hundred?

A couple of years ago, I read and reviewed a book called *All the Countries We've Ever Invaded: And the Few We Never Got Round To* (The History Press, 2012) by a British author, Stuart Laycock, asking the same questions about Britain. His answer was that Britain has invaded or fought conflicts in almost 90 percent of the world's countries. I thoroughly enjoyed his book, and eventually we met for a pint in London, and a friendship blossomed. We decided to team up, using Stuart's passion for world history and my passion for American history to answer the questions about my country that I'd wondered about for so long. This book is the result.

Obviously, when you set out to write a book like this, you first have to define what you're researching. It's fairly easy to decide what "militarily involved with" means (not a mere posting of US marines to an embassy for security), but what about "invading"?

If satellite reconnaissance counts as an "invasion," then clearly the answer is a very large figure. Ditto for NSA telephone surveillance. If you count American cultural invasions such as Elvis, McDonald's, or Hollywood, for example, we could include nearly every country in the world. That, however, seems a bit of a linguistic stretch.

The nature of what constitutes an invasion has, of course, changed dramatically over the years. The old cry of "Send in the Marines!" could, in the days of cyber-warfare, be replaced by "Send in the nerds!" Should the introduction of a computer virus be considered an invasion?

In the end, we decided to define an "American invasion" as an "armed attack or intervention in a country by American forces." That still leaves a few countries where the question is open to some debate, but by the time we'd finished doing the research, we'd come up with some pretty amazing results.

America hasn't invaded just thirty or forty countries. It has invaded or fought in eighty-four out of 194 countries (countries recognized by the United Nations and excluding the United States) in the world. That's 43 percent of the total. And it hasn't been militarily involved with just ninety or a hundred countries. It has had some form of military involvement with a spectacular 191 out of 194. That's more than 98 percent. Yep, we haven't really been militarily involved with Andorra, Bhutan, or Liechtenstein. Sometimes for better, sometimes for worse, America has had a vast impact around the globe.

This book outlines American military activity around the globe from the birth of the United States (and sometimes even before—see, for example, "Colombia") up to the present day. This is, in a sense, the book that never ends, as we continue to intervene in conflicts in the twenty-first century. We plan to update future editions of this book as necessary.

Obviously, it's a vast subject, and inevitably, we haven't had space to include every battle, every campaign, and every deployment, and even where events are included, constraints of space in a book like this mean that only brief details can be given. We've also tended to concentrate more on the less widely known aspects of US military activity around the globe and less on the better-known ones. Nevertheless, we hope we've given a real taste of US military history in regard to each nation on earth and where you find an event or action of interest it may spur you on to read more about it elsewhere.

This book is most definitely not intended to judge the morality or wisdom of individual US military actions. Each reader can decide that for himself or herself.

Most people would probably agree that much of what America has done around the world has clearly been wise and noble (as in helping liberate Europe from Nazi tyranny). Some, however, has been wrong and/ or unwise (sometimes propping up repressive regimes, for instance). And some of what America has done has been in-between. In some sense, it's like looking at the history of your own family. And indeed all of it—the liberations, the fiascoes, and the follies—is, in some sense, part of the history of every American citizen. Writing this book made me feel different about America and what it means to be an American. Maybe it will do the same to you.

We Americans have had an ambivalent attitude to the nature of war and invasions throughout our history. Many early colonists fled the war-ravaged continent of Europe hoping to find peace for themselves and their families. Some Americans, such as the Quakers, were explicitly anti-war in accordance with their religious principles. Yet our nation could not have been founded without fighting the American Revolution against George III's Britain.

Americans are always hoping for peace but usually preparing for war. The American eagle is an ambivalent bird holding arrows in the talons of one foot and an olive branch in the other.

Thomas Jefferson, author of the Declaration of Independence and our third president, encouraged us to found an "Empire of Liberty." He encouraged James Madison in waging the War of 1812 with Britain and suggested that the conquest of Canada would be "a mere matter of marching." We failed to conquer Canada, but we would carve much of the American West out of the Mexican Republic (see "Mexico").

In the late nineteenth century, we were caught up in the imperialistic frenzy that swept up much of the globe and annexed Puerto Rico and controlled the Philippines after the Spanish-American War.

Consider the examples of three distinguished and quintessential Americans—the inventor Benjamin Franklin, politician Charles Sumner, and writer Mark Twain. All three expressed powerful anti-war sentiments, and all three became enthusiastic war proponents.

Founding Father Benjamin Franklin said, "There hardly ever existed such thing as a bad Peace, or a good war." In an amusing 1782 letter to Joseph Priestley, Franklin went even further writing:

> Men I find to be a Sort of Beings very badly constructed, as they are generally more easily provok'd than reconcil'd, more dispos'd to do Mischief to each other than to make Reparation, much more easily deceiv'd than undeceiv'd, and having more Pride & even Pleasure in killing than in begetting one another, for without a Blush they assemble in great Armies at Noon Day to destroy, and when they have kill'd as many as they can, they exaggerate the Number to augment the fancied Glory; but they creep into Corners or cover themselves with the Darkness of Night, when they mean to beget, as being asham'd of a virtuous Action. A virtuous Action it would be, and a vicious one the killing of them, if the Species were really worth producing or preserving; but of this I begin to doubt.

Yet, Franklin was an ardent patriot whose support for the American cause estranged him from his own son who became the Tory governor of New Jersey. Franklin's assistance in negotiating a treaty and alliance with France was a decisive component of the American victory in the Revolution.

Charles Sumner was a zealous opponent of the Mexican-American War (1846-1847). In a Fourth of July speech delivered in Boston in 1845, he asked, "What is war but organized murder?" Senator Sumner of Massachusetts was also firmly opposed to slavery. In 1856, following an abolitionist speech in the US Congress, he was assaulted by Preston Brooks, a pro-slavery congressman from South Carolina. Sumner would lead the radical Republican faction of the Senate where he was a staunch supporter of the Union war effort.

In the summer of 1861, Mark Twain, our third quintessential American, had a brief and unsuccessful career as a soldier in the Marion Rangers of the Confederate forces. He soon fled to Nevada partly to find silver but mainly to avoid the war. In 1867, long before "shock and awe" and after a visit to Ottoman-controlled Syria, Twain wrote, "I wish Europe would let Russia annihilate Turkey a little—not much, but enough to make it difficult to find the place without a divining rod or a diving bell." Yet after the American occupation of the Philippines, which followed the Spanish-American War, Twain would become a strident anti-imperialist who railed that America had debauched her "honor" with imperialism.

During the twentieth century, we fought in two world wars and won the Cold War. We triumphed over both forms of totalitarianism—fascism and Communism.

In a 2002 interview, Colin Powell, secretary of state at the time, said:

> *Far from being the Great Satan, I would say that we are the Great Protector. We have sent men and women from the armed forces of the United States to other parts of the world throughout the past century to put down oppression. We defeated Fascism. We defeated Communism. We saved Europe in World War I and World War II. We were willing to do it, glad to do it. We went to Korea. We went to Vietnam. All in the interest of preserving the rights of people. And when all those conflicts were over, what did we do? Did we stay and conquer? Did we say, "Okay, we defeated Germany. Now Germany belongs to us? We defeated Japan, so Japan belongs to us"? No. What did we do? We built them up. We gave them democratic systems which they have embraced totally to their soul. And did we ask for any land? No, the only land we ever asked for was enough land to bury our dead. And that is the kind of nation we are.*

In the twenty-first century, the United States, though challenged by Russia and China, is the sole remaining superpower. The global responsibilities that we began to shoulder in the twentieth century seem today more burdensome than ever. Nation building seems highly problematic and fraught with difficulties. The cost of being the world's policeman seems exorbitant in terms of both lives and treasure.

Yet former secretary of defense Robert Gates reminds us, "We are the indispensable nation." The United States, with its network of bases and alliances that spans the globe, would find it hard simply to retreat from its engagement with the world. The United States is or can be a force for principled action in the afflicted parts of the world. The US military, by virtue of its global reach, is almost invariably the first to respond to natural disasters as they occur around the world. If not us, then who will?

The United States assisted in the removal from power of a long list of dictators and tyrants, including George III, Kaiser Wilhelm, Mussolini, Hitler, Saddam, Gaddafi, Osama bin Laden, and many more.

In 2014, a hundred years on, prominent historians are vigorously debating whether World War I was a necessary war or not. I suspect that one hundred years hence historians will also be arguing whether the 2003 invasion of Iraq was necessary or not.

World War II, often referred to as a "good war" that unified the nation, is the exception rather than the rule. Most American wars have been controversial. Much of New England gave serious consideration to secession during Madison's War of 1812.

Much of what we Americans know about our foreign wars is derived from media and entertainment. At the close of Puccini's opera, Madame Butterfly, just before her suicide, plants a little US flag in the hand of her unrecognized son (named "Dolore" in Italian, or "Pain" or "Sorrow") with her lover, USN Lieutenant Pinkerton. In film, George C. Scott blusters and swaggers his way through World War II as the legendary American titan of war, General George S. Patton Jr. Martini-swilling surgeons cut and sew their way through the Korean War in Altman's M*A*S*H and the TV series. Robert Duvall rides with the Wagnerian Valkyries over the Vietnamese rice paddies in his screaming Hueys in *Apocalypse Now*.

These fictions may have shaped many of our attitudes and beliefs, but what about the realities of US overseas interventions? What has been their cost? What are the consequences of these deployments?

We have written this book according to modern country names and boundaries. These may not, of course, have applied at the time of all the events described, but it seemed the most sensible method of making the geography accessible to the modern reader and demonstrating quite how amazingly broad has been our military reach. We have not covered US military activity that took place within current US boundaries (like the Civil War and numerous conflicts with Native Americans) because that is a different subject.

The story of Americans in combat is NOT limited to the actions of those brave men and women who wear the uniform of the US military. Americans, not always willingly, fought at Waterloo, Trafalgar, and the Battle of the Nile under British colors. In spite of the Neutrality Acts of 1794 and 1818, Americans have fought in conflicts that were not supported by our government. William Walker of Nashville, Tennessee, invaded Central America with a group of fellow adventurers in the 1850s (see "Nicaragua" and "Honduras"). Irish Americans conducted Fenian raiding parties into Canada in the 1860s and were the first ever to fight under the banner of the Irish Republican Army (see "Canada"). Americans fought on both sides during the Boer War in South Africa. Some Americans joined the Lafayette Escadrille and the Foreign Legion to fight for France. Some Americans joined the RAF's American Eagle Squadrons to fight in the battle of Britain.

Nor have all American combatants been loyal to the US flag. Many American, of course, fought as Tories remaining loyal to their King in the American Revolution. In the Mexican-American War, the San Patricio battalion was largely made up of US Army deserters who fought on the Mexican side (see "Mexico"). The most famous of about a dozen Tokyo Roses, Iva Taguri, was born in Los Angeles. More recently, a few Americans have even volunteered to fight or propagandize on behalf of al-Qaeda and the Taliban.

We have included some of the stories of the volunteers and even a few of those who fought against the United States. Benedict Arnold, one of America's most notorious traitors, wrote a letter on behalf of a descendent of mine who was engaged in our 1776 invasion of Canada.

Napoleon once said, "The boundaries of an empire are marked by the graves of her soldiers." America has sent its sons and daughters to the far corners of the world. Today the sacrifice of over 218,000 American servicemen and servicewomen is memorialized in American military cemeteries in twenty-four different overseas cemeteries in eleven different countries. The boundaries of Jefferson's Empire of Liberty, therefore, stretch around the globe.

The story of America's foreign interventions is a story of families as well. Many have paid the ultimate sacrifice, but many more have been wounded in body and mind. Every victim of war is someone's son or daughter. Family members, too, suffer under the strains of long deployments.

Neither Stuart nor I have ever served in our nation's armed forces. We both, however, share a deep respect for those warriors who have stood guard over our nation's freedom.

I, however, have had numerous family members serving in the armed forces. Similarly, Stu has had a number of close members of his family serving in the British military. We have included some of my old family stories to add color where relevant. This book is, in part, a story of my family's involvement in US military history.

In writing history about the recent past, there is something I like to call the "Bletchley effect." Imagine that you were an objective fair-minded historian in the year 1970 attempting to write a history of World War II. Your account would necessarily suffer from an unawareness of the extraordinary impact of Bletchley Park and other Allied decoding efforts on the conduct of the war; these disclosures did not emerge until the mid-1970s, or thirty years after the war's conclusion. In fact, the UK government to this day maintains some documents relating to Rudolf Hess's flight to Britain in 1941 on a classified basis. Time must pass to allow political passions to cool, memoirs to be published, and secrets to be declassified—without this, history cannot be brought to light. In writing about recent American campaigns, our account—and those found in other sources—can be no more than a provisional judgment. Therefore, our accounts of the last thirty years or so are as much journalism as history.

This volume covers US military operations from the first large scale American invasion in Colombia in 1741 right up to the present. It is a world tour of an enormous subject. Inevitably, we will have missed some things out that really should be in and maybe gotten a few things wrong as well; plus some situations may have changed between the time of writing and actual publication. Please forward your comments, corrections, and suggestions to our website, www.AmericaInvades.com.

Some of our readers may feel pride in America's military exploits around the world. Others may feel ashamed. Many will feel a more complex mixture of both sentiments. Regardless of how one feels on these issues, we believe it is our duty to support the many men and women who, together with their families, have made enormous sacrifices while serving in our nation's military. It is for that reason we have decided to donate 5 percent of the proceeds of this work to military charities. Thank you for helping us to support our military with your purchase of this book.

AFGHANISTAN

QUITE A COUNTRY TO START THIS BOOK WITH, but that's the alphabet for you. Afghanistan has plenty of terrain that challenges even the toughest invaders logistically and a complex mix of ethnic and cultural identities and loyalties that defies even the cleverest of invaders politically.

Afghanistan's long history of turmoil and violence has given it the label "graveyard of empires." In the fourth century BC, bitter fighting in the mountains of Afghanistan took the shine off Alexander the Great's dreams of world conquest. And even the British Empire could not tame Afghanistan. During the First Anglo-Afghan War in 1842, a British force of 4,500 was pretty much reduced to just one man, Dr. William Brydon, after a retreat from Kabul to Jalalabad. And even though the British had more success with later efforts, Afghanistan would never be a part of the empire. The Soviets' invasion of Afghanistan in 1979 turned into a ten-year-long quagmire—the Russian Vietnam. Today it seems to be our turn.

For some of the twentieth century, Afghanistan had an uncharacteristically peaceful time. Despite flirting with Germany, Afghanistan remained neutral in World War I, and despite doing it again with the Axis powers in the 1930s, the nation once more remained neutral during World War II.

It was in the decades after World War II that we started to have some involvement in Afghanistan. For instance, from 1949 until 1979 the US government (USG) built the Helmand Valley Authority, which was modeled on the Tennessee Valley Authority. In 1963, King Zahir Shah of Afghanistan visited the United States, meeting President Kennedy and even touring Disneyland, and in 1964 the king introduced a new constitution that included a number of liberal measures.

The king, however, was toppled by a coup in 1973, orchestrated by his cousin Daoud, and Afghanistan was declared a republic. Then in 1978, Afghan Communists seized power in another coup and introduced a secular and Marxist-Leninist program of action. This, in a strongly Muslim country, in turn, led to a spreading insurrection against the government.

Amidst increasing rebellion and Afghan Communist disarray, in December of 1979, the Soviets then launched their invasion. An army of over 120,000 was deployed to occupy the country. If the Soviets thought this would stabilize the country, they were very wrong. Very, very wrong. The presence of foreign invaders, instead, increased support for the insurrection, which led to increasingly brutal Soviet counter-measures, which obviously didn't win them many local friends either.

President Carter reacted to the Soviet invasion with a boycott of the 1980 Moscow Olympics, and after Ronald Reagan was elected in the fall of 1980, US support for the Afghan resistance increased substantially. Amidst other measures, the CIA began shipping Stinger missiles to the mujahideen to help counter Soviet air superiority that had caused the resistance so much trouble.

Rather than providing direct assistance to the mujahideen, the United States chose generally to use Pakistan's intelligence service, ISI, as a proxy intermediary with them. While this may have saved some American lives, it also meant that few firm links between Americans and the mujahideen were formed. Saudi Arabia also provided financial support and volunteers to the mujahideen. One of the mujahideen who emerged from obscurity in this conflict was a young Saudi called Osama bin Laden.

The ten-year-long war would cost the Soviets over fourteen thousand lives. However, it would cost Afghanistan much, much more. Over a million Afghans (mostly civilians) were killed, and the economy and infrastructure of the country were devastated.

By the end of it, however, the Afghan tribesmen, with outside help, had humbled a superpower.

When the Soviet occupation came to an end in 1989, Najibullah, the pro-Soviet ruler, managed to remain in power until 1992. In January 1992, all Russian aid to Afghanistan was cut off, and mujahideen warlords captured Kabul in April 1992; they were, however, soon fighting amongst themselves. The United States took little interest. With the Soviet withdrawal and the end of the Cold War, Afghanistan seemed to lack importance to American policymakers.

And soon a new force arose to challenge the warring warlords. The Taliban, a fundamentalist Islamic movement, which had links to the ISI, started taking ground from often fragmented and ineffective opposition. In 1996, they took Kabul. Najibullah, who had been sheltering with the UN, hoping for safe passage out of the country, was castrated, dragged through the streets behind a truck, and then hung from a lamp post.

The Taliban instituted a harsh regime that denied many basic human rights and dealt brutally with opposition. For instance, education for females was suspended. Singing, dancing, and even kite-flying were banned. In March of 2001, the Taliban destroyed the two monumental, fifteen-hundred-year-old Bamiyan Buddhas.

Two days before the 9/11 attacks, the leader of the Northern Alliance, Ahmad Shah Massoud, was assassinated by al-Qaeda operatives posing as cameramen. And soon after 9/11, President George W. Bush visited the smoking ruins of Ground Zero in New York. He seized a bullhorn and gave an impromptu speech, "I can hear you. The rest of the world hears you. And the people who knocked down these buildings will hear all of us soon." To this day, the 9/11 memorial site remains a popular venue for enlistment and re-enlistment ceremonies for our serving military. Many of the first bombs that fell on Afghanistan were inscribed with "FDNY" to commemorate those firemen killed on 9/11.

The Taliban had won themselves very few friends in the international community. This and the sympathy generated by the 9/11 attacks helped the United States gain considerable support from its traditional allies for the invasion of Afghanistan. Over twenty-five different nations would contribute troops, equipment, or services to Operation Enduring Freedom.

This first covert team inside Afghanistan, code-named "Jawbreaker," arrived on September 27, 2001. The CIA operatives in Jawbreaker carried three million dollars in one-hundred-dollar bills to distribute to Afghan warlords. Nearly 1.7 million pounds of supplies were also airdropped to the tribal leaders of the Northern Alliance.

On October 7, 2001, the air campaign against Taliban-controlled Afghanistan began. F-14 and F/A-18 strike fighters were launched from the decks of two USN supercarriers, *Carl Vinson* and *Enterprise*. A combination of massive air power, US (and other nations') special forces, and the Northern Alliance soon looked set to eradicate the Taliban as a military force. Rapidly, US Marines would join the battle as well.

Kabul was captured on November 13, 2001. The first American casualty in Afghanistan was Johnny Michael Spann, a CIA operative and former Marine, who was killed in a Taliban prisoner-of-war uprising on November 25, 2001.

From December 12 to 17 of 2001, the battle of Tora Bora raged. The United States deployed only less than one hundred US Special Forces (Delta) along with about one thousand Afghan militia. Air strikes were called in, and Gator cluster mines were dropped on the snowy passes of Tora Bora. Around December 16, bin Laden managed to escape from Tora Bora across the mountains with hundreds of al-Qaeda followers.

At year end, Hamid Karzai was sworn in as the president of the Afghan Transitional Administration, and the UN Security Council established ISAF, the International Security Assistance Force.

The Taliban had not, however, been eliminated. After the initial shock of the invasion, they regrouped and switched from fighting as the army of a government to fighting as a guerrilla army, in particular making devastating use of roadside bombs (IEDs).

Our ongoing war in Afghanistan is far too big a subject for just one chapter of this book. The war has been long, tough, and complex, and it is impossible to cover the campaigns and battles and combat in the detail they deserve here, so we will mention just a few points in this continuing story.

In 2003, the invasion of Iraq (Operation Iraqi Freedom) diverted US military strength and resources and political attention from the campaign in Afghanistan. On August 11, 2003, NATO assumed peacekeeping duties in Afghanistan.

The next year in April, Pat Tillman, a former NFL player with the Arizona Cardinals, was killed in a friendly fire incident in Afghanistan.

In 2005, Hamid Karzai became the first democratically elected president in Afghanistan's history. That same year, on a mission in Afghanistan, Marcus Lutrell became the lone survivor of the worst debacle in the history of the USN SEALs. The same code of Pashtunwali that harbored Osama bin Laden in Afghanistan helped to save Lutrell's life. In some ways, Lutrell's fate paralleled that of Dr. Brydon, except the Englishman never got a movie deal.

President George W. Bush ordered a "silent surge" in the fall of 2006, raising US troop levels from twenty-one thousand to thirty-one thousand to counter a deteriorating security situation on the ground.

In 2007, Defense Secretary Robert Gates increased the length of military tours in Afghanistan from twelve months to fifteen. Suicide bombings continued.

In the fall of 2008, President-elect Obama interviewed Bush's secretary of defense, Robert Gates. Gates asked if Obama would go after violent extremists wherever they lived. Obama replied, "Yes, I'm no peacenik." Obama had campaigned on the pledge to raise the US commitment in Afghanistan—a conflict that his party approved of in distinction to the war in Iraq.

The following year, Obama appointed General Stanley McChrystal to head up the US forces in Afghanistan. McChrystal was an expert in counterinsurgency who had successfully implemented the surge in Iraq and was credited with helping to track down and kill al-Qaeda's leader in Iraq—al Zarqawi. In December 2009, Obama announced an additional thirty-thousand troop surge into Afghanistan, raising our total strength to just over one hundred thousand.

Obama's presidency also saw a massive expansion of drone attacks on the other side of the Afghan border in Pakistan (see "Pakistan").

In 2011, a drawdown of US forces committed to Afghanistan began. On May 2, 2011, the raid that killed Osama bin Laden in Abbottabad (Operation Neptune Spear) was launched from a US airbase in Jalalabad, Afghanistan. August 6 of that same year, however, proved to be the deadliest day for the United States in Afghanistan when Taliban forces managed to shoot down a CH-47 Chinook helicopter killing thirty Americans.

At the time of this writing, 2,187 Americans in the military have been killed while serving in Afghanistan, and over nineteen thousand have been wounded. Many soldiers from other countries and many thousands of Afghans have also been killed or wounded. The war in Afghanistan, spanning two administrations and over twelve years, is now the longest war in American history. The difficult terrain, Afghan society's cultural and ethnic complexity, its reaction to foreigners, the role of drugs in subsidizing the Taliban and spreading corruption in official circles, and Taliban links inside Pakistan have all played a major role in making America's experience so frustrating.

Using however many years it needs, Afghans now bear the weight of stabilizing their country. As of 2014, hundreds of thousands of Afghan troops have been trained, and NATO forces are now steadily being withdrawn from Afghanistan. Yet the future of Afghanistan looks very uncertain. Also uncertain is what role, if any, America will play in it.

The attitude towards warfare in Afghanistan is very different from that in the technologically focused West. "Our enemies have the watches," some Afghans used to say, "but we have the time." It appears the Western presence may have run out of time in Afghanistan.

ALBANIA

Y OU MAY NOT HAVE HEARD AS MUCH ABOUT ALBANIA as other European countries—France and Britain and Germany, for example—but that's partly because, for a number decades after World War II, it was largely closed off to the outside world by its somewhat eccentric Communist ruler, Enver Hoxha.

OK, obviously the Cold War didn't do much to encourage Western tourists to visit Communist countries, but Albania under Hoxha was a bit in a league of its own, which is a shame because it's an interesting place with an interesting history and we've played a key part in it.

Albania is situated on the eastern side of the Adriatic, with Montenegro to its north, Greece to its south, and Kosovo and Macedonia (the former Yugoslav Republic of Macedonia, or FYROM) to its east. It has a lot of beautiful scenery and a rich history that involves, along with the locals themselves, Greeks, Romans, Byzantines, Bulgarians, Venetians, Turks—and all that even before World War I.

In 1912, after the Ottomans were defeated in the Balkan Wars, Albania became independent. What euphoria there was, however, wore off pretty fast, as Europe collapsed into the chaos of the First World War and Albania ended up fragmented and fought over. We got involved with the fighting in Albanian waters, with American subchasers (small boats aimed, not surprisingly, at chasing submarines) playing a brave role in the 1918 Battle of Durazzo (named after the Albanian port city of Durrës—Durazzo in Italian). By the end of the war, Albania had assorted victorious Allied troops controlling big chunks of it.

And some of our own troops got pretty close to Albania at this time. After the war, units of the 332nd Infantry Regiment were briefly stationed just next door in what is Montenegro while it was being decided what exactly to do with the territories of the old and defeated Austro-Hungarian Empire. There was also an international force under British Brigadier-General G. F. Phillips that was actually occupying the major northern Albanian city of Shkodër at the same time. We haven't yet been able to trace any Americans in this force, but if you know of any, do please let us know.

Just as some American names no doubt have a humorous air to Albanians, some Albanian names can raise a smile in America. For instance, Albania actually has a city named Pukë ("I was born in Pukë, I grew up in Pukë, I want someday to be buried in Pukë!") And between the two world wars, the key figure in Albanian politics was King Zog. King Zog was purported to have survived no less than fifty-five assassination attempts, including one in Vienna where he saved himself by returning fire with the revolver he habitually carried.

Zog's days, however, were numbered. In April 1939, even before the actual start of World War II, the Italian Army seized control of Albania. World War II was almost as chaotic in Albania as World War I had been, and into the middle of it all boldly strode the Americans of the OSS (Office of Strategic Services, the forerunner to the CIA). As in a lot of Albanian history, our role there during the war is unfamiliar to most Americans, but it deserves to be a lot better known.

In 1943, after the Allied invasion of Italy, OSS agents, following in the footsteps of the British Strategic Operations Executive, or SOE (who were tasked by Winston Churchill to "set Nazi-occupied Europe ablaze" and about whom you will read more in this volume), were dispatched to Albania. At the time, Enver Hoxha was leading a partisan band of Communists. The Albanian Balli Kombëtar (National Front), on the other hand, was anti-Communist but was also accused of collaborating with the Nazis. A third Albanian group, the Legalitetei (Legality Party), sought the return of King Zog but weren't as interested in fighting.

The main goal of the American OSS and their British SOE allies was the defeat of Hitler and his allies, so this left them with little choice but to assist the Hoxha-led partisans (the enemy of my enemy is my friend) and to hope for the best.

The OSS supplied food, ammunition, and advisors to the Albanian partisans, and they called in air strikes from the USAAF to help Hoxha's forces. Captain Tom Stefan was an Albanian-American from Laconia, New Hampshire. Fluent in Albanian, he was recruited by the OSS and served as a direct liaison with Enver Hoxha.

Two famous actors were involved in helping the Albanians fight the Nazis. The British actor, Anthony Quayle, was with the SOE. Quayle would later star in *Guns of Navarone* and *Lawrence of Arabia*. The American actor, Sterling Hayden, gave up a Hollywood career to become a US Marine captain and member of the maritime division of the OSS. A skilled captain, Hayden piloted boats laden with American supplies from Italy to Albania. In the movie *The Godfather*, Hayden played the role of Captain McCluskey—the crooked cop who gets an extra dollop of marinara in the forehead from Michael Corleone.

After Southern Italy was occupied by the Allies in 1943 and the Italian government surrendered (leaving many desperate Italian solders trapped between the Germans and the partisans), airbases in Italy were used to bomb southern Axis targets, such as the vital Ploeşti oil fields in Romania. Inevitably, therefore, Allied planes sometimes went down in Albania and Yugoslavia. On November 8, 1943, a Dakota C-53 transport plane carrying thirty Americans, including thirteen army flight nurses, crash-landed in Albanian territory. Albanian Communist partisans helped them make their way back to Allied territory.

On November 17, 1944, after heavy fighting, Tirana, the capital of Albania, was liberated from Germans occupation by Albanian partisans with the assistance of Allied air support. Also, several German divisions, which could otherwise have fought the Allies in Italy or France, were pinned down in Albania. That night, OSS forces raised the flag at the American legation in Tirana for the first time in years.

But this wasn't to be the end of our secret war in Albania. Although in the next round of it, we were on the opposite side to Hoxha and his Communists. Things hadn't quite turned out how we had hoped, and after the war in 1949, the CIA tried to foment a resistance movement in Albania with a ragtag army of exiled royalists and anti-Communists.

Over a period of about three and a half years, the exiles were sent into Albania by land, sea, and air. A ship, for instance, was launched from Malta with nine Albanians in a commando-type raid. Three were killed immediately, and the rest were rounded up. At the end, there was little to show for the effort, apart from hundreds dead or in prison. How much success the operation could have had anyway is uncertain, but information given to the Russians by the notorious British mole Kim Philby, and perhaps information from others, meant that too often Hoxha's forces had been tipped off before the infiltrators arrived in Albania.

After remaining a fan of Stalin, even when the Soviet Union denounced the moustachioed Uncle Joe, and after a flirtation with Maoist China, Enver Hoxha died of natural causes in 1985. Communism officially collapsed in 1992, seven years after his death.

In 1997, as chaos and unrest swept across Albania in the wake of a collapsed savings scheme, US Marines were sent into Albania to secure American property and rescue US citizens.

Two years later, in 1999, American forces were in Albania again. With the Kosovo crisis erupting just next door, Albania became a key area of American and NATO interest with American troops, aircraft, and helicopters arriving in quantity. Kosovar refugees who had fled across the border needed help, and there was the possibility of a ground offensive into Kosovo if the Serbs did not give in. Indeed, before a peace deal was signed, US General Wesley Clark already had troops repairing the main road from the Albanian capital Tirana to Kukës, near the Yugoslav border, to ease the passage of invasion troops and US heavy tanks. Other Americans were also there on a rather different basis—members of the Atlantic Brigade of the Kosovo Liberation Army to fight the Serbian forces in Kosovo.

More recently, Albania has sent troops to Afghanistan, and today Albania is a NATO member. Among other military links, the New Jersey National Guard is partnered with Albania. Albania today is attracting increasing interest from tourists, which is quite a change considering that not that long ago it was perhaps the most hardline and closed-off Communist state in all Europe.

ALGERIA

L IKE LIBYA, ALGERIA IS A BIG NORTH AFRICAN COUNTRY. In fact, it's huge—the tenth largest country in the world. It has quite a lot of oil and gas and even more desert. It also has plenty of fertile areas and a lot of people, about thirty-seven million of them. Algeria's capital is, not surprisingly, Algiers.

Algeria is an ancient land with a long and culturally rich history. Among its early glories are the amazing Tassili n'Ajjer rock paintings, the product of a prehistoric culture that emerged when the Sahara was green. Yep, surprising but true.

More recently, although not that recently, some areas of Algeria, particularly in the coastal region, became part of the Carthaginian Empire. With Rome's conquest of Carthage, it was then absorbed, like so much else, into the Roman Empire. One of the oldest cities in America, St. Augustine, Florida (founded in 1565), is named after the hugely influential Catholic theologian St. Augustine of Hippo (Hippo being his home city) who was born in what is today Algeria.

During part of its long history, Algeria, like much of North Africa, became a home for the Barbary pirates. It's easy to forget quite how extensive piracy was then. From the sixteenth to nineteenth century, these raiders are said to have captured and enslaved over one million Europeans. That's a lot of Europeans.

And it wasn't just Europeans suffering. Algerian pirates captured their first American ship in 1785.

American independence from Britain obviously had its advantages, but one of its disadvantages was that merchant ships from the United States would no longer be under the protection of the powerful Royal Navy. In May 1794, war secretary Henry Knox decided it was time to do something about the Barbary pirates, and he appointed Philadelphian Joshua Humphreys "Constructor of the Navy of the United States." Humphreys was a gifted naval architect who designed the 44-gun frigates (which could, in fact, carry over fifty guns), such as the USS *Constitution*, that were faster and more powerful than their European counterparts. By contrast, a typical British frigate had just thirty-two to thirty-six guns. Amazing, considering how old it is, the USS *Constitution* is still afloat today.

Despite having ships under construction, however, our government was still cautious at that stage about picking a fight with the Barbary pirates, preferring instead to pay ransoms and tribute. In 1795, for instance, to ransom 115 sailors, we paid one million dollars in cash, supplies, and a frigate to the dey of Algiers alone, a staggering amount at the time. Assorted treaties with Algiers and the other Barbary pirates followed, but the problem never seemed to go away permanently.

Thomas Jefferson, understandably in this situation, eventually got fed up with paying tribute, and when in 1801 the pasha of Tripoli (see "Libya") rather unwisely declared war on the United States, Jefferson sent ships and troops against the pasha's forces in the First Barbary War. We won that war, while Algiers, wisely kept out of it. However, despite that, we were still in a position where the Treaty of Peace and Amity of 1805 obliged us to a pay a ransom of sixty thousand dollars to the dey of Algiers for each sailor.

In 1815, however, having dealt with the rather urgent matter of the War of 1812, we were determined that things were going to change between Algiers and the United States. Stephen Decatur of the USN commanded a squadron in the Second Barbary War, also known, reasonably enough, as the Algerian War since it was basically us versus Algiers. It wasn't much of a war, really. Decatur managed to capture the Algerian flagship *Mashuda* with 406 sailors aboard. Soon after that, our ships turned up off Algiers and, after assorted threats, pretty much dictated terms to Algiers. There was to be no tribute ever again; there were to be no American slaves ever again. Oh … and Decatur wanted an immediate ten thousand dollars compensation payment.

During World War I, we were in the waters off Algeria again. In 1918, the USS *Lydonia*, which was basically a converted yacht, was helping escort a convoy from Bizerte in Tunisia to Gibraltar. Off the Algerian coast, she and a British warship got into a battle with the German submarine UB-70, which seems to have been sunk.

In November of 1942, we returned to Algeria. In the period after the Barbary Wars, France had become the colonial power in Algeria (or Algérie, as they put it), which meant that, after the German invasion of France, it was under the control of the pro-Nazi Vichy regime.

Operation Torch was launched with the British to invade Vichy-controlled parts of northwest Africa, so that, with the British advancing from the east, the Axis troops in the region would be squeezed between two Allied forces. The operation posed many risks as there were nearly 120,000 French troops in North Africa and US commanders weren't at all sure what kind of fight they might put up.

Major General Fredendall led US forces that landed near Oran and Algiers. Their mission was to push on into Tunisia as rapidly as possible into the rear of Rommel's forces that had been threatening British-held Egypt and the Suez Canal.

On November 7, 1942, US paratroopers in thirty-nine C-47s flew eleven hundred miles from airfields in Cornwall to two airfields near Oran. It was the first American airborne operation of the war, and it wasn't a great start. In fact, it was a near total disaster. Many of the planes got lost. Others were hit by anti-aircraft fire. Some landed in Spanish Morocco where the men would be interned for three months.

The next day, on November 8, 1942, American troops landed near Algiers. They had hoped the French would surrender immediately to troops from America's oldest ally. In fact, the battle with the French lasted just over three days. Resistance was strongest near Oran where the Big Red One (the 1st Infantry Division of the US Army) suffered more than three hundred casualties. After the battle, though, Oran, a deep-water port, was rapidly transformed into a vast Allied supply depot. By November 12, thanks to a deal with Admiral Darlan, all Algeria, as well as Morocco, was under Allied control. Allied forces would soon be making a push eastwards into Tunisia.

Brigadier General Theodore Roosevelt Jr. was among those leading forces in this invasion of Algeria. The filmmaker Darryl Zanuck, who would later make *The Longest Day*, also landed in Algeria with American troops, serving as a colonel in the Signal Corps.

The Allies' deal with French Admiral Darlan meant putting him in charge of civil administration throughout North Africa. This then inevitably ignited a political firestorm of criticism in the United States over the question of working with a Vichy representative and collaborator. The problem, however, was removed finally (very finally) by Darlan's assassination at his headquarters in Algiers by a young monarchist on December 24, 1942.

After a bloody seven-year civil war, Algeria gained its independence from France in 1962.

We have had some military involvement with the country since then. For instance, in October 1980, after a devastating earthquake in the country, US Air Force planes rushed in hundreds of tons of humanitarian aid. USN ships now call on ports in Algeria on a regular basis, and the United States has developed a number of other military links with Algeria, including bilateral exercises.

ANDORRA

ATINY COUNTRY WITH SOME BEAUTIFUL MOUNTAINS and places to ski, located in the Pyrenees between Spain and France, Andorra, not surprisingly, has only a tiny army, basically used for ceremonial duties. We have not really invaded Andorra or seen much military involvement here.

It did, however, declare war on Germany in 1914. What's more, because it was so small, nobody bothered to include it in any peace deal at the end of World War I, so technically it went on fighting World War I decades longer than anybody else.

Now, with such a small military track record and so little land within its borders, it might seem pretty unlikely that we would have had much involvement with trying to take it over, but strange as it seems, there are stories of an American connection in two attempts to take control of Andorra, both in 1934. Yep.

The year 1933 had been a bad one for Andorra. The two princes of Andorra—who, because of Andorra's vulnerable position squeezed between Spain and France, are always the bishop of Urgell and the president of France—had, unusually, intervened in Andorra's internal affairs over an election dispute. French gendarmes had ultimately been sent in as well. There had been resentment among some Andorrans.

Perhaps because of this, some may have thought 1934 would be a good year to offer the Andorrans a new ruler. In March 1934, it was reported that the Council of Andorra had received a letter from an unidentified American originally from Chicago offering to buy Andorra. There was wild speculation (well, some speculation) in the press about the identity of the mystery American and some suggested Samuel Insull, a former utilities operator from Chicago who had fled to Greece after the collapse of his utilities empire and some questions over the possibility of things like fraud. If the offer was real, the Andorrans seem to have rejected it.

Meanwhile in late 1933, one Boris Skossyreff, a man with a very varied past, turned up in Andorra, and at his side was an American divorcee with whom he'd been living, one Florence Marmon, ex-wife of an automobile magnate from Indiana. In December 1993, Boris acquired Andorran citizenship, and in May 1934, he presented his plans for reform of the government of Andorra. Then at some stage, he declared himself king of Andorra, allegedly with some local support but apparently definitely not with the support of the bishop of Urgell, who sent the Spanish police to get him and end his brief reign. It seemed unlikely that American Florence was ever going to be queen of Andorra.

During World War II, Andorra stayed neutral, and it became a major destination for escaping Allied airmen who had been shot down, including some Americans. Not all, though, made it to Andorra. Some tragically died of cold and exhaustion in the Pyrenees.

ANGOLA

A LARGE AFRICAN COUNTRY, Angola lies north of Namibia with a long Atlantic coast. Plus there's a little extra bit of Angola in the north, the Cabinda enclave, which is separated from the rest of Angola by a strip of the Democratic Republic of the Congo. Angola gets its name from the ngola, the ruler of the Kingdom of Ndongo.

Some of Angola used to be major slave-trading territory, so not surprisingly, our first military involvement with Angola was when the USN's Africa squadron was sent to the area in the nineteenth century to try to suppress slavery. In fact, our ships even had a base at the time in Angola. In 1859, our ships' depot was moved from Cape Verde to St. Paul de Loando. Two areas of particular concern for our navy in Angola were Cabinda itself, situated at the mouth of the Congo, and Ambriz. For instance, in 1850, the USS *John Adams* and the USS *Perry* between them seized three ships at Ambriz. Two ships were seized at Cabinda in 1845, another two in 1846, one in 1859, and another in 1861. It wouldn't be right to claim that the navy's efforts did huge damage to the slave trade, but they did some.

But our navy didn't just concern itself with slavery. In March 1860, Commander Thomas W. Brent sent marines and seamen ashore from the USS *Marion* to protect American property at Kissembo in Angola.

Angola was for a long time a Portuguese colony. In the second half of the twentieth century, oil extraction became a major industry, and by 1973, it had replaced coffee as Angola's biggest export. Then in 1974, a leftist military coup in Portugal signaled the beginning of the end of the Portuguese Empire, and in 1975, Angola became independent. Tragically, what followed was twenty-seven years of civil war as different factions, with the support of assorted outside countries, fought for control of the country. We played our own secret and semi-secret role in supporting first the FNLA (National Front for the Liberation of Angola) and then UNITA (National

Union for the Total Independence of Angola) against the MPLA (Popular Movement for the Liberation of Angola) that was supported by Cuba and the Soviet Union. The Clark Amendment to the US Arms Export Control Act of 1976 was supposed to restrict aid from America to warring factions in Angola, but the amendment was repealed in 1985, much to UNITA's delight.

The 1990s saw occasional periods of peace and others of renewed fighting. In 1991, the USAF flew some emergency relief supplies into Luanda, the capital of Angola, and in 1992, the US Air Force, as part of Operation Provide Transition, flew demobilized soldiers home in Angola. However, it was only in 2002, after Jonas Savimbi, UNITA's long-time leader, was killed that the civil war finally came to an end.

In recent years, things have gotten a bit more friendly between Angola and the United States. In 2009, Hillary Clinton declared Angola a "strategic partner" of the United States. In 2010, a Memorandum of Understanding enshrined the Strategic Partnership Dialogue between the two countries. And the USN, over 150 years since it first operated in Angola, is again a visitor to Angolan ports. For instance, in 2011, commander of US 6ᵗʰ Fleet, Vice Admiral Harry B. Harris Jr. called in at the Angolan capital Luanda to celebrate the thirty-fifth anniversary of the Angolan navy.

ANTIGUA AND BARBUDA

ANTIGUA'S HIGHEST PEAK used to be called Boggy Peak (elevation 1,319 feet). Not anymore. In 2009, the highest peak on this popular Caribbean island was renamed Mount Obama.

In 1798, the US ship, the *Retaliation* under Lieutenant William Bainbridge, was cruising off Antigua when it came across two French warships. Unfortunately for Bainbridge and the *Retaliation*, we were in state of quasi-war with France at the time, and the ship was captured.

However, for most of the colonial period, Antigua and Barbuda were controlled by the British, so much of our military involvement with the islands has involved them as well. When were at war with Britain, assorted ships from Antigua and Barbuda were a target for American warships. For instance, in 1814, the American privateer *Frolic* captured the schooner *Encouragement* carrying sugar, molasses, and rum from Antigua to Nova Scotia. And in October 1814, US Marines assisted in the capture of the British ship *Mary* by the US sloop *Peacock* off Barbuda.

Since then, of course, US warships have visited the islands on a more friendly basis, and during World War II, Antigua featured in the 1940 Destroyers for Bases deal in which, in return for the right to bases in assorted territories then controlled by Britain, we gave the destroyers to the British to help in their fight against Hitler.

In Antigua, we built a naval air station at Crabbs Peninsula and built Coolidge Air Force Base on the other side of Parham Harbour. During the war, Coolidge was used, and air transport and anti-submarine patrols were flown from here. The closure of wartime bases, however, was not the end of US forces in Antigua. For instance, we kept a missile tracking facility there.

Antigua and Barbuda became an independent state in 1981. In 1983, Antigua and Barbuda offered military and political support to the invasion of Grenada.

Since then, we've developed assorted military links with the islands, including exercises. For instance, in 2011, the Tradewinds 2011 Exercise, sponsored by US Southern Command and featuring US forces and those from partner nations in the area, took place in Antigua and Barbuda. In 1995, we turned over a former USN support facility to the Antigua and Barbuda government, and it's being turned into a coast guard training facility.

ARGENTINA

THE TANGO, THE PASSION, the Perón. Yep, the wife of Argentine President Juan Perón was the inspiration for the hit musical *Evita*.

The United States and Argentina are two great American nations, but with a long geographic distance between them and, on occasions, a political distance as well.

Argentina wasn't exactly our area of most major interest in the nineteenth century, but we did send in the marines when things looked dangerous ashore.

In October 1833, marines and seamen from Commodore Woolley's squadron landed in the capital, Buenos Aires, on a mission to protect US citizens and property. Not for the last time.

In February 1852, more US marines arrived in the same location and on the same mission, though this lot were from Commodore McKeever's squadron.

No big break this time because just a few months later, in September of the same year, the US sloop *Jamestown* was offloading marines into Buenos Aires to protect American property.

And then in 1890, as political unrest hit again, the schooner USS *Tallapoosa* turned up in Buenos Aires to protect American diplomats.

It was during the twentieth century, however, that we were to take a closer interest in Argentina. Signs of things to come were our attempts to encourage Argentina into the First World War, but in the Second World War, tensions between Argentina and us really rose.

Argentina had a large German population, and because of that and other reasons, it just wouldn't declare war on Germany and Japan. Argentine neutrality angered President Roosevelt who expected more support after his introduction of a "good neighbor" policy towards Latin America. We put huge pressure on Argentina, and finally, in March 1945, Argentina declared war on our enemies. However, the dispute left a sour taste on both sides, and stories of Nazis in Argentina after the war didn't exactly improve the American opinion of Argentina.

However, after the war, links between the United States and Argentine military did develop as Argentina eventually began to be seen as a bulwark against Communism. A coup put a military junta in power in Argentina in 1976, and what followed was the so-called Dirty War involving appalling human rights abuse as the junta's forces sought to crush left-wing opposition. American did eventually impose restrictions on its military cooperation with the junta, but the question of how much was known by some members of US intelligence and the US government remains.

The 1982 conflict involving the UK and Argentina in the Falkland Islands (or the Malvinas, as Argentina calls them) posed a bit of a dilemma for the United States as we were aligned to both the UK via NATO and Argentina via the OAS (Organization of American States). Jeane Kirkpatrick, US ambassador to the United Nations, declared that Latin America had become "the most important place in the world for us." President Ronald Reagan clearly, however, tilted towards Britain, which was led at the time by the "Iron Lady," Margaret Thatcher. In spite of our neutrality, the United States provided surveillance, satellite intelligence, and significant supplies that helped Britain win back the islands.

In 1991, Argentina did send ships to help free Kuwait, and Argentine forces have taken part alongside US forces in assorted exercises and SOUTHCOM (or Southern Command, in the US Department of Defense covering Central and South America) has helped with humanitarian projects. But in recent years, some tensions have arisen again between the Argentine and US governments.

ARMENIA

A NATION WITH A LONG AND FASCINATING Christian tradition, Armenia is a land of the Caucasus. It is also famous these days as a land with a Kardashian connection.

During the period after World War I, the American Military Mission in Armenia toured the area, including Yerevan, the capital of Armenia, before returning and reporting to the US government.

American Colonel William Haskell was appointed Resident Allied High Commissioner in Armenia in the period with one of his jobs being to supervise relief efforts by the Allies in Armenia. Even though Haskell's administration was not without some controversy, huge amounts of American aid were distributed in Armenia saving many lives.

Armenia eventually became part of the Soviet Union and consequently received some attention from us during the Cold War. For instance, on November 20, 1956, a U-2 plane piloted by Francis Gary Powers flew over Armenia observing targets there.

In 1988, though, USAF personnel flew into Armenia for a very different reason, helping rush in aid after a devastating earthquake hit the area.

Armenia became independent again in 1991, and in 1992, we opened an embassy in Yerevan. In recent years, we have started to develop military links with Armenia. For instance, Armenians served alongside our troops in Iraq and Afghanistan. We've given millions of dollars of communications equipment to Armenia's Peacekeeping Battalion. Armenia was the host for the forward operating site of EUCOM-sponsored exercise Combined Endeavor 2007, and in 2010, the Third Air Force and Kansas Air National Guard medics found themselves training alongside the Armenian military. The Kansas National Guard is partnered with Armenia.

AUSTRALIA

SINCE AUSTRALIA WAS PART OF THE BRITISH EMPIRE for a long time, it still has strong connections with Britain, but that doesn't mean we haven't been militarily involved there. Not at all.

During World War II, for instance, almost a million US service personnel passed through Australia. That's a lot of military personnel. The first American forces arrived in Australia as early as December 1941 and were there, among several reasons, to help the Australians defend themselves against any attempt by the advancing Japanese to invade Australia.

But Australia rapidly became a major base for training US troops before they were sent to the battle front and a major destination for US troops' rest and recuperation. It was also a major base for the US Army Air Forces (USAAF) conducting combat missions against the Japanese forces. The Fifth Air Force established its headquarters in Australia in 1942, and large numbers of US aircraft operated out of Australian bases. For example, on April 5, 1942, B-26 Marauders took off from bases in Queensland, Australia, refueled at Port Moresby, and hit Japanese targets at Rabaul. In May of 1942, a B-17 flying out from Australian bases spotted a Japanese invasion fleet at the start of the Battle of the Coral Sea.

Maintaining the shipping lifeline between the US West Coast, Hawaii, and Australia was vital for Allied prosecution of the war in the Pacific. When Douglas MacArthur withdrew from the Philippines, he retreated to Australia and set up his headquarters in Melbourne. After the decisive battle of Midway, the Allies began to advance in the Pacific using Australia as their launch pad and supply depot.

Generally, Americans and Australians got along well. Sometimes, extremely well. Over twelve thousand Australian women became American war brides. But tensions arose occasionally as well. On November 26, 1942, for instance, the so-called Battle of Brisbane erupted as US and Australian troops brawled.

In the period after World War II, military links between Australia and the United States remained strong. Both countries, for instance, became members of SEATO (Southeast Asia Treaty Organization) and ANZUS (Australia, New Zealand, United States Security Treaty), and we conduct regular exercises, training, and visits with the Australians. Australia sent troops to fight in Vietnam, and more recently, it has sent troops to both Iraq and Afghanistan.

We have had facilities in Australia after the war, in particular the Nurrungar (now closed) and Pine Gap bases. Both bases have been linked to tracking missiles, but some people have also suspected involvement with a range of other military and intelligence roles. The Pacific is becoming an area of increasing strategic interest for the United States, and in 2011, President Obama announced he eventually wants twenty-five hundred US marines to be located in Australia. Hundreds have already been sent, and the Australia government is building new facilities at Robertson Barracks and the Royal Australian Air Force base in Darwin to cope with the increasing numbers rotating through.

AUSTRIA

AUSTRIA IS, AMONG MANY OTHER THINGS, THE LAND OF MOZART, Viennese waltzes, and, of course, the *Sound of Music*.

We fought Austria-Hungary during World War I after our entry in 1917. Most of this fighting took place in the mountains of northern Italy. The Treaty of Versailles, in which the United States played a major role, broke up the Hapsburg Empire forever.

Sadly, Versailles would not prevent another world war. In 1938, as featured in, yes, the *Sound of Music*, Adolf Hitler (himself born in Austria) sent troops into Austria to join it to Germany. Inevitably, therefore, as World War II raged, targets inside Austria were to receive a lot of attention from the USAAF. Oil refineries and aircraft factories in the vicinity of Vienna were, for instance, regular targets for our bombers.

And soon, Americans would be operating on the ground inside Austria as well. For instance, Lieutenant Colonel Franklin Lindsay of the OSS had parachuted in to work with the Slovene partisans in 1944, and along with them, he had attempted to advance in southern Austria. Other OSS teams were dropped into Austria itself.

In the last weeks of the war, as General Dwight Eisenhower ordered American troops to halt their advance into Czechoslovakia (see "Czech Republic"), US troops pushed south into Austria. At the same time, US troops were also pushing towards Austria from the south, from Italy, and on May 4, 1945, the two thrusts met.

By the end of the war, in addition to the corridor in Western Austria linking with Italy, US forces held a big chunk of northwest Austria, including Linz and (yes, it's Mozart and the *Sound of Music* again) the beautiful city of Salzburg (liberated on the same day as the link-up with troops from the Italian front).

Austria's capital, Vienna, was and remains the home of the famous white Lipizzaner stallions. Colonel Alois Podhajsky was the head of the Lipizzaners and a former Olympic equestrian. He removed the horses from the capital and brought them to the attention of the US Army and, finally, General George S. Patton Jr., begging for their protection. Patton, a fellow Olympian (modern pentathlon, Stockholm 1912) and cavalryman, responded and enthusiastically offered to make the horses "wards of the US Army."

Austria was divided into four Allied occupying zones after the war, and Americans held Salzburg and Upper Austria. Vienna itself was also divided amongst the four powers.

Austria regained its independence in 1955 and was declared a permanently neutral country.

During the Cold War, this neutrality and Austria's strategic location between east and west made it a popular destination for espionage agents from both sides.

Austria today remains neutral but has granted overflight rights for Operation Enduring Freedom and Operation New Dawn. Austrian troops have trained alongside US troops, and Austrian troops have served alongside US troops, for instance, in Kosovo.

AZERBAIJAN

AN OIL-RICH NATION IN THE CAUCASUS, Azerbaijan is bordered by the Caspian Sea on the east, and in that Caspian, they find some amazing caviar.

After the Russian Revolution in 1917, like people of other nations in the area, the Azeris wanted to break away from Russian control and form their own country. However, President Wilson wasn't keen on this (though he did say nice things about the Azeri delegation he met), preferring instead that the Azeris form part of a confederation with other peoples in the area.

Ultimately, considerable fighting took place in the area in the period around the end of the First World War. Of the Allies, the British were more involved in the fighting than we were, though the American Military

Mission to Armenia did, during its investigations, travel to Baku, the oil-rich capital of Azerbaijan.

Eventually Azerbaijan became part of the Soviet Union.

During the Second World War, Baku played a key role in our efforts to aid the Soviets against the Nazis. We sent supplies and aircraft up through Iran and through Baku, which at that stage was part of the Soviet Union.

During the Cold War, American-made aircraft were in the sky over Baku once again. For instance, on November 20, 1956, a U-2 flown by Francis Gary Powers flew over Baku.

In 1991, Azerbaijan became independent again. Our government then got involved in trying to help sort out the Nagorno-Karabakh conflict between Azerbaijan and Armenia.

Friendly military links between the Azeris and the United States increased after 2001. For instance, Azerbaijan became a vital route for US military aircraft and supplies being taken in and out of Afghanistan. Azerbaijan has taken part in operations alongside us in Afghanistan and in Kosovo and Iraq as well. US and Azeri military personnel have shared cooperative training. The Oklahoma National Guard is partnered with Azerbaijan.

THE BAHAMAS

AH, THE BAHAMAS. Where Christopher Columbus made his first landfall in the New World all those centuries ago. It's well known that the Bahamas have some amazing and beautiful beaches, but a lot of Americans will probably be surprised at how much armed involvement we've had over the years with the islands.

For a start, in the early eighteenth century, Anglo-American pirates operated out of the Bahamas, and both British and American ships set out to hunt them. For instance, Colonel William Rhett, a plantation owner in the Province of Carolina fitted out and led ships in an attempt to stop pirates operating. By 1730, a concerted campaign by the authorities had largely forced the pirates out.

But the Revolutionary War was to see plenty of American military activity in the area. On March 3, 1776, Commodore Esek Hopkins, in the first amphibious assault in US military history, landed marines and sailors on New Providence Island and managed to seize Fort Nassau. The

American forces occupied this for two weeks and, during that time, loaded on board much badly needed gunpowder and many artillery pieces.

And in 1778, we did it again. On January 27 of that year, Captain John Rathbun arrived at New Providence Island with the appropriately named US ship, *Providence*. Rathbun landed his men and captured Fort Nassau, this time freeing American prisoners held there and capturing more weapons and vessels as well.

American military involvement with the Bahamas during the Revolutionary War wasn't finished yet. Not at all. Both American supporters of the revolution and opponents were about to get even more deeply involved. In May 1782, a Spanish and American fleet, including twelve American ships, arrived off New Providence Island and demanded its surrender, and on May 7, the British governor of the islands did indeed surrender. But the islands were not to remain out of the control of the Crown for long because, in May 1783, American Major Andrew Deveaux, fighting on the Crown's side, successfully led an expedition to recapture the islands.

During the Civil War, the Bahamas became a key location for Confederate blockade-runners. In early 1862, the sloop of war USS *Adirondack* was sent to attack blockade-runners off the Bahamas, which it did until it hit a reef. And in August 1862, the Confederate commerce-raider CSS *Florida*, having been built in Liverpool in the UK, was commissioned at Green Cay in the Bahamas. There, it took on coal on that occasion and again later before being finally captured in 1864.

Eventually, the United States and the UK became friends, and at times since then, we've had assorted bases on the islands. For instance, during World War II, the USN had a base in the Exuma area. We've also had rocket-tracking facilities on the islands. And after World War II, the USN established an underwater research facility on Andros Island.

The US and the Bahamas cooperate on a number of security issues these days, for instance, on the fight against illegal narcotics. The Rhode Island National Guard is partnered with the Bahamas.

BAHRAIN

BAHRAIN, IN THE PERSIAN GULF, is home to our 5th Fleet.

From 1861 until 1971, Bahrain was closely aligned with Britain, which managed its foreign affairs and maintained a naval presence. Oil was discovered in the 1930s.

Bahrain joined the Allied side alongside Britain with the start of World War II in 1939. After Mussolini joined the Axis cause, in one of the more extraordinary but little-known episodes of the war, Bahrain's oil refineries were bombed in 1940 by Italian aircraft flying from the distant Mediterranean island of Rhodes. This attack, while it did not cause extensive damage, exposed the Gulf nation's vulnerability to hostile action (see also "Saudi Arabia").

We didn't get heavily involved militarily with Bahrain at this stage. That came later. During World War II, however, we did use the then-RAF base at Muharraq in Bahrain for air transport and air-ferrying purposes.

Britain still has connections with Bahrain, but from the 1970s onwards, American influence in the Gulf, including Bahrain, expanded.

We've assisted Bahrain with military training, exercises, and sales of huge quantities of military equipment, including a frigate as well as Apache and Black Hawk helicopters. In 1991, Bahraini planes flew missions during the Gulf War. In October of 2001, the Bahraini navy, in a show of post-9/11 solidarity, deployed a frigate in support of US operations against the Taliban in Afghanistan. And Bahrain has sent troops to both Iraq and Afghanistan.

We've also made use of Bahrain's air facilities again. For example, US aircraft were based in Bahrain during both Operation Enduring Freedom and Operation Iraqi Freedom.

However, most people think of the USN when they think of Bahrain and the US military. Bahrain has been a base for USN activity in the Persian Gulf since 1947. In 1971, when the British withdrew, the United States took over the naval base from them. And, for instance, USN ships operated from Bahrain against the Iranians during the Tanker War of the 1980s (see "Kuwait").

In 1996, Bahrain became the headquarters for the USN's 5th Fleet, and it is today one of the most important USN bases in the world, home to thousands of US personnel.

In 2011, the Arab Spring spread to Bahrain with demonstrators demanding greater political rights.

Recently the USN has dramatically increased its footprint in Bahrain with an expansion in process that will almost double the size of the USN base there.

BANGLADESH

BANGLADESH, A COUNTRY ABOUT THE SIZE OF WISCONSIN, is almost entirely surrounded by India on its land frontiers, but it does have a short border with Burma in the south and a coastline facing the Bay of Bengal. The royal Bengal tiger is its national animal.

What is now Bangladesh was part of the British Empire until 1947, so our main military involvement up until then was during World War II. With Burma so close, extensive fighting against the Japanese took place nearby.

US forces and supplies moved through the area and, we had a number of important airbases there. US transport planes based at Tejgaon Airport near the capital of Bangladesh, Dhaka, and at Kurmitola Airfield, now Shahjalal International Airport, moved supplies from there into southern China. The airfield at Chittagong, now Shah Amanat International Airport, being close to the fighting was used also for combat and reconnaissance missions. Among US aircraft based there were P-38 Lightnings and C-46s that could drop supplies to Allied troops in the field. The USN also made use of port facilities in what is now Bangladesh, including those at Chittagong.

Between 1947 and 1971, the area was part of Pakistan and became known as East Pakistan. We did have military links with Pakistan, but these were suspended in 1965 during the war between India and Pakistan and were not resumed until 1975. In 1971, after the Bangladesh Liberation War, however, the country separated from Pakistan and became independent Bangladesh.

Since Bangladesh became independent, we have developed some links with the country's forces. For instance, Bangladesh sent troops to join the 1991 Gulf War coalition. We've also assisted with training and developing the country's peacekeeping and anti-terrorist procedures, provided expertise in dealing with emergencies, and helped the Coast Guard of Bangladesh buy boats.

In addition, US military forces have played a major role in helping Bangladesh deal with some of the disasters that have hit it over the years. For instance, after the catastrophic March 1991 cyclone, a US Naval Task Force was rushed in, and US forces are thought to have saved up to two hundred thousand lives. And, in 2007, after another cyclone, two USN vessels and US troops assisted with relief efforts. The Oregon National Guard is partnered with Bangladesh.

BARBADOS

TODAY'S MOST FAMOUS BARBADIAN IS RIHANNA. Huge numbers of Americans have enjoyed visiting Barbados, and in 1751, George Washington visited. He wasn't a man who spent much time outside the United States, so that's got to be pretty special.

We also have some military links with the place. During the Revolutionary War and the War of 1812, our warships targeted assorted ships bound for Barbados and ships departing Barbados. For instance, in January 1814, the US frigate *President* with marines on board captured a number of British ships off Barbados.

Things didn't always go to plan, though. In 1779, the 16-gun privateer *Cumberland*, under the command of John Manley, was captured by a British frigate, and ship and crew were taken to Barbados where they were imprisoned. In the end, though, Manley and his men managed to bribe a jailer, seize a British government tender, place the crew in irons, and escape to the United States.

During World War II, Barbados wasn't part of the Destroyers for Bases deal, but US forces did make some use of the island.

And there was more US military activity after the war. For instance, in the 1950s, we commissioned the United States Naval Facility Barbados, at Harrison's Point in Saint Lucy. That operated there for twenty-two years.

In 1983, Barbados played a major role in Operation Urgent Fury, the invasion of Grenada, offering political and military support, and with Barbados being used as a staging post for the invasion.

In recent years, we've been involved militarily with Barbados through assorted training, exercises, ship visits, and humanitarian operations.

BELARUS

BELARUS IS NEXT TO RUSSIA, more than just geographically. We used to call Belarus, Belorussia, or Byelorussia. Even the name is close to Russia because it means White Russia.

Belarus has long been close to Russia politically, as well, so it's perhaps not surprising that we haven't had vast amounts of military involvement with it. But we have had a small bit.

In the period just after World War II, the CIA and other Western intelligence agencies, which envisaged using nationalists within Belarus to oppose the Soviet regime, re-established in the area after the wartime Nazi occupation. The CIA's controversial efforts with assorted exiles and exile groups had little effect in the end, however.

Among other Cold War operations linked to Belarus were U-2 spy flights over it. For instance, on July 9, 1956, a U-2 set off to fly over targets in Ukraine and Belarus.

In the uncertain period following the break-up of the Soviet Union, our Department of Defense and military, along with various charities, commenced assorted humanitarian efforts in Belarus under Operation Provide Hope. As part of this effort, USAF Airlift Wing aircraft have flown into Minsk with emergency supplies and airlifted children affected by Chernobyl out for specialist medical care.

BELGIUM

THEY HAVE GREAT CHOCOLATE, GREAT BEER, AND GREAT FRIES IN BELGIUM. Excellent.

Belgium seems as if it's been around forever but isn't even as old as the United States. In fact, at least one American was fighting on what is now Belgian soil before Belgium, as we now know it, even existed.

In June of 1815, Sir William Howe De Lancey and his new bride, Magdalene Hall, were invited, but did not attend, the famous Duchess of Richmond's ball in Brussels that preceded the Battle of Waterloo. De Lancey, born in New York City, served as the British Duke of Wellington's deputy quartermaster general in the Waterloo campaign. His father, Stephen De Lancey, had also served as an officer in the 1ˢᵗ New Jersey

Loyal Volunteers in the American Revolution. Sadly, while accompanying the Duke of Wellington at the Battle of Waterloo on June 18, 1815, De Lancey was struck by a bouncing canon ball and fatally wounded.

In August of 1914, with the outbreak of World War I, Belgium was invaded, and mostly occupied, by the Kaiser's army. After President Woodrow Wilson led the United States into war on the side of the Allies in 1917, in part due to the violation of Belgian neutrality, many Americans would fight in and over Belgium.

For example, Robert Lovett, a Yalie who would become secretary of defense in the Korean War, served as a pioneering naval aviator in World War I. One of his missions was to bomb German submarine pens based in Bruges, Belgium. And Americans played a vital role in campaigns that liberated large chunks of Belgium in the last months of the war. In August and September 1918, the American II Corps helped the British wipe out the German-held Lys salient, and in October, the 37th and 91st Divisions joined in an attempt to cross the Scheldt. Finally, on November 2, 1918, just a few days before the Armistice, the 37th managed to get across the Scheldt at Heurne.

Over one hundred thousand Americans were involved in the fighting in Belgium then, and many of them would never return home. Hundreds of American soldiers from the American Expeditionary Forces (AEF) are buried at the Flanders Field American Cemetery in Belgium at Waregem, only a few miles from the scene of the crossing of the Scheldt by the 37th.

In May of 1940, Belgium was once again invaded by the Germans who occupied the country until the fall of 1944.

On September 3, 1944, the US First Army crossed the Belgian border and liberated the city of Mons and the surrounding area. Advancing American troops reported being greeted by bottles of cognac and champagne and by pretty girls. Twenty-five thousand Germans would soon be captured in the Mons pocket.

However, anyone expecting a quick end to the fighting was in for a surprise. One of the largest battles in American military history was fought primarily on the soil of Belgium—yes, it's the Battle of the Bulge.

Hitler had begun planning operation Wacht am Rhein (Watch on the Rhine) shortly after the D-Day landings in June. In spite of the Ultra decrypts, the Germans managed to achieve strategic surprise with a massive counterattack through the Ardennes. At 5:30 a.m. on December 16, 1944, a huge German artillery barrage broke out near the Ardennes forest.

The Germans advanced against inexperienced US divisions or the remnants of shattered units that had been put into a quiet part of the front in order to recuperate, and the attackers were helped by bad weather, which countered Allied air superiority. The 101st Airborne, which had been rushed forward via trucks, was soon completely surrounded at Bastogne.

On December 22, 1944, Von Lüttwitz, commander of the German forces besieging Bastogne, sent two officers to request the surrender of the American garrison. Brigadier General McAuliffe, in temporary command of the 101st Airborne Division, laughed and famously exclaimed "Nuts" in response.

It was near the Belgian town of Malmedy that the most notorious massacre of unarmed American soldiers in our history took place. Sixty-seven men of Battery B of the 285th Field Artillery Observation Battalion who had surrendered were killed by machine gun fire from SS panzers. At least four hundred, including over one hundred Belgian civilians, were killed by Joachim Peiper's 1st SS-Panzer Division. After being tried and sentenced to death, Peiper managed to cheat the hangman's noose, and he was released from prison in 1956.

The German offensive had already caused considerable chaos in the American rear, and Skorzeny's English-speaking German commandos disguised as Americans just added to it. David Niven, an actor who moved to Hollywood seeking fame and fortune, served in the British Army during World War II and found himself caught up in it. When suspicious GIs demanded he tell them who had won the World Series in 1940, he had to confess he had no idea, but he was able to point out to the GIs that he had made a picture with Ginger Rogers in 1938. They let him pass.

In an Allied strategy conference held on December 19, General George S. Patton Jr. assured Eisenhower that he would be ready to counterattack in forty-eight hours. Eisenhower expressed skepticism. Patton, however, was not going to be put off. His view was that the Germans had put their heads in a mincer, and he wasn't going to miss the opportunity to mince them.

Patton kept his word attacking two days later with the US 4th Armored Division and relieving the "Battling Bastards of Bastogne" on December 26. With the weather now improved, allowing Allied air superiority to reassert itself, as German supplies ran out and Allied support began to arrive in force, the German offensive stalled.

The Ardennes Offensive was Hitler's last in the West. With its collapse, the Germans were once again forced into retreat, and by February 1945, Belgium was finally free from the Nazis. But it had come at a heavy price. Thousands of American soldiers from both world wars are buried in three American battle monument cemeteries in Belgium.

American soldiers who had fought in Belgium would go on to play roles small and large in other key scenes from American history. For instance, Officer J. D. Tippitt, shot and killed in Dallas on November 22, 1963, by Lee Harvey Oswald, had won a bronze star for his service in the US Army at the Battle of the Bulge in Belgium.

Since the war, very close military ties have developed between the United States and Belgium. The country became a founding member of NATO in 1949. The headquarters of the NATO alliance is now located just outside Mons in Belgium. And assorted US military units have been based in Belgium since the war. For instance, today, the US Air Force's 309th Airlift Squadron operates at Chièvres Air Base in Belgium.

BELIZE

IT'S NOT A COUNTRY WE'VE HAD THE MOST MILITARY INVOLVEMENT WITH, but we have had just a little bit.

For most of the nineteenth and twentieth centuries, Belize was a British colony, and British influence remained strong after independence, so that limited our involvement somewhat. Plus we've focused more on neighboring Guatemala, and since Guatemala and Belize have had a long-running border dispute, that's perhaps limited our involvement in Belize as well.

Obviously, however, the United States hasn't always been friends with Britain, and during the War of 1812 (actually in January 1813), the USN brig *Viper* was in waters off Belize when it was captured by HMS *Narcissus* under Captain Lumley.

And a force sent by William Walker, American adventurer (see "Nicaragua"), didn't exactly enjoy their time in Belizean waters either. Their schooner, the *Susan*, hit a reef, and their mission had to be abandoned.

However, some Americans who had been involved in a war received more of a welcome in Belize. A number of Confederates fleeing after the Civil War ended up in Belize and founded New Richmond there.

During the 1960s, Guatemala and Belize turned to America to try to mediate the border dispute between them, and LBJ appointed a US lawyer to consider the matter. However, the Belizeans rejected the resulting proposal, and despite a lack of US enthusiasm, Belize became independent in 1981.

Since independence, however, things between the United States and Belize have gotten more friendly, and the US military has developed a number of links with the country.

We opened a military assistance office in Belize in 1983 and have helped provide the Belize Defence Force (BDF) with some training and equipment. The US military has been involved in humanitarian projects there, and the US and Belizean governments cooperate in fighting illegal narcotics. The US Military Liaison Office worked with the BDF to establish the Belize National Coast Guard. And the Louisiana National Guard is partnered with Belize.

BENIN

ITUATED ON THE AFRICAN COAST with Togo to its west and Nigeria to its east, Benin was the home of the great African kingdom of Dahomey.

The port of Ouidah in Benin used to be a major slave port, so not surprisingly the town appears in a lot in descriptions of what our Africa Squadron did in its attempts to stop slaving ships from operating. For instance, in July 1854, Commodore Mayo, on board the USS *Constitution*, dropped anchor at Ouidah. In three days, he then proceeded to send boarding parties aboard at least eight ships. All were then released, but at least he was looking.

What is now Benin eventually became the French colony of Dahomey. In 1960, Dahomey became independent, and in the 1970s, Dahomey acquired a Marxist-Leninist government under Major Mathieu Kérékou and became Benin. Perhaps not surprisingly, considering the Marxist-Leninist bit, we didn't have major military involvement with Benin at that time. Kérékou was president from 1972 to 1991 and then again from 1996 to 2006.

In recent years, however, we have had some links with the Beninese military. For instance, US marines and Beninese soldiers carried out an exercise in silent scouting and observation in Benin in Shared Accord 2009. More broadly, we're involved with Benin in helping it develop the expertise necessary for multinational peace-support operations. Benin has supplied hundreds of troops to the French-led effort in Mali, to which we have also given political and logistical support.

BHUTAN

MILITARILY, BHUTAN HAS A STRONG TRADITION of archery, which is not surprising since that's its national sport. But it also now has an army trained by India. Bhutan is a kingdom situated at the eastern end of the Himalayas with China to the north and India surrounding it to the south.

Mao once described Bhutan as one of the five fingers of Tibet that he aimed to take control over, so it has been a potentially strategic location. However, perhaps because its close foreign policy and defense ties to regional superpower India made links to a global superpower of less interest, we don't seem to have ever had much planned military involvement with the country. Though, someone from Bhutan did recently attend the Asia-Pacific Center for Security Studies' Comprehensive Security Responses to Terrorism (CSRT) course in Honolulu.

Unfortunately, however, American servicemen have died in Bhutan. The time when we had our highest military presence in the region (though not in Bhutan itself) was during World War II, particularly with our program of flying supplies over the Hump from India to China.

During this period, American planes entered Bhutanese airspace on a number of occasions, and some of them crashed there. For instance, on November 3, 1945, just over a month after the war ended, an American C-45 took off from Chabua in northern India, which was a major airbase for flying the Hump, taking men to Karachi in what is now Pakistan, so they could return home. They never made it. The plane crashed in Bhutan near Chhukha killing all on board.

In spite of these incidents or accidents, we have not invaded or seen military involvement with Bhutan.

BOLIVIA

BOLIVIA DERIVES ITS NAME FROM SIMON BOLIVAR. Officially, it is known as the Plurinational State of Bolivia because of the different peoples it contains. Plurinational. Interesting word with something of *e pluribus unum* going on.

We have played a significant role in various periods of Bolivia's history. For instance, in the 1920s, the United States was given control over

Bolivian taxation services in return for a thirty-three-million-dollar loan. And at times, we have had very close links with the Bolivian military. For instance, in the 1960s, significant numbers of Bolivian troops, including most of the senior army officers, had received US training either in America or in the Panama Canal Zone. And America had supported the general, René Barrientos, who was in power in Bolivia in 1967.

In this context, we need to take a look at our most famous military involvement in Bolivia, which is surely the capture and killing of Che Guevara.

Two little-known facts about Che are that "Che" just means "pal," and that Che's father had the name Ernesto Guevara Lynch and had Basque and Irish ancestors.

By the time of his encounter in Bolivia, former Argentinian medical student Che had already had a couple of brushes with the CIA. Che had fled a CIA-supported coup that took power in Guatemala in 1954, and he had subsequently played a hugely significant part in the Cuban revolution. But Che was a dedicated Marxist and, perhaps even more, a dedicated revolutionary. Not content with revolution merely in Cuba, he was determined to export revolution across the globe. After Cuba, he ended up fighting alongside guerrillas in the Congo (see "Democratic Republic of the Congo") against CIA-supported forces. And he ended up losing. Bolivia was to be his next attempt at revolution, his next conflict with the CIA, his next defeat, and indeed his last.

When in early 1967 the CIA began to be aware that Che was operating with a band of guerrillas in Bolivia's southern mountains, they sent weapons, equipment, and special forces trainers to help the Bolivian army against the rebels. It worked. After a few initial successes by Che's forces, Bolivian Special Forces managed to surround his encampment, and Che was captured and wounded but very much alive on October 8, 1967. He was interrogated by a Cuban working for the CIA, Felix Rodriguez, but the Bolivian high command ordered his execution, and he was killed the next day. His body was then photographed and put on public display to prove he was really dead.

Our involvement in Bolivia, however, did not end with Che Guevara's death. For instance, some suspect that the Nixon administration gave significant support to right-wing General Hugo Bánzer Suárez who launched a failed coup attempt in 1970 and a successful coup attempt in 1971 that toppled a left-leaning president.

Today, once again, the US government has its differences with a left-leaning Bolivian president, this time, Evo Morales, and in 2008, the US DEA was expelled from that country.

BOSNIA AND HERZEGOVINA

SAREJEVO, THE CAPITAL OF BOSNIA AND HERZEGOVINA, was the site in 1914 of the assassination of the Archduke Franz Ferdinand that eventually led to the First World War and the scene, a lot less bloody, of the 1984 Winter Olympics.

On June 2, 1995, Captain Scott O'Grady was shot down over Bosnia, and in 2001, the movie *Behind Enemy Lines* came out. The O'Grady incident was one of the reasons for the development of the unmanned drone program we have today. Yes, Bosnia is a land that saw a terrible war in the 1990s, but we've shared other history with it too.

In 1941, the Germans invaded Yugoslavia, a country of which Bosnia was then a part. We sent aircraft to target the German war machine in Bosnia and to help those resistance groups on the ground that were bravely fighting it. Bombing missions would hit targets, such as rail facilities and airfields. For instance, in January 1944, B-24s bombed the airfield at Mostar. Meanwhile, other aircraft would fly supplies and OSS teams in to assist the resistance fighters and to evacuate the wounded and allied aircrew who had been shot down.

Winston Churchill had formed the SOE and commanded them to set Nazi-occupied Europe ablaze with support for local resistance movements. Wild Bill Donovan, the leader of the OSS, wanted to use American resources to accomplish the same mission. Soon, nearly sixty OSS agents were serving directly with Tito, and arms shipments were pouring into Yugoslavia to the partisans and to other resistance fighters.

For example, the first army air force aircraft to land in the Balkans were two C-47s that landed on a rough airstrip at Medeno Polje near Tito's headquarters at Drvar in Bosnia on the night of April 2/3, 1944. They airlifted out thirty-six partisans that night. And in the next few weeks, hundreds more were airlifted out. After a German attack on Tito's headquarters almost captured him, we airlifted out members of his staff. And the amount of supplies being taken in was impressive as well. US aircrews made a huge contribution to the defeat in Bosnia of German forces and their allies.

During World War II, the internal politics of who among the locals was fighting whom in Bosnia were complex, and in the 1990s, they were to be complex again. In 1992, Bosnia and Herzegovina declared independence from Yugoslavia. Civil war was already raging in neighboring Croatia between those who wanted independence and local Serbs who didn't, and soon it would be in Bosnia as well. In addition, though, in the middle of that civil war, Croats and Bosniaks who had previously been fighting the Serbs side by side turned on each other. That was sorted out only with the help of a US government keen to prevent the Croat/Bosniak war further destabilizing Bosnia. And a mini-civil war took place inside the Bihać pocket.

Early in the war, the UN agreed on an arms embargo on Bosnia, and NATO helped enforce that by sea and by air. Then in April 1993, NATO began Operation Deny Flight, an operation to impose a no-fly zone over Bosnia. This was not without incident. For instance, on February 28, 1994, US F-16s shot down a number of Serb jets that had violated the no-fly zone during a bombing attack on an arms factory at Novi Travnik. And soon NATO's role extended to assisting UN ground forces, for instance, hitting Serb targets when the Gorazde safe area was threatened. In June 1995, Scott O'Grady was shot down and rescued after days spent evading capture. And then in August 1996, NATO began Operation Deliberate Force, again unambiguously named, which involved widespread bombing of Serb targets in Bosnia. Meanwhile, since the start of the war, Croat and Bosniak forces had improved considerably both in terms of training and weapons, and some have speculated about a US role in that. The bombing, advances on the ground by Croat and Bosnia forces, and changes in Slobodan Milosevic's attitude eventually led to the Dayton peace conference and the end of fighting in Bosnia.

This did not, however, mean the end of a US military role in Bosnia. Not at all. After the Dayton Peace agreement, NATO ground forces, including US ground forces, moved into Bosnia to help secure the peace and begin the task of stabilizing the country and allowing it to rebuild. We led Multi-National Division North, which took control of the northeast part of Bosnia. The initial force IFOR (Implementation Force) handed over in 1996 to SFOR (Stabilization Force), which in turn handed over in 2004 to a European Union Force EUFOR.

Bosnia has assorted military agreements with the US and participates in exercises with US forces. Bosnia has sent troops to Iraq and Afghanistan, and the Maryland National Guard is partnered with Bosnia.

BOTSWANA

BOTSWANA IS LOCATED IN CENTRAL SOUTHERN AFRICA. It's a little smaller than Texas. Mma Precious Ramotswe, of the No. 1 Ladies' Detective Agency, as featured in the works of novelist Alexander McCall Smith, is based in Gaborone, capital of Botswana. A big chunk of the country is the Kalahari, but it also has places like the Okavango Delta. Considering it's quite a big country, it doesn't have a lot of people.

We have had some significant military involvement in the country.

America is friends with Botswana, and we do conduct some military activities there. A significant percentage of the officer corps of Botswana, for instance, has received training from the United States.

Recently, we've been involved with a variety of actions there, including US Army Africa soldiers helping integrate women in the Botswana Defence Force, but a lot of our involvement in Botswana has been focused on Thebephatshwa Airbase and facilities there. A lot of Southern Accord, a major bilateral US and Botswana exercise in 2012, for instance, took place there.

BRAZIL

A BIG COUNTRY WITH A BIG FUTURE, Brazil is actually one with which we've had quite a lot of military involvement over the years.

It wasn't long after our independence that US ships were involved in military operations in the waters off Brazil. For instance, in December 1812, the USS *Constitution* faced HMS *Java* in a three-hour engagement off the Brazilian coast and defeated the British ship.

And in 1813, the USS *Hornet* was blockading British sloop *Bonne Citoyenne* in Salvador, Brazil, before the arrival of British reinforcements forced *Hornet* to abandon the blockade and head for the Caribbean instead.

In the nineteenth century, the USN had its own Brazil Squadron, originally formed in 1826 to protect American commercial interests but later also used in the fight against slavery. It seized six ships between 1845 and 1849.

The waters of Brazil were to see more action by American warships during the Civil War. In October 1864, the Confederate cruiser *Florida* was captured by Commander Napoleon Collins of the USS *Wachusett* while it was anchored in Bahia.

In 1894, however, we were more worried about events ashore in Brazil, and with conflict raging, we sent US ships as a display of force to Rio de Janeiro to help protect US property and interests in that city.

During World War I, Brazil declared war on Germany in 1917 and took part in some operations. The Brazilian navy, for instance, conducted patrols off West Africa. And links between the US and Brazilian navies continued after the war, with a US naval mission being sent to Brazil.

In World War II, Brazil was again neutral at first but increasingly looked to the Allied side. In 1942, Brazil allowed us to establish airbases in Brazil for air ferrying/transport purposes. Two particularly important airfields were at Belém and Natal.

Brazilian ships were torpedoed, and in August 1942, Brazil declared war on Germany and Italy. At sea, once again, the Brazilian navy fought to keep merchant ships safe from the U-boats. On land, the Brazilian Expeditionary Force fought alongside US troops and, with US assistance, in Italy. In the air, Brazilian pilots flew P-47 Thunderbolts as part of the 350th Fighter Group of the USAAF.

In the period after the war, too, we had assorted links with the Brazilian military, including the US Military Assistance Program. US involvement with the military coup in Brazil in 1964 and in the repression that followed it is another matter.

Recent links between the US military and the Brazilian military include participating in multinational exercises.

BRUNEI

SURROUNDED, ON ITS LAND SIDE BY MALAYSIA, Brunei is a small sultanate that's big in oil and natural gas. Brunei also has a long history, and we've played a brief role in it.

As early as 1845, the USS *Constitution* dropped in hoping to acquire rights to coal deposits. And in 1850, as Brunei began to get a little nervous about British intentions on it, they signed with us a Treaty of Peace, Friendship, Commerce and Navigation, which apparently is still in force.

In 1865, the US consul general to Brunei, Claude Lee Moses, even managed to get from the sultan of Brunei a ten-year lease over a big chunk of northern Borneo, but since this area is now part of Malaysia, we'll cover the story in that chapter.

Eventually, as the nineteenth century wore on, Brunei became an area of British influence, and when in 1945 the Allies arrived to liberate Brunei from Japanese occupation, it was mainly Australian troops that did so. However, American ships and aircraft were a vital part of the invasion forces, being involved in extensive operations against targets in the Brunei area.

More recently, since Brunei gained full independence from Britain, we've conducted joint exercises and assorted other forms of military cooperation with Brunei. In 1994, we signed a memorandum of understanding on military defense cooperation with Brunei.

BULGARIA

BULGARIA'S ON THE BLACK SEA. Well, the coast of it is.

The Bulgars have a fascinating history. Already by the seventh century AD, they had built an empire that was scaring the mighty Byzantines, and the Bulgars even laid siege to Constantinople itself. Yep.

American missionaries first began visiting Bulgaria in the nineteenth century when the area was still part of the Ottoman Empire, and actually Americans built up quite a lot of influence in nineteenth-century Bulgaria. For instance, they opened schools in Bulgaria, and Robert College opened a campus in Istanbul. Soon, over half of its students were Bulgarian, and three future prime ministers of Bulgaria attended.

In 1876, a rebellion broke out in Bulgaria against Ottoman rule. The Ottoman authorities crushed the rebellion, and massacres ensued. The American consul general in Istanbul and an American journalist with the (unusual and rather interesting) name of Januarius MacGahan played key roles in telling the world about the massacres.

Eventually, Russia demanded the Ottomans enact measures to ensure the protection of, among others, the Bulgarians. When the Ottomans refused, Russia went to war and, after fierce fighting, defeated it, leading to Bulgarian independence under nominal Ottoman rule.

Bulgaria declared itself fully independent in 1908, and because of its close links to Russia, it might have seemed likely that, with the arrival of World War I, Bulgaria would have joined the Allied side. However, territorial disputes with Serbia, Romania, and Greece eventually meant the country, instead, joined the war in 1915 on the side of Germany and Austria-Hungary. Bad decision.

The United States, however, had no particular quarrel with Bulgaria, and the influence of American missionaries was still significant there, and when we declared war on Germany and subsequently on Austria-Hungary in 1917, we did not declare war on her ally Bulgaria. This led to the slightly improbable situation of us still being at peace with a country that a short distance beyond its southern borders was fighting bitter battles against our allies.

Eventually in 1918 as Allied forces broke through Bulgarian defenses, the country was forced to ask for peace and lost a lot of territory in the peace deal that followed. The inter-war years were often not easy ones for Bulgarians. In 1939, another world war broke out, and once again, Bulgaria joined the losing side. Another bad decision.

In January 1941, "Wild Bill" Donovan went on a whirlwind tour of the Balkans that was paid for by MI6. Donovan met Tsar Boris III of Bulgaria who thought the American naïve and ignorant of Balkan politics and history. Donovan, for his part, thought Boris an extremely frightened man. He would not be deterred from joining the Axis, which seemed supremely victorious at the time.

Donovan accompanied George Earle, the US ambassador to Bulgaria, to a Sofia nightclub. Meanwhile, Abwehr agents broke into his room at the Bulgarie Hotel and stole his traveling bag. When the bag was later recovered by Bulgarian police, a list of questions posed by the USN was the only missing item.

In World War II, although Bulgaria joined the Axis, it refused to send its troops to fight in Operation Barbarossa. On December 13 of 1941, Bulgaria, less than a week after the Pearl Harbor attack, declared war on the United States, and the United States would soon be targeting Bulgaria. In 1943 and 1944, for instance, the USAAF conducted multiple bombing raids on Sofia. Hundreds of Allied airmen, including many Americans, were shot down and became POWs in Bulgaria.

While the British SOE focused its Balkan efforts on Yugoslavia, it encouraged the OSS to penetrate Bulgaria and Romania where it did not operate. The Cereus network was designed to encourage widespread sabotage in Bulgaria.

In August 1943, Tsar Boris III died under suspicious circumstances after paying a visit to Adolf Hitler who had berated him for not assisting in the invasion of the Soviet Union. Perhaps Boris was the naïve one about the threats to himself and his country.

In September of 1944, the Red Army invaded Bulgaria, and Bulgaria abandoned Germany and joined the Allies. However, Soviet influence was strong, and a pro-Soviet government soon took control in Bulgaria.

An American Military Mission with General Crane initially in command formed part of the Allied Control Commission for Bulgaria. By mid-1945, fifty American officers and enlisted men were stationed in Bulgaria, mainly living at the American college near Simeonovo, a few miles from the capital. The ground section under Lieutenant Colonel John Bakeless continued intelligence activities, including gathering information about Soviet forces. Bulgaria soon came under firm Soviet domination.

One of the better-known Bulgarians of the Cold War period was Georgi Markov. He was a Bulgarian writer who defected to the West in 1969. He later worked for Radio Free Europe out of London before being poisoned by a ricin pellet that had been injected into his thigh with an umbrella while crossing Waterloo Bridge. He is buried in a small country churchyard in Dorset.

Radio Free Europe was financed by the CIA. The exposure of this fact in a 1967 *Ramparts* magazine story caused some embarrassment in the West, but actually may have enhanced its credibility in the Eastern bloc. An American invasion of the Iron Curtain via radio waves began with the Voice of America broadcasting into Russia in 1947. An astonishing 92 percent of the Soviet visitors to the 1958 Brussels World Fair admitted to listening to the Voice's broadcasts.

This American radio invasion had a significant impact on the Warsaw-pact nations, including Bulgaria. Vaclav Havel of Czechoslovakia, for instance, said that, if his fellow citizens had heard of him before he was made president, then it was due to these stations. When Lech Walesa was asked to comment on the impact Radio Free Europe had on the Polish Revolution, he simply asked whether the world could exist without the sun.

The Communist regime in Bulgaria tried to stamp out the impact of this American invasion by offering free overhauls on radios, the only catch being that after the free overhaul, you could only get Radio Sofia on them.

Since the collapse of Communism in Bulgaria, close links have been established between the US and Bulgarian militaries.

Bulgaria, for instance, sent a contingent to fight in Iraq in 2003. Bulgaria joined the NATO alliance in 2004. And a Bulgarian contingent serves alongside us in Afghanistan as of this writing. Currently, about twenty-five hundred US military personnel are serving at a number of bases within Bulgaria. The USN pays regular visits to Bulgarian ports. The Tennessee National Guard is partnered with Bulgaria.

BURKINA FASO

A LANDLOCKED COUNTRY IN WEST AFRICA, Burkina Faso is about the size of Colorado. It used to be called Upper Volta, if you ever wondered what happened to Upper Volta. Its football team is named "Les Étalons," the Stallions, after a legendary twelfth century warrior, horsewoman, and mother of the Mossi Empire, Princess Yennenga. Basically, we (unlike Princess Yennenga) haven't had a lot to do with this country militarily until quite recently.

In recent years we have, however, trained three battalions of 750 troops, each from Burkina Faso for peacekeeping operations in Darfur. Also, Burkinabé troops took part alongside US forces in Flintlock 10, an AFRICOM-sponsored exercise, centered on Ouagadougou (capital of Burkina Faso) and designed to boost Special Operations Forces' capabilities in the region.

Burkina Faso is strategically located close to areas where the United States is concerned about the activities of Islamist jihadists. Burkina Faso has recently become a member of Trans-Sahara Counterterrorism Partnership (TSCTP), and Ouagadougou has become a focus of some US counterterrorism interest.

BURMA

O NE FAMOUS NAME THAT WILL BE FOREVER LINKED to US military involvement with the land of Burma is Merrill's Marauders. The story of Merrill's Marauders is an epic of endurance, courage, and daring, fighting behind enemy lines in Japanese-occupied Burma against larger numbers of Japanese and having to cope with the challenges of warfare in very difficult conditions and very far from base. The Marauders caused large numbers of casualties to the Japanese and extensive disruption to their communications, and the culmination of their efforts was the capture, with the assistance of Nationalist Chinese troops, of Myitkyina in the summer of 1944.

However, the brave efforts of Merrill's Marauders were certainly not the only US military involvement in Burma during World War II.

For instance, "Vinegar Joe" Stilwell led Nationalist Chinese troops in Burma, the USAAF flew large numbers of missions in the area in support of Allied ground troops, and OSS Detachment 101 helped train and organize and fought alongside Kachin resistance groups.

The end of World War II wasn't to be the end of our military involvement with Burma either.

The CIA has been involved in Burma. For instance, in 1951, during the Korean War, the CIA began helping train and arm Nationalist Chinese troops in the part of Burma near the Chinese border, encouraging them to infiltrate China. The operation was not, however, a success. Their infiltration attempts were ruthlessly countered by the Communist Chinese, and some of the Nationalist Chinese switched to harvesting opium poppies in Burma's Golden Triangle instead.

In 1962, General Ne Win took power in Burma in a coup and instituted policies that for decades left Burma isolated from the international community in many senses. Now, though much less isolated, the country still faces many challenges.

After the devastating Tropical Cyclone Nargis hit Burma in 2008, the US military rushed to send humanitarian help. The first US military relief flight flew to Rangoon in May. Opposition from the Burmese authorities has, however, impeded some assistance from our forces.

BURUNDI

A SMALL COUNTRY IN CENTRAL AFRICA, Burundi is about the size of Maryland. And this isn't going to be a big chapter either.

Like its rather better-known neighbor, Rwanda, Burundi has had at times a turbulent history, involving coups and ethnic conflict between Hutus and Tutsi.

In April 1994, President Bill Clinton sent troops to Burundi in order to be ready to evacuate American and other civilians from Rwanda. And in

September 1996, a US Air Force C-141 flew into Bujumbura, the capital of Burundi to evacuate civilians threatened by the situation in the country.

Burundi's history is not something we've really played a big part in. In recent years, however, Burundi has seen some better times, and we're now involved in training the Burundian military.

Burundi has contributed peacekeepers to Somalia, and much of our military involvement with Burundi is aimed at developing its forces' peacekeeping expertise. For instance, in the summer of 2012, the Burundians created the First Sapper Company of the Burundi National Defense Force with help from marines from Security Cooperation Team-2, Special-Purpose Marine Air-Ground Task Force Africa. And in March 2013, US troops were giving Burundian soldiers deployment logistics training at Gakumbu Camp in Burundi. In December 2013, as the French moved into the Central African Republic (CAR) to try to stop the fighting, the United States offered to help by sending planes to airlift Burundian troops to the CAR in support.

CAMBODIA

A NAME VERY, VERY FAMILIAR TO MOST AMERICANS, Cambodia was a French protectorate from 1867 to 1953 when it gained its independence. It was, however, occupied by the Japanese during World War II, which brought about our first military involvement with the country. For instance, on February 7, 1945, US B-29s bombed targets in and around Phnom Penh. Obviously, it wasn't to be the last time US heavy bombers would pound targets inside Cambodia.

On April 7, 1954, President Dwight Eisenhower articulated the domino theory: "You have a row of dominoes set up, you knock over the first one, and what will happen to the last one is the certainty that it will go over very quickly." Cambodia was, perhaps, the domino that fell the hardest of all.

Cambodia was to see appalling tragedy as competing forces battled for control in a complex and sometimes confusing (and confused) pattern of changing alliances.

In 1965, during the Vietnam War, Prince Sihanouk allied Cambodia with North Vietnam and China. Sihanouk allowed Communists from North Vietnam to use the Ho Chi Minh trail that wound through his country to resupply the Viet Cong in South Vietnam. The VC also found sanctuary from American air attack in neighboring Cambodia.

However, battling to balance forces within the country, Sihanouk also allowed his pro-American defense minister Lon Nol to crack down on Cambodian leftists. The result was the rise of the Khmer Rouge and the beginning of the Cambodian Civil War as the central government battled increasingly bitter and effective Communist guerrillas.

In March of 1970, a coup deposed Prince Sihanouk from power while he was out of the country. Lon Nol, the premier and defense minister who led the coup, immediately asked for American support.

Sihanouk was soon in Beijing and renewed his Communist alliance, teaming up with the Khmer to fight the new government. If ever a chance had existed of keeping Cambodia out of the carnage that had engulfed Vietnam, it was now almost gone.

In April of 1970, President Richard Nixon launched an "incursion" into Cambodia aimed at smashing the infrastructure within Cambodia that helped enable the Viet Cong to operate within South Vietnam. Direct US ground forces involvement lasted about three months; about thirty thousand US troops and fifty thousand ARVN troops took part. Most US forces were withdrawn from Cambodia by June 30, 1970, but the US bombing of targets inside Cambodia continued.

At almost the same, though, the Communists were also starting to advance inside Cambodia, and US air power was used also to try to support government troops against them. The United States dropped more than 540,000 tons of explosives in Cambodia, claiming at least thirty thousand lives, until Congress cut off funds in August 1973.

Well before 1975, signs of strain had been showing between the Khmer Rouge, primarily supported by Beijing and the North Vietnamese who were looking more to Moscow, but the Cambodian government and its forces were in total disarray and unable to stop the Khmer Rouge's advance on Phnom Penh.

Lon Nol resigned on April 1 to give negotiations a chance, but on April 12, with the city about to fall, Operation Eagle Pull evacuated US diplomats from Phnom Penh.

In May of 1975, a US-flagged merchant ship, *Mayaguez*, was seized by a Khmer Rouge gunboat. Thirty-nine crew members were held hostage. President Gerald Ford, determined to avoid a second *Pueblo* incident (see "North Korea"), ordered F-4 Phantom fighters based in Thailand to attack Koh Tang Island. On May 14, an assault force of about 175 US marines assaulted dug-in Khmer Rouge positions. The *Mayaguez* crew were later rescued from a fishing boat. Forty American servicemen were killed in the operation.

Pol Pot took over in Cambodia and launched a vast genocide. Pol Pot's Khmer Rouge were responsible for approximately two million deaths as Cambodia was transformed into a "killing field" from 1976 to 1979.

Many different groups, including various religions, were targeted for destruction. Only one thousand out of approximately sixty thousand Cambodian monks survived the terror. The Muslim Cham were slaughtered, and their mosques were converted or razed to the ground. The Catholic cathedral in Phnom Penh was destroyed along with nearly half of Cambodia's Catholics.

Pol Pot also persecuted ethnic minorities, such as Vietnamese. Vietnam eventually decided it had had enough of Pol Pot and launched a full-scale invasion of Cambodia on Christmas Day 1978. Phnom Penh was captured in 1979, and Pol Pot was driven into exile in Thailand.

The US government wasn't too enthusiastic about a new status quo in Cambodia dictated by Vietnam, but in recent years, ties between the US military and the Cambodian government have restarted in a limited sense. For example, in 2002 the USN deployed a medical research unit to Phnom Penh. Since 2006, the USN has resumed port visits to Phnom Penh and assisted the Cambodian Navy in training exercises.

CAMEROON

CAMEROON IS LOCATED TO THE SOUTH AND EAST OF NIGERIA. And like Nigeria, it's had quite a few triumphs on the soccer pitch. Its soccer team even won the gold medal at the Sydney Olympics in 2000.

It's a fairly big country by world standards, about the size of California, but this is going to be quite a short chapter, since basically we haven't had that much military involvement with Cameroon. Cameroon, for instance, still has military links with France, one of the former colonial powers.

However, USN ships were in the area in the nineteenth century during anti-slaving operations, and USN ships have been in the area occasionally since. For example, in 2005, the USS *Emory S. Land* landed some naval personnel in Douala for a visit. And the USS *Robert G. Bradley* visited in 2011. Cameroon has taken part in maritime exercises and training alongside US forces.

On land, over the years, we've also supplied training, for instance, recently training Cameroonian peacekeepers. The USAF has also flown humanitarian relief missions there. For instance, in November 1988, the 9th Military Airlift Squadron flew an ambulance to Douala.

CANADA

OH, CANADA, LAND OF THE MAPLE LEAF, is now one of our oldest and closest allies (it couldn't get much closer geographically either). The Peace Arch marks the border between Washington State and British Columbia. We fought alongside them in two world wars. They are founding members of NATO. They have been supportive of Operation Enduring Freedom in Afghanistan. The recent Oscar-winning movie *Argo* reminded us of the heroic role of the Canadian ambassador in rescuing Americans trapped in Iran during the hostage crisis. So surely we have never invaded our hockey-loving friends to our north?

Of course we have! Even before America was a country, Americans were invading Canada. We, along with the British, invaded French Canada during the Seven Years War (or French and Indian War, 1754–1763). In fact, George Washington gained his first military experience fighting in the Ohio Valley in this conflict.

At the battle of Quebec, which took place on September 13, 1759, Wolfe defeated Montcalm, with six companies of American rangers participating alongside British forces in the battle. The French lost Canada to the British.

Voltaire's cynical verdict on the Seven Years War was that "the two nations are fighting each other over a few acres of snow on the Canadian frontier and this lovely war is costing them rather more than the whole of Canada is actually worth." This fight over "a few acres of snow" in Canada was, however, to have rather far-reaching consequences. The cost of paying for this war compelled the British to raise taxes on their American colonies. The rest, as they say, is history …

And even before the actual declaration of independence, the American colonials were invading Canada. In 1775, General Philip Schuyler, an ancestor of mine (Chris Kelly's) led the Continental Army on an invasion of Canada. The patriot forces hoped to rally the French-speaking Canadians to their cause. It wasn't a great success for us. In fact, it was a bit of a disaster. We took Montreal and besieged Quebec, but we failed to take it, and British reinforcements launched a counter-offensive that drove our forces out.

I have in my possession a letter dated March 17, 1776, and written on behalf of another ancestor of mine, James Van Rensselaer. The letter was a gift from my grandmother, Georgina Van Rensselaer, of Bedford, New York. James Van Rensselaer was, at the time, a Captain in the American army invading Canada. He was a leader of the New York colonial militia who fought in the American Revolution and evidently longed to go home. The letter is signed simply "B. Arnold." Here is the full text:

> Sir [General Wooster],
>
> Captain Van Rensselaer being anxious to go home I have permitted him to go to Montreal, until your pleasure is known. The troops who have lately arrived here are not mustered. Neither have I any person here fit for that office, that can be spared from their office.
>
> I am your obedient servant,
> B. Arnold
>
> Camp before Quebec
> March 17, 1776

How many members of invading armies from the dawn of time from all nations have been "anxious to go home"? How many young Americans in our military now stationed around the world have had similar feelings?

After the American Revolution was won, many American Tories fled to Canada. Other Americans, however, were casting covetous glances on our northern neighbor. Benjamin Franklin, a revolutionary with pacifist leanings, suggested that we should purchase Canada from the British. Thomas Jefferson, more bellicose and a believer in an "Empire of Liberty," wrote in a letter dated August 4, 1812, "The acquisition of Canada, this year, as far as the neighbourhood of Quebec, will be a mere matter of marching; & will give us experience for the attack of Halifax the next, & the final expulsion of England from the American continent." The Anglophobic Jefferson encouraged his protégé and fellow Democrat James Madison to declare war on Britain, which he did in 1812.

During the War of 1812, the hapless Stephen Van Rensselaer III (yet another ancestor of Chris's), led the New York militia in an invasion of Canada at the Battle of Queenston in October 1812. Historian George Daughan, in *1812: The Navy's War* (Basic Books, 2011), wrote, "Van Rensselaer, as he had throughout the battle, stayed on the New York side of the river away from the fighting."

Many of us know that the British burned the White House in 1814 during the 1812 war (Tony Blair offered a belated apology to George W. Bush not long ago). Fewer, however, are aware that the burning was a reprisal for the American burning of York (now Toronto) that followed the American victory at the Battle of York on April 27, 1813. And it wasn't just burning. A fair bit of plundering took place as well. The parliamentary mace of Upper Canada, for instance, disappeared off to Washington, and the Canadians got hold of it again only in 1934, courtesy of President Franklin D. Roosevelt (FDR).

During the war, Master Commandant Oliver Hazard Perry led the fledgling USN to victory over the mighty Royal Navy in the Battle of Lake Erie on September 10, 1813. After the battle, Perry wrote to his commanding officer, "We have met the enemy and they are ours."

The War of 1812 was a war of choice, which was divisive and tremendously unpopular in Federalist strongholds, such as New England. Support or opposition to the war ran very closely along partisan political lines. Many farmers in New England sold cattle and supplies to the British during the war. A secessionist movement even convened at the Hartford Convention of 1814 in opposition to "Mr. Madison's war." The Federalist governor of Massachusetts, Caleb Strong, actually wrote a letter to his counterpart, the governor of Nova Scotia, offering a separate peace in exchange for settling the border with what later became the state of Maine.

The War of 1812 was essentially a draw for America and Britain. It was, however, a decisive victory for Canada, which was never really invaded again by the United States. But it was also a decisive defeat for the First Peoples of Canada, who lost their great leader Tecumseh and any real hope of halting the American westward expansion. Native Americans who had fought loyally alongside the British in North America were not even invited to attend the peace conference at Ghent, which concluded the war.

That did not, however, mean the end of border disputes between the United States and Canada. For instance, we had the Aroostook War of 1838-1839. This actually ended without violence, in a compromise, though militias had been called out.

In 1844, the Democratic presidential candidate and eventual winner, James K. Polk, ran on a platform of taking control over the entire Oregon Territory and adopted the famous campaign slogan, "Fifty-four Forty or Fight!" after the line of latitude serving as the northern boundary of Oregon at 54°40'. Polk's plan was to claim, and go to war over, the entire territory for the United States. Under Polk's scheme, virtually all present-day British Columbia would have formed part of the United States. After he was elected president, however, Polk instead turned his attention south fighting the Mexican-American War (see "Mexico") from 1846 to 1848.

And then, we come to the famous, or possibly infamous, Pig War of 1859. The San Juan Islands lying between Vancouver Island and the North American mainland were the subject of dispute between the United States and Britain. In 1859, things got serious, particularly for a certain pig, after an American farmer on the island found it in his garden and shot it. Unfortunately for the situation between the United States and Britain, the pig had belonged to an employee of the Hudson's Bay Company. The conflict began to escalate. US troops landed on the island, and soon after that, British warships turned up. A tense stand-off began. In the end, however, the dispute did go to arbitration, and the United States got the islands. The only casualty of this "war" was porcine.

As absurd as the Pig War may seem to us now, it raises some fascinating historical conjectures. What if President James Buchanan had led the United States into a shooting war with Great Britain in 1859? Would the US Civil War have been postponed or deferred as all states, slave and free, rallied against a common enemy … over bacon?

From 1866 to 1870, the Fenian Brotherhood (Americans of Irish descent who supported independence for Ireland) mounted five unsuccessful raids into British Canada. The Fenians, most of them veterans of the US Civil War, sought to influence events in Ireland by attacking British-held Canada. A Fenian bard wrote …

> We are a Fenian Brotherhood, skilled in the arts of war.
> And we're going to fight for Ireland, the land that we adore.
> Many battles we have won, along with the boys in blue.
> And we'll go and capture Canada, for we've nothing else to do.
> — Fenian Drinking Song, 1866

The Fenians were led by Union Army veteran officers, such as John O'Neil who had a distinguished record in the Seventh Michigan Cavalry. The Fenian raiders were the first forces to serve under the banner of the

Irish Republican Army. The Fenians even tried out a submarine in New York's East River!

Some have speculated that the American government may have turned a blind eye to these activities in part due to British support for the Confederacy during the American Civil War. In any event, the decisive Canadian defeat of these raiding parties at the Battle of Ridgeway in 1866 helped to bind the Canadian confederacy and form a stronger national Canadian identity.

A border dispute between Alaska and Canada was solved by compromise and without violence after arbitration in 1903.

The interesting thing is that, though we are such good friends with Britain and Canada today, even as late as the 1920s and 1930s, we had a secret war plan for what might happen if we ended up fighting a war against the British Empire. This is War Plan Red, and a key part of it was, yep, an American invasion of Canada!

CAPE VERDE/CABO VERDE

NOT ONE OF THE BIGGEST COUNTRIES IN THE WORLD, Cape Verde/ Cabo Verde is a group of islands off the coast of Africa. Nevertheless, hundreds of thousands of Americans have ancestors from Cape Verde, with a particularly big community located in New England.

It's not surprising, therefore, to find that we have a long history of links, including some military ones, with the islands. Already by the eighteenth century, American whalers were recruiting crew from the islands, and we had a consul there by 1818.

In addition, for much of the time, it was conducting anti-slavery operations off the African coast. In the nineteenth century, the USN's African Squadron was based at Porto Praya in the Cape Verde Islands. And they even captured a number of slavers in and around Porto Praya. For instance, in 1846, the schooner *Robert Wilson* had been forced into Porto Praya by bad weather. When Captain Skinner of the USS *Jamestown* investigated the ship, he found evidence on board that it was indeed a slaving vessel. The vessel was confiscated, and in the United States, its master was given a one-thousand-dollar fine and a three-year jail sentence. But he was pardoned in April 1847.

U-boats operating off Cape Verde were a concern during World War II, and US ships were accordingly dispatched to patrol the waters.

At one stage, General Marshall apparently authorized spending five hundred thousand dollars to draw up a plan to have US commandos invade the Cape Verde Islands, but it never happened.

Cape Verde became independent in 1975, and in recent years, we've again had assorted military links with the country. For instance, the USN and USCG have been working with the Cape Verde Coast Guard and police to boost their abilities in dealing with suspect vessels. And Cape Verde was one of the nations participating with the USN in the multinational maritime exercise Saharan Express 2013.

CENTRAL AFRICAN REPUBLIC

THE CENTRAL AFRICAN REPUBLIC is located, not surprisingly, in Central Africa. It seems to be, though, one of those countries that comparatively few people in America know much about.

It's faced some very difficult times over the last decades, including its brief transformation into the Central African Empire under Emperor Bokassa the First (who was almost certainly also Bokassa the Last), and it's still facing them.

We haven't exactly had a huge military involvement with the country, but we have had some. There were three mutinies against the government in 1996 and 1997, and in May 1996, President Bill Clinton reported the deployment of US military personnel to the capital of the Central African Republic to help evacuate US citizens and boost the security of the US embassy there.

In 2002, Operation Shepherd Sentry again saw US troops on a mission to evacuate people from the Central African Republic.

In recent years, the US military offered some assistance and advice to the Central African Republic's military in attempts counter the activities of the notorious militia, the Lord's Resistance Army, with American teams based in Obo and Djema.

Sadly, in 2013, the fighting between different militias in the Central African Republic started to get much worse, and large numbers have been killed there. In December 2013, as the French moved into the Central African Republic to try to stop the fighting, the United States, among other actions, sent thee C-17s and USAF personnel to airlift Burundian troops and supplies into the country in order to help them.

CHAD

YEP, IT'S A GUY'S NAME, and what about those hanging chads from the 2000 election? But Chad is also the name of a huge landlocked African country that has long sat astride important and often valuable trans-Saharan trade routes and is now an oil producer as well.

It was a French colony from 1920, and during World War II, unlike some other French colonies, which stayed under the control of the pro-German Vichy regime, Chad rapidly (and wisely) joined the free French side. That meant it was open for use by the Allied war effort and open for use by our own trans-Saharan efforts. The French airbase at what was then Fort Lamy (now Ndjamena, the capital) was a vital transit base for Allied airplanes crossing from African ports on the Atlantic coast to the Middle East, which meant visits from American aircraft and aircrew.

But it was sometime after Chad gained its independence in 1960 that we really started taking an interest in Chad militarily.

The independent nation faced plenty of challenges, including conflict between southerners and northerners, but that wasn't primarily why we were interested in Chad. In fact, the person who made us interested in Chad wasn't even Chadian. It was Colonel Gaddafi.

Libya is Chad's northern neighbor, and in the repeated conflicts that spread across Chad, Gaddafi saw opportunity for himself there leading to repeated Libyan interventions, both military and diplomatic.

In 1981, after the Gulf of Sidra incident where US planes were fired on by Libyan planes and two Libya planes were subsequently shot down (see "Libya"), the US government was desperately looking for greater leverage in its dealing with Gaddafi.

So the CIA began funneling arms and support to Hissène Habré and helped him take power in Chad and fight Gaddafi. It has been estimated that a massive half billion dollars' worth of support went to Chad in the 1980s, and in August 1983, President Ronald Reagan even reported the deployment of eight F-15s, two AWACS planes, and ground support staff to help fight the Libyans.

The story has more plot twists and turns than many Hollywood thrillers, but by 1987 after thousands of Libyans had been killed and they had finally fallen out with their main local allies at the time, the Libyans were pushed out of Chad. It was a massive defeat for Gaddafi, but Habré's success came at a high price for Chad as well.

Habré turned out to be not exactly an ideal leader, and he was deposed in 1990. Further periods of conflict followed, including cross-border tension with Sudan.

More recently, the US government has been taking a renewed interest in the area, for instance, offering counterterrorism training to Chadian troops.

CHILE

EVER HEARD OF THE CHILEAN-AMERICAN WAR? No? Well that's, of course, because it never actually happened, but it almost did.

As US horizons began to expand in the early nineteenth century, it was inevitable that pretty soon the United States would come into close contact with the new, young state of Chile.

And indeed as early as 1811, with the Chilean struggle for independence from Spain still in progress, one Joel Roberts Poinsett appeared in Chile. He was appointed by President James Madison as consul general in the area, but this was a man who didn't limit his diplomacy to that of the more conventional type. Instead, in his mission to protect American ships from seizure, he ended up fighting as part of the Chilean Army.

At about the same time, we also fought a battle in Chilean waters, though this one wasn't against the Chileans. In the Battle of Valparaiso, the USS *Essex* fought bravely but eventually lost against British warships, the fearsomely named HMS *Phoebe* and HMS *Cherub*.

By the late nineteenth century, Chile with a certain amount of support from Britain was making itself something of a regional power. The Chilean Navy, for instance, modeled after the British Royal Navy, became a formidable force, including for instance, the *Almirante Cochrane*, a 3,560-ton ironclad frigate built in Hull (UK) in 1874. In the War of the Pacific from 1879 to 1883, Chile took on both Peru and Bolivia and won. As a consequence of that war, Bolivia lost her entire coastline and remains a landlocked nation to this day. And Chile even began a modest overseas territorial expansion of its own, annexing the Easter Islands in 1888.

With Chile's links to Britain and with the United States having its own ambitions in South America, Chile's expanding power wasn't entirely to our liking. The United States had, for instance, lent some support to Peru during the War of the Pacific. And things between the Chileans and us didn't get any friendlier when the Chileans rejected our attempts to bring an earlier end to the War of the Pacific.

In 1891, civil war broke out in Chile, and we supported one side, while Britain supported the other. We seized an arms shipment bound for the other side, and when our side lost, we gave asylum in the US mission to some of its leaders. So, when in October 1891 sailors from the USS *Baltimore* came ashore on leave in Valparaiso, things were already tense, and they were about to get a lot tenser as fighting broke out leading to the deaths of two US sailors. The United States demanded immediate reparations; the Chileans refused until a judicial investigation was complete. War was a strong possibility for some time, but in the end, it never happened.

During the 1891 crisis, some in the US military actually feared that Chilean ships might start shelling American coastal cities. However, in the end, Chilean fears that the United States would attack it eventually led it to agree to US terms.

In 1908, America's Great White Fleet called in at Punta Arenas on its epic voyage around the world.

Chile was the last nation to join the Allies in World War II, declaring war on Japan in 1945 near the war's end. Still, as the saying goes, better late than never.

During the Cold War, many Americans feared Communist expansion into central and Latin America. The Monroe Doctrine provided American foreign policymakers with a rationale for intervening to prevent the spread of Soviet and Cuban influence in this region.

In Chile's 1964 presidential election, the CIA secretly helped to fund the successful candidacy of Eduardo Frei Montalva against his Socialist rival Salvador Allende.

The presidential election of Salvador Allende in a three-way election by a 1.5 percent margin in 1970, therefore, represented a dilemma for American policymakers who were already facing severe problems in Vietnam. Henry Kissinger called Chile "a dagger pointed at the heart of America." The CIA received orders to plan for a coup. The CIA identified General Camilo Valenzuela as a "general with balls" who could lead a successful coup. Chilean General Schneider was assassinated among rumors of CIA involvement.

The Chilean coup occurred on September 11, 1973. Allende had accepted the support of Fidel Castro and alienated the Chilean military. Surrounded in his own presidential palace, he ended up shooting himself with an AK-47 that had been a gift from Castro. Ironically and, in spite of repeated allegations of CIA involvement, there is little evidence for its direct meddling in the coup that toppled Allende. At most, the CIA was aware of the plot and may have lent encouragement.

Augusto Pinochet, the chief plotter against Allende who received US government support after the coup, was accused of murdering more than thirty-two hundred people over his seventeen-year reign.

In recent years, the US military has worked closely with Chile on assorted security matters, including the development of a joint Chilean and US base for peacekeeping training at Fort Aguayo in Chile. Also, the USAF sent teams to Chile to help after an earthquake in 2010. The Texas National Guard is partnered with Chile.

CHINA

GIVEN ITS VAST SIZE AND ECONOMIC IMPORTANCE, it's no surprise outsiders have had their eyes on the potential China holds for hundreds of years. Our latest "invasion" is led by Starbucks, which plans to open 1,500 stores in China by 2015, hoping to convert an ancient tea-drinking culture to the pleasures of coffee.

China, a huge land with an amazing history and culture and such resources and potential, seems certain to be one of the great powers of the twenty-first century. In fact, China's now such a major military power that it seems almost surprising that US forces have ever been in action on Chinese soil. But, they have. In fact, our troops were regularly in action in China for about an entire century from the 1840s to the 1940s.

In the nineteenth century, America was one of the Western powers eager to open up China to Western trade and influence. It was far from always a peaceful process, and from 1843 onwards, we regularly sent in troops to protect American citizens and American interests in China, particularly in the so-called treaty ports in which Western traders held a privileged position. A particular focus of American concern was the American part of the Shanghai International Settlement.

Most of these incidents were small, short-term operations, like our brief involvement bombarding Chinese forts in the Second Opium War, the 1855 Battle of Ty-Ho Bay against Chinese pirates, or the punitive Formosan Expedition of 1867. But as the nineteenth century turned into the twentieth century, that was all about to change.

The Society of the Harmonious Fist (Boxers) was a Chinese secret society that led an anti-foreign and anti-Christian uprising in China from 1899 to 1901. In the summer of 1900, there was a famous siege of the international legations area in Beijing, including the American legation, in which American soldiers under the command of Captain John T. Myers played a heroic role in hanging on against huge numbers of attackers. Eventually in August, after a battle at Yangcun in which troops of our 14th Infantry Regiment played a key role, an international force broke through to Beijing and lifted the siege of the legations. Looting and reprisals followed.

In 1908, part of America's Great White Fleet called in at Amoy during its epic voyage around the world.

China managed pretty much to stay out of the First World War, though the Kaiser's Germany lost her colonial foothold in Tsingtao.

Throughout the First World War, our 15th Infantry Regiment remained stationed in China, and although a lot of Americans today don't know it, the regiment actually was based there until 1938, which is why its regimental crest is a dragon.

Another element of our deployment in China was the Yangtze Patrol, a fascinating part of our naval history that deserves to be much better known, in which US ships long cruised China's mighty river.

In the period between the wars, China saw plenty of major political turmoil, and we continued regular deployments in China to protect Americans and American interests. For instance, in 1925, we sent in troops to protect civilians in the Shanghai International Settlement from rioting and fighting. In 1926, with fighting going on in Hankow and Kiukiang, we sent in troops again. And in 1927, with fighting going on in Shanghai and Nanking, we again deployed troops and warships. Then in 1932, in a sign of things to come, we sent in troops to protect Americans in Shanghai as the Japanese entered the city.

In the 1930s, Imperial Japan took advantage of a weakened China to invade and occupy Manchuria and much of coastal China. Ahead lay a bitter and brutal war that lasted until the defeat of Japan in 1945 and saw the deaths of vast numbers of Chinese, often in appalling and horrifying circumstances, like the Rape of Nanking.

Our government's main concern initially was still the protection of American lives and interests, but increasingly, individual Americans and America itself were sucked into the war.

Arthur Chin, a Chinese-American (Chinese father, Peruvian mother) from Portland, Oregon, volunteered for service in the Nationalist Air Force and became the first American fighter ace (five confirmed Japanese planes shot down) of World War II.

America, in spite of isolationism, had strong pro-Chinese leanings fed by a pro-China lobby. FDR saw in Chiang Kai-shek and the Nationalists a valuable ally against the rising power of Japan. Claire Chennault, an LSU Tiger, had become an American air advisor to Chiang Kai-shek in 1937. In April 1941, months before the Pearl Harbor attack, FDR authorized, formally or informally, the creation of the American Volunteer Group of pilots that made up the Flying Tigers. These pilots were drawn from the US Navy, Marines (including "Pappy" Boyington, later of the Black Sheep Squadron), and the Army Air Corps. Twelve days after Pearl Harbor, Flying Tigers forces were already engaged with Japanese forces in China shooting down three Japanese bombers near Kunming. With the snarling teeth painted on their aircraft that became such a legendary sight, the Flying Tigers fought heroically against far larger numbers of Japanese planes and did significant damage to the enemy.

After Pearl Harbor, any hesitance about helping the Chinese against the Japanese was a thing of the past, and from late 1941 until victory in 1945, we made great efforts to help the Chinese war effort. For instance, first inheriting the mantle of the Flying Tigers (and some of their pilots) but with huge additions of American manpower, planes, and supplies in the region was the China Air Task Force of the USAAF. In August of 1942, Chennault became commander of the 14th Air Force.

Most of the Doolittle Raiders of April 1942 landed in China where the Japanese authorities pursued them, killing hundreds of thousands of Chinese in the process.

Eventually our air forces achieved air superiority over the Japanese and launched a vast strategic bombing campaign, Operation Matterhorn, with B-29s partly based in China. In addition, our transport planes airlifted invaluable supplies to the Chinese force over what became known as the Hump, the eastern end of the Himalayas. Later in the war, Allied advances on the ground also allowed the opening of a land route for supplying Chinese forces, the Ledo Road. American generals, including General Albert C. Wedermeyer, worked with Chiang Kai-shek in trying to modernize and improve the Nationalist Chinese forces.

The OSS operated in China long before Pearl Harbor and continued to do so throughout the war.

In August 1945, shortly after atomic bombs were dropped on Hiroshima and Nagasaki, the Japanese surrendered. Peace did not, however, come to China. With Japan out of the picture, the stage was set for a final, long-awaited showdown between Chiang's Nationalists and the Communists led by Mao Zedong and supported by Stalin's Soviet Union.

On August 25, 1945, Captain John Birch, an intelligence officer attached to Chennault's 14th Air Force, was shot and killed by Chinese Communists at a roadblock.

As well as the Nationalists, we had worked alongside the Chinese Communists in fighting the Japanese during the war, but now, with the Cold War making the situation icy between the Soviets and us, we took the side of the Nationalists in China. It didn't turn out well. Despite the supplies, training, and occasional deployment of US forces to help them, the Nationalists hampered by too-often corrupt and ineffective leadership, gradually gave way to the advancing Communists. Eventually, we withdrew our forces from China, and in 1949 Chiang Kai-shek retreated to the island of Taiwan, starting the separation of Taiwan from the rest of China that is still in operation today. In 1950, the Chinese Communists took control of Tibet.

Ahead lay decades of animosity between the United States and Communist China, which saw plenty of Cold War and occasional Hot War.

For instance, we started training and supplying Chinese Nationalist forces in Burma, stuck there after the war, and Tibetan rebels as well.

The biggest donnybrook ever between American and Chinese forces came during the Korean War (see "North Korea" and "South Korea"), which started on June 25, 1950. Mao, believing the United States was a "paper tiger," was willing to roll the dice on the Korean peninsula. In August of 1950 over two hundred thousand troops of the People's Liberation Army moved south to support the North Korean war effort. They conducted costly human-wave mass attacks. The war eventually evolved into a stalemate around the thirty-eighth parallel, dividing the country into two equal but unequal parts. This remains pretty much the situation to this day.

And Taiwan became a source of long-term tension between Communist China and us. In 1955, the USN helped evacuate the Dachen Islands before the Communists took control there. Chairman Mao believed that international tension could help mobilize the population. On August 23, 1958, the People's Liberation Army rained thirty thousand artillery shells in just one hour on the Nationalist-controlled island of Quemoy killing six hundred of Chiang's soldiers. The United States, obligated by a 1954 defense treaty, responded immediately with a massive naval deployment to the straits of Taiwan and the dispatch of two hundred aircraft. From 1958 to 1979, the USAF maintained a presence at Ching Chuan Kang airbase in Taiwan. It remains a Republic of China airbase today.

Mao sought to export the socialist revolution by supporting the North Vietnamese during the Vietnamese war (see "Vietnam").

In February 1972, though, President Nixon went to China and shook Chou En Lai's hand. The era of Ping-Pong diplomacy was born, and the Sino-Soviet Communist monolith was, thereby, broken up.

Deng Xiaoping , the de facto leader of the People's Republic of China from 1978 to the early 1990s, is reputed to have advised his countrymen that "to get rich is glorious." The quote may be apocryphal, but nevertheless, millions of Chinese acted on it, transforming China into an economic superpower. In 2010, China passed Japan to become the second largest economy in the world, and currently, China is our largest trading partner and debt holder.

Today, Chinese historians exalt the eunuch Admiral Zheng He, the fifteenth-century commander of the treasure fleet and master of the Indian Ocean. A vastly more prosperous and powerful China is now disputing with its ancient rival Japan the ownership of the uninhabited Senkaku Islands that may contain offshore oil resources. China is building a "blue seas" fleet complete with its first aircraft carrier, the *Varyag*, purchased from the Ukrainian Navy and now being refitted, that is, designed to project Chinese power and influence over the wide Pacific.

Today, the century of US deployments in China seems a distant part of history, and few Americans know much about it. Even the decades of Cold War are starting to seem a long time ago, but there are still sources of potential tension between the United States and China. Who knows what the future holds for these great powers? Recent tensions over islands in the Pacific have shown how easily problems can occur.

COLOMBIA

EVEN BEFORE OUR NATION HAD BEEN FOUNDED, Colombia was the site of the very first large-scale American invasion of a foreign country. During the War of Jenkins' Ear in 1741, the Royal Navy Admiral Edward Vernon, known as "Old Grog," landed a party of British and about thirty-six hundred American colonial troops in an assault on Cartagena, Colombia. They failed to take the city and suffered heavy losses from disease. Lawrence Washington, George's older half-brother, participated in the Colombia expedition. George Washington's Virginia home, Mount Vernon, was later named after the British admiral.

For many years Colombia formed part of the Spanish Empire which possessed many precious metals. Colombia gained her independence from Spain in 1811 and soon was known as New Grenada.

In 1846, the United States signed a treaty with New Grenada to uphold their sovereignty over the isthmus of Panama. We would later have second thoughts about that policy.

Ten years later in 1856, USN ships landed 160 Marines and bluejackets to protect American citizens in Panama City, which was part of Colombia at the time. More naval and marine landings would follow in 1860 and twice in 1873.

During a local uprising in 1885, the US consulate in Colon was burned by insurgents. Six USN ships and the full East Coast Marine Corps comprising about two thousand men arrived in Colombia. The Panamanian railway track, which provided transit from the Atlantic to the Pacific, was guarded by US marines.

In 1899, a civil war, called the Thousand Day War, erupted in Colombia. Four US warships were dispatched to Colombia in 1901 over concern about foreign lives and property. A truce that ended the conflict was negotiated aboard the USS *Marietta*.

During the Panamanian revolt of 1903, we intervened to protect the Panamanian rebels from their Colombian overlords (see "Panama"). The USS *Nashville* was sent to Colon to prevent the movement of Colombian troops. US marines under the command of Major John Lejeune (Camp Lejeune, North Carolina) also were landed to intimidate the Colombian forces. A bribe of eight thousand dollars was paid to the Colombian commander, and transportation for his men on a British Royal Mail Steamer (RMS) was provided.

President Teddy Roosevelt recognized Panamanian independence on November 6, 1903. The United States acted as midwife at the birth of Panama through which Teddy Roosevelt (TR) planned to build a canal.

In 1921, seven years after the canal was built, the US government agreed to compensate Colombia twenty-five million dollars for the loss of Panama.

During World War II, we sent naval and military aviation missions to Colombia to assist Colombia's defenses. The Panama Canal was obviously an area of particular strategic concern for us. And we supplied Colombia with military equipment under lend-lease. After U-boats attacked a number of Colombian ships, Colombia entered the war on the Allied side in 1943.

In November of 1950, Colombia dispatched an infantry battalion to fight alongside American and UN forces in Korea. Colombia was the only Latin American nation to fight in the Korean war.

But in Colombia itself, civil war had broken out. In 1948, the assassination of presidential candidate Gaitá marked the beginning of a period known as La Violencia. It was a period of often intense political and military conflict, and out of it grew a variety of guerrilla groups. In the late 1950s and early 1960s, US advisors offered recommendations on developing a Colombian counter-insurgency strategy. The Special Survey Team issued its final report in May 1960, and in 1962, the Yarborough Team headed for Colombia. In 1962, the Colombian security forces began to implement Plan LAZO. A key element of this plan was targeting leftist guerrilla groups in assorted enclaves. In 1964, Operation Marquetalia attacked one of these guerrilla enclaves, the so-called Republic of Marquetalia. Many of the guerrillas escaped, but the increased threat from security forces led a number of guerrilla groups to amalgamate and create the Revolutionary Armed Forces of Colombia—FARC.

Along with FARC, more urban-based guerrilla movements were also to emerge, first the ELN (National Liberation Army) and, then in the 1970s, the 19th of April Movement, or M-19. Also, in the 1970s, the Medellin Cartel, led by drug lord Pablo Escobar, headquartered its drug production and trafficking operations in Colombia. And the growing illegal drug trade would add another source of huge instability in Colombia.

In the early 1980s, things seemed to be calming down a bit on the political front, but in November 1985, M-19 launched an attack on the Palace of Justice in Bogota. More ceasefires and more progress towards a peace process but also more violence on some fronts followed in the late 1980s and early 1990s. M-19 eventually ceased their guerrilla war and became a political party. Meanwhile, drug gangs had killed three presidential candidates. However, Pablo Escobar himself was killed in late 1993.

Despite this, drug-gang violence continued during the 1990s and on into the twenty-first century, and so did the activities of FARC and ELN. It has been a brutal war.

The United States has provided extensive military aid and training to help combat cocaine production and violence. In 1999, Plan Colombia was launched, and over the years, billions of dollars' worth of support from the US government has been delivered to tackle a range of Colombia's most urgent problems. And US military personnel have played an important role.

US Special Forces have played a significant role in Colombia. For instance, in 2003, the United States expanded its involvement with the country by deploying special forces in Colombia to train Colombian soldiers in anti-terrorism. US personnel have operated out of a number of bases in Colombia. A 2009 agreement to give US personnel access to more bases in Colombia caused huge controversy. The South Carolina National Guard is now partnered with Colombia.

COMOROS

THE COMOROS IS NOT EXACTLY THE MOST WELL-KNOWN NATION on earth among Americans. It's a group of small islands in the Indian Ocean between Mozambique and Madagascar. Apparently, the Comoros is the only state that's a member of the Arab League, the African Union, the Organization of Islamic Cooperation, Francophonie (for French-speaking nation), and the Indian Ocean Commission. Anyway, yes, we have attacked them, or at least, one of them.

In 1850, the American whaler *Maria* and its captain and crew were seized by locals on the Island of Johanna, also known as Anjouan Island.

In 1851, the USS *Dale*, a 16-gun sloop under Captain William Pearson turned up at Mutsamadu to find out what was happening and demand from the sultan the release of the American ship, plus a hefty compensation fee of twenty thousand dollars.

The sultan instead offered five hundred dollars cash, plus another five hundred dollars' worth of bullocks and trinkets. That's probably quite a lot of bullocks and trinkets in 1851 terms. But Pearson was playing hardball. He refused the offer and pulled his ship up not far from the beach, with eight guns trained on the port's fortifications. The offer from the sultan went up to five thousand dollars, leaving Pearson unsure how to proceed next. However, when he saw local military reinforcements arriving in the town, Pearson decided it was time to act and opened fire. After six shots, a white flag went up on the fort, and Pearson ceased fire, while sending a launch with marines and Lieutenant Fairfax to find out what was going on. When, however, negotiations could still not be satisfactorily accomplished,

Dale opened fire again, and after about another hour of firing, Lieutenant Fairfax returned to the town. This time, he was given the whaler's captain, one thousand dollars, an offer of a bond for five thousand dollars, a plea from the sultan to stop the bombardment, and an offer to surrender the town. With the addition of a treaty giving America favored trading status, Pearson accepted the deal on offer, and the war was finished.

In 1887, the USS *Alliance* investigating the allegedly fraudulent sale of an American schooner on Anjouan Island, turned up and seized parts of the outfit of the ship.

In recent years, US military personnel have returned to the Comoros on a much friendlier basis. In 2007, for instance, the USS *Forrest Sherman* became the first USN ship to visit the Comoros in thirty-three years, and in 2010, a US Maritime Civil Affairs Team was sent to the Comoros in support of Combined Joint Task Force–Horn of Africa. They've helped with assorted projects, including school renovations, but they've also helped train the Comorian Coast Guard on operating a boat given to them by us.

COSTA RICA

A H, COSTA RICA, sandwiched between Panama to its south and Nicaragua to the north. "Costa Rica" means "Rich Coast."

Many American observers in the nineteenth century had high hopes for Costa Rica considering it to be "the New England of Central America." Some believed that Costa Rica was free from the contagion of revolutionary sentiment that afflicted much of Central America.

Costa Rica played a leading role in the alliance of Central American nations against William Walker's filibuster movement in Nicaragua (see "Nicaragua"). It was Costa Rica's General Joaquin Mora, the brother of President Mora, who led his allied troops against the Yankees in 1856. Many of the Costa Rican officers were the European-educated sons of coffee barons and excellent horsemen, and their raw conscripted troops wore white trousers and shirts with straw hats circled with red bands.

General Walker's force of mostly American filibusters invaded Costa Rica from Nicaragua. On March 20, 1856, the Battle of Santa Rosa was fought, which resulted in the deaths of nineteen Costa Ricans and fifty-nine of Walker's men. The filibusters had been driven from the field by a peasant army.

After Walker's subsequent defeat in Nicaragua, USN ships, such as the *Decatur* and *St. Mary's*, helped to evacuate Walker filibusters from Costa Rica. Lieutenant David McCorkle was assigned the duty of marching three hundred filibusters from Nicaragua to Punta Arenas in Costa Rica.

The USS *Decatur* celebrated July 4, 1857, at Punta Arenas where they fired a salute, which was answered by a Chilean warship, and a marine from the *Decatur* who had drunk too much ended up being jailed for breaking down a door.

In 1921, as tensions rose between Panama and Costa Rica over a border dispute, we sent ships to both sides of the isthmus to calm things down.

Costa Rica joined the allies along with other Central American nations on December 8, 1941, and German business interests were seized by the government. Costa Rica wasn't exactly a major focus of our military interest during the war, but at one stage, the USAAF considered building an airbase on Cocos Island to protect the Panama Canal. In the end, it was never built. We did put early warning radar on the island, though.

In 1948, Costa Rica experienced a month-long civil war, which claimed about two thousand lives. We did not intervene directly in the conflict, but we did have a clear preference in the outcome. The existing Picado regime was supported by the Popular Vanguard Party—a Communist party. The Truman administration, concerned about the spread of Communism in North America, mobilized our forces in the neighboring Panama zone and sought to cut off supplies to the Picado regime.

José Figueres eventually became the victorious rebel leader who toppled Picado in Costa Rica. Figueres had initial CIA support for his activities. He served three times as president of Costa Rica between 1948 and 1974. In 1959, however, Figueres would send arms to Fidel Castro in Cuba. And some have alleged CIA operations against him.

Since 1949, Costa Rica's constitution has banned a standing army. In the 1980s, the Contras had some presence in Costa Rica.

In 2010, a decision by Costa Rica to allow US military access to Costa Rica caused some local controversy, and in recent years, the US has been heavily involved with helping Costa Rica fight illegal narcotics smuggling.

We've also been involved in a number of emergency relief operations there. For instance, in 1968, the USAF's southern command helped evacuate people put at risk by Mount Arenal's eruption and flew in emergency supplies to help those suffering. Again in 1970 and 1978, the US Air Force helped when floods hit.

The New Mexico National Guard is partnered with Costa Rica.

CROATIA

ROATIA IS A LAND WITH SO MUCH SUPERBLY BEAUTIFUL ADRIATIC COASTLINE. The cravat, forerunner of the necktie, is a Croat invention, and indeed, the word "cravat" derives from the word "Croat."

Croatia had been part of the Austro-Hungarian Empire, and at the end of World War I, American troops were sent to occupy parts of what is now southern Croatia until it was established exactly who would rule the area after the war. A certain amount of friction developed with the Italians who were keen to take over the area, and at Trogir, for instance, the USS *Cowell* moved in to prevent the Italians taking control. Meanwhile a rather similar situation was also developing in northern parts of the country, for instance, in the Croatian port of Rijeka (then frequently known by its Italian name, Fiume). Here Italian moves prompted the withdrawal of an Allied force, including some of our forces and the USS *Pittsburgh*. American forces were prepared to take action, but a real risk of war with Italy existed. In the end, the Italians got Rijeka and Istria in the north (until they lost it again), and the new country of Yugoslavia got most of Croatia.

In 1941, during World War II, the Germans invaded Yugoslavia. Some Croats resisted them, including obviously Croat partisans, but other Croats formed an independent state allied to the Nazis. As such, Croatia, both the part that had been occupied by the Italians and the part allied to the Germans, became major targets for American military activity. Rijeka, for instance, was heavily bombed. And our aircraft flew missions specifically to support partisan operations in Croatia. OSS personnel on the ground in Croatia also assisted the partisans. The Allies even had a base on Croatian soil, on the island of Vis in the Adriatic. It was fortunate for one George McGovern that they did. In December 1944, McGovern's B-24, based in Italy, was badly damaged on a mission to bomb a factory at Pilsen. Unable to make it to Italy, McGovern managed to land the plane on a challenging airstrip on Vis and save his crew.

The end of World War II produced in some sense a similar situation to the end of World War I, and once again, our forces were sent in to try to help sort things out. The main area of contention was in the north of Yugoslavia, in the area that had been held between the wars by the Italians. Consequently, the beautiful Croatian city of Pula on the tip of the Istrian peninsula was put under Allied Military Control, with US troops, among others, stationed there for a couple of years until it could be decided who would administer it permanently. In the end, it became part of Yugoslavia.

But that was not truly the end. Yugoslavia was not to last forever. In 1991, as a desire for independence grew among the different peoples making up the Federal Republic of Yugoslavia, Croatia declared independence. A bitter civil war followed in which Serbs living in parts of Croatia bordering Bosnia and Serbia, with the help of Milosevic's Yugoslav Army, seized control of big chunks of Croatian territory and continued to hold them while the civil war in Bosnia-Herzegovina raged next door.

Bosnia, of course, was the main focus of American military activity during this period, but we did get involved a bit in Croatia again as well. For instance, planes from the Serb-held area of Croatia were being used against targets inside Bosnia, in contravention of NATO's Operation Deny Flight. In response, US aircraft were involved in attacking Serb-held Udbina airbase inside Croatia's border.

In 1991, the new Croatian Army, short of weapons and training, had not been able to prevent the secession of much Croatian-Serb territory. In 1995, however, it swiftly retook all the areas held by the Serbs. Partly this was due to the changed attitude of Milosevic to the Croatian Serbs, but some people have also speculated about the role of American advisors from private companies in the rebuilding of the Croatian Army during this period.

Since the end of the war, the USG has developed assorted links with the Croatian military. We've supplied some equipment and training, and Croatian forces regularly take part alongside US forces in exercises. We have a variety of military agreements in force with Croatia, and the Croats have sent troops to Afghanistan.

CUBA

THE BEAUTIFUL ISLAND OF CUBA IS JUST NINETY MILES FROM FLORIDA, so it's hardly surprising that over the years we've taken a close interest in it.

Already by the early nineteenth century, American forces were in action there. At this stage, our main concern was combating piracy, and in the 1820s, we made a number of landings, including, for instance, one in July 1823 when three American vessels attacked a pirate schooner off Matanzas, Cuba. When some of the pirates managed to make it ashore, an

American landing party went after them. It was a scrappy kind of conflict, but a conflict nonetheless and helped make the seas a little bit safer for shipping.

But already we were beginning to imagine a rather bigger US involvement in Cuba than pursuing a few pirates. In the same year that the pirate schooner off Matanzas was being put out of business, John Quincy Adams, then secretary of state, wrote, "If an apple, severed by the tempest from its native tree, cannot choose but fall to the ground, Cuba, forcibly disjoined from its unnatural connexion [sic] with Spain, and incapable of self-support, can only gravitate towards the North American Union."

In December of 1823, President Monroe produced the Monroe Doctrine. The Monroe Doctrine (nothing to do with Marilyn, obviously) basically stated that we could accept existing European colonies in the Americas, but from then on, we were going to regard outside interference in South and North America as interference with our own interests. Having chucked King George's army out of America, Americans felt a natural fellowship for any other locals wanting to chuck out Europeans who were oppressing them. But over the decades, as our power grew, the Monroe Doctrine also began to be interpreted as a concept that we, as the biggest power in the Americas, had a special responsibility for what goes on here. Both attitudes, with a bit of belief in manifest destiny added in as well, were to be much in evidence in our involvement with Cuba.

In 1858, in the Ostend Manifesto, a bunch of American diplomats in Europe recommended that the United States buy Cuba and suggested that if, by any chance, it wasn't for sale, the United States would be justified in seizing the island from Spain. The manifesto is named after a port in Belgium because that's where the diplomats ended up meeting. Nothing came of it in the end partly because some Northerners saw in it a Southern attempt to add another slave-owning Southern state to the Union.

Spain had very-long-term ties to the island of Cuba, with Columbus having reached it on his first voyage on October 28, 1492, but by the four hundredth anniversary of that event, things were beginning to look a bit problematic on the island for Spain. In 1868, a local insurrection burst out and dragged on for about ten years, from which, not surprisingly, it got the name of the Ten Years War. Then again in 1895, another rebellion was launched. Harsh measures taken by the Spanish in their attempts to smash the rebellion boosted natural fellow feeling in America for those fighting for freedom from a European power, but we still weren't yet about to go to war. Not quite yet anyway.

The newspaper publisher William Randolph Hearst (of *Citizen Kane* fame) wanted a war in order to help sell newspapers. Hearst had a famous exchange of telegrams with his photo-journalist Frederic Remington who was in Cuba prior to the Spanish American war. Hearst received a telegram from Remington that said, "Everything is quiet. There is no trouble here. There will be no war. I wish to return. Remington." Hearst sent the answer, "Please remain. You furnish the pictures, and I'll furnish the war."

On January 25, 1898, the USS *Maine*, an armored cruiser, arrived in Havana harbor. The largest island in the Caribbean had been experiencing an insurrection by local Cuban rebels against their Spanish overlords for the past three years. On February 15, 1898, at 9:40 p.m., one or perhaps two explosions rocked the battleship. About three-quarters of her crew (266 lives) were killed.

What really happened that night remains a mystery that will, perhaps, never be solved. The USN's Sampson board of inquiry ruled unanimously that a foreign device or mine triggered the explosion and sinking. A variety of suggestions and counter-suggestions have since been put forward for what really happened that night.

If the *Maine* was, in fact, destroyed by a mine, it is by no means even certain that the Spanish government placed it there, although they did have motivation. It could be that the Cuban rebels themselves might have used a mine in order to get the Americans more deeply involved in Cuba …

Many in Cuba today are convinced that a false-flag conspiracy (the USN sank its own ship) was to blame. There is no evidence to suggest such a thing.

What we do know for certain is that President McKinley, who had only the USN Sampson report to go by, pressed for war with Spain.

The US Congress debated and passed resolutions calling for Cuban independence. Spain responded by declaring war. President William McKinley's opening move was to impose a naval blockade of Cuba.

In late June 1898, American troops landed in Cuba. On July 1, Teddy Roosevelt, with the assistance of the African-American Buffalo Soldiers, led his Rough Riders to victory over the Spanish in the Battle of San Juan Hill. The Americans and their Cuban allies had won the war in just over three months at a cost of just under three thousand killed—most of these attributable to disease. Nearby Puerto Rico was annexed as part of the peace settlement.

At the time, we also got another bit of real estate that you've heard of. The United States began construction of its oldest overseas naval base,

Guantanamo Bay, in 1898. A long-term lease was negotiated with the Cuban government in 1903.

Having helped free Cuba from a European colonial power, we weren't about to turn Cuba into our own colony—not officially anyway—but we did regard it as part of our sphere of influence, and we reckoned we had a right to protect our growing interests there.

President Teddy Roosevelt dispatched US forces to occupy Cuba again from 1906 to 1909. The Cuban rebels laid down their arms at the sight of US troops, and there was no bloodshed. The US Army built fifty-seven miles of roads and supervised the free election before their withdrawal.

In 1912, President William Taft sent the navy and US marines to support the Cuban government in suppressing another rebellion.

And in 1917, during World War I, US forces, with the excuse of being invited to practice drilling in a warm climate, helped combat political unrest that was causing damage to the sugar industry and sugar harvest. This became known, not entirely unreasonably, as the Sugar Intervention.

By the end of 1941, of course, we had quite a lot else on our minds apart from Cuba, like the need to win a world war. Cuba wasn't exactly on the frontlines during World War II, and for one resident, it was all just too quiet. Ernest Hemingway, a resident of Cuba and avid fisherman, could not stand the idea of missing a war. From the summer of 1942 to the end of 1943, Hemingway, based on Cuba, took *Pilar*, his wooden fishing yacht, armed with machine guns and hand grenades, out into the Caribbean hunting for German U-boats. He did allegedly finally sight one, only for it to submerge before he could reach it.

After the war, Cuba became a fleshpot with casino gambling and the US mafia. Batista, realizing that he could not win electoral victory, seized power in a coup in 1952. Organized crime leaders such as "Lucky" Luciano, Meyer Lansky, and Santo Trafficante helped turn Havana into a Latin Las Vegas.

Fidel Castro was the illegitimate son of a wealthy Galician immigrant to Cuba. Six foot three and powerfully built, he became an accomplished athlete. In 1949, he was offered a contract to pitch for the New York Giants baseball team, but he turned them down. History might have been so different, and so might the Giants.

Instead of playing ball with us, Castro began launching attacks on the Moncada army barracks in 1953 to start the Cuban revolution, which lasted until the collapse of the Batista regime in 1958. Batista fled the country on New Year's Day 1959.

Fidel Castro, who had not started as a Communist, had become America's worst Cold War nightmare—a revolutionary Communist government on America's doorstep that was allied with the Soviet Union. We hadn't been too keen about Spain ruling Cuba, and we were even less keen about Russia moving in next door.

On March 4, 1960, another ship explosion in Havana harbor influenced the course of Cuban-American links and history. This time it was the Belgian *La Coubre*. Loaded with ammunition, it blew up, causing widespread devastation. This explosion was probably the result of negligence, though Fidel used it as an excuse to accuse the United States of sabotage and to request more arms from the Soviet Union.

The Bay of Pigs fiasco must rank among the more disastrous interventions in US military history. On April 15, 1961, eight American B-26s bombed Cuban airfields as the CIA's brigade of Cuban exile volunteers approached the Bay of Pigs. JFK, however, refused to provide additional air support for the doomed invasion and the bitter fighting that followed.

After the Bay of Pigs fiasco, the US government tried other ways of getting at Castro. The Kennedy brothers initiated Operation Mongoose, which attempted many times to assassinate Fidel Castro. They tried exploding cigars and poisoned ice cream, among others.

JFK retaliated against Cuba in February 1962 by banning the importation of Cuban cigars—a ban that persists to this day. JFK, a devoted smoker, had stocked up on his personal supply in advance.

During the Cuban missile crisis in the fall of 1962, the world came closer to thermonuclear war than any time in its history after a US reconnaissance flight over the island took photos of a missile site under construction. Many options were explored on how to deal with the introduction of Soviet medium-range nuclear missiles on Fidel's Cuba, some of them involving a US invasion of the island. Ultimately, cooler heads prevailed, and we opted for a naval blockade of Cuba.

Soviet ships that were delivering more missile parts turned around, but the Soviets gained their original strategic objective by forcing the United States to withdraw its own medium-range missiles from Turkey, and Cuba gained a pledge that the United States would never again invade Cuba.

And since then, there have been more plots and a continued Cold War. We've remained in Guantanamo, and the Communist government has remained in power in Havana.

CYPRUS

A BEAUTIFUL ISLAND IN THE EASTERN MEDITERRANEAN, Cyprus was famous for copper mining in the ancient world. The word "copper" is derived from the Greek name for this island, Kupros. Cyprus has seen plenty of conquerors come and go over the millennia, including Alexander the Great and Richard the Lionheart of England.

For much of the nineteenth and twentieth centuries, Cyprus was controlled by the British, so much of our military involvement there has been linked to our alliance with them.

Although, on one occasion, it was rather aimed at them. In October 1956, in defiance of American wishes, Britain and France invaded Egypt over the Suez Crisis. In the run-up to that invasion, in September 1956, two U-2 spy flights were sent over Cyprus and Malta and the Eastern Mediterranean in an attempt to photograph any British military build-up there.

This, however, was the exception. Due to Cyprus's key strategic location, close to the conflicts of the Middle East, we have a history of sharing communications and intelligence facilities with Britain on the island. In 1956, William P. Boteler, American vice consul on the island, was killed in a bomb attack by the Greek Cypriot guerrilla organization EOKA; though EOKA claimed they were intending to target Britons. In February 1964, two more bombs exploded at the rear of the US embassy in Cyprus.

American planes have also used British air facilities on the island on a number of occasions. For instance, during the 1970s, American U-2s flying from RAF Akrotiri in Cyprus were used to monitor the Arab-Israeli situation in the Middle East. And American casualties were evacuated to RAF Akrotiri after the 1983 Beirut bombing. Technically, however, British bases on Cyprus have not actually been in the nation state of Cyprus since independence in 1960. They are legally British sovereign territory.

In the 1960s and 1970s, America played a significant, but still controversial, role in the crisis between Cyprus, Greece, and Turkey that led to the Turkish invasion there in 1974. And in July, after the Turkish army landed on the island, ships from the USN were deployed to evacuate US civilians.

CZECH REPUBLIC

THE CZECH REPUBLIC AS WE KNOW IT TODAY didn't come into existence until January 1, 1993, and to anyone over forty, the name Czechoslovakia will also be very familiar.

The Czechs have a long and proud history, but much of it is in the history books as in places like Bohemia and Moravia. In 1918, that all changed. As the Austro-Hungarian Empire fell apart, new nations were born, among them Czechoslovakia, the land of the Czechs, and to the east, the land of the Slovaks, united in one state. And even before the new state existed, we were involved with it.

During World War I, Czechs and Slovaks hoping that an Allied victory would lead to independence for their peoples formed Czechoslovak Legions to fight for the Allies, but ultimately to fight for their own freedom as well. Czech and Slovak volunteers fought alongside the Russian Army, but various Czechoslovak units were also formed in France, and among those fighting in these units were several thousand Americans of Czech and Slovak ancestry. Men from the Czechoslovak Legions would go on to form a key part of the armed forces of the new country.

And we had quite a lot to do with the formation of the country politically as well. The tenth of Presidents Woodrow Wilson's Fourteen Points demanded, "The peoples of Austria-Hungary, whose place among the nations we wish to see safeguarded and assured, should be accorded the freest opportunity to autonomous development." The new state of Czechoslovakia actually declared its independence in October 1918, even before the First World War was finished. However, its borders were to be discussed in the Paris Peace Conference in 1919. Among the considerations was the future of German-speaking parts of the new country. In the end, it was decided that German-speakers should not be separated, and international acceptance of the new state was formalized in the Treaty of St. Germain in 1919. German speakers within Czechoslovakia were, in less than two decades, to be at the heart of the Sudetenland Crisis, a key point on the road to World War II.

In 1938, British prime minister Neville Chamberlain hoped he had won "peace in our time" with the concessions he made to Hitler over the fate of Czechoslovakia. Instead, in the end, it turned out that appeasement bought a little time by selling out an ally.

In October 1938, German troops entered the Sudetenland. But that was not enough for Hitler, and in March 1939, German forces occupied Bohemia and Moravia as well. In addition to territory, Hitler also acquired some very useful heavy industry, including that in advanced armaments. Many of the German tanks, for instance, that participated in the invasion of France and the low countries in 1940 had actually been produced by the Czech company Škoda. And that was one reason, when we started our bombing campaign in Europe, some of our targets were in what is now the Czech Republic. Not surprisingly, yes, the Škoda armaments plant at Plzeň came in for particular attention.

In 1945, though, as German resistance began to crumble away, the crucial question for us became not what to bomb in the country but what to do about a land invasion.

Near the end of the Second World War in Europe, there was a certain amount of turmoil in the Allied ranks over how best to proceed in Czechoslovakia. On April 12, 1945, FDR, America's wartime president, died. In late April of 1945, Patton's Third Army crossed the Czech border.

Winston Churchill wanted the Allied forces to liberate Prague before the Soviets arrived. Dwight Eisenhower, however, was more concerned with minimizing US casualties and adhering to the Yalta agreements in order not to upset the Soviets. Patton, predictably, was all for pressing on and liberating more of Czech territory and heading for Prague.

The situation led to some tension among the US military leadership. On May 6, Omar Bradley found himself phoning Patton to try to get Patton to obey Eisenhower's orders and shouting at him, ordering him to halt.

The situation was made even more difficult by the return of an OSS team from Prague, which reported that news of the American advance into Czech territory had set off a rising against the Germans in Prague and that the SS were ruthlessly crushing the rebels, even as the American advance had, because of Eisenhower's wishes, ground to a halt just forty miles away. Patton again pleaded for permission to advance and liberate Prague, and again he was denied. Unsure who was going to liberate them, some Czech villagers erected signs saying "Welcome Americans" on one side of their village and "Welcome Russians" on the other side.

In the end, Eisenhower managed to halt the advance along a line between Plzeň and Karlsbad in Bohemia.

The Red Army would take Prague instead, and post-war Czechoslovakia would become part of the Soviet sphere of influence. And in 1968, Soviet tanks would once again advance into Prague, this time to crush the Prague Spring.

It was not until the Velvet Revolution of 1989 that the Czechs would once again be free of Soviet influence. In 1993, Czechoslovakia separated peacefully into the Czech Republic and Slovakia.

The Czech Republic has been a NATO member since 1999. The Texas and Nebraska National Guards are partnered with the Czech Republic. Czech units have participated alongside American forces in recent campaigns in Afghanistan and Iraq. However, President Obama did scrap a missile defense program in the Czech Republic in 2009.

DEMOCRATIC REPUBLIC OF THE CONGO

A LOT OF PEOPLE TEND TO GET THIS COUNTRY CONFUSED, understandably, with the Republic of the Congo, which is also on the list (see "Republic of the Congo"). Basically, this Congo is the former Belgian colony straddling much of the mighty Congo River (Joseph Conrad, author of *Heart of Darkness*, served as captain on a steamship) and has a capital at Kinshasa, while the Republic of the Congo is the former French colony on the north bank of a bit of the Congo River with a capital at Brazzaville. Between 1971 and 1997, the Democratic Republic of the Congo was called Zaire, and it's tended to be in the news more than the other Congo often for not very positive reasons.

The mouth of the Congo was a major slaving area and received a lot of attention from our Africa Squadron in its anti-slaving activities. In fact, it seized more vessels in the Congo area than in any other one location. Between 1853 and 1861, it captured twelve vessels here, not including those taken at nearby Cabinda (see "Angola").

In May 1879, the USN returned (not all of it, obviously) as the USS *Ticonderoga* ventured a short distance into the Congo River on a mission to promote American trade with the area.

One American (or Anglo-American) who played a major though controversial part in the history of the area is the (very) controversial figure of Henry Morton Stanley. He was born John Rowlands in Wales. By 1859, he had reached the United States, and there he managed to become adopted by a rich merchant, Henry Hope Stanley, and changed his name. During the Civil War, he first joined the Confederate Army and fought at the Battle of Shiloh. Then after being taken prisoner, he briefly joined the Union Army and eventually ended up in the Union Navy. By the 1870s, he was in Africa, sent by a New York newspaper magnate to locate the well-known missionary Dr. David Livingstone. This he did, and later in the decade, in an expedition that only about a third of those who set out on it made it through, he traced the Congo River to the sea. This and subsequent exploration work in the area on behalf of King Leopold II of the Belgians eventually led to the creation of a Belgian-controlled territory in the area, the Congo Free State, that would eventually become the Democratic Republic of the Congo. The Congo Free State, however, saw some particularly brutal and nasty atrocities perpetrated by some of those in authority. These abuses eventually led to a major international human rights movement, one that received support from, among many others, Mark Twain and Sir Conan Doyle.

During World War II, the USAAF used the airports at Léopoldville and Élisabethville for transport aircraft on one of its trans-Africa routes.

The Democratic Republic of the Congo became independent in 1960. Soon after independence, the mineral-rich province of Katanga tried to secede, and the prime minister Patrice Lumumba was killed.

A UN mission was sent in to help sort out the Katanga problem, and we were involved with that, for instance, with the USAF helping airlift UN troops into the Congo and the USN transporting troops and supplies as well. To what extent America was or was not involved with the death of Lumumba remains controversial. His death would eventually lead to the seizure of long-term power in the country by Mobutu, with whom America developed a lot of friendly links, seeing him as an ally against Communism in the Cold War. For instance, when a few years later Che Guevara turned up in the Congo to assist rebels there, we assisted the Congolese to defeat him. And in 1978, we flew in Belgian and French forces to help tackle rebels.

However, by the early 1990s with the end of the Cold War, Mobutu began to lose his value as an ally, and America was less inclined to ignore the shortcomings of his dictatorial rule. Inside the country, Mobutu's authority was starting to crumble as well. In 1991, when unpaid troops started looting Kinshasa, we again flew in Belgian and French paratroopers to evacuate civilians. Mobutu was forced out of the country in 1997.

By 1996, the country was about to enter a horrific period of civil wars. Even after the main war, sometimes known as Africa's World War because of the involvement of nine African countries, ended in 2003, instability and conflict have lasted in some parts of the country until very recently. It has been a period in which violence, disease, and hunger have killed millions, and other atrocities, like rape, became appallingly frequent.

In 1996, President Bill Clinton sent US planes to assist in surveying part of the east of the country for humanitarian relief efforts. Some of the aircraft got shot at.

In 1997, Clinton sent an evacuation force to nearby Gabon, ready if we needed to evacuate civilians from the Democratic Republic of the Congo.

The United States has played a role in trying to negotiate peace in the Democratic Republic of Congo and has had some military involvement as well. For instance, it has helped train some of the peacekeepers from other African countries who have been operating in the Congo and has trained some Congolese troops in military medical operations and in demining techniques. US troops have also been in the Democratic Republic of the Congo training a battalion there as part of efforts to defeat the notorious Lord's Resistance Army.

DENMARK

ELEVEN HUNDRED YEARS AGO, THE WORD "DANES" STRUCK TERROR into the hearts of people across Europe as Danish Vikings went on extended raiding and pillaging sprees. These days, though, we might instead think of Lego, Prince Hamlet, and, yes, the Little Mermaid.

Denmark consists of a peninsula and a bunch of islands at the mouth of the Baltic, which means that pretty much ever since USN ships have been venturing into the Baltic, they've been close to Denmark.

The country was invaded and occupied by Germany on April 9, 1940, during the German campaign to occupy Denmark and Norway. The Danes didn't stand much of a chance. They had tiny military forces compared to Germany, and they were situated right next door to Germany, with the Jutland peninsula giving the invaders direct access by land to much of Denmark. The Danish government surrendered within hours.

However, there were two bits of land that were part of the Kingdom of Denmark that the Germans were never going to get their hands on. One was Iceland (though that became independent during World War II), and the other was Greenland, which today remains part of the Kingdom of Denmark.

As the war progressed and the Atlantic convoy routes and air-ferry routes from the United States to Britain became ever more important, control of Greenland and Iceland also become vital. The Danish government and king remained in Denmark under German occupation and were clearly not in a position to authorize occupation of Greenland or Iceland by forces of which the Germans would not approve.

The British had invaded Iceland in 1940 (before handing it over to us in 1941), and on April 9, 1941, a year after the German invasion of Denmark, FDR announced that the United States had concluded an agreement with the Danish envoy to the United States and with the support of the Greenlanders themselves to occupy Greenland and set up bases there.

Subsequently, thousands of US troops were sent to garrison Greenland, and airbases and a naval base were established.

And soon the war came even to Greenland. The Germans attempted to establish clandestine weather stations on the eastern side of Greenland in order to support their sea and air operations. And it was the job of US forces working with the Northeast Greenland Sledge Patrol to stop them. Greenland's army consisted of only a few people and was the smallest in the Second World War. Nevertheless, this tiny war was a real one with important implications for the wider war, and people did die. One corporal in the Sledge Patrol was killed fighting in Greenland.

Sabine Island saw a number of incidents in this distant front of World War II. For instance, in spring 1943, a German post there was detected but then withdrawn before it could be attacked. Later, another German station was detected on the island, and this time, it was attacked by USAAF bombers based in Iceland, and then the Coast Guard went in.

In 1946, there was apparently discussion in US government circles about the possibility of purchasing Greenland from Denmark for one hundred million dollars in gold, but when the offer was made, no deal was agreed.

Despite that, however, we kept bases on Greenland after the war. For instance, Bluie West One became Narsarsuaq Air Base until 1952, and Bluie West 8 became Sondrestrom Air Base, and we stayed there until 1992.

In the post-war period, though, it is Thule that has become the main focus of our military activities in Greenland. Thule Air Base in Qaasuitsap Greenland lies within eight hundred miles of the Arctic Circle. The 12th Space Warning Squadron located there is in charge of monitoring arctic air space for missile attack. Outside temperatures there drop to sixty below zero.

During World War II, our forces weren't in action in just Greenland; they were also involved with Denmark itself. The USAAF, for instance, conducted a variety of operations over Denmark during the war, including bombing missions against a major Luftwaffe base at Aalborg.

But other mission types took place as well. For instance, on May 12, 1944, five B-17s dropped 1.74 million propaganda leaflets over Denmark. Even such non-bombing missions, however, carried risks. On that mission, two airmen were killed and three wounded. And in Operation Carpetbagger, the so-called Carpetbaggers of the 492nd Bombardment Group dropped supplies to resistance groups in assorted countries, including Denmark and Norway.

We have had military personnel based in Denmark also in the post-war period with, for instance, US Air Force planes based at Kastrup Airport Copenhagen. And assorted other activity has taken place, like future CIA director Colby setting up a program of stay-behind agents in Denmark who would start operations in the event of a Soviet invasion.

Denmark became a founding member of NATO in 1949 and remains a key member today. US military links with Denmark are strong, and in recent years, for example, Danish contingents have served alongside the US military in Bosnia, Iraq, and Afghanistan and in air operations over Libya.

In the spring of 2014, Denmark was the target of the most recent American invasion (as of this writing) when American hackers "invaded" Minecraft Denmark raising a virtual Stars and Stripes over virtual Copenhagen.

DJIBOUTI

DJIBOUTI IS A TINY NATION ON THE HORN OF AFRICA and currently of big importance to the United States.

Djibouti was a French colony from the late nineteenth century until it gained its independence in 1977.

The French Foreign Legion used to have a base in Djibouti, called Camp Lemonnier. The base was named after Emile Lemonnier—a French general beheaded by the Japanese for refusing to sign a surrender document while serving in Indochina in the last months of World War II.

Camp Lemonnier is conveniently located next to Djibouti-Ambouli International Airport and is close to the Djibouti port as well. Djibouti itself is in a strategic location, especially because of its vital sea routes (for instance, about 10 percent of the world's petroleum passes near Djibouti's waters every year), particularly those affected by Somali pirates. It is handy for Somalia (next door), Yemen (less than fifty miles distant, across the sea), and other areas of conflict where extreme Islamists are active. And it is handy for Sudan, South Sudan, and areas where the Lord's Resistance Army has been active. Djibouti, worried about Islamic extremism, has had friendly relations with the United States. Thousands of French troops, including some from the Foreign Legion are still stationed there. Great location then for a US base, particularly after a civil war was brought to a final end in 2001.

In 2002, the USS *Whitney* arrived at Djibouti and landed a party of US marines. The marines began cleaning up Camp Lemonnier, which had been abandoned and fallen into extreme disrepair.

In recent years, many have speculated about the extent of US involvement in Africa and the number of bases it might have there, but the existence of Camp Lemonnier, AFRICOM's main African facility, is not in dispute. It is a United States Naval Expeditionary Base and home to the Combined Joint Task Force Horn of Africa. Thousands of Americans, including Special Forces, have been based in Camp Lemonnier with access to large amounts of equipment, including manned aircraft and unmanned type, in other words, drones. Though, recently, it has been suggested that drone operations will be moved from Camp Lemonnier and Djibouti airport, some ten kilometers distant to Chabelley Airfield.

As AFRICOM's premier African facility and with a long history of drone and special forces activity in counterterrorism and anti-piracy operations in the surrounding region, Camp Lemonnier has been involved in a wide variety of actions, many of them secret.

One action reported in 2012 involved a mission to rescue an American and a Danish worker held hostage for ransom for months in Somalia. Navy SEALs from Camp Lemonnier parachuted in, hiked to where the hostages were held, killed nine of the hostage-takers, and flew out with no losses of their own and the hostages safe.

DOMINICA

THE SISSEROU PARROT IS UNIQUE TO DOMINICA and, as the island's national bird, is featured on its flag. Dominica is not to be confused with the Dominican Republic. Dominica is an island we've not had much to do with militarily.

But, yes, we have had a little connection with the area. For instance, in December 1800, during the quasi-war against the French, the US frigate *Philadelphia* captured French privateer *La Levrette* off Dominica. "Levrette" means "female greyhound" so, unfortunately for the French, the greyhound didn't run fast enough.

Dominica seems to have been an area of some interest to our warships during this conflict because the USS *Constitution*, also on the trail of French privateers, is recorded as joining up with Commodore John Barry's squadron at Dominica during this period and calling into Prince Rupert's Bay on Dominica.

Dominica lent its support to the invasion of Grenada in 1983, and in recent years, personnel from Dominica have taken part in assorted exercises alongside US personnel, for instance, training for the fight against illegal narcotics and organized crime. In 2012, the United States gave Dominica two patrol boats to help with law enforcement and maritime security.

DOMINICAN REPUBLIC

THE DOMINICAN REPUBLIC LIES ON THE EASTERN SIDE of the Caribbean island of Hispaniola, with Haiti on the western portion. It has long had strong and close ties with the United States, and today more than a million people of Dominican origin live in the United States. The Dominican Republic is famous for (among many other things) beaches, a temperate climate, and amazing baseball players—today there are more Major League Baseball players from the Dominican Republic than from any other nation except the United States.

The Dominican Republic has also at times had a tumultuous political history. We have taken an interest in the Dominican Republic pretty much from the beginning of our history, and we have sent in the Marines a few times. Well, quite a lot of times, actually.

The Dominican Republic was first colonized by the Spanish and then the French. And some of our first military engagements in the area were against them. During the Undeclared War against the French, for instance, in 1800, marines from the USS *Constitution* under Captain Daniel Carmick captured the French ship *Sandwich* before spiking guns at Puerto Plata.

African slaves were imported to work the sugar-cane plantations. Toussaint L'Ouverture's Revolution in the first decade of the nineteenth century (see "Haiti") meant that Haiti ruled the Dominican Republic until it gained its independence in 1844.

During the US Civil War, the Dominican Republic reverted to Spanish rule. Our distraction with fighting the Civil War made it difficult to enforce the Monroe Doctrine.

Teddy Roosevelt's corollary to the Monroe Doctrine held that "the US had the responsibility to protect foreign lives and pay foreign debts" while keeping European powers from encroaching on the Western hemisphere. President Woodrow Wilson would cite Roosevelt's corollary to justify his intervention in the Dominican Republic.

In April 1903, marines from the USS *Atlanta* landed to guard US diplomats in Santo Domingo City during conflict there.

Things got even busier in 1904 as the USS *Detroit* was dispatched to try to bring peace between the different factions in the country and protect US interests. In January, the USS *Detroit* landed marines at Puerto Plata. A few days later, the ship landed marines at Sosua. After a few more days, the USS *Detroit* and this time the USS *Hartford* were landing more US marines and sailors in the country. In February, it was the turn of USS *Newark* and *Columbia* to land marines and sailors, this time at Santo Domingo. The Clyde Line steamer *New York* had been fired upon by revolutionaries, and the revolutionaries also had opened fire on our landing party. With the assistance of naval gunfire, our men drove the revolutionaries out of the city.

Things were a little more peaceful in 1905–1906. We kept a floating battalion in Dominican waters on board the USS *Yankee*, but in the end, they were withdrawn. Something similar happened with the USS *Prairie* in 1912.

In 1914, US ships intervened with gunfire to prevent the bombardment of Puerto Plata.

And in 1916, our forces went in again. President Wilson intervened on behalf of Jimenez, who was the fifth Dominican president since 1911. Jimenez was engaged in a civil war with the anti-American defense minister Arias.

Admiral Caperton of the USN landed a party of six hundred bluejackets and marines at Santo Domingo on May 12, 1916, and on May 13, he delivered an ultimatum to Arias to get himself and his forces out of the city.

US occupation of the country followed with assorted operations. For instance, the USN gunboat *Sacramento* landed 130 marines at Puerto Plata on June 1, 1916. That day, H. J. Hirshinger became the first US marine to be killed in the Dominican Republic. Colonel "Uncle Joe" Pendleton led an assault that captured Santiago. He declared, "We are not in an enemy's country though many of the inhabitants may be inimical to us."

The US Marines would occupy the country from 1916 to 1924. They brought a kind of peace to the country and helped bring baseball to the Dominican Republic.

During World War II, the Dominican Republic joined the Allied side, and accordingly, we sent lend-lease military aid, including aircraft to the Dominican Republic. To some extent, military links continued after World War II. For instance, in 1947, the USN helped the Trujillo government intercept craft carrying rebels who were supported by Cuba. And throughout the 1950s, the United States sent military aid to the Dominican Republic, along with a variety of training missions.

Gradually, however, the United States began to distance itself from the repressive Trujillo regime. Military assistance was cut off in 1960, and in 1961, Trujillo was assassinated. And following the re-emergence of two of Trujillo's brothers in the Dominican Republic, the USN put on a show of force to demonstrate US disapproval.

A few years later, we sent in the troops again. After another civil war broke out, LBJ intervened in the Dominican Republic in 1965. The US Marines and two brigades of the 82nd Airborne were deployed alongside the forces of other OAS nations. Nine US soldiers were killed, mainly by snipers in Santo Domingo.

US military links with the Dominican Republic were strong in the period after the intervention. President Balaguer was in power from 1966-1978, and the United States increased its military aid during his first term. During the rule of President Guzman after that, President Jimmy Carter's administration sent hundreds of US military personnel to help after the devastation caused by Hurricane David.

Recent years have also seen extensive links between the US military and the Dominican Republic. For instance, the Dominican Republic sent troops to fight alongside US forces in Iraq, and the United States and Dominican Republic have cooperated in the fight against the traffic in illegal substances. US forces have shared training exercises with Dominican military personnel and have been involved in humanitarian projects in the Dominican Republic. The Puerto Rico National Guard is partnered with the Dominican Republic. And the US government has financed the construction of a $1.5 million naval base in Saona Island in the Dominican Republic.

ECUADOR

ECUADOR MEANS "EQUATOR" IN SPANISH and, yep, it's on the equator. The amazing Galapagos Islands are part of Ecuador.

We haven't had as much to do militarily with Ecuador as we have had with some other South American countries. But we have had some involvement.

And some of it was quite early. For instance, during the War of 1812, the USS *Essex* under Captain David Porter captured a number of British ships off the Galapagos Islands before heading across the Pacific to the Marquesas (see "France").

Also, during World War II, we had a naval and air base (Seymour Island Airfield) on Isla Baltra (Galapagos Islands), and from 1942 to 1943, we had an airbase at Salinas on the mainland. A major aim of both was to combat any threat from Japanese submarines and any threat to the Panama Canal.

And at times we've assisted the Ecuadorian military with training and equipment. What links the CIA may have had with the Ecuadorian military is a different question.

Relations between the United States and Ecuador haven't always been friendly. Starting in the 1960s, we've had Ecuador versus the United States in the great "tuna war." OK, not actually a war, but it does, involve tuna. Ecuador decided it needed a two-hundred-mile territorial limit off its coast. We decided it didn't. In 1963, a US fishing boat was seized and fined, and many more vessels were seized after that. We responded by assorted measures, including intermittently suspending military aid. In 1971, tension increased when an Ecuadorian warship fired warning shots to stop a US ship hundreds of miles off the coast of Ecuador. Later, however, an apology was given.

In recent years, the United States and Ecuadorian governments have seen matters very differently on a number of other subjects. The two countries have cooperated on anti-narcotics measures, but in 2009, the Ecuadorean government refused to renew the ten-year lease on a base at Manta Airport, from which our E-3 AWACS and P-3 Orion surveillance planes had carried out anti-narcotics work.

However, this did not put an end to all links between the US military and Ecuador. For instance, the Kentucky National Guard is partnered with Ecuador.

EGYPT

THE LAND OF THE PHARAOHS AND PYRAMIDS, Egypt is also the land of the Nile. Although it won't surprise you to know the Battle of the Nile against Napoleon was not fought by the US fleet, some Americans were present at it.

In 1798, Ralph Willet Miller served under Admiral Nelson as captain of the HMS *Theseus*. Miller had been born in New York in 1762 to a Tory father. This American was one of Nelson's hardy forces that destroyed the French fleet on August 12, 1798.

But we have had American state forces on Egyptian soil. For instance, during the Urabi Revolt in July 1882, the British seized control of Alexandria, and US troops landed in the city to protect US interests and help the Brits keep order. OK, it's not exactly an Egyptian military operation on the scale of what Ramses II or, indeed, 1920s Hollywood might have dreamt up, but it's something nonetheless.

Interestingly enough, though, at roughly the same time, a number of American military men were themselves also serving in the Egyptian army of the Khedive of Egypt. For instance, American soldier and explorer Charles Chaillé-Long, whom we'll mention again later in this book, was second-in-command to General "Chinese" Gordon in the 1870s, and Charles Pomeroy Stone, who had had, to put it mildly, a controversial career during the Civil War, was basically head of the Egyptian Army in the early 1880s.

In 1909, America's Great White Fleet called in at Suez on its epic voyage round the world.

During World War II, even before the Pearl Harbor attack, the United States supplied lend-lease equipment and support to Britain. FDR recognized that arms and war material would do more good in British hands than in American storage facilities. Winston Churchill told Parliament the Lend-Lease Act was "the most unsordid act in the history of any nation." American Sherman tanks and other equipment were sent directly to Egypt where they played an important part in the fight against Rommel.

But Egypt was also an important base for US air crew and US air operations during World War II. For instance, US 9th Air Force bombers and fighters operated out of Egypt in support of the British Eighth Army's drive westwards along the North African coast against Rommel, and we actually built our own airbase in Egypt at Payne Field near Cairo.

After the removal of King Farouk in 1952, Gamal Abdel Nasser came to power. During the Cold War, Nasser at first attempted to steer a neutral course but also bought weapons from Soviet and Warsaw-pact sources. On July 26, 1956, Nasser ordered the nationalization of the Suez Canal, which had been built by the British and the French in the nineteenth century. The British and the French weren't happy about it. They weren't happy about it at all. Both were still imperial powers, despite a battering during World War II, and neither had entirely come to terms with their new reduced role in a post-war world dominated by the two superpowers of the United States and the USSR. They thought that invading Egypt, even against US wishes, was a good idea. It wasn't.

In 1956, the United States played an enormous role in the Suez crisis by NOT intervening militarily in Egypt and by opposing the intervention of her closest World War II allies and Israel. This is particularly remarkable, given how close President Dwight Eisenhower was to many British on account of his role in planning Operation Overlord (see "France"). Early on, Eisenhower wrote to British Prime Minister Anthony Eden saying, "I must tell you frankly that American opinion flatly rejects the thought of using force, particularly when it does not seem that every possible peaceful means of protecting our vital interests has been exhausted without result.'" And when subtle hints didn't work, Eisenhower began to put up the pressure, including heavy financial pressure. At the same time that British amphibious forces were landing in Egypt in Operation Musketeer, Ike ordered an American-fuelled run on British currency while America also prevented Britain accessing IMF funding. Eventually Britain and France succumbed to US and international pressure and withdrew their forces. Israeli forces were successful in invading the Sinai but were compelled to withdraw under American pressure.

During all this chaos, however, US forces did play one active role in Egypt. Eisenhower ordered the deployment of a USMC battalion in Egypt to help evacuate US nationals and others from Alexandria during the Suez Crisis.

After 1956, Israel recognized the problems of acting against the wishes of the US government and seemed to drift closer to the Soviet orbit, in spite of their enormous ideological differences. And in 1957, fearing that Egypt might interfere with the movement of US merchant ships headed for Israel and Jordan, the USN instituted a destroyer patrol in the Straits of Tiran and the Gulf of Aqaba.

During the 1973 Yom Kippur War, Soviet naval and armed forces were deployed towards the Middle East in support of Egypt, and US security was raised to DEFCON 3 (defense readiness condition three; USAF's alert state requiring readiness to mobilize in fifteen minutes).

Egypt's major initial successes in this war were followed by devastating Israeli counterattacks, and after the war, Egypt turned sharply away from the Soviets, and eventually Anwar Sadat chose to make a historic visit and speech to Israel's Knesset in 1977 and to barter land for peace.

The Camp David accords returning the Sinai to Egypt as part of a peace deal were signed in 1978. Billions of dollars of American military and economic support began flowing towards Egypt and has continued in every subsequent American administration to the present.

Another consequence of the peace deal was the return of US forces to Egyptian soil and their long-term stationing there. It's definitely one of our lesser-known international postings, but first in the Sinai Field Mission and subsequently as part of the Multinational Force and Observers (not a UN mission because the UN Security Council couldn't agree on it), Americans have been deployed in Sinai helping keep the peace between Egypt and Israel.

Anwar Sadat was assassinated on October 16, 1981, by Islamic extremists who opposed peace with Israel. And that wasn't the only challenge Egypt was facing by any means. For instance, in 1983, AWACS were sent because of fears of a threat from Libya after a Libyan plane had bombed a Sudanese city.

Ever since 1980, we had been conducting joint exercises with the Egyptian military deploying troops and aircraft into Egypt, in particular in the series of Bright Star exercises.

In 2011, Sadat's successor, Hosni Mubarak, however, was swept out of power in the Arab Spring. And the military toppled President Morsi in 2013. The Bright Star series of exercises has consequently been suspended until the US government can work out exactly what's happening and what is likely to happen in Egypt.

EL SALVADOR

IN 1906, EL SALVADOR INVADED ITS NEIGHBOR GUATEMALA, and the USS *Marblehead* was used to arrange a truce between combatants by American officials. Otherwise, El Salvador wasn't an area of huge concern for the United States, until the civil war in El Salvador.

In 1979, after a period of instability characterized by increasing radicalization among both left-wing and right-wing factions, a junta toppled President Carlos Humberto Romero. The junta's failure to deliver all the improvements it promised and the revolution in nearby Nicaragua gave a boost to the left-wing guerrilla groups of the FMLN (Farabundo Marti para la Liberacion Nacional).

On March 24, Roman Catholic archbishop and human rights campaigner Oscar Romero, who opposed US support for the Salvadoran government, was assassinated, and in the aftermath of the murder, El Salvador descended into civil war. Right-wing death squads killed thousands.

The Cold War was in full swing at this time after the Soviet invasion of Afghanistan in 1979, and El Salvador's Sandinista-controlled neighbor, Nicaragua, had aligned itself openly with Cuba. Determined to prevent left-wingers from coming to power in El Salvador as well, the Reagan administration gave extensive military support to the Salvadoran government—a massive six billion from 1981 to 1992.

A bitter struggle ensued in which, in the end, an estimated seventy-five thousand people were killed.

In 1981, hundreds died in what has become known as the El Mozote Massacre. In 2011, Salvadorian Foreign Minister Hugo Martinez asked forgiveness for what he called the "blindness of state violence."

The guerrillas took control of parts of north and east El Salvador and launched a campaign aimed at sabotaging the economy.

The guerrilla campaign would also claim some American military victims. On June 19, 1985, the FMLN rebels attacked a restaurant in San Salvador, which killed four US marines and three US businessmen.

Not all our military involvement during the period was linked to the guerrilla war, however. For instance, in 1986, after an earthquake devastated large parts of El Salvador's capital, the USAF rushed in emergency supplies.

The war dragged on through the 1980s and into the 1990s. Finally, in January 1992, a ceasefire was signed.

In the 2004 election in El Salvador, the George W. Bush administration openly supported Antonio Saca, the winning candidate, over his opponent who was a former Communist guerilla.

In 2009, though, former rebel Mauricio Funes of the FMLN was elected president.

El Salvador has sent troops to both Iraq and Afghanistan, and strong security links exist on a number of other levels, including counterterrorism and the fight against illegal narcotics, plus ship visits, military exercises, and humanitarian missions. The United States operates a facility at Comalapa in El Salvador, which exists for the purpose of, among other things, supporting US aviation units assigned to counter illicit trafficking operations. The New Hampshire National Guard is partnered with El Salvador.

EQUATORIAL GUINEA

A S THE NAME SUGGESTS, Equatorial Guinea straddles the equator. Well, sort of. Its mainland chunk, by far the biggest part of the country, is actually north of the equator, but Equatorial Guinea also has some islands to the south of the equator. As the Guinea part of its name suggests, it is not far from the Gulf of Guinea; although somewhat confusing, it's a long, long distance from two other African countries with similar names, Guinea and Guinea-Bissau, which are further north and much further west.

One of the islands that are situated south of the equator is now called Bioko, but Western seamen used to know it as Fernando Po, after the Portuguese explorer who landed on it in 1472. Britain's anti-slaving patrol had a base on Fernando Po, and it was also a regular stop for our anti-slaving naval operations in the nineteenth century.

For much of the nineteenth and twentieth centuries, what is now Equatorial Guinea was a Spanish colony, and a sort of mini-Spanish civil war even took place in the colony while the main Spanish civil war was being fought far to the north. Equatorial Guinea became independent from Spain in 1968.

The country has faced some very challenging situations and some major human rights issues at times, and the United States and Equatoguinean (yes, that's the adjective) governments haven't always been that close. For instance, we suspended diplomatic relations with Equatorial

Guinea in 1976, and they didn't resume until 1979. And then again in 1995, we closed our embassy in Equatorial Guinea and transferred its functions to the embassy in neighboring Cameroon. In recent decades, Equatorial Guinea has become a significant oil-producer, and our embassy in Equatorial Guinea reopened in 2006 as a result of growing US interests in the country.

We have had some military involvement with Equatorial Guinea in the past decades as well. In 1988, for example, we gave the navy of Equatorial Guinea a patrol boat and provided some training of Equatoguinean forces in the 1980s and 1990s. In more recent years, a number of American ships have been to the country for official visits and for some training with Equatoguinean personnel, including the US Coast Guard Cutter *Dallas*, the USS *Fort McHenry* visiting the capital Malabo, and the USS *Robert G. Bradley* visiting Bata.

ERITREA

THE NAME ERITREA DERIVES FROM THE GREEK WORD FOR "RED," and yes, it's located on the Red Sea. In the early twentieth century, Eritrea was an Italian colony. In 1941, as part of the war between Britain and Italy, Britain occupied Eritrea. Then after the war in 1952, under a UN resolution that we supported, Eritrea was joined to Ethiopia. This marriage didn't entirely work out, and after a very, very long war, Eritrea got its independence in 1993.

After Britain took Eritrea from the Italians, we had a wartime air-transport and plane-ferrying base and Technical Services Command depot at Asmara, the capital of Eritrea. After the war, we had a continuing major presence in the area as well. This was Kagnew Station, near Asmara, an old British base that we took over and turned into one of our major communications centers in the region that, at its peak in the 1960s, was home to thousands of Americans.

Supplies either were flown in from Saudi Arabia or came in by ship to the main Eritrean port of Massawa. We even had R & R centers for the staff on the coast at Massawa and in the mountains at Keren. In the end, however, increasing use of satellite communications, a growing rift with the Ethiopian government after Haile Selassie had been toppled, and the growing war between Ethiopia and Eritrean guerrillas led to Kagnew's closure in 1977.

We did play a significant role in the negotiations that led to the independence of Eritrea from Ethiopia, but we haven't had much to do politically or militarily with the current regime in Eritrea. In 2008, for instance, the United States condemned Eritrea for aggression against our friends in Djibouti and called on both sides to resolve the border dispute peacefully.

ESTONIA

ESTONIA, WITH ITS CAPITAL AT TALINN, is the most northern of the three Baltic countries, which means that it's just along the coast from St. Petersburg in Russia.

Historically, it's been at a junction where competing spheres of influence from great powers, particularly Sweden and Germany to the west and Russia to the east, have met, which has not made for the smoothest of rides.

By contrast, we came quite late to the area. Plus, it's a long distance across the Atlantic, so we haven't played a huge military role in Estonia's history, but we have played a small one.

In 1918, in the chaos after the end of the Russian Revolution, Estonia declared independence from Russia, and after fighting off both Bolshevik and German forces, the Estonians managed to establish the freedom of their country.

We had naval forces in the area at the time, protecting US interests and assisting with US relief efforts. For instance, the USS *Pittsburgh* operated in Estonian waters, calling in, among others, at Tallinn, the capital. On one occasion in 1920 when the USS *Pittsburgh* sighted Soviet submarines off Estonia, it enthusiastically asked to be allowed to regard them as hostile. Washington, however, was less keen on the whole idea and refused.

A number of Americans also played a role in helping Estonia during its war of independence. Some US military officers, for instance, became advisors to the Estonian army.

In the aftermath of the failure of the Allied intervention in Russia, Estonia became a friendly base from which we could observe the USSR. American officers conducted intelligence operations there, and American foreign-policy luminaries, such as Chuck Bohlen and George Kennan, worked in Estonia while studying Russia and the Russian language. But it wasn't all work. Bohlen commented that he could never entirely stop being surprised by the sight of nudism on Estonia's beaches. He served as an advisor to every American president from FDR to Nixon and became the American ambassador to the Soviet Union under Eisenhower.

Estonian independence was, however, short-lived. In June 1940, with the eyes of the world on the German occupation of France on the other side of Europe, Stalin ordered the blockade of Estonia. On June 14, 1940, Harry Anthiel, a twenty-seven-year-old American State Department employee and courier, was among those killed when a commercial aircraft, the Kaleva, was shot down by Soviet planes after taking off from Tallinn. A few days later, Soviet forces invaded and occupied Estonia, and Stalin annexed it to the Soviet Union, a move the United States refused to recognize.

The chaos and the carnage of the Second World War was to come, and then decades under Soviet rule. Assorted US intelligence efforts inside Estonia, including those to help the anti-Soviet Baltic resistance at the end of and just after World War II were also to follow.

Finally with the end of the Cold War, the US government once again recognized a free Estonia on September 4, 1991, and military links between Estonia and the United States have been re-established. For instance, Estonian forces operated alongside US forces in Baghdad, and Estonia has contributed a small force to the conflict in Afghanistan. Estonia joined NATO in 2004, and today, NATO's Cooperative Cyber Defense Center of Excellence is headquartered in Tallinn.

The Maryland National Guard is partnered with Estonia.

Decades after the USS *Pittsburgh* first called there, the USN has visited the port of Tallinn on many occasions. In 2008, the USNS *Pathfinder*, for instance, went to look for the remains of the Kaleva shot down on that tragic day in June 1940.

ETHIOPIA

EARLY AMERICAN INVOLVEMENT WITH ETHIOPIA involves the fascinating stories of some individual Americans. A significant number of American Civil War veterans joined the army of the Khedive in Egypt, and many of them, including William Wing Loring, Charles Chaillé-Long, and William Dye, were involved in his Ethiopian wars. Some were unlucky. The British general Gordon, also fighting for the Khedive, records an unnamed American killed during the fighting in 1875, and Surgeon Major Thomas D. Johnson, a Confederate veteran, was wounded and captured by the Ethiopians.

In 1903 a USMC detachment was sent to Ethiopia as security accompanying a diplomatic mission to the country.

Then, when Mussolini's Italian Army attacked Ethiopia in 1935, the head of the small Ethiopian Air Force at the time was an African American pilot and colonel, John C. Robinson, who would later find fame in the United States as the Father of the Tuskegee Airmen. As the Ethiopians struggled to resist the overwhelming might of the Italian Army, many other African Americans volunteered to fight for Ethiopia but were prevented from doing so at the time by America's Neutrality Act.

America, however, refused to recognize Italy's occupation of Ethiopia, and it wasn't to last long. In 1941, British Commonwealth and Ethiopian troops defeated the Italians and on May 5, Emperor Haile Selassie returned to Addis Ababa. In 1945, President Franklin Roosevelt met with Haile Selassie on board the USS *Quincy* to strengthen links, and in the post-war years, we cooperated closely with the Ethiopians. For instance, in 1953, we signed a mutual defense assistance agreement with Ethiopia under which we would supply military equipment and training, and we were Ethiopia's main arms supplier from 1945 to 1977.

However, in 1974, Haile Selassie was toppled, and in the ensuing years, the Ethiopian revolutionary government got steadily closer to the Soviet Union and Cuba.

During the 1990s, though, we began to get a little friendlier again with the Ethiopians, and although some political differences between the United States and Ethiopia remain, some military links resumed as we got involved in sponsoring assorted training programs.

In recent years, Seabees and other US military personnel have been involved in various Ethiopian towns on humanitarian projects, such as drilling wells, offering medical and veterinary help, and building schools and health clinics.

And American troops have been located in a number of places in Ethiopia. For instance, in 2006, at Camp Hurso in Ethiopia, US soldiers from the 294th Infantry Regiment in Guam spent a year training members of the Ethiopian Army. We have also been on the same side as Ethiopian troops against Islamist militiamen in Somalia, and Ethiopia is strategically located in an area of importance for the United States.

In 2011, it was reported that the US 17th Air Force started flying drones out of Arba Minch in southern Ethiopia, near Somalia. though the drones are apparently unarmed due the sensitivities of the Ethiopian government.

FIJI

FIJI IS A PACIFIC ISLAND NATION that includes hundreds of islands. Fiji, whose national motto is "Fear God and honour the Queen," dropped the image of Queen Elizabeth II from its currency in the twenty-first century.

For a country that, in the late nineteenth century, was firmly within the British sphere of influence, we actually had a surprising amount of military involvement with Fiji prior to that. Mostly this was concerned with the USN attempting, sometimes rather forcefully, to secure recompense on behalf of Americans who'd had their property on the islands damaged in some of the conflicts that occurred during that period.

Already by 1840, the United States Exploring Expedition was doing a bit more than just exploring Fiji. Somehow, two USN personnel were killed by locals, and in a response, a force of US sailors was landed. Two villages were burned, and a number of Fijians were killed.

Then we come to a certain John Brown Williams. John Brown Williams owned a store in Fiji, and he also happened to be the US consul. His store suffered assorted damage, and by 1855, the USN was returning to the island again demanding tens of thousands of dollars in compensation for damage to US property. Now tens of thousands of dollars is a lot of money these days but it was a lot, lot more then. Marines and sailors from the USS *John Adams* went ashore in an attempt to capture the local ruler Cakobau. The landing party defeated local resistance, but one sailor was killed and two marines wounded, and Cakobau escaped.

In 1858, the USN was once again in Fiji, with USS *Vandalia*, demanding compensation. And in 1867, USS *Tuscarora* arrived at Levuka and threatened to open fire unless compensation was paid.

Eventually Cakobau decided that forming a government with assorted settlers and, in the end, having the islands taken over by Britain was his best option for dealing with his problems, so that's what he did.

The US military returned to Fiji during World War II, though this time it was on a much friendlier basis. New Zealand forces had previously been assisting the local defenders of the islands, but in 1942, we took over. Bomber squadrons were based at Nadi. We assisted with 155mm coastal defense artillery and anti-aircraft defense, and the 37th Division, which had originally intended to go to Northern Ireland, arrived in Fiji and Tonga instead. Quite a change. Assorted US facilities were built, including the Martintar Naval Air Station. Some of our troops trained on a Fijian island prior to the attack on Guadalcanal, and while the situation on Guadalcanal remained uncertain, Fiji remained at risk from a Japanese invasion.

Fiji became independent from Britain in 1970. After the coup in Fiji in 1987, the United States suspended defense cooperation. Another government was toppled in 2000, and another coup took place in 2006, which the United States condemned.

FINLAND

THE FINNS LOVE THEIR SAUNAS so much that Finnish peacekeepers have built saunas around the world.

Finland had spent a long time under Russian control when in 1917 it declared independence, or perhaps Finndependence. But was Russian control finished or indeed Finnished?

The early years of Finnish independence included intervention by the Germans (who were our enemies at the time) and a civil war between White Finns and Red Finns. It sounds a bit like a battle in an aquarium but was, in fact, between nationalist Finns and Bolshevik Finns.

We delayed recognizing Finland until we were sure what was going on. The White Finns eventually won the war, and between the world wars, we got quite friendly with the country. But by 1939. things weren't looking great for Finland.

A secret protocol of the Nazi-Soviet non-aggression pact that preceded the start of World War II in Europe provided for an assault on Finland. On November 30, 1939, Stalin's Soviet Union attacked Finland, but the outnumbered Finns, trained skiers and skillful in using their home territory to their military advantage, fought the Soviets nearly almost to a standstill in the Winter War.

Americans, including many Finnish-Americans, had great sympathy for the gallant Finns who defended their homeland from Stalin. And an American-Finnish legion made up of about 350 Americans, primarily of

Finnish descent, volunteered to serve in the Winter War and finally arrived on the front line just as the war was finishing. Kermit Roosevelt, the son of Teddy Roosevelt, led a group of British volunteers who fought in the Russo-Finnish war. Sheer Soviet might did, however, tell in the end, and the treaty of Moscow finished the Russo-Finnish war in March of 1940. The disappointing performance of the Red Army in the Winter War encouraged Hitler in his plans to invade the Soviet Union.

In spite of the fact that Finland allied herself with the Nazis in their 1941 invasion of the Soviet Union, the United States remained at peace with the Finns, even after Pearl Harbor. In 1942, the OSS recruited Thérèse Bonney, a war correspondent and photographer, for a mission to Finland. She had a clandestine meeting with Marshal Carl Mannerheim in Helsinki where she attempted to persuade him to abandon Hitler. She failed but returned to Washington with detailed information on Finland's military and political status.

And despite their alliance with Hitler, the Finns sent a steady stream of information to the OSS office in Stockholm. Wilho Tikander, a Finnish-American, worked for the OSS in Scandinavia. The Finns offered Russian Army communication codes to Tikander for sale to the Americans. In spite of our wartime alliance with the Soviets, "Wild Bill" Donovan approved the $62,500 payment.

Eventually, however, in September 1944, the Finns did sign an armistice with the Soviets and the British (but not with us since we weren't officially at war with them).

Finland was heavily influenced by the Soviets during the Cold War period, though not actually occupied by them. With the might of the Red Army just next door and with a previous history of Russian control and Russian invasion, it's hardly surprising that the Finns wanted to avoid antagonizing the Soviet Union. The term "Finlandization" was coined to describe nations whose foreign policy had to tow the Soviet line.

Having said that, there were some links, for example, intelligence links, between Western forces, including ours, and the Finns during this period. In addition, we flew occasional spy flights that went over Finnish territory.

Since the end of the Cold War, more open links have developed between the United States and Finnish militaries. For instance, Finland has sent troops to Afghanistan, we've sent USN ships on port visits in Finland, and US and Finnish military personnel have cooperated in exercises.

FRANCE

AH, THE BEAUTIFUL LAND OF FRANCE, *la belle* France.
France is our oldest ally and the site of the most famous American invasion of all time. More American military cemeteries (eleven) are located in France than in any other foreign country in the world.

When the American Revolution broke out, Louis XVI saw aid to the thirteen colonies as a means of avenging England's defeat of France in the Seven Years War, but he was reluctant to commit to the American cause until gentleman Johnny Burgoyne surrendered his force after the Battle of Saratoga in October 1777. The Marquis de Lafayette arrived in American that same year serving as a major-general in the Continental Army where he grew very close to General George Washington, who thought of him as a son. The great inventor, author, and statesman Benjamin Franklin helped to negotiate a treaty of alliance with France in 1778. The direct intervention of the French began with Rochambeau landing a force of about six thousand French soldiers in Providence, Rhode Island. These forces and, critically, the French Navy led by the Comte de Grasse helped secure the surrender of Lord Cornwallis's army at Yorktown.

John Paul Jones led his 1778 raid on Whitehaven (see "United Kingdom") from the French port of Brest. His frigate that defeated the British *Serapis* in 1779, the *Bonhomme Richard* (during which he uttered his famous "I have not yet begun to fight") was a converted French merchant ship, the *Duc de Duras*.

Even though France is our oldest ally, we have fallen out with the French on occasion as well. The Quasi-War with revolutionary France was fought by the USN on the high seas between June 1798 and March 1801. On February 9, 1799, for instance, Captain Thomas Truxton of the *Constellation* fought and captured the French frigate *L'Insurgente*. The war was settled by the treaty of Mortefontaine after Napoleon Bonaparte assumed control as first consul.

France and the United States also very nearly came to blows over the French invasion of Mexico, which was launched by Napoleon III during the US Civil War. The United States supplied Mexico with arms and support to drive the French out of North America (see "Mexico").

In 1886, the people of France sent us an iconic gift—the Statue of Liberty that would welcome immigrants to our shores ("*La Liberté éclairant le monde*," "Liberty enlightening the world").

But it was to be with the two world wars that our forces became most deeply involved with France.

Even before America's entry into the Great War, Americans were fighting and dying in France. For instance, young American pilots volunteered to serve in the French air force forming the Lafayette Escadrille hoping to repay America's debt to France. Ten out of the "Valiant 38" American men who served in the Lafayette Escadrille were killed in action.

Americans had also volunteered for the French Foreign Legion, and it's worth mentioning here some of the better-known names that have been linked to the legion over the decades:

1. John F. "Jack" Hasey, CIA
2. Peter Julien Ortiz , one of the most decorated US marines of WWII, OSS, actor in John Ford's *Rio Grande*
3. William Wellman, director of the legion epic, *Beau Geste*, and many more
4. Alan Seeger, poet
5. Arthur Bluethenthal, member of College Football All-American Team from Princeton, pilot killed in WWI
6. Eugene Bullard, first African American military pilot
7. Norman Kerry, actor

Cole Porter told many of his friends that he had joined the French Foreign Legion, though conclusive evidence is lacking. The lyrics for "War Song," written for the London stage during World War I have been attributed to Cole Porter …

> *And when they ask us, how dangerous it was,*
> *Oh, we'll never tell them, no, we'll never tell them.*
> *We spent our pay in some cafe,*
> *And fought wild women night and day.*
> *'Twas the cushiest job we ever had.*
> *And when they ask us, and they're certainly going to ask us,*
> *The reason why we didn't win the Croix de Guerre,*
> *Oh, we'll never tell them, oh, we'll never tell them,*
> *There was a front, but damned if we know where.*
> (Source: A *Fine Romance, Jewish Songwriters,*
> *American Songs*, David Leahman, 2009)

After President Woodrow Wilson led the nation into war on the Allied side, American doughboys were shipped to France and the trenches of the Western Front. They were called "doughboys" because they tended to be larger and better fed than their French comrades in arms.

The earliest units of the American Expeditionary Forces to see action were engineering units rushed into the British line in November 1917. But it was in 1918 that our men were really to have an impact on the Western Front. Eddie Rickenbacker, flying French-built aircraft, such as the SPAD S.XIII, became the leading American fighter ace of World War I scoring twenty-six air combat victories. A few American land and air units and even our First Gas Regiment were committed to action in April 1918 to stem the German Spring Offensive, which used German troops released from the Eastern Front by peace with Russia in an attempt to deal a knockout blow before American troops could be deployed in large numbers.

In late May and June, the Germans tried to push forward in the Chemin des Dames along the Aisne River. Aisne bridges were captured, Soissons fell, and the Germans reached Château-Thierry on the Marne with Paris less than forty miles distant. American troops battled fiercely to prevent the Germans from crossing the Marne and then, on June 6, a date that would later become famous for other reasons, successfully counterattacked at Belleau Wood, where the US marines earned the nickname *"teufel hunden,"* or "devil dogs." Further German attacks on the Marne followed and were fought off by American troops, earning the 38th Infantry of the 3rd Division its name "Rock of the Marne." The Germans were now exhausted, and it was the turn of the Allies to attack. American troops played a key role in July in helping destroy the German-held Marne salient. From then on, American units assisted major campaigns by the British and the French, but Pershing had also gotten his wish for an independent American operation, and in September, about half a million Americans of the US First Army went into action against the German-held St. Mihiel salient. The operation was a significant success. Finally, from September to November 1918, First Army ground through the Meuse-Argonne offensive. The fighting was bitter, and casualties were at times heavy, but major progress was made, and by the Armistice, First Army had dealt a huge blow to the German divisions facing it.

The American Expeditionary Forces had played a vital role in liberating France and in winning the war against Germany, but it had come at a high cost in American blood. The beautiful Aisne-Marne American Cemetery, for instance, next to Belleau Wood and just six and a half miles from Château-Thierry, contains almost twenty-three hundred war dead, most of whom fought in the area and in the Marne valley in summer 1918.

After the guns fell silent ending the "war to end all wars" on November 11, 1918, President Wilson came to Versailles with his Fourteen Points. A bitter peace was settled that helped sow the seeds of the next war.

Between the wars, Paris was subjected to an "invasion" of Lost Generation American writers, such as Ernest Hemingway, F. Scott Fitzgerald, Gertrude Stein, and others. Hemingway said Paris was the city he loved best in the world. Wealthy American philanthropists, such as John D. Rockefeller and J. P. Morgan, helped to restore the Reims Cathedral that had been shelled by the Kaiser's artillery in the Great War.

In 1942, shortly after the Pearl Harbor attack and America's entry into World War II, the United States invaded French colonies in North Africa that were under the control of the Vichy government (see "Algeria," "Morocco," and "Tunisia"). After about three days of fighting, the French switched sides and joined with the Allies to drive the Axis out of North Africa.

Even before D-Day, Americans began the liberation of France with the invasion of Corsica in the fall of 1943. Joseph Heller, the author of *Catch 22*, served as a bombardier on a B-25 based on Corsica. The USAAF dropped its share of the six hundred thousand tons of bombs on occupied France. The French national railway system was smashed to prevent the Germans from making a strategic redeployment against the Normandy landings.

D-Day, June 6, 1944, marked the start of the most famous American invasion in all history. With a terse, "OK, let's go," Eisenhower had resolved all doubts in the Allied deliberations over weather conditions prior to the invasion. The time had finally arrived. Ike later wrote comparing the invasion force to a coiled spring ready to "vault the English Channel."

The vaulting began on the night of June 5 when private John Steele, a paratrooper with the 82nd Airborne, got his chute caught on the tower of the church at Ste.-Mère-Église. He survived the conflagration and firefight that shook the sleepy Norman town that night by playing dead. A visitor to Ste.-Mère-Église today will find a stained-glass window in the church has the Virgin Mary surrounded by American paratroopers. The American paratroopers of the 82nd and 101st Divisions would secure the western flank of the Normandy invasion.

On Utah Beach, fifty-six-year-old Brigadier General Theodore Roosevelt Jr. (oldest son of President TR) was landed about a mile away from his intended target and, when asked whether to re-embark the 4th Infantry

Division, said simply, "We'll start the war from right here!" Bloody Omaha had received an abbreviated naval bombardment from ships such as the battleship *Texas* lasting only thirty-five minutes. Its bare beaches offered no cover for the American invaders as German machine guns from fortified gun emplacements swept the beaches. The US Rangers, who had trained earlier on the cliffs of Dorset, scaled the sheer cliffs of Pointe Du Hoc while being shot at by German soldiers; their mission was to destroy artillery pieces that threatened to sweep the landing zones. Their commander that day was Lieutenant Colonel James Rudder. Unknown to Rudder's Rangers, most of the artillery had already been moved by the Germans. They held the position for two days in the face of fierce counterattacks by the 916th Grenadiers. At the Ranger memorial at Pointe du Hoc, one can still see massive craters created by Allied naval bombardment on D-Day.

As commander of the US Third Army after D-Day, General Patton, led an army that advanced farther and faster than just about any army in military history, crossing twenty-four major rivers and capturing 81,500 square miles of territory, including more than twelve thousand cities and towns. Patton loved to quote Danton who said, *"De l'audace, et encore de l'audace, toujours de l'audace!"* ("Audacity, more audacity, always audacity").

In August of 1944, American troops participated in a much less widely known invasion, Operation Dragoon that landed in the south of France. Everyone knows about June 6, 1944, but how many know about August 15, 1944? Yet the parachute drop by the 1st Airborne Task Force, landings by American troops, primarily the 3rd, 36th, and 45th Infantry Divisions, and a French armored division were highly successful. Allied casualties were light, and German resistance mainly crumbled fairly fast. By mid-September, they had pushed their way up the Rhone Valley near the German border. Some of the invasion targets, like the beach of St. Tropez, famous for film stars in the post-war era, are now more readily associated with pleasure than with war, which may be one reason Dragoon is less familiar to Americans.

Meanwhile to the north, on August 25, 1944, the French 2nd Armored Division, led by General Leclerc, was allowed the honor of being the first Allied force to liberate Paris. Ernest Hemingway personally led a group of irregulars that liberated the Ritz Hotel drinking seventy-three martinis that night in its bar. General Charles de Gaulle spoke from a balcony at the Hotel de Ville, "Paris outraged! Paris broken! Paris martyred! But Paris liberated! Liberated by itself, liberated by its people, with the help of the whole of France!" De Gaulle seems to have temporarily ignored the contribution of the Americans, British, Polish, Canadian, and other Allied troops that fought so hard to liberate France.

Robert Capa, the famous war photographer, rode into Paris on an American-built tank that day.

And there was still much fighting remaining before all France was liberated. It wasn't until November 22, 1944, after American troops had captured the vital, strategic pass at Saverne, that French troops liberated Strasbourg, the most easterly major city in France. And at about the same time, after bitter fighting, to the northwest, the US Third Army was finally taking Metz, a heavily fortified French city, close to the border with Germany.

The liberation of France would claim 134,000 American casualties. Thousands of Americans would be buried in French cemeteries, such as the beautiful one that overlooks Omaha Beach.

France became a founding member of NATO in 1949. France, though strained by its Indochina and African commitments, contributed an infantry battalion that served alongside Americans in the Korean War. My (Chris Kelly's) father, Robert E. Kelly, served as a clerk typist in the US Army based in Verdun, France, during the Korean War. He liked to say that he "kept the North Koreans out of France."

Fifty-six French troops would be killed alongside American marines in the Beirut bombing in October 1983. French forces would also serve in the Gulf War of 1991 that liberated Kuwait. And French forces have served alongside Americans in Afghanistan.

France still has assorted territories around the world, which used to be part of its empire. So we need to deal with American military involvement there in this chapter.

For instance, our navy built an advance base on Nuku Hiva Island in the Marquesas Islands, now part of French Polynesia, in 1813. Captain Porter briefly claimed Nukuhiva for the United States and named it Madison Island and the fort built there Madison's Ville, and the water next to it, Massachusetts Bay. Yep.

It's also worth mentioning Nouméa, in the French territory of New Caledonia, which is situated east of Australia. This became an important US base during World War II. In fact, it became, the US headquarters for the whole of the South Pacific with tens of thousands of US personnel stationed there.

The most fun of the French territories from the point of American invasions is Clipperton Island. Few people have heard of it, and even fewer know how we invaded it. It doesn't sound very French (unless you call it

Île de Clipperton or its other name, Île de la Passion, when it does sound a lot more French).

It's an uninhabited coral atoll lying in the Pacific Ocean west of Costa Rica and northwest of the Galapagos Islands. The French were the first Europeans to find it, and it's French today, and, even though it's not the most attractive bit of real estate in the world, it's been invaded by others over the years, including, yes, Americans.

The Guano Islands Act of 1856 was supposed to promote American use of islands that had plenty of guano on them, and this being one of the few things Clipperton did have on it, the American Guano Mining Company claimed it. Guano mining caused a minor diplomatic incident in 1897 when the French found that three American guano miners had raised the Stars and Stripes. The State Department eventually gave in to the French. However, during World War II, we returned because FDR thought the place might be useful as a flying base. In December 1944, we occupied the island and raised the American flag again, not admittedly against much, or indeed any, resistance, sending in a meteorological team protected by troops. However, the mission didn't last long and was eventually withdrawn, leaving Clipperton and its seabirds to the French.

GABON

THE NAME "GABON" COMES FROM THE PORTUGUESE WORD *"gabão,"* which means a type of cloak.

Gabon is another country on Africa's Atlantic coast where our first military contact was due to anti-slaving operations. Our Africa Squadron seized a number of vessels in the area, though not always with ultimate success. They seized the ketch *Brothers* at Mayumba on September 8, 1858, believing the vessel to be equipped for slaving, but the charges were later dismissed in the United States. And they seized the *Emily* at Loango on September 21, 1859, again because they believed it was equipped for slaving, and here too, the charges were dismissed in the United States.

But not all our naval visits have been linked to fighting slavery. The USS *Ticonderoga*, for example, called in on Gabon in 1879 on a cruise down the African coast designed to promote to the locals the advantages of trade with the United States.

In the later twentieth century and into the twenty-first century, Gabon became a significant oil producer. In recent years, we've had some military involvement, though France is the former colonial power and quite a lot of French influence remains. For instance, in 1997, US military personnel deployed to Gabon as part of an evacuation force ready to rescue Americans and others from problems in nearby Zaire (now Democratic Republic of Congo). We've been involved with the Gabonese military in peacekeeping training. For example, US and Gabonese military medics teaming up in Medical Accord Central 12, and in naval visits, like the arrival of the USS *Bradley* in Libreville, the capital of Gabon, in 2011.

THE GAMBIA

LOCATED ALONG THE BANKS OF THE GAMBIA RIVER, The Gambia is the smallest country on the African mainland.

The Gambia is another of those African countries where slaving posts on the Atlantic coast brought early attention from the USN's Africa Squadron.

Since The Gambia was a British colony, not surprisingly during World War II, our military used facilities there. The navy used the port at what was then Bathurst (now Banjul, the capital). For example, the USS *Memphis* was sent to Bathurst, so that on the night of January 13, 1943, Franklin Roosevelt could sleep there before going on to the conference at Casablanca. While he was in the city, Roosevelt took a boat trip along the seafront at Bathurst. The USAAF also used the airport at Bathurst during World War II, for instance, for aircraft being ferried north to Morocco.

The Gambia became independent in 1965. A coup in 1994 interrupted our military links with The Gambia, but they have resumed to some extent since then. For instance, in 2009, the High Speed Vessel (HSV) *Swift* paid a visit to Banjul in the most important US naval visit since the coup, we ran exercise Africa Endeavor 2011 in The Gambia, and The Gambia was one of the nations participating with the USN in exercise Saharan Express 2013.

GEORGIA

NO, THIS GEORGIA IS NOT THE US STATE and has not so much to do with Jimmy Carter either. This is the nation in the Caucasus, which has Russia to its north and Turkey, Armenia, and Azerbaijan to its south.

Having said all that, neatly enough, the US state of Georgia has had a partnership program with the country of Georgia since 1995. So, American guardsmen from the Georgia National Guard have trained alongside Georgians (from Georgia the country) in the Georgian military. Georgia (the country), though, also has a Georgian National Guard, so it's neat but frankly, it could all get pretty confusing at some stage.

After the Russian Revolution of 1917 brought the Russian Empire to an end, Georgia became independent for a few years, along with other nations in the Caucasus. We had a bit of military involvement in the area at this point. For instance, the American Military Mission in Armenia visited the Georgian capital Tblisi during its investigations in the area.

In 1921, Georgia became part of the Soviet Union. Stalin was Georgian, and if you've ever wondered about the name Operation Bagration, the epic Soviet offensive that almost entirely destroyed German Army Group Centre in 1944, its name has nothing to do with bags or rations. It's the name of a Georgian royal family and also of the famous Georgian general in the Russian army, Pyotr Bagration, who among other things led Russian troops against the Revolutionary French in Italy. In 1991, Georgia became independent again, and by 1992, the Soviet Union's former foreign minister, Eduard Sheverdnadze, became its president. Lost one job, found another.

During the Cold War, Georgia was occasionally the target of US surveillance efforts, but since the end of the Cold War, we have developed close military links with Georgia (which also involve Americans from states other than Georgia). For instance, Georgia has sent large contingents of troops, many of them trained by the United States, to fight alongside ours in Iraq and Afghanistan. In 2008, with the war between Russia and Georgia, President George W. Bush announced that US air force and naval personnel would deliver humanitarian and medical aid to Georgia, and the US government sided with the Georgian government, offering air transport for Georgia troops to return home from where they were serving in Iraq.

GERMANY

THE FIRST MILITARY INTERACTION BETWEEN THE UNITED STATES and Germans saw Germans in action on our soil. The British, in fact, used Hessian troops to help fight the colonists in the American Revolution while a certain "Baron" von Steuben from Magdeburg Prussia became a major general in the Continental Army and wrote the drill book (*Revolutionary War Drill Manual*) that was used by the US Army until the War of 1812.

But it wasn't just German soldiers that were coming to the United States. German civilians were coming too to make a new home for themselves and new lives. German-Americans at one stage formed the largest non-English ethnic group in the United States.

In World War I, the United States was at first neutral in the struggle of the Triple Entente of England, France, and Russia against the Central Powers of Germany and the Austro-Hungarian Empire. The violation of Belgian neutrality, unrestricted submarine warfare, and fears of a German conspiracy to bring Mexico over to the German side (revealed in the Zimmerman telegram), however, eventually propelled America into the war on the Allied side. In addition, it's worth pointing out that the United States had an enormous financial stake in Allied victory as the largest bondholder to the Allied governments.

In the Great War, American forces would fight the Germans in the trenches on the Western Front, dog-fighting in the skies, and on the high seas against the Kaiser's U-boats. US forces would never, however, actually fight on German soil in World War I.

American troops did, though, march into Germany as victors after World War I. American troops of the Third Army were given the job of occupying the Koblenz bridgehead. And even though much of the army gradually returned to the United States, it wasn't until 1923 that President Warren Harding ordered our last men home from Germany.

World War I stirred up strong anti-German sentiment in the United States. For a time, frankfurters were renamed "victory dogs," sauerkraut became "victory cabbage," and Beethoven and Bach were banned from repertoires. Some have even partly blamed the passage of Prohibition on the backlash against German-American brewers that followed the war.

The war to end all wars, of course, did not succeed in doing so. In 1933, Hitler came to power in Germany. By September 1939, Europe was at war once more.

At first, as with World War I, we kept out of it, but ultimately, as Hitler's tanks crushed France and the Luftwaffe bombed Londoners, the sympathies of a lot of Americans increasingly lay with Britain in its lonely struggle against Nazi tyranny. In Brest, France, a monument had been erected to commemorate the USN's efforts in the First World War. On July 4, 1941, prior to Pearl Harbor, the Germans destroyed this monument and replaced it with a naval command bunker. Meanwhile, an undeclared naval war was raging in the waters of the Atlantic with the US Navy and Merchant Marine fighting German U-boats. On October 31, 1941, Nazi submarines torpedoed and sank the USS *Ruben James* while it was escorting merchant ships to Britain.

Shortly after the Pearl Harbor attack, Hitler declared war on the United States fulfilling his treaty obligations to Imperial Japan. The United States would face a two-front war.

One of the great ironies of World War II is that so many individuals with German-American connections played such a vital role in leading the Allies to victory. Dwight D. Eisenhower's grandfather Jacob was a Protestant preacher in Pennsylvania who delivered his sermons in Plattdeutsch. The name of the Supreme Allied Commander in German means "iron hewer." Wags in London even referred to Grosvenor Square, where Ike helped formulate the plans for Operation Overlord, as "Eisenhowerplatz." Chester Nimitz, the American Fleet admiral in WWII, was born in Fredericksburg, Texas, which had been named after the German crown prince Frederick.

America's first chance to strike at German soil directly was from the air.

German cities faced an increasingly relentless bombing campaign from the USAAF. The RAF flew missions by night, and the USAAF flew daylight raids. Eventually, P-51 Mustang escort fighters would be deployed that could reach Berlin and provide vital air protection for the bombers.

American aircrews showed enormous bravery, did extensive damage to the German war effort, and often suffered appalling casualties, particularly in the early days of limited fighter cover. For instance, in an August 1943 raid against factories working on German aircraft components in Regensburg and Schweinfurt, sixty bombers were lost and many more heavily damaged. And in a follow-up raid on Schweinfurt, even more bombers were lost and even more damaged.

German civilians also, however, suffered terribly. Bombing left four hundred thousand Germans dead and 7.5 million Germans homeless. After the fire-bombing of Dresden, which claimed about twenty-five thousand lives, a private first class also of German-American descent, one

Kurt Vonnegut, who had been captured earlier in the war, was pressed into service by the SS gathering bodies and carrying them to pyres.

But soon the chance to strike at German soil on land would also present itself.

On D-Day, June 6, 1944, American forces landed alongside those of our allies in Normandy. The liberation of Paris in August 1944 and Brussels shortly afterwards fueled Allied optimism that the war could be brought to a swift conclusion by Christmas of 1944. This optimism was misplaced. American strategy, somewhat cautious, called for advance on a broad front. The Allies also faced fuel and logistical difficulties due to scarce port facilities—most had been destroyed by the retreating Germans.

Nevertheless, in October of 1944, Aachen, burial place of the emperor Charlemagne, was the first major German city to fall to the Allies when American troops took it after fierce fighting. German forces towards the end of the war would include children and men of retirement age, but there were still plenty ready to fight our advancing forces. A series of bloody battles was fought in the Hürtgen Forest in the last months of 1944, and then the Germans launched a massive counterattack with the Battle of the Bulge (see "Belgium" and "Luxembourg").

However, as the German counterattack faltered and then stalled in the face of Allied reinforcements and Allied airpower, the advance eastwards resumed. The Americans and their allies raced on to the Rhine. On March 6, 1945, units of the US 9th Armored Division managed to cross the bridge at Remagen, which allowed forces to cross over the Rhine into the heart of Germany.

On March 17, 1945, US troops captured the German city of Koblenz, which other US troops had occupied after World War I. Suitably enough, just as the US Third Army had occupied it then, General George Patton's Third Army took it this time.

As Western armies firmly established themselves on the eastern side of the Rhine, some Western leaders like Churchill and Patton were tempted to ignore the agreement reached at Yalta on zones of influence between the Allies and to push on, to try to take Berlin before the Russians could. There was even a plan drawn up, Operation Eclipse, to drop American and British paratroopers on key airfields in the Berlin area, but eventually fears of high casualties and conflict with the Russians led to the abandonment of the idea.

As the worst war in human history drew to a close, the Americans discovered the horrors of the Nazi concentration camps. After Eisenhower visited Ohrdruf Concentration Camp that had been liberated by American troops on April 4, he declared: "We are told that the American soldier does not know what he is fighting for. Now at least he will know what he is fighting against."

On April 18, Magdeburg, home to von Steuben who wrote our drill book all those decades ago, fell to troops of the 30th Infantry Division, and on the same day, resistance in the Ruhr pocket finally collapsed. When it was all finished there, hundreds of Germans had been taken prisoner.

On April 20, the Seventh Army took Nuremberg, scene of all those Nazi rallies, and two days later, they crossed the Danube.

Then on April 25, elements of our First Army met up with Russian forces advancing from the east, splitting Hitler's Reich in two, and on the next day, an official link-up ceremony was held at Torgau.

On April 30, units of the Seventh Army captured Munich, scene of Hitler's Beer Hall Putsch in 1923, and on the same day, far to the north, in Berlin, Hitler committed suicide. A few days later, American troops reached Berchtesgaden, site of Hitler's mountain residence, the Berghof.

The much feared Alpine Redoubt where Nazis were alleged to be planning a ferocious last stand, in fact, fell quickly and easily to our troops.

On May 8, 1945, V-E Day, we celebrated the end of the European part of the most destructive war in history.

The war's conclusion forced a measure of reflection onto many American soldiers. They found they had things in common with the German civilians, but they had also been shocked to the core by the evidence of atrocities in the concentration camps.

Steps were immediately taken to exorcize the ghosts of fascism from Germany with a program of de-Nazification and targeting the symbols of Nazism. For instance, GIs blew up the huge stone swastika that overlooked Zeppelin Field in Nuremberg. We even converted the Hitler Youth stadium in Nuremberg into a baseball park. It was here at Soldier's Field that the European Theatre of Operations World Series was played in September of 1945.

In July 1945, the same month that President Harry Truman headed for the Potsdam Conference, just outside Berlin, the first US army unit, troops of the 2nd Armored Division, entered the former Nazi capital of Berlin.

After the war, Germany was divided into British, French, Soviet, and American zones of occupation. With the onset of the Cold War, the situation between Western allies and the Soviets became increasingly tense. In June 1948, the tensions between the Western allies and the Soviets over plans for the future of Germany erupted as the Russians instituted the Berlin Blockade. In reply, we and our allies instituted the Berlin Airlift.

Just a few years previously, the Luftwaffe had failed to supply the Sixth Army, surrounded in Stalingrad, from the air. Admittedly, by 1948, it was no longer wartime, but the Berlin Airlift had to supply not just an army but also a big chunk of one of the world's major cities.

Despite the enormous difficulties faced, a combination of Allied determination, wartime experience of airlifts, and the hard work of Berliners eventually saw the targets of necessary daily supplies achieved. In fewer than ninety days, German civilians under French direction even built a new airport, often using their bare hands. And a French general took the risk of blowing up a radio tower controlled by the Soviets that was causing problems on the approach to the new airport.

By April 1949, the Russians had to admit that the blockade was not working, and they called it off. Seventeen American aircraft had been lost, and thirty-one Americans killed in the race to supply Berlin.

The NATO alliance was formed in April 1949, and West Germany was declared an independent state in May 1949. It became a key ally of ours during the Cold War, joining NATO in 1955. But the other German state, the German Democratic Republic, declared independent in October 1949, became a major opponent of ours during the same period, and we conducted assorted espionage operations on their soil during the period, which are outside the remit of this book.

In November 1989, free passage through the Berlin Wall was allowed, and its demolition was begun almost immediately. Less than a year later, West Germany and East Germany were one country again.

In recent years, German troops have served alongside Americans in Kosovo and in Afghanistan, and the United States maintains a significant military establishment in Germany to this day.

GHANA

GHANA IS A COUNTRY THAT TOOK ITS NAME from the ancient African kingdom of Ghana.

Some major slave-trading ports were located in what is now Ghana, so the area received quite a lot of attention from our Africa Squadron during its anti-slaving operations, though much of their time was spent cruising up and down the coast and the ability of comparatively few navy ships to do much about the slave trade was limited. On December 28, 1858, the USS

Vincennes did seize the barque *Julia Dean* at Cape Coast Castle in what is now Ghana and sent the vessel to the United States. There the case was dismissed by the courts.

What is now Ghana became the British Gold Coast colony, and in World War II, we were back. Although Ghana is a long way from where the main World War II action took place, our bases there became, in fact, vital in winning the war. With the Mediterranean and North Africa a battleground, the area became a key site on the route that enabled aircraft from the United States to be shipped safely across the Atlantic, across Africa, and up to the Middle East and beyond. In fact, the entire operation is sometimes called the Takoradi Route, named after Takoradi in what is now Ghana. There, planes that had been shipped disassembled across the Atlantic were reassembled for flight onwards across Africa. We also had another airbase at Accra, now the capital of Ghana. Despite the distance from the fighting, the job at these bases still had its dangers. US records contain a list of accidents and incidents involving American aircraft in the area. The route became less important after the Allied conquest of North Africa in 1942 and 1943, but it had still been vital to victory.

After the war, as Britain began to give up its empire, Ghana again became something of a focus for America. Kwame Nkrumah had arrived in America from the Gold Coast in 1935. He studied hard, picking up a number of degrees and associating with a number of leading left-wing thinkers and intellectuals. On his return to Ghana in 1947, he started campaigning for self-governance. The British authorities eventually jailed him, but when they held an election in 1951, Nkrumah's party, even though he was still in prison, won by a landslide. The British set Nkrumah free, and in 1952, he became prime minister. By 1957, he was leader of an independent and free Ghana. Not everybody, however, liked Nkrumah's left-leaning and sometimes authoritarian politics, and in 1964, he was toppled in a coup. There has been huge speculation and controversy over what America and the CIA did or did not know about the coup and did or did not do to support it. Nkrumah died in exile in 1972.

Relations between the America government and Ghana haven't always been easy since then. There were some particularly difficult moments during the years when Jerry Rawlings was in power in Ghana, like, for instance, the whole Soussoudis situation.

However, there have also been good times, and in recent years, our military has had extensive links with Ghana's military, including many joint training exercises and assistance in assorted construction projects. The North Dakota National Guard is partnered with Ghana.

The United States also has a history of assisting Ghana's troops on peacekeeping missions. For instance, the USAF flew Ghanaian troops to Liberia for the peacekeeping operations of ECOMOG (Economic Community of West African States Monitoring Group) there, and more recently, AFRICOM has included Ghana in its program of helping a number of African countries further develop their peacekeeping expertise.

GREECE

Yes, Greece. The ancient Greeks played a vital role in the creation of Western civilization. For instance, they brought to the world the gifts of poetry, philosophy, drama, and yes, the Olympic games. The Romans' vast and enduring empire (or at least enduring in the West until 476 AD) owed so much to the glories of Greece.

This sun-dappled land in the Eastern Mediterranean Sea was the cradle of democracy. And, although as we watch politicians in action and see how democracy can have its problems, in the famous words of Churchill, "It's the worst form of government, except for all those other forms that have been tried from time to time."

For all these reasons and more, when in 1821 the Greeks rose against their Ottoman rulers, philhellenes across Europe and America urged them on. And some of them did more than urge—they went to fight. From Britain, for instance, came the famous, or infamous, or perhaps famous AND infamous, Lord Byron. And from America came assorted volunteers like George Jarvis, a New Yorker who arrived in Greece in 1822 and became a guerilla fighter, wearing the foustanella, the traditional skirt of warriors, and serving as adjutant to the aforementioned Lord Byron. He died in 1828 and is buried in Argos. Other Americans, too, would head for Greece to fight for its freedom, including Captain Jonathan P. Miller and James Williams, a former slave who died fighting there.

But not all military links between Americans and Greeks in this period were of the friendly type. Between 1825 and 1828, we had warships in the Aegean to protect our merchant ships against attack by Greek pirates. Sometimes the action was at sea, as when Lieutenant Goldsborough of the USS *Porpoise* and his men freed a British ship taken by pirates killing or wounding something like ninety of them in the process. But sometimes the action involved landings, as when US sailors and marines landed on

Mykonos (now a popular holiday destination) to recapture stolen goods and, in the fighting that followed, one pirate boat was burned and the town was shelled.

When much of what is now modern Greece was free from Ottoman control, other Americans would follow in their footsteps. Some of those would struggle to match the classical Greece they knew from leather-bound books in American libraries with the realities of a country trying to restore itself after centuries of occupation and long, bitter years of rebellion and war. In 1867, an American Civil War veteran named Samuel Clemens paid a visit to Greece. In *The Innocents Abroad*, he wrote under his pseudonym, Mark Twain, "We saw no ploughed fields, very few villages, no trees or vegetation of any kind, scarcely, and hardly ever an isolated house … The fleets that were the wonder of the world when the Parthenon was new, are a beggarly handful of fishing-smacks now."

Greece faced plenty of challenging times in the nineteenth century, and the period saw the beginning of mass emigration to the United States and the development of a large Greek-American community here.

Gradually, though, modern Greece began to develop and expand towards its modern frontiers, adding other Greek-populated regions previously controlled by the Ottomans.

And the USN was in Greek waters again. In January 1909, for example, part of Teddy Roosevelt's Great White Fleet spent a week in Piraeus. Soon our ships would be there not just to visit but to fight again as well, though not, this time, against Greeks.

In World War I, Greece, like the United States, declared war on the Central Powers in 1917. American submarine chasers were based on the Greek island of Corfu to help enforce a mobile barrage of ships of the Strait of Otranto across the Adriatic, placed there to prevent enemy submarines escaping from their Adriatic bases into the Mediterranean. Some of these Corfu submarine chasers ended up being involved in one of the biggest sea battles of the war, the Battle of Durazzo (see "Albania").

In 1940, Greece was invaded from Albania by Mussolini's Italian forces, but the Greeks not only managed to repel the invasion but even pushed into Albania as well. The Germans, however, launched an attack on Greece in the spring of 1941 forcing Greek's British and Commonwealth allies to evacuate after a second Battle of Thermopylae. Crete was captured by an airborne invasion, and Allied forces were compelled to withdraw from that as well, though resistance by locals there to the German invaders started pretty much as soon as the first German paratroopers landed in Crete and lasted until the last Germans left or surrendered.

The British SOE, based in Cairo, began guerilla operations in Crete and in the Greek mountains, and subsequently, the OSS, including many Greek-Americans, also began carrying out commando attacks on railroads, bridges, and telephone exchanges. The OSS parachuted Special Forces into Greece and used caiques (light skiffs used for fishing) to take personnel in and out and to send in supplies. The OSS tended to be a bit more pragmatic than the SOE in their support for Greek resistance forces, being more ready to support the left-wing Communist ELAS (Greek People's Liberation Army) as well as the right-wing nationalist EDES (National Republican Greek League). In light of US policy in Greece after the war, this seems, as we shall see, somewhat ironic.

During the war, also, the USAAF conducted raids against a variety of targets in Greece and on the Greek islands. For instance, in 1943, USAAF bombers based in Cyprus provided air support for the brief and ultimately disastrous British invasion of the island of Leros (which, because of the large Italian coastal guns on Leros may have partly inspired Alistair Maclean's *Guns of Navarone*). On July 28, 1944, American bombers attacked a marshalling yard at Florina. And on October 4, 1944, P-51s strafed the airfields at Tatoi, Kalamaki, and Eleusis.

By the fall of 1944, however, German forces were retreating throughout Europe. British forces landed in Greece, and Athens was liberated on October 14, 1944. That same month, Churchill and Stalin held a conference in Moscow where they allegedly agreed that Britain would have prime influence over post-war Greece whereas Russia would have more influence in assorted parts of the Balkans.

Friction between Communist and nationalists first led to fighting in late 1944 and early 1945. But a ceasefire was patched up (it has been suggested that Stalin may here have been trying to keep his side of the bargain with Churchill) and held until just about November 1946. From there, it was bitter civil war until 1949. This conflict marked the commencement of the global Cold War and claimed the lives of about eighty thousand Greeks, and while it was the British who had taken the lead over America in Greece during World War II, in the period after that war, we came to play a very major role.

The Truman Doctrine, announced on March 12, 1947, declared that the United States would "support free peoples who are resisting attempted subjugation or by outside minorities or by outside pressures." The US Military Advisory and Planning Group Greece, launched in 1948, was one of the first Cold War organizations that helped to assure the Greek government's victory over the Communists. We sent huge amounts of military equipment for the Greek government's armed forces and hundreds of US military personnel to help them win. In the end, the Communists gave in and announced a ceasefire in October 1949.

Greece joined the NATO alliance in 1952, and US military influence remained strong in Greece after its civil war.

In 1967, days before the start of an election campaign that could have brought to power a politician keen on improving links with the Soviet Union and not hugely keen on NATO, a Greek junta, dubbed "the Colonels," seized power in Athens. The junta had strong links to the United States. Its rule was brutal and authoritarian and came to an end in 1974 after its attempt to topple Archbishop Makarios in Cyprus had helped lead to the Turkish invasion of the island. The American ambassador in Cyprus and the CIA station chief in Athens were killed in a wave of anti-American fervor.

Democratic elections were held in November 1974, and by 1981, Greece was joining the European Union.

Greece was still a part of NATO, and we retained some close military connections with the country. For instance, in 1990, we had thirty-seven hundred US military personnel in Greece, mainly at the Nea Makri Communications Station at Marathon, at the Hellenikon Air Base in Athens, and on Crete at the Souda Bay base and the Iraklion Communications Station.

American personnel and facilities in Greece have been the target of some terrorist attacks, as, for instance, on January 12, 2007, when a rocket-propelled grenade hit the US embassy.

Today we still have access to some key facilities in Greece, most important, Naval Support Activity Souda Bay with its deep-water port and airfield. Greece is still a significant member of NATO, for instance, sending troops to Afghanistan and taking part in NATO's Ocean Shield counter-piracy operation.

GRENADA

GRENADA IS A BEAUTIFUL SMALL ISLAND IN THE CARIBBEAN with a population of about one hundred thousand, which is also known as the "Island of Spice"—it produces cinnamon, cloves, and about 20 percent of the world's nutmeg. It's a popular tourist destination, especially for cruise ships to its capital, St. George's. And yes, as you already know, we have invaded it.

Grenada was a former French and, then from 1763, British colony. So inevitably there was a certain amount of French and British invading that went on then. During the British period, we first got involved militarily with Grenada. Nothing major but still worth mentioning.

During the Revolutionary War, for instance, American privateers targeted ships leaving Grenada's ports. Mind you, we didn't have it all our own way. There were also privateers operating out of Grenada that preyed upon our shipping.

Then during World War II, US forces occasionally visited the island, on one occasion allegedly attempting to set up an artillery post on Richmond Hill, but finding no suitable site.

Grenada gained its independence from Britain in 1974 but remains part of the Commonwealth.

In 1983, Grenada was the site of America's largest military intervention since the Vietnam War. Ronald Reagan had defeated Jimmy Carter in the election of 1980 to become our fortieth president. Reagan took a more aggressive view about confronting Communism than his Cold War predecessors. Political upheaval on the island of Grenada gave Reagan an opportunity to reverse militarily what he saw as a dangerous expansion of Cuban and Soviet influence.

On October 19, 1983, Bernard Coard, a hard-line Communist deputy prime minister, led a coup against Prime Minister Maurice Bishop, a Marxist who had assumed power after a coup in 1979. A few days later, Bishop and two other members of his cabinet were assassinated.

Even before the coup, Reagan had been agonizing about exactly what was happening on Grenada and what it meant for the United States. There were intelligence reports indicating that Russia and Cuba had been building military infrastructure, in particular a ten-thousand-foot airstrip. That summer, he had already told vice president George Bush to make contingency plans, and now Reagan didn't hesitate for long in enacting them.

With the Organization of East Caribbean States calling for a military response from the United States and despite being warned that there would be "a harsh political reaction" to a US invasion, on October 22, just a few days after the coup, Reagan decided the invasion should go ahead.

Operation Urgent Fury was launched on October 25, 1983. The US Army Rapid Deployment Force, including Ranger battalions, the 82nd Airborne Division, marines, and Navy SEALs, was augmented by a few hundred troops from Jamaica and other countries. These forces engaged about fifteen hundred troops from the Grenadian Army and about a few hundred Cuban military special forces. The fighting was short (three days) and sometimes sharp, costing nineteen American lives and over one hundred total fatalities, including some civilians.

The UN General Assembly condemned the US invasion calling it "a flagrant violation of international law" and voting 108 to 9 against it. Reagan's ideological soulmate, Prime Minister Thatcher, was thrust into an awkward position by the US invasion as Grenada was still a member of the Commonwealth. Thatcher was disappointed by the American lack of consultation prior to taking action in Grenada.

However, there was also widespread American support for the invasion, particularly after the ABC broadcast *Nightline* featured an interview with American medical students from St. George's University School of Medicine who expressed their gratitude for the invasion and towards the US Army Rangers. Americans were obviously particularly anxious about the potential for hostage taking after the Iranian crisis of 1979, so anything that took Americans out of a potentially dangerous political situation was likely to be popular.

US troops were withdrawn in December of 1983, and Grenada held elections in December of 1984. The operation can be seen as having laid to rest some of the inevitable reluctance for overseas military interventions evident in the period after the end of the Vietnam War.

October 25, the day American forces arrived, is celebrated in Grenada as a national holiday—Thanksgiving Day. The airport has been renamed "Maurice Bishop International Airport" in honor of the assassinated prime minister.

GUATEMALA

GUATEMALA IS LOCATED JUST TO THE SOUTH OF MEXICO in Central America and has a fascinating history, including its amazing Mayan culture.

Guatemala gained its independence from Spain in 1821 and later joined forces with other Central American republics to fight General William Walker's American-led invasion of Nicaragua in the 1850s (see "Nicaragua").

In 1920, US forces had to protect American diplomats and American interests during turmoil in the country.

Guatemala, home to a substantial German overseas population, remained neutral at the start of World War II. However, on December 9, after the Pearl Harbor attack, Guatemala declared war on Japan, and shortly after that, it declared war on Germany. Guatemala wasn't going to play a vast role in World War II, but it did play some.

We've occasionally had forces based in Guatemala. For instance, we made use of assorted airbases in the country during World War II. In particular, we had aircraft based at Guatemala City Air Base, some of them conducting anti–U-boat operations.

By the 1950s, the United Fruit Company (known to some as "El Pulpo," or "the octopus") owned 42 percent of the arable land in Guatemala. In 1901, the US-based company even started running the Guatemalan post office. In 1953, a government led by Jacobo Arbenz, inspired by the New Deal, began expropriating land. The Eisenhower administration feared the spread of Communism in Central America. Arbenz's wife publicly declared that the triumph of Communism was inevitable in the world. The United States imposed an arms embargo on Guatemala and airlifted arms to neighboring Honduras. A USN force was sent to the area for potential evacuation duties.

Told by CIA director Allen Dulles that the chances of success were somewhere between 40 and 50 percent, Ike gave the green light for a coup attempt, code named PBSUCCESS. Mercenaries were trained in Florida and in neighboring Honduras. The CIA helped to provide air support and jammed the government airwaves. The 1954 coup removed Arbenz and replaced him with Colonel Carlos Castillo Armas, who would be assassinated by a security guard in 1957.

In the summer of 1960, anti-Castro Cubans began training in Guatemala to prepare for a CIA-sponsored invasion of Cuba, and in 1961, the Kennedy administration used airbases in Guatemala to support its failed Bay of Pigs invasion.

A long bloody civil war raged in Guatemala from 1960 until 1996, in which left-wing guerrillas fought army and government. Fearing the growth of Communism, the United States gave extensive support to the army and government. Huge numbers were killed during the war, very many of them unarmed civilians, very many of them killed by government forces. Mayan suffering was enormous. In 1999, President Bill Clinton visited Guatemala after an independent report on the war and expressed regret, "It is important that I state clearly that support for military forces or intelligence units which engaged in violent and widespread repression of the kind described in the report was wrong, and the United States must not repeat that mistake. We must, and we will, instead continue to support the peace and reconciliation process in Guatemala."

In recent years, links between the US military and Guatemala have focused on fighting drug traffickers, ship visits, humanitarian efforts, and exercises such as Medical Readiness Training Exercises.

In 2010, after Tropical Storm Agatha and a volcano eruption, helicopters and teams from Joint Task Force Bravo, based in Honduras, rushed relief supplies to some of those affected in Guatemala. And in 2012, two hundred US marines flew into Guatemala City and proceeded to patrol the coastline looking for drug smugglers.

The Arkansas National Guard is partnered with Guatemala.

GUINEA

GUINEA IS ABOUT THE SIZE OF OREGON and located on West Africa's Atlantic coast. At one stage, it formed part of some of the great West African empires, like the Mali and the Songhai empires.

Rio Pongo, in what is now Guinea, was a major slaving area and, therefore, of great interest to our anti-slaving patrols. On March 24, 1845, for instance, at Rio Pongo, the USS *Truxtun*, acting on intelligence about an American slaving ship in the area, seized the New Orleans ship *Spitfire*. The USS *Truxtun* was operating alongside a British ship, and when the anti-slaving vessels approached, the *Spitfire* ran up the Stars and Stripes to try to deter the British vessel, only to find that it was facing a US vessel as well. There were no slaves yet on board, but three hundred were waiting to be loaded, and one of the officers of the *Truxtun* noted the appalling conditions in which hundreds of slaves would be packed into the comparatively small ship. In June 1845, Peter Flowery was sentenced in Massachusetts for the slaving expedition, but because he had not actually loaded the slaves yet and because the jury recommended mercy, he was sentenced to only five years' imprisonment and a two-thousand-dollar fine. In the end, after only twenty-one months, he was released on grounds of ill health.

Guinea became a French colony and eventually gained independence in 1958. It has had a difficult history involving many coups, extensive human rights abuses, and much authoritarian rule.

Ahmed Sékou Touré became president of the newly independent country and stayed president until his death in 1984. Touré had links to a variety of nations at different stages of his career, including the United States and Soviet Union. Ours included, in 1960, US Air Force planes flying into the capital Conakry to airlift Guinean troops to take part in the UN operation in the Congo.

Touré's death, unfortunately, didn't bring Guinea's problems to an end, and the country has seen periods of instability in the years since then. Our military involvement with the country has been limited. US military personnel have, for instance, visited the country to supply disaster management and medical training. Recently, Guinea was one of the countries participating in Western Accord 2012 in Senegal, an AFRICOM-sponsored multi-lateral exercise led by US Marine Corps Forces Africa.

GUINEA-BISSAU

GUINEA-BISSAU IS ON AFRICA'S ATLANTIC COAST to the north of Guinea, and its capital is, perhaps not surprisingly, Bissau.

Slave trading posts were located in Guinea-Bissau, so its coast and the waters off them were of interest to the USN's anti-slaving patrols in the nineteenth century.

Guinea-Bissau became independent after a long guerrilla war against Portuguese colonial authorities, and we established diplomatic relations with Guinea-Bissau in 1975. The country has had, at times, a fairly turbulent history.

We have had some military involvement there. For example, we signed an international military training agreement with Guinea-Bissau in 1986, and prior to 1998, we were helping the Guinea-Bissau Navy with training and some communications and navigation equipment.

In 1998, the Guinea-Bissau civil war broke out. In June of that year, US military personnel and aircraft were sent to Dakar in neighboring Senegal to be ready to help evacuate US citizens. In fact, by then, forty-four Americans had already left Bissau on a Portuguese boat and a Senegalese ship.

African peacekeepers trained under a US program have served in Guinea-Bissau.

GUYANA

UYANA ON SOUTH AMERICA'S NORTHERN COAST used to be British Guiana, although in the colonial period, the French and Dutch also controlled different bits of it at various times. And, in fact, Guyana still has its own New Amsterdam. Yep.

Because of the British influence, we didn't have much military and political involvement there until after Guyana's independence, but even before, we did have some. For instance, during the War of 1812, in February 1813, the USS *Hornet* under Captain James Lawrence defeated HMS *Peacock* after the *Hornet* chased a British merchant ship into the mouth of the Demerara River in British Guiana.

In the late nineteenth century, after Venezuela appealed to the United States for help over a border dispute with British Guiana, President Grover Cleveland got involved and persuaded Britain to agree to international arbitration.

Under the Destroyers for Bases deal during World War II, we got two bases in what was then British Guiana, a USAAF base at Atkinson Field, and a seaplane base at Makouria. Atkinson had a mission to combat U-boats in the area and protect other US interests, including bauxite deposits, but it also rapidly developed into a vital link in the South Atlantic air-ferry and transport route connecting to Africa and beyond to the Middle East.

Guyana became independent in 1966, but in the years prior to that, the US government had become worried about a possible spread of Communism in British Guiana. Cheddi Jagan was a dentist who had been educated in the United States and was married to a woman from Chicago. He was also, however, a left-winger and, despite British opposition, had been elected into power three times in British Guiana. In 1961, he visited President Kennedy in the Oval Office. However, US government concern about Jagan's politics continued, and it has been alleged that Kennedy and the CIA launched an extensive campaign against him. Jagan lost power in 1964. Though he would eventually return to be president of Guyana from 1992 until his death in 1997, and his wife, Janet, would be elected president shortly after his death.

The Jonestown tragedy of 1978 put major US focus on the area once again, and USAF aircraft flew hundreds of bodies from Guyana to the United States at that time.

From 1964 to 1985, one man, Forbes Burnham was basically in control of Guyana. Finally, in 1982, because of its dislike of the Burnham government, the US government suspended aid to Guyana. However, links began to improve after Burnham's death in 1985, and in the 1990s, the US military was occasionally training alongside the Guyana Defence Force and was involved in humanitarian projects in the country. Such links continue today. In 2012, for instance, in Exercise Fused Response, members of the US military and of the Guyana Defence Forces teamed up to improve interoperability.

HAITI

HAITI MAY BE KNOWN FOR ITS EXTREME POVERTY TODAY, but in the eighteenth century, it was the richest jewel in the French overseas empire.

Haiti produced 60 percent of world's coffee supply and 40 percent of the world's sugar supply. Labor was supplied in brutal working conditions by African slaves whose life expectancy was extremely short. The slave population outnumbered the white planter population by a factor of ten to one.

The French Revolution broke out in 1789 heralding the rights of man. Toussaint L'Ouverture, a former slave who had been born on the island, asserted that human rights belonged to ALL men, and the Haitian Revolution followed in 1791.

While some Americans in the South were terrified by the prospect of a slave revolt on Haiti, other Americans saw the uprising as an opportunity for profit. American merchants, mainly from New England, sold thirty thousand muskets to Toussaint and his rebels. And we were even, to a certain extent, attacking the French in and around Haiti. During the quasi-war against the French, we attacked many French ships in the area. For instance, in 1800, marines from the USS *Constitution* assisted in the capture of the French schooner *Esther* off Cap Francois.

In 1801, Napoleon dispatched his brother-in-law, General Leclerc (married to Pauline Bonaparte), to invade Haiti and restore French rule, the property rights of the planters, and slavery. The French had some success against the rebels and captured Toussaint, who was sent back to prison in France.

However, news of his death and concern over other French actions reignited the rebellion, and thousands of French troops were killed by yellow fever, including Leclerc who died in 1802.

Leclerc had not been able to fulfill the second part of his orders, which was to proceed to New Orleans to strengthen the French presence in the New World. As a direct result of this Haitian debacle, Napoleon chose simply to sell the Louisiana Territory to the Jefferson administration. The Louisiana Purchase, negotiated in 1803, accounts for about 23 percent of the total area of the current United States.

Meanwhile in Haiti, in what had become an increasingly bitter fight, the rebels finally defeated the French, and on January 1, 1804, Jean-Jacques Dessalines, known as Emperor Jacques I of Haiti, declared independence.

The road that lay ahead for independent Haiti was not an easy or smooth one, featuring extensive political instability and turmoil, and an embargo aimed at securing payments to France for loss of Haiti did its share of damage.

In the nineteenth century, we started a pattern of regularly getting involved in Haiti. Marines landed in 1817 to protect American interests and property, and again in 1818 and in 1821.

We put on a show of force in 1888 and compelled the Haitian government to release an American steamer they'd seized.

In the late nineteenth century, Germans began migrating to Haiti setting off alarm bells in Washington. Two German ships threatened to shell Port au Prince in 1897. Did the Kaiser want a colony in the Caribbean?

In 1914, US marines landed in Haiti a number of times, for instance, at Port au Prince, which was convulsed by a civil war at the time. Captain Smedley Butler led the marines in numerous firefights against the Cacos, or peasant guerillas. A squad of eight US marines removed five hundred thousand dollars in gold from the Banque Nationale in Port au Prince for safekeeping; the funds were shipped to New York via the USS *Machias*.

The next year, in 1915, President Woodrow Wilson sent in the US Marines to safeguard US interests amidst political and economic turmoil in Haiti and concerns that the Germans might exploit them. And the marines were going to stay there a long, long time. In fact, the United States would basically run Haiti for almost the next twenty years. The United States took control of Haiti's customs receipts, and the US naval commander there dissolved Haiti's congress and introduced a new constitution. US marines were to be garrisoned on the island until 1934.

However, the US occupation would not come without resistance. USMC aviators in De Havilland DH-4 and Curtiss Jenny biplanes were used to dive-bomb Haitian guerillas. The US Marines would fight no fewer than two hundred firefights in Haiti in one year alone. In 1919, Captain Herman H. Hanneken managed to infiltrate the rebel camp and shoot rebel leader Charlemagne Péralte dead with a pistol.

Due to the large role played by the USN and USMC, Wilson's secretary of the navy, Josephus Daniels, was greeted by other Cabinet members as "Josephus the First, King of Haiti." The term "cup of Joe" was coined due to Daniels's enthusiasm for encouraging coffee-drinking in the USN.

FDR's Good Neighbor Policy shifted the United States away from direct control over Haiti.

After the attack on Pearl Harbor, Haiti declared war on Japan and then on Germany and Italy. We supplied extensive amounts of lend-lease equipment to Haiti, including aircraft, artillery, and tanks. We helped train and equip a Haitian Air Force, and the US Coast Guard stationed a detachment at Bizoton to help the fight against U-boats.

The end of the war meant the end of much of this activity, but we did have assorted military links with Haiti in the post-war period as well. For instance, the USAF used the airbase at Bowen Field. And from 1959 to 1963, in response to a request from President Duvalier for help in reorganizing the armed forces, a US Naval Mission was present in Haiti.

The Kennedy administration had had its doubts about the Duvalier regime for some time and taken some measures against it, but things got rapidly worse in April 1963 when the regime announced it had exposed a plot against it. The thirty-strong US Marine Corps training force was withdrawn, and USN vessels, including USS *Boxer*, evacuated over two thousand civilians.

Duvalier died in 1971 and was followed in power by his son Jean-Claude Duvalier. Eventually, in 1986, the Haitian army forced him out. In 1990, elections put into power Jean-Bertrand Aristide, but in September 1991, a coup toppled him and installed a military regime.

In July 1994, President Clinton ordered twenty thousand troops to Haiti in Operation Uphold/Support Democracy to restore Aristide to power. Ten Haitians were killed in a brief firefight with US marines.

A disputed parliamentary election and a presidential election boycotted by the opposition in 2000 created another political crisis in Haiti, and Aristide finally resigned in disputed circumstances in 2004. After Aristide's departure, President George W. Bush quickly dispatched one thousand marines to Haiti who, along with forces from other nations, helped restore order. Subsequently, MINUSTAH, the United Nations Stabilization Mission, arrived in Haiti with US support.

But it hasn't been just political conflict that has taken our forces to Haiti. For instance, on January 12, 2010, a massive earthquake measuring 7.0 on the Richter scale hit Haiti. Over one hundred thousand people were killed, and millions made homeless. The United States intervened with military assets, including the supercarrier *Carl Vinson* and a brigade of the 82nd Airborne Division to provide emergency relief assistance.

The Louisiana National Guard is partnered with Haiti.

HONDURAS

I N 1821, HONDURAS GAINED ITS FREEDOM FROM SPAIN. It's had a pretty eventful history at times since then, and we've played a pretty significant part in that.

For instance, General William Walker, a native of Nashville, Tennessee, who managed to get elected president of Nicaragua after leading a group of filibusters (the word is derived from the Dutch *vrijbuiter*, or "freebooter") arrived in 1860 in Honduras. At the age of thirty-six, he was leading his third attempt to invade Nicaragua by first landing in neighboring Honduras. It was to be his last attempt to do that and pretty much his last attempt to do anything, in fact. He was captured by Honduran troops who were aided by Royal Navy warships and Royal Marines. Captain Norvell Salmon of the Royal Navy handed Walker over to the Hondurans, who then carried out an execution on the beach at Trujillo on September 12, 1860.

But soon our armed involvement with the country was to become a lot more official. By the end of the nineteenth century, the Honduran banana industry was becoming a major industry, and US financial and strategic interest in the country was increasing. One result would be an increase in our military involvement there.

In 1903, we sent warships to the seas off Honduras after a revolution there, and marines were sent ashore to protect American diplomats.

Again, in 1907, we sent marines ashore to protect US interests, and later that same year, we got involved with sorting out a war between Honduras and Nicaragua.

On February 11, 1911, the USN cruiser *Tacoma* landed men again to protect US banana interests in Puerto Cortez, Honduras, and we got involved with arranging a deal to end a civil conflict that had hit Honduras.

In 1912, troops were once again landed, this time to prevent the Honduran government from taking over an American-owned railroad. But official US disapproval forced withdrawal of the troops.

Another US landing force was sent in again in 1919, and we helped install an interim government after internal disputes once more hit Honduras.

Three major fruit companies, Standard, United, and Cuyamel ran much of the economy. Standard was organized by the Vaccaro brothers—a Sicilian family out of New Orleans. A civil war broke out in Honduras in 1924 where different political factions sought the support and patronage of the banana magnates. US warships were sent in, and detachments of US marines were landed in Honduras, one setting up its headquarters in the Vaccaro brothers' warehouse. In April of 1924, the American secretary of state, Sumner Welles, arrived in Honduras to settle the Honduran conflict.

And in 1925, once more, US troops were sent in to protect foreign civilians.

After that, things quieted down a bit, though we did retain military links with the country. For instance, in 1934 the Military Aviation School of Honduras was founded with, perhaps inevitably, a US colonel as its commandant. From 1932 to 1949, Tiburcio Carías Andino was in power, despite seeing a number of challenges to his rule.

And on December 8, 1941, the day after the Pearl Harbor attack, Honduras joined the Allied cause in World War II.

In 1954, the US government feared the growth of Communism in neighboring Guatemala. Part of our response to this was to rush weapons to Honduras to counter any attempt to invade it. The crisis, however, passed (from a US government point of view) when a military coup toppled the Guatemalan government.

Plenty of sports fans feel passionate about their teams, but usually that passion stops short of actual war. Not so in Central America. In 1969, Honduras and El Salvador fought the famous, or indeed, infamous, Football War. The catalyst for the four-day-long war was violence at a series of qualifying matches between El Salvador and Honduras for the 1970 World Cup. Basically, the only direct US involvement in this conflict, however, was the use of US equipment, including WWII vintage fighters, such as P-51s and Corsairs by both sides in the fighting.

In the 1980s, as it became concerned about events in both neighboring El Salvador and Nicaragua, the United States began to concentrate on building up the Honduran military. Questions arise about the human rights records of some Honduran personnel during these years and how much the US government and CIA knew about, for instance, Battalion 316's alleged operations in Honduras.

And Honduras became the base for a massive secret war fought with huge US support. The United States helped established Contra ("Counterrevolutionary") bases in Honduras with the intention of subverting the Sandinista regime in neighboring Nicaragua.

And the 1980s generally saw a peak in the involvement of the US military in Nicaragua, which included major construction projects, particularly on airfields.

In 1983, the US government, fearing that neighboring Nicaragua might invade Honduras, sent one hundred Green Beret military advisors to the country and a powerful naval task force to the seas off Nicaragua.

In 1988, President Reagan authorized Operation Golden Pheasant, which deployed three thousand US troops to Honduras. Sandinista forces, which had invaded Honduras, were compelled to withdraw to their own country.

Joint Task Force Bravo has been operational in Honduras since the 1980s and is now stationed at the Palmerola/Soto Cano Air Base. It consists of hundreds of US military personnel there basically to provide the United States with the ability to respond to civilian emergencies (hurricanes and such) and security threats in the region and to promote coordination with other militaries in the region.

In recent years, US security concerns in Honduras have focused increasingly on efforts to counter narcotics smuggling there. This drug war has, for instance, seen the United States set up a series of bases in Honduras, including Forward Operating Base Mocoron.

The Puerto Rico National Guard is partnered with Honduras.

HUNGARY

HUNGARY, LAND OF BEAUTIFUL BUDAPEST, set astride the mighty Danube River, is also land of delicious food, gorgeous salami, and spicy paprika.

The Hungarians call themselves Magyars and have a language very unlike most others. It's part of the Finno-Ugric group, which also includes Estonian and Finnish (not surprising bearing in mind the Finno bit but quite surprising given it's quite a long way from Hungary to Finland). Hungary includes place names like Székesfehérvár, which looks as if it ought to be pronounced Sexyforever but probably isn't pronounced quite like that.

Some have claimed that the first king of Hungary was Attila the Hun, one of those characters in history that can at best be described as controversial and at worst something rather ruder. The first definite king of Hungary, though, was Saint Stephen I. He is said to have been crowned either on December 25, 1000, or on January 1, 1001 (and a long time before anyone was worrying about the millennium bug). Saint Stephen I is linked to the famous and beautiful Holy Crown of Hungary, which today appears on the coat of arms of Hungary. America, too, has quite a role to play in the history of this amazing crown because at the end of World War II it ended up in the hands of the US Army. It was then kept safe in good old Fort Knox until 1978 when Jimmy Carter sent it home to Hungary.

By 1867, Hungary was a key part of the Austro-Hungarian Empire, which found itself on the losing side in World War I. Our navy clashed with Austro-Hungarian forces in the Adriatic, and our army fought Austro-Hungarian units in Italy, but we didn't make it into Hungary at that stage. The Treaty of Versailles, which ended the First World War, dismembered the Austro-Hungarian Empire. The Treaty of Trianon, signed by the United States and other Allied powers in 1920, created the new nation of Hungary.

On October 22, 1913, Endre Friedmann was born in Budapest. He would later become Robert Capa, one of the greatest war photographers of all time. As an accredited war correspondent of the US Army, he would document the heroism of ordinary GIs in Tunisia, Sicily, Italy, and at Normandy.

During World War II, landlocked Hungary was ruled by Admiral Horthy, who had served in the Austro-Hungarian navy. Under duress, he allied his country with Adolf Hitler during the Second World War, and Hungarian units participated in Operation Barbarossa, the invasion of the Soviet Union, which began in June of 1941.

Just as in World War I, Hungary was a bit too far into Eastern Europe for our armies to reach, but this time, our air force did pay it some visits. For instance, on June 2, 1944, as part of Operation Frantic, bombers took off from Italy, bombed Debrecen in Hungary, and then landed at Poltava in the then Soviet Union. And, on September 13, 1944, the Eighth Air Force bombed the steelworks at Diosgyor in Hungary.

However, while our boys were in the air over Hungary, there were also some American feet on the ground. During World War II, "Wild Bill" Donovan of the OSS plotted to bring Hungary out of its alliance with Hitler's Germany and over to the Allied side—just as the Italian government had a few months earlier. Operation Sparrow went in March of 1944 to convey an American peace proposal to Hungary. At that point, it was already clear that the Allies would win the war.

Colonel Florimund Duke (amazing name) and two of his subordinates were parachuted by a British Halifax into Hungary near the border with Croatia. Duke had been a football star at Dartmouth and then worked for *Time* magazine as an advertising manager.

The Sparrow team planned to infiltrate Hungary by becoming prisoners of war of the Hungarian army. They then hoped to make contact with General Stephen Ujszaszi, the army's chief of intelligence. They succeeded and were cordially received. Ujszaszi helped to set up meetings with two Hungarian cabinet members to discuss the possibility of a Hungarian defection from the Axis.

On Sunday, March 19, the OSS team were roused before dawn for a meeting with Ujszaszi. Three German panzer divisions had just crossed the border from Austria, and 240 Gestapo agents were on their way to Budapest. German intelligence had learned of the American plans and acted to foil any separate Hungarian peace plot. Colonel Duke and his OSS agents spent the remainder of the war as prisoners in the infamous Colditz Castle, a medieval German castle, originally designed to keep people out, which the Germans had turned into a POW camp designed to keep people in and reserved for prisoners likely to try to escape or of high value or both.

After the war, in 1956, the United States once again attempted to shape events inside Hungary. Stalin had died in 1953, and there was uncertainty about Khrushchev's willingness to use force. Spontaneous demonstrations against Soviet power erupted in Hungary that fall. In October, a crowd at Budapest City Park tore a statue of Stalin from its pedestal and Imre Nagy, a former prime minister, denounced the crimes and mistakes of the previous decade.

The Eisenhower administration was optimistically hoping for a miraculous unraveling of Soviet control. John Foster Dulles, the secretary of state, wanted to roll back Communism. His brother Allen Dulles, the CIA director, assumed that 80 percent of the Hungarian army would defect to the rebel side.

The Soviets responded to the uprising by dispatching two hundred thousand troops and twenty-five hundred tanks to crush the uprising. About twenty thousand were killed, and twenty thousand more were sent to prison camps in Siberia. Furthermore, about two hundred thousand Hungarians fled the country. Nagy was secretly tried and hanged.

American military intervention would not be forthcoming because Eisenhower was unwilling to risk World War III over Hungarian independence.

In recent years, with the Cold War long finished, US forces have spent time based in Hungary. During operations in Former Yugoslavia, Taszár Air Base in the south of the country became an important base for our military, and today Papa Air Force Base (great name) in Hungary is home to US personnel serving with the international Heavy Airlift Wing. Hungary is a NATO member and has sent troops to Afghanistan, and among many other military links, the Ohio National Guard is partnered with Hungary.

ICELAND

ICELAND HAS THE NORTHERNMOST CAPITAL IN THE WORLD, Reykjavik. From Iceland, the Vikings expanded to Greenland and then went in search of Vinland (not Finland; that's in the other direction entirely).

Most Americans have heard of the Vikings and Vinland, but not many know we occupied Iceland during World War II—and we occupied Iceland even before we were officially in the war.

The British launched an unopposed invasion with Operation Fork in 1940 to prevent any attempt by the Germans to occupy it and threaten the vital Atlantic convoy routes. In the summer of 1941, prior to Pearl Harbor, American forces relieved and replaced the British garrison with the US government making an agreement with Icelandic and Danish officials (at the time, the Danish king was also king of Iceland) that the US occupation force would be withdrawn after the war.

Task Force 19, including the First Provisional Marine Brigade, and numerous warships departed Newfoundland on July 1 and arrived off Reykjavik on July 7, landing there on July 8. In the end, tens of thousands of Americans were based on Iceland during the war. The island was a crucial transit point for aircraft moving between America and Europe and was also used as a naval and airbase from which to fight the German U-boats that menaced merchant shipping through the Atlantic waters.

In 1942, we started building what would become Keflavik airbase (and is, today, Iceland's main airport, Keflavik International). The fighter field, Patterson Field, went into operation first. And that was followed in 1943 by the bomber field, Meeks Field.

On June 17, 1944, while the war was still going on with bitter fighting in Normandy and while we were still occupying Iceland, the island became an independent nation after the Icelanders voted overwhelmingly in a referendum to split from Denmark, which at the time was still occupied by the Germans.

In 1949, amidst some controversy (there were riots), Iceland became a NATO member. But Iceland has no standing army, so the Iceland Defense Force, made up of US Navy, Marines, and Air Force was based in the country to protect it from 1951 until its withdrawal in 2006.

US naval forces in Iceland during the Cold War played a significant role in countering Soviet submarines in North Atlantic waters.

In October 1986, President Reagan and Gorbachev, president of the USSR, met in Reykjavik. In a meeting at Hofdi House on a bleak stretch of Icelandic coast, the United States and USSR narrowly missed agreeing on the elimination of their nuclear arsenals. Reagan refused to back down on his Strategic Defense Initiative program. When George Schulz later asked Gorbachev what was the turning point in the Cold War, he replied immediately, "Reykjavik."

A small Icelandic contingent (mainly coast guard forces) was deployed in the Iraq War. And in the years since our withdrawal from Iceland in 2006, we have still taken part in exercises there. For instance, in 2011, we jointly led planned exercise Northern Viking (those Vikings again) with Iceland. The Reserve 459th Air Refueling Wing was one of the US units taking part.

INDIA

A LAND WITH SO MUCH FASCINATING HISTORY AND CULTURE and a country that looks to be one of the great powers of the twenty-first century, India is already the world's largest democracy in terms of population.

Because it's such a major nation, it's surprising we haven't had more military links with India. However, India's association with the Non-Aligned Movement during the Cold War, India's development of nuclear weapons in the 1990s, and the long-running tensions between Pakistan and India have all created barriers to closer military links between the United States and India.

Indian prime minister Nehru is said to have been sometimes unenthusiastic about America. During France's war in Indochina, India banned US cargo planes from bringing supplies through Indian airspace. He also closed US Information Agency centers in India.

However, in 1962, during the war between India and China, Nehru asked for US fighters for possible missions against China. Some armaments were sent, and a US aircraft carrier was dispatched, but this turned around shortly afterwards when the crisis passed.

Things got a bit tense during the Bangladesh crisis of 1971 when President Nixon deployed the USS *Enterprise* to the Bay of Bengal in a show of support for Pakistan. Prime minister Indira Gandhi, though, directed her Indian navy officers to invite the USN officers aboard their ships for tea!

In recent years, India has become a partner in the war against terror. For example, India provided intelligence and other aid for the coalition attack on Afghanistan in 2001. And more generally, we developed links on a number of levels, including naval visits and joint exercises. For instance, in November 2013, Indian and US naval forces, including the guided-missile destroyer USS *McCampbell* (DDG 85), cooperated in Exercise Malabar, which featured both ashore and at-sea training in the Bay of Bengal.

However, during World War II, we did have large numbers of US military personnel stationed in India and using its facilities. In fact, during the war, something like 350,000 US troops served in India in support of operations in Burma and China.

For instance, Merrill's Marauders trained in India before heading into Burma. And we had large numbers of USAAF personnel and planes based there. One major mission was flying supplies from India to China. Another major mission was supporting ground troops in action in Burma. We made use of a large number of airbases in India during the period. Chabua Airfield, for instance, was one of the most important airbases in northeast Assam. B-24 Liberators flew combat missions from there, but its major significance was as a base for aircraft and air crews flying supplies over the Hump (the Himalayas) to China. The airbase was attacked by Japanese aircraft, but the major danger for the brave crews was flying in hugely challenging mountainous conditions without many of the modern aids used by pilots today. Americans even got involved in fighting on Indian soil during the bitter battles around Imphal and Kohima after the Japanese invaded India in 1944.

INDONESIA

BEAUTIFUL BALI IS AMONG THE FASCINATING ISLANDS OF INDONESIA.
Indonesia's not exactly a next-door neighbor to the United States, so it's a bit of a surprise to find out how early our military involvement with the area actually was. Already by 1800, Captain Edward Preble and the USS *Essex* were conducting escort duties for merchant ships in the Sunda Strait, and in 1815, the USS *Peacock* carried out one of the last actions of the War of 1812 in the same area. It came across a small British East India Company ship that tried to point out to Captain Warrington of the *Peacock* that the war had finished months before. Warrington had obviously, however, been out of contact for some time and thought the British were trying to trick him, so he fired a broadside and boarded the British ship anyway, only to find out later that they had been telling him the truth.

And in the 1830s, threats to merchant ships led to two US military expeditions into what is now part of Indonesia. In 1831, a US merchant ship, the *Friendship*, got a rather unfriendly reception in the Aceh town of Kuala Batee. In fact, pirates attacked the ship, killed some of its crew, and stole its cargo. In response, Commodore John Downes and the USS *Potomac* were sent to exact retribution. This they did in 1832 with considerable force, sending an attack party into the harbor, burning shipping, and bombarding the town and its forts.

In 1838, another American ship, this time, the *Eclipse*, was attacked in the area, and its crew massacred. This time, the USS *Columbia* and USS *John Adams* carried out the retribution. First, they bombarded Kuala Batee, and then they headed for the village of Muckie. An American landing party went in and destroyed the village.

Eventually, the Dutch became the dominant colonial power in the region. That meant, in 1941, their colonial possessions in the region suddenly became a target for the advancing Japanese.

American, British, Dutch, and Australian forces in the area combined as ABDACOM in a desperate attempt to halt the Japanese onslaught, but the scale and speed of the Japanese attack made that a tough mission. For instance, small numbers of American troops were among the Allied defenders on Java, but within two weeks, the Japanese were in control of the island. On land, Allied forces suffered a series of defeats.

And at sea, things were little better. The Battle of Badung Strait, the Battle of the Java Sea, and the Battle of Sunda Strait (Sunda again!) were all naval defeats for the Allies.

By the time the Japanese advance in what is now Indonesia had been halted, a lot of territory had fallen, and much would need to be recaptured. It would be a long, tough, series of campaigns by land, by sea, and by air. For instance, the New Guinea campaign saw a series of dramatic Allied amphibious assaults on islands, like Morotai and Biak, and on the coast of New Guinea, like the landing at Hollandia. And American forces made a major contribution to the Allied campaign in Borneo in 1945.

Soon after the war, Indonesia became independent, but a rough road lay ahead. In 1958, as fears grew among some in Washington that Indonesian leader Sukarno was getting too close to Communists, rebels attempted to topple him. The coup, however, was crushed.

Over the years, the United States has had assorted military links with the Indonesian military, including shared training, visits, etc. But political disputes, particularly in the past over East Timor, caused disruption to some links.

Examples of links from recent years follow. In 2012, building work began with US funding on barracks for the Indonesian Peace and Security Center in West Java. In 2013, US and Indonesian naval personnel trained alongside each other in Cooperation Afloat Readiness and Training 2013. The Hawaii National Guard is partnered with Indonesia.

IRAN

PERSIA, THE ANCIENT LAND OF XERXES AND DARIUS, Iran has been, in more recent times, the land of the shah and the Ayatollah Khomeini. It's not going to come as a shock to many Americans that we have long been involved with the country, sometimes in a friendly sense, sometimes less so.

To begin with, it was definitely in a friendly sense. In the late nineteenth and early twentieth centuries, Iran, or Persia as it then was, found itself squeezed between two empires, the Russian (and after the Revolution, Soviet) Empire to the north and the British Empire to the south and east. America, by contrast, with much less influence in the region, was seen as something of a safe alternative. Americans like Arthur Millspaugh and Morgan Shuster held high rank in the country offering advice on modernizing and westernizing. Americans opened schools and colleges. One American at the time even fought and died for constitutional democracy in the country. Howard Baskerville, born in North Platte, Nebraska, became a teacher at the American Memorial School in Tabriz. In 1909, aged twenty-four, with royalist forces besieging the city, Baskerville led a volunteer force against them. He was killed by a sniper, but even today he is honored in Iran.

During World War II, Iran was vital to Allied victory. After the Anglo-Soviet occupation of the country, about eighteen billion dollars' worth of American lend-lease material poured through Iran on its way to the Soviet Union. Our Persian Gulf Command took control of US efforts in the country, organizing improvements to infrastructure to help the flow of war supplies and setting up a plant at Abadan near the coast with the 17th Air Depot Group where aircraft could be assembled before onward transmission to Tehran and then the Soviet Union. American influence was seen elsewhere as well. For instance, in 1942, H. Norman Schwarzkopf (not the leader of Operation Desert Storm—see "Kuwait" for that—but his father) was put in charge of organizing the Iranian police force.

And, of course, the principal Allied leaders of the war, FDR, Churchill, and Stalin all met for a wartime conference in Tehran. FDR had flown in from Cairo on November 27, 1943. FDR mixed martinis for Churchill and Stalin. FDR asked Stalin how he liked his drink. Stalin answered that it was OK but cold on his stomach.

Stalin pressed the Western allies to commit to opening up a second front. FDR settled on Dwight Eisenhower to be the supreme commander in Europe, responsible for Operation Overlord. Little discussion was given over to the question of post-war Iran or the Persian Gulf.

After the war, Iran emerged as the fourth largest oil exporter in the world, supplying 90 percent of Europe's petroleum. In the early 1950s with the Cold War raging, people in the UK and US governments and intelligence agencies started to get nervous about what might happen in Iran.

Iran shared a thousand-mile border with the Soviet Union and had an active Communist (Tudeh) party. The crisis really began, however, when Mohammad Mossadeq, the democratically elected prime minister, looking to take more of the profits from Iran's oil, started to nationalize the Anglo-Iranian Oil Company, a move deeply unpopular with Britain, which imposed sanctions.

In 1953, President Eisenhower authorized a CIA-led coup against Mossadeq in favor of Shah Mohammad Reza Pahlavi. Kermit Roosevelt

(Teddy Roosevelt's son) was put in charge of Operation Ajax, and funds were used by the CIA to recruit Iranian mobs, which eventually helped drive Mossadeq from office. Eisenhower subsequently awarded Kermit Roosevelt the National Security Medal in a closed-door ceremony in December 1953.

In the period after the coup, we helped build up the shah with military and other aid, and the shah became a firm partner of the United States in the Cold War. Our Military Assistance Advisory Group in the country, for instance, had widespread involvement with Iran's military and security structures prior to the 1979 revolution.

In 1973, Iran accounted for 10 percent of world's oil output and was a vital strategic interest for the United States and the rest of the West. A 1978 National Intelligence estimate had confidently reported that Iran was not in a "revolutionary or even a pre-revolutionary situation." In 1979, the Iranian revolution broke out, and soon the shah was gone from Iran forever.

So much has happened between the United States and Iran since the revolution that this can only be a summary of some of the main events.

In 1979, American hostages were seized in Teheran after the US embassy was stormed. The CIA working closely with the Canadian ambassador managed to "exfiltrate" six Americans under the noses of the Iranian militants. Ross Perot also hired a retired ex–Green Beret officer to free two of his EDS employees from Iranian kidnappers. Fifty-two Americans remained in custody. President Jimmy Carter authorized Operation Eagle Claw, an attempt to rescue the hostages using navy helicopters and a Delta Force under the command of Colonel Charles Beckwith. Carter's secretary of state, Cy Vance, resigned over the decision. In the early hours of April 25, a helicopter rotor struck a Lockheed C-130 on the ground causing a massive explosion. The bodies of eight Americans were left in the Persian desert. The mission's failure severely weakened the Carter presidency.

And then the Iran-Contra arms-for-hostages scandal of the Reagan years nearly brought down Carter's successor. Meanwhile, in Lebanon, another hostage crisis was brewing with Iran's ally Hezbollah.

Because of its problems with post-revolution Iran, the United States tended to favor Saddam's Iraq in the brutal Iran-Iraq War that he launched and which lasted from 1980 to 1988 and claimed over a million lives. US and Gulf Arab support for Iraq led to huge tensions with Iran in the Persian Gulf and eventually actual violence.

In an attempt to put pressure on Iraq's Gulf allies, Iran commenced attacks on their oil tankers in the Persian Gulf. In response, in Operation

Earnest Will, America agreed to offer naval protection to tankers reflagged under the Stars and Stripes and took a number of other actions as well.

In October 1987, after a missile hit the *Sea Isle City*, a Kuwaiti-flagged oil tanker, we launched Operation Nimble Archer against two Iranian oil rigs, which had been used to coordinate attacks on merchant shipping. After four warships shelled the platforms, US Special Forces boarded them and planted explosives.

During Earnest Will, in early 1988, the USS *Samuel B. Roberts* hit a mine and was almost sunk. Operation Praying Mantis was launched four days later. US forces again attacked and destroyed two Iranian oil rigs, and when the Iranian navy tried to counterattack our forces, the Iranian frigate *Sahand* disabled another Iranian frigate, destroyed the missile patrol boat *Joshan*, and sank or damaged a number of other Iranian patrol boats. Iran's fleet was not big, and by the end of the action, half of it was sunk or severely damaged.

On July 3, 1988, the USS *Vincennes* accidentally shot down an Iranian commercial jet liner with 290 passengers, all of whom were killed. The USG agreed to pay over $130 million in compensation. The Iran-Iraq War came to an end shortly after this tragedy.

In the State of the Union address George W. Bush delivered on January 31, 2002, he accused Iran of forming part of "an axis of evil" in the world. In August of 2002, evidence emerged that Iran was building a uranium-enrichment facility in Natanz and a secret heavy water production plant in Arak. In June of 2005, Mahmoud Ahmadinejad was elected president of Iran. In power, Ahmadinejad used rhetoric widely against countries such as the United States and Israel. Iran claimed its nuclear program was for peaceful purposes, but Iran's support for Shiite forces in Iraq opposed to the United States and for Hezbollah and Hamas inevitably raised concerns about whether the Iranian nuclear program was in reality mainly designed to create nuclear weapons.

Over the years, Iran has been the target of assorted US surveillance and intelligence operations, and it has been speculated that the United States has had contacts with groups mounting cross-border operations into Iran, as well as other activities inside Iran.

In 2010, the Stuxnet worm targeted cascades and centrifuges at the Natanz uranium enrichment plant in Iran and is reputed to have delayed the process by as much as two years. It is widely speculated that United States and Israeli intelligence organized the Stuxnet operation. Has the American battle cry evolved from "Send in the Marines" to "Send in the Nerds"?

Recent negotiations have raised hopes that problems over Iran's nuclear program might be solved peacefully, but little is certain at this stage.

IRAQ

IRAQ IS THE ANCIENT LAND OF THE TIGRIS AND EUPHRATES RIVER VALLEY— this area marks the very beginnings of human civilization. Unless you have just returned from a very long space journey (and one with communications failure), you are aware that the United States invaded and occupied Iraq.

But 2003 didn't mark the beginning of our military involvement with the country.

For instance, during World War II, we had forces in Iraq, though they weren't there to fight. Instead, they were there to help with air-ferry routes and particularly with the supply of military aid to Russia in its fight against the Nazis. For instance, we had a presence at the airbase at Basra at this time and also at RAF Habbaniya near Baghdad.

In the post-war era, we had friendly links with the royal government of King Feisal II of Iraq, and in 1952, he came to the United States to meet President Harry Truman. He also met, among others, Deborah Kerr, James Mason, and Jackie Robinson. By 1958, however, Feisal was dead, murdered along with other members of his family in a military coup.

Immediately after the coup, King Hussein of neighboring Jordan (who had been at Harrow School in the UK with Feisal) requested Western support to prevent any threat from the new Iraqi regime. The British led in responding, but we also offered support. And pretty much the same situation occurred in 1961 when the Iraqi regime briefly threatened Kuwait. Not, of course, the last time that was going to happen.

In 1963, another coup took place in Iraq, this time putting the Baath party in power.

For much of the 1960s and 1970s, fighting took place between the Iraqi government and the Kurds. The Kurds received much help from Iraq's neighbor and rival, Iran, at that stage run by the shah. The shah was a major US ally, and the United States gave some support to the Kurds in their efforts against the Soviet-linked Baghdad regime. However, in 1975, the shah did a deal with the Iraqi government.

In some senses, 1979 would change everything. Saddam Hussein took total control, while in Iran the revolution toppled the shah and brought to power the Ayatollah Khomeini. The change, however, did not end the competition for regional power between Iran and Iraq, nor did it solve the problems faced by the Kurds. In addition, Saddam feared the influence of Khomeini on Iraq's own large Shia population. In 1980, Saddam invaded Iran.

With the shah gone, though, and the United States now a major focus for Khomeini, US priorities in the region had somewhat changed. Despite the USS *Stark* incident in which an Iraqi missile killed thirty-seven US personnel in 1987, the United States played an active part in defending Arab oil tankers, which were being targeted by the Iranians because of Arab governments' support for Saddam. The full extent of US support specifically given to Iraq during this period is still a matter of debate.

In March 1988, Saddam's forces launched their notorious and horrifying chemical weapons attack on the Kurdish town of Halabja. In August 1988, hostilities ceased between Iran and Iraq, with both sides having suffered appalling casualties. Two years later in August 1990, Iraq went much further than it had in 1961, and this time it invaded Kuwait.

Although the story of the liberation of Kuwait mainly belongs in the chapter on Kuwait, it did also involve extensive US military activity inside Iraq. For instance, coalition aircraft extensively bombed targets inside Iraq, and coalition Special Forces operated there. Plus when the ground campaign to liberate Iraq actually began, a thrust through Iraqi territory to the west of Kuwait was a major component.

In the aftermath of the war, as President George H. W. Bush in a radio broadcast called upon Iraqis to topple Saddam, rebellions broke out in the south of the country and in the Kurdish north. Saddam unleashed massive force against the rebels and crushed the southern rebels, though he had less success in the north. In 1991, in Operation Provide Comfort, US troops were sent along with other troops to the Kurdish areas to assist with the crisis there, and in 1992, we helped impose no-fly zones over areas of both southern and northern Iraq. Massive sanctions that had been imposed on Iraq after the invasion of Kuwait were maintained in order to put pressure on the Iraqi regime and force it, among other things, to pay reparations and eliminate weapons of mass destruction, or WMDs.

On June 26, 1993, after receiving information from the CIA that blamed Iraqi Intelligence for an attempted assassination plot against former President George H. W. Bush in Kuwait, President Clinton ordered the launch of twenty-three Tomahawk cruise missiles at targets inside Iraq.

In September 1996, in response to an Iraqi attack on Kurdish areas and Iraqi targeting of US fighters, we launched Operation Desert Strike, a cruise-missile and bombing attack on Iraqi targets, particularly air-defense targets.

In December 1998, after Iraq had impeded the work of WMD inspectors, Britain and the United States followed up with Operation Desert Fox, a three-day bombing and cruise-missile campaign aimed at facilities believed to be associated with WMDs, as well as other targets, including some associated with the Iraqi secret police and Republican Guard.

In March of 2003, President George W. Bush ordered the execution of Operation Iraqi Freedom, a US-led invasion of Iraq. Bush declared that the purpose of the operation was "to disarm Iraq of weapons of mass destruction, to end Saddam Hussein's support for terrorism, and to free the Iraqi people."

Some have argued, on the other hand, that Iraq was an unnecessary war, a war that diverted US focus from confronting al-Qaeda, finishing the job in Afghanistan, and dealing out justice to Osama bin Laden. Senator Barack Obama, in a 2002 speech, characterized the idea of invading Iraq as "a dumb war."

The causes of few other wars have been the subject of so much debate and controversy as the invasion of Iraq, but a variety of causes obviously had at least some impact.

Saddam Hussein's regime had a history of appalling brutality and barbarity that had already been responsible for the deaths of hundreds of thousands. He also had a track record of invading other countries, of using poison gas against both defenseless civilians and the Iranian military on a mass scale, and of attempting in the past to acquire nuclear technology. Many genuinely believed at the time of the invasion of Iraq that he still possessed WMDs, and even today, questions remain about exactly what happened to some of the stockpile of chemical weapons he had once had. He had supported terrorism against Israel. He had continued to challenge the international community in the decade after his invasion of Kuwait, and the rigorous sanctions aimed at his regime were causing the Iraqi population far more suffering than they were causing to Saddam and his cronies. Saddam had two sons, Uday and Qusay, who might one day succeed Saddam and who were both generally regarded as cruel and brutal too.

Ironically, well before 9/11, President Bill Clinton made, in some sense, the most cogent case for a regime change in Iraq. In a 1998 televised speech, he said:

The hard fact is that so long as Saddam remains in power, he threatens the well-being of his people, the peace of the region, and the security of the world.

The best way to end that threat once and for all is with a new Iraqi government—a government ready to live in peace with its neighbors, a government that respects the rights of its people …

Heavy as they are, the costs of action must be weighed against the price of inaction. If Saddam defies the world and we fail to respond, we will face a far greater threat in the future. Saddam will strike again at his neighbors. He will make war on his own people.

And mark my words, he will develop weapons of mass destruction. He will deploy them, and he will use them.

International interventions in Sierra Leone and Kosovo had created an environment in which many politicians had come to believe, wrongly as it turned out, that a military intervention in Iraq could lead within a short space of time to a stable and peaceful situation. And 9/11 had created an environment in which Americans were suddenly aware of the real possibility of an attack on their home soil causing thousands of deaths and devastating destruction.

It is also clear that Iraq, with its vast oil resources and its key Middle East location (next door, for instance, to Iran), is a country of genuine strategic interest for the West. And it is clear some might have hoped that if a successful pro-Western democracy could be created in Iraq, it might serve as a valuable example in a region that has suffered so much from dictatorships.

All that is clear. What is less clear, and perhaps may never be entirely clear, is in which order this complex assortment of motivations and aspirations ranked. Which were ultimately less important and which were ultimately more important in leading to war? Inevitably, all the causes that contributed to the Iraq invasion and occupation are now judged through the lens of a conflict that was not the quick, low-casualty, successful intervention those who decided it should go ahead had hoped for.

The war has had tremendous impact on Iraq, on the United States, and on the other countries that fought alongside the United States there, and this one chapter in this book can deal with only a few of its aspects.

That war began on March 20, 2003, with the launch of forty Tomahawk cruise missiles from USN vessels near the Middle East in an attempt to "decapitate" Iraqi leadership. The strikes failed to kill Saddam Hussein. By the eighteenth day of the war, over seven hundred Tomahawks had been fired by the USN.

The Shock and Awe air campaign began the next day. More than fifteen hundred sorties a day were flown by the USAF and USN.

General Tommy Franks led the coalition forces that were made up primarily of about 148,000 US forces. A significant force (about forty-five thousand troops) from Great Britain fought alongside us. Ultimately, over forty different nations, including Australia, Poland, Italy, Japan, Albania, Mongolia, and the Dominican Republic, made up the Coalition of the Willing that contributed troops to this conflict.

The greatest Iraqi resistance was composed of the fedayeen, or "martyr" battalions, irregular forces that were armed with AK-47s and RPGs.

On March 26, the 173rd Airborne brigade conducted the first US Army combat jump since World War II landing near Bashur Airfield in Northern Iraq. By April 10, these troops, along with Kurdish fighters, liberated Kirkuk—Iraq's largest northern city.

By April 3, US armored forces were on the outskirts of Baghdad. The Iraqi information minister was proclaiming to the media that no Americans had entered Baghdad, even though a battle could clearly be heard raging and tanks were not far off. Thunder runs made up of Abrams tanks and Bradley fighting vehicles began charging through downtown Baghdad on April 5. The A-10 Warthog, whose production had been championed by the legendary fighter pilot John Boyd, proved to be effective in destroying Iraqi vehicles with its 30 mm cannon.

On April 9, Iraqis pulled down a large statue of Saddam in al-Fardous square in downtown Baghdad.

On July 23, members of the 101st Airborne Division tracked down and killed Saddam Hussein's sons Uday and Qusay. Uday had personally ordered the torture of Iraqi Olympic and other athletes who did not perform up to his expectations. Qusay had conceived the destruction of Iraq's southern marshes (a massive environmental disaster) and ordered the deaths of many political prisoners.

Saddam himself was captured by US forces near Tikrit in December 2003. After his trial and conviction, he was executed on December 13, 2006.

US and allied forces were well prepared and trained to defeat Iraqi forces on the battlefield but not so well prepared to win the peace. In the spring of 2003, the mood of Baghdad swiftly changed from jubilation at the collapse of Saddam to despair at the chaos and looting that ravaged the nation's capital. The regime's police force collapsed, and Allied forces did not manage to fill the void.

Looters stole some fifteen thousand objects from Baghdad's National Museum. They broke into the Iraq Central Bank. Saddam Hussein was a brutal repressive dictator, but it seemed to many Iraqis that the Americans brought chaos in their wake. Huge problems occurred with restoring basic services, such as power, telephone service, and water supplies in many areas. Saddam himself had contributed to the chaos by emptying the prisons prior to being overrun.

Many mistakes were made during the occupation. Many Iraqi Army ammunition dumps were not secured, which allowed insurgents access to high explosives for IEDs (improvised explosive devices). Our greatest error may have been the dismissal of the Iraqi Army, which effectively made many armed young and trained Iraqi men unemployed and unhappy.

The upshot of this was an insurgency movement that also received arms, support, and some manpower from hostile states, such as Iran and Syria.

In the spring of 2004, US forces were unable to drive the insurgents out of Fallujah. The increasing level of violence and particularly IEDs forced the United States to extend military tours of duty by ninety days. The US Marines spearheaded the second battle of Fallujah in the fall of 2004, which finally drove insurgents from the city. Ninety-five Americans were killed.

In the same year, the Abu Ghraib prison scandal erupted into the open. Donald Rumsfeld has recently expressed his regret over President George W. Bush's rejection of his offer to resign, which followed disclosures about Abu Ghraib.

In January 2005, nationwide elections were held in Iraq. It was the first Iraqi election since 1958. In a third election held that same year in December, nearly 80 percent of the population voted. The purple-stained fingers of Iraqi voters may have contributed to the Arab Spring, which continues to reverberate throughout the Middle East.

After the bombing of the Shia Golden Mosque of Samarra on February 22, 2006, sectarian violence exploded throughout Iraq. Three years after the invasion, over twenty-five hundred Americans had been killed. By 2006, the war had become deeply unpopular with many of the American people.

In the fall of 2006, President Bush accepted the resignation of Donald Rumsfeld as defense secretary. To replace him, Bush tapped Robert Gates who had been the president of Texas A&M University but also had an extensive Washington résumé with a focus on defense and intelligence issues. For the new US commander in Iraq, Gates soon settled on General David Petraeus, who literally wrote the book on counter-insurgency (*Field Manual 3-24: Counterinsurgency*). Secretary Gates also championed the introduction of MRAPs (mine-resistant ambush-protected vehicles) that dramatically reduced the vulnerability of our troops to IEDs.

On January 10, 2007, President George W. Bush announced a surge of five brigades to Baghdad and two battalions of marines to Anbar. In all, about thirty thousand additional troops were eventually sent to Iraq. The surge was hugely controversial, but later Secretary of State Hillary Clinton would simply state, "The Iraq surge worked."

Another crucial development was the rise of the Sunni Awakening that, with US and Iraqi government support, began to fight against al Qaeda.

Suicide bombings and casualties did not suddenly and entirely stop, but the level of violence steadily declined.

Shortly after being inaugurated president, Barack Obama announced on February 27, 2009, the withdrawal of US troops from Iraq. US troops' combat role in Iraq finally ended on August 31, 2010, about seven and a half years after our invasion. Our losses included 4,427 Americans killed and 34,275 injured. Figures for Iraqi casualties in the period have been a subject of much debate, but over one hundred thousand Iraqis have also been killed.

Only in the future will we be able to tell whether the Iraq War was "a dumb war" that failed to find WMDs and did lasting damage to international consensus on how and when international military interventions should occur or was the necessary removal of a criminal regime that helped the Middle East move beyond repressive dictatorships to new and better political structures.

Currently the Iraqi government is locked in conflict with a renewed Sunni insurgency. As we go to press, President Obama has deployed three hundred American military advisers to aid the Maliki government in its battle against the insurgent forces of ISIS (the Islamic State in Iraq and the Levant). They are now directing a bombing campaign against ISIS.

IRELAND

AS A RESULT OF MASSIVE IMMIGRATION FROM THE EMERALD ISLE to the United States, about 10 percent of Americans are of Irish stock, and many more exuberantly celebrate St. Patrick's Day every year. Many Irish have served in the US military over the years, including John Barry of County Wexford who is widely acclaimed (along with John Paul Jones, of course) as being the "Father of the American Navy."

But have we ever sent forces to what is now the Republic of Ireland?

For a start, during the Revolutionary War, John Paul Jones and assorted privateers cruised in and operated in Irish waters. More American privateers operated in Irish waters during the War of 1812. Captain Hailey in the *True Blooded Yankee* went as far as landing on Irish soil and burnt seven ships in one harbor. He even sailed into Dublin harbor and destroyed a schooner there.

During World War I, we had substantial military involvement with Ireland. About four million Americans were shipped through the Irish Sea from 1917 to 1918 to bring the AEF to Europe. This is roughly eight times the massive deployment of Allied troops to Saudi Arabia for the 1991 Gulf War. It should come as no surprise, therefore, that the USN took an active interest in Ireland and its surrounding waters. For example, USN ships, including six American submarines, were based in Cork, and US submarine chasers were based at Queenstown. The USN also built a naval air station in Wexford, Ireland, to help counter the Kaiser's submarines.

This was at a time when the whole island of Ireland, both north and south of what is now the border, was part of the United Kingdom. That was soon to change after World War I, as an IRA campaign and resentment caused by some British tactics against the insurgents led eventually to partition off the island. American volunteers went to join the fight on the Irish Republican side. In January 1921, for instance, the Philadelphia correspondent of the *New York Tribune* reported that five companies of Irish volunteers had been raised willing to fight, wearing uniforms similar to the Republicans in Ireland, and that individuals and small groups were headed for Ireland through "roundabout channels" to avoid interception by the British. Éamon de Valera, a leading Irish Republican, was born in New York City in 1882, but moved to Ireland at the age of two. After his release from prison in 1917, he fled to America where he toured and raised about six million dollars in funds for the Irish Republican cause.

By the time of World War II, Ireland was partitioned. Northern Ireland was still part of the UK and took a major part in the war. Even before the December 1941 attack on Pearl Harbor, for instance, the United States was drawing up possible plans to send over thirty thousand troops to Northern Ireland. Derry, in particular became a major naval base for the Atlantic escort ships that kept the vital convoy routes to Britain.

The Republic of Ireland, however, maintained its neutrality during World War II. Some Irish Republicans did have contacts with the Nazis, but the Irish government itself and much of the Irish population clearly leaned in the Allied direction. For example, over 350 Allied airmen who went down over Ireland were released during the war while Axis airmen were interned for the duration. American planes refueled during the war at Shannon Airport, and Allied planes were allowed the use of the Donegal Corridor, a short stretch of airspace linking Northern Ireland to the Atlantic through Irish airspace. Over seventy thousand Irish volunteers fought alongside American forces while serving in the British Army. Irish weather stations offered critical reporting on atmospheric conditions prior to D-Day.

During the Cold War, Ireland again remained neutral.

The IRA had not, of course, disappeared after the Anglo-Irish Treaty of December 1921 that partitioned Ireland. Some members of the IRA rejected the treaty and went on to fight and lose a civil war against Irish pro-treaty forces, and subsequently engaged in repeated campaigns of bombings and shootings against Britain in an attempt to unite Northern Ireland with the rest of Ireland. The Provisional IRA Campaign lasted from 1969 until the last ceasefire in 1997 and was mainly fought in Northern Ireland, with occasional campaigns on the UK mainland but did involve some Irish living south of the border as well. As before, support, particularly financial, from some Americans was a significant factor in assisting Irish Republican activity during this period.

In recent years, Shannon Airport has been used as a staging area for American troops and supplies headed for Iraq and Afghanistan. And Ireland has long held a significant role in international peacekeeping forces, including in Kosovo.

ISRAEL

DUE TO RELIGIOUS, CULTURAL, AND ETHNIC LINKS, America has long had a strong, deep, and lasting commitment to this land.

And for a long time, Americans have been going there. On an 1867 visit to the Holy Land, Mark Twain and a group of American tourists were shown some of the holy sites: "We visited the places where Jesus worked for fifteen years as a carpenter, and where he attempted to teach in the synagogue and was driven out by a mob. Catholic chapels stand upon these sites and protect the little fragments of the ancient walls which remain."

Most pilgrims feel blessed just to experience the sanctity and beauty of such sites, but some of Twain's pilgrims on that occasion went too far with their enthusiasm. "Our pilgrims broke off specimens … Our pilgrims would have liked very well to get out their lampblack and stencil-plates and paint their names on that rock, together with the name of the village they hail from in America, but the priests permit nothing of that kind."

But it was during World War II that our forces first arrived there. US air crews used the RAF based at Lydda (which later became Lod Airport and eventually Ben Gurion International Airport) for air transport and air-ferrying missions. And during the fighting between Rommel and British/Commonwealth troops in nearby Egypt to the west, American bombers were based at a number of locations in the Palestine Mandate with, for instance, B-17s at Lydda and B-24s at Ramat David.

After the Second World War, Britain eventually announced its withdrawal from a fractious Palestine Mandate, and on May 14, 1948, the modern state of Israel was launched. The US government recognized the state of Israel only eleven minutes after Ben Gurion declared its independence. Fighting intensified between Arabs and Jews, and neighboring Arab countries invaded.

Foreign volunteers, or Machal, came from a wide range of countries to help Israel, and American volunteers played a role in that war as they have done in other wars involving Israel. Most were veterans of World War II, including the famous Micky Marcus, a colonel in the US Army who went to Israel, became a brigadier general, and helped break the Siege of Jerusalem in 1948.

We had some official US involvement as well. In June 1948 when the US consul general was killed by sniper fire, a marine force from the USS

Kearsarge was ordered to Jerusalem. And on July 23, flying a UN flag, the USS *Putnam* evacuated UN team members from the Israeli port of Haifa.

By 1949, Israel had joined the United Nations.

The Holocaust had created massive American sympathy of the concept of a Jewish homeland. American arms and financial support began flowing to Israel during the Truman administration. A tradition of shared training and military exchange between the United States and Israel was established.

US government support for Israel, however, was not automatic (or unconditional). For example, in 1956, President Dwight Eisenhower refused to endorse the invasion of the Suez Canal and Sinai by forces from Britain, France, and Israel. U-2 intelligence gave the president vital information on what was happening on the ground at the time. In the end, Israel withdrew its forces from the Sinai.

During the Six-Day War of 1967, Israel delivered a preemptive strike on the Egyptian air force destroying most of its Soviet-made aircraft while they were still on the ground. The conflict more than doubled the amount of territory under Israel's direct control, including the addition of the Sinai Peninsula. On June 8, 1967, units of the Israeli air force and navy attacked the USS *Liberty*—an intelligence-gathering ship, which was cruising in international waters off the coast of the Sinai Peninsula. Thirty-four Americans were killed. The Israeli government apologized for the tragic mistake and paid thirteen million dollars in compensation.

In the 1973 Yom Kippur War (October 6–24), Israel was attacked by Egyptian forces near the Suez Canal and by Syrian forces near the Golan Heights. After recovering from the initial surprise, Israeli forces managed to counterattack across the Suez Canal and were soon driving towards Cairo itself. The Nixon administration, though crippled by the Watergate scandal, flew over twenty-two thousand tons of supplies to Israel in Operation Nickel Grass. The Soviets resupplied the Arab forces. On October 24, Moscow announced the mobilization of seven airborne divisions for possible deployment to Egypt. The next day, US armed forces were moved to DEFCON 3—planes ready to launch in fifteen minutes. Yuri Andropov, KGB chief, declared, "We are not going to start the Third World War." Egypt withdrew its request for Soviet troops, and a UN truce was soon agreed to.

American shuttle diplomacy eventually helped to secure the Camp David accord of 1978, which significantly reduced Middle East tensions when a "land for peace" agreement was hammered out between Egypt and Israel. The Sinai Peninsula was returned to Egypt, and Sadat broke decisively with his former Soviet ally. Billions in US aid soon began flowing to Egypt, as well as to Israel.

During the first Gulf War, Saddam Hussein launched Scud missile attacks on Israel, which killed two and wounded hundreds. He was desperately trying to drive a wedge between coalition forces by prodding a neutral Israel into a military response.

Prior to the start of the 1991 Gulf War, the Israeli government agreed to allow a US Army Patriot unit into Israel—the first time that foreign troops had ever been stationed in that country. And in the end, Israel did stay out of the conflict.

More diplomatic action followed the Gulf War, again with extensive US involvement. In 1994, President Clinton was there when a peace deal between Israel and Jordan was signed, and in 1995, the Oslo II agreement was signed between Israel and the Palestinian National Authority.

In 2006, war broke out in Lebanon between Israel and Hezbollah, and the United States offered Israel extra fuel and munitions.

Today, the search for a complete end to the Arab-Israeli conflict continues, and so does the search for a solution to problems over Iran's nuclear research. In the desert in southwest Israel is located a small US military installation operated by US personnel with hugely powerful radar watching what goes on in the region.

In the context of all the uncertainties about the future in the Middle East, America's partnership with Israel on a wide range of exercises, training, planning, supply, development, intelligence, and other military matters remains a central part of our strategy.

ITALY

A LAND FOREVER TO BE ASSOCIATED WITH SUCH CULTURAL WONDERS as Michelangelo, Leonardo da Vinci, and, of course, pizza, Italy is also a land with a formidable military history. This is Italy, land of the rulers who built one of the mightiest empires the world has ever seen. Although interestingly enough, quite a lot of the Roman emperors didn't come from Italy in the first place, including Septimius Severus who came from Libya.

It's amazing how far Roman power did reach, all the way to Scotland in the northwest and as far in the East as parts of what is today Iraq (yes, they went there too). America, however, seems to have been a bit too far even for them. There was a Roman emperor called Philip the Arab, but there was never going to be one called Philip the American. So when our military got involved with Italy, it was by us going to them.

And it didn't take long after independence from Britain until our forces were in Italian waters and on Italian soil. By 1801, for instance, we were at war with the Barbary pirates, and Commodore Edward Preble of the USN dropped anchor in Messina, Sicily, to see if he could get any help from King Francis of the Two Sicilies (he wasn't seeing double; it's what the kingdom was called). King Francis happened to be very helpful and gave our commodore access to men, supplies, and port facilities.

During the mid-nineteenth century, American volunteers, a number of whom fought bravely at the Battle of Caserta, helped Garibaldi in his campaign to reunify Italy and establish the foundations of today's modern state.

Another early encounter took place amidst a devastating tragedy. On the morning of December 28, 1908, a severe earthquake measuring 7.1 on the Richter scale struck near Messina on the Italian island of Sicily. The quake was followed by tsunamis with waves measuring thirty-nine feet in height. More than seventy thousand people were killed, and over 90 percent of all buildings in Messina collapsed. Immediately, the word went out, and the USN supply ships, USS *Celtic* and USS *Culgoa*, along with other ships from the American Great White Fleet, were diverted from their Mediterranean cruise to provide humanitarian assistance (food and a prefabricated hospital) to the Italians. It's interesting to note that the humanitarian emergency relief operations our armed forces have been involved with recently aren't a new thing.

There were even rougher times ahead for Italy. Another great cataclysm was to strike Europe in 1914. World War I had arrived, though it didn't arrive until 1915 for Italy. At the start of the war, Italy was technically allied with Austria-Hungary and Germany, but a large portion of what is now northern Italy was under Austrian control. Italy wanted it so didn't join the war on the side of its allies. Instead, it waited and, finally in May 1915, joined the war on the Allied side (that is on the side of the Allies with a big A, not on the side of its former allies with a small *a*, who can't have been very pleased at the turn of events).

It was not an easy war for the Italians. As we were to find out even more in World War II, fighting in Italy, which has a fair bit of mountainous territory, can be a pretty rocky experience. Heavy fighting led to few major gains by the Italians, and in late 1917, the Austro-Hungarians, with German reinforcements, inflicted a devastating defeat on the Italians at Caporetto.

it all his way ending up being very nearly court-martialled for slapping
dier suffering from battle fatigue.

With Sicily under Allied control, it was on to mainland Italy. The
nd World War in Italy was a long grueling affair in which Americans
t with great tenacity and bravery. For instance, The 442nd Regimental
at Unit, composed mainly of Japanese-Americans, became the most
ted American military unit in our history winning a staggering 9,486
Hearts. There were times when the possibility of a rapid advance
owards the heart of Europe seemed possible, for instance, after
mans were initially surprised by the Allied landings at Anzio, but
w the enemy collapse never came, at least not until right at the end
ar itself.

pite of the surrender of the Italian government and their switching
he Allies, the German defense of Italy under the able "Smiling
esselring was stubborn and tenacious. After Southern Italy was
ne Americans used airbases in Italy to bomb Axis targets, such as
oil fields in Romania. George McGovern, the future presidential
piloted his B-24 Liberator bomber on thirty-five missions from
ani Air Base in Apulia.

Mussolini's former capital, was liberated by American forces
1944, an extremely newsworthy event but preempted by what
ys later far to the north — D-Day. As Allied armies swept across
rope towards the Reich, American and other Allied armies
eir slow, tough advance north through Italy. In fact, fighting
ue in Italy all the way until May 8, 1945 — V-E Day.

n Italy came at a heavy price. There were about 114,000
in the Italian campaign. Today you will find two American
ssion cemeteries in Italy, one in Florence and another near
o) where visitors can sit and think about the huge sacrifice
young troops.

war, we were involved in border disputes between Italy

have strong and extensive military links with Italy. Italy
nd we positioned important military bases in Italy. The
maintains about eleven thousand service personnel in
aesars. For instance, a little way north of beautiful and
viano remains a strong USAF base, and the headquarters
6th Fleet is located at Naples, not far from Pompeii and
uthwest coast of Italy.

The year 1917 saw even more major develo
Woodrow Wilson led the United States in joining
World War I, and just as American doughboys were
France, so they were also soon on their way to fight
An American regiment (the 332nd Infantry Regime
attached medical and supply units), was sent to 1
1918 in response to urgent requests from the Ita
Hemingway volunteered for the Red Cross An
in Italy and was wounded in 1918. The 332nd 1
the retreating enemy after the decisive Allied v
October 1918.

After being in the winning side in the Fi
began to hope for a new Roman Empire. V
word fascism that we sometimes don't think ;
comes from the word "fasces," the bundle of
of power in ancient Rome and adopted by

On June 10, 1940, Mussolini, cynical
the German blitzkrieg and hoping for his
on the Allies. Then after Pearl Harbor, I
States of America dragging his Italian ;
(and in spite of Christopher Columbu;

After Northern Africa was finall
to take the fight to mainland Europe
prior to an attack on northern Eurc
eventually joined the Brits and othe
Italy in 1943. Dwight D. Eisenhov

We're not going to be able 1
the full heroism, sacrifice, and ul
campaign, so we'll give just a bri

It all started on July 10, 19
Sicily. The first day of the can
504th Parachute Infantry Regi
was decimated by friendly fir
tragically killed by fire from
From this painful experien
Allied aircraft participating
and white stripes prior to t'

Once ashore, Gene
competed in the famous
To Montgomery's irrita'

have
a so

Seco
fough
Com
decor
Purple
north
the Ge
someho
of the w
In s
sides to
Albert" I
cleared, t
the Ploești
candidate,
San Giova
Rome
on June 4,
came two d
northern Eu
continued th
was to contin
Victory
US casualties
Battle Comm
Anzio (Nettun
made by many
After the
and Yugoslavia.
Today, we
joined NATO, a
US military still
the land of the
historic Venice, A
for the mighty US
Vesuvius on the so

IVORY COAST

vory Coast is located between Liberia to the west and Ghana to the east and has a flag that looks a bit like the Irish flag.

The area received a certain amount of attention from the USN's anti-slaving patrols in the nineteenth century, and in 1843, US marines came ashore in the Ivory Coast region to demonstrate US resolve after two Americans had been killed.

The area eventually, however, became a French colony (also known as Côte d'Ivoire) until independence in 1960, and links with France have remained strong.

In 1997, the USAF used Abidjan in Ivory Coast as a base for Operation Assured Lift into neighboring Liberia, but soon, sadly, Ivory Coast was going to be in need of peacekeepers itself.

In September 2002, the First Ivorian Civil War started as a military uprising took place in several cities. The government eventually managed to retain control of the main city of Abidjan but lost control of the north of the country to the rebels, including the city of Bouake. In Operation Autumn Return, US C-130s flew into Yamoussoukro, and US Special Forces went into Ivory Coast and worked with French forces, among others, to help rescue Americans and people of some other nationalities, particularly those in Bouake.

UN troops were eventually sent into Ivory Coast with US support to try to stabilize the situation, but violence persisted in the country until a peace accord in 2007.

Once more, a crisis broke out, in 2010, leading to the brief Second Ivoirian Civil War in 2011. French forces again played a major role in resolving the situation.

Recently, the US military has been developing more links with Ivory Coast, with Ivorian personnel, for instance, taking part with US personnel in 2013 in counter-piracy exercise Obangame Express 2013 and in Africa Endeavor 2013.

JAMAICA

A FASCINATING ISLAND, Jamaica has inspired many people. James Bond's author, Ian Fleming, for instance, had his home Goldeneye (also the title of one of the Bond films) there, a house also later connected with Jamaican legend Bob Marley.

Some armed Americans were active around Jamaica even before the Revolution, though not at that stage fighting the British. They were fighting on their side. For instance, Thomas Paine of Jamestown, Rhode Island, was a privateer with a commission from Jamaica's then British governor, Sir Thomas Lynch. And in 1740, a large contingent of Virginia troops was shipped to Jamaica to assist the British war effort.

But during the Revolutionary War and the War of 1812, our ships were active in targeting assorted ships bound for Jamaica or coming from there. In 1779, for instance, the frigates *Providence* and *Queen of France* with the sloop *Ranger* suddenly found themselves in fog in a British convoy headed for Jamaica and managed to capture eleven ships.

In 1873, a ship sailing under the American flag, the *Virginius* that had been running guns to insurgents in Cuba, picked up another load on Jamaica, only to be pursued and captured in Jamaican waters by a Spanish ship. The Spanish executed some of its crew before a diplomatic deal was finally worked out.

As we've already noted elsewhere, the use of our forces for humanitarian purposes isn't just a modern idea. In 1906, US marines and seamen landed at Kingston, Jamaica, to help in the aftermath of an earthquake.

However, during World War II when we were on the same side as Britain, we took most interest in the island militarily. Under the Destroyers for Bases agreement of September 1940, the UK got some old destroyers, and we got access to much British-controlled territory to establish bases there. One of the areas involved was Jamaica.

The USN got a naval air station on Little Goat Island and the use of naval facilities at Port Royal. And the USAF got Vernam Army Airfield. A group of officers and enlisted men known as "Force Tuna" arrived there in late 1941 to set things up. Vernam was initially used for anti-submarine flights, but eventually it became a major destination for long-range training flights. It closed in 1949.

Jamaica became independent from Britain in 1962, and in 1972 democratic socialist Michael Manley came to power. His attitude towards

Cuba scared some in Washington, and there has been speculation by some that America may have conducted covert attempts to undermine him.

In 1983, Jamaica offered military and political support to the American invasion of Grenada.

In the years since World War II, we've had assorted other military links with Jamaica, including training, exercises, exchanges, ship visits, and shared humanitarian projects. Jamaica's military connections to the United States and Canada grew as its connections to the UK decreased. The District of Columbia National Guard is partnered with Jamaica.

General Colin Powell, who also served as secretary of state, is of Jamaican descent.

JAPAN

IN 1791, SIXTY-TWO YEARS BEFORE MATTHEW PERRY'S ARRIVAL, an American merchantman landed in Japan. The Japanese reported that it belonged to "American Red Hairs." Obviously, it would have been unusual if the entire crew of an American ship had had red hair, but presumably to those generally used to jet-black Japanese hair, red, blond, and brown hair must have seemed both exotic and noteworthy.

By the middle decades of the nineteenth century, the race was seriously on among Western nations to open up the East to lucrative trade. Both Commander James Biddle and Captain James Glynn took American ships to Japan in the 1840s with very mixed results.

But it was in 1853 that Commodore Matthew Perry (NOT the Matthew Perry who was in *Friends*) sailed into Tokyo Bay with a squadron of four ships. Perry, a native of Newport, Rhode Island, was the younger brother of the impressively middle-named Oliver Hazard Perry (known for his concise report of "We have met the enemy and they are ours" in the Battle of Lake Erie, War of 1812). Matthew Perry had served in the Mexican-American War and commanded the Africa Squadron, which was responsible for attempting to suppress the slave trade. Two of Perry's ships were steamships that belched black smoke; they came to be known to the Japanese, not unreasonably, as the "Black Ships."

Perry bore with him a letter from President Millard Fillmore, not now the best known of US presidents, to the emperor of Japan: "I have directed Commodore Perry to assure your imperial majesty that I entertain the kindest feelings towards your majesty's person and government, and that I have no other object in sending him to Japan but to propose to your imperial majesty that the United States and Japan should live in friendship and have commercial intercourse with each other."

Fillmore went on to request coaling depots based in Japan to serve American ships and a humane response to shipwrecked American mariners in Japanese waters.

Japan under the Tokugawa Shogunate had gone through a period of isolation from the rest of the world that lasted over two hundred years. Japan was a highly militaristic feudal culture that had opted for near total seclusion (*sakoku*) from foreigners. Japan did not allow foreign visits with the exception of a small Dutch trading enclave near Nagasaki, and the Japanese were, on pain of death, prohibited from leaving as well. Their Samurai used some of the finest swords in the world, but many of their coastal battery guns were extremely outdated.

Perry delivered his letter and said he would return for an answer.

In February 1854, Perry once again arrived in Japan, this time, with ten ships that comprised nearly one quarter of the USN at that time. He got what he was after. The Treaty of Kanagawa, signed on March 31, 1854, was negotiated under the guns of the USN. The treaty represented a capitulation to all of Perry's demands and a humiliation for Japan.

But the battle to open up Japan was not yet entirely won. In 1863, the emperor issued an order to expel "barbarians" once again. The mighty Chōshū clan of Shimonoseki rushed to obey and started shelling any foreign ship that tried to pass through the crucial Shimonoseki Straits. An American merchant ship, the *Pembroke*, was among those ships targeted. It managed to escape, but not unreasonably, the crew weren't happy, and the USS *Wyoming* was sent in to do something about it. The result was the Battle of Shimonoseki Straits in which *Wyoming* exchanged fire with Japanese shore batteries and managed to sink two Japanese ships before withdrawing, having suffered significant damage. It wasn't a defeat for the *Wyoming*, but it wasn't a massive victory either.

It wasn't until September 1864 that a multinational Western naval force inflicted a decisive defeat on the Chōshū and ensured safety of passage for Western merchant ships.

Japan would now embark on a tumultuous period of radical change and military growth.

The Boshin War was fought between 1868 and 1869 as supporters of the Tokugawa Shogunate battled supporters of the emperor for control of Japan. The United States didn't get officially involved, but there were already plenty of Western weapons and some Western military advisers involved, and we did send troops to protect American citizens.

The Bakufu ("Tent Government") of warlords led by a Shogun and a titular emperor were eventually replaced by a modern industrial nation state under the rule of the emperor Meiji. The Imperial Japanese Navy was modeled on Britain's Royal Navy, and their army was modeled on the Prussian example. Japan quickly adopted the imperial ambitions that were sweeping the Western world in the nineteenth century, colonizing Okinawa, Formosa, and later, Korea.

If there were any doubts of the radical military advances being made by Japan, they were dispelled in the first decade of the twentieth century when, in 1904-05, Japan fought the Russo-Japanese War and destroyed two Russian fleets. President Teddy Roosevelt incidentally picked up a Nobel Prize for himself for helping to secure a peace treaty between Imperial Japan and tsarist Russia to end the war, the Treaty of Portsmouth.

And we were keen to show off our own growing naval power. On October 18, 1908, TR's Great White Fleet was welcomed to Yokohama while on their round-the-world cruise.

In World War I, Japan was on the Allied side, a wise strategic decision that allowed it to take control of many of the Pacific islands that had previously belonged to the Kaiser's German Empire.

Of course, in World War II, it was all to be a very different story. Japan achieved strategic surprise attacking the United States fleet at anchor at Pearl Harbor on December 7, 1941. Some Americans, not realizing, how advanced Japan's navy and air force had become, made the assumption that German pilots must have been involved. And Japan, in its onslaught in the East, would later launch attacks on American allies, such as the Philippines, and occupy American territory, such as Guam, Wake Island, and Alaska.

The American riposte to Pearl Harbor was the spectacular and very daring Doolittle Raid, which took place on April 18, 1942. Sixteen B-25B Mitchell aircraft were launched from the deck of the USS *Hornet* to bomb Tokyo and proceed to China afterwards. The raiders inflicted minimal physical damage, but the psychological impact was enormous as the Japanese felt compelled to initiate the disastrous (for the Japanese) Midway campaign to prevent future American air attacks on their homeland.

As the war progressed, slowly, US forces began to edge closer towards Japan. From 1943 to 1945, the American island-hopping campaign using US naval and marine landings drove closer and closer to the Japanese home islands. From April to June of 1945, US forces fought the ferocious Battle of Okinawa, also known as the "typhoon of steel." This battle claimed the lives of virtually all the 117,000 Japanese defenders, as well as more than a third of the island's total civilian population. Japanese kamikaze strikes resulted in the highest losses ever suffered in a single battle by the USN.

On September 2, 1944, USN pilot George H. W. Bush was shot down in his Grumman Avenger while flying off the coast of the island of Chichijima. After spending about four hours in a raft, the fortunate future president was rescued by the USS *Finback* submarine.

Advances in the Mariana Islands had given us airbases within practical reach of the Japanese mainland in late 1944, and the use of incendiary munitions dropped by B-29 Superfortress bombers proved devastating in 1945. Cities such as Kobe, Nagoya, Osaka, Yokohama, and Kawasaki were burnt to ashes. Over one hundred thousand were killed by the fire-bombing in Tokyo in a single day — more even than the atomic bombs that followed in August.

And we weren't attacking Japan only from the air. Captain Eugene Fluckey (later admiral) commanded the USS *Barb*, which sank many Japanese merchant ships in World War II. Around 56 percent of Japanese merchant shipping was sunk by USN submarines such as the USS *Pampanito* (now found in San Francisco) during the war, which crippled Japan's ability to feed its population. On July 23, 1945, the USS *Barb* approached Patience Bay near Kashiho, Japan. A cutting-out party was sent ashore in rubber raft; their mission was to mine the tracks on a nearby railway. The team detonated their explosives under a Japanese train and watched as the engine exploded into the air and train cars smashed into each other and toppled off the track.

In August of 1945, the United States dropped atomic bombs on Hiroshima and Nagasaki avoiding the massive sacrifices that would have been made in any invasion scenario. The Soviets had also, at long last, begun their promised offensive against Manchuria. On August 15, Emperor Hirohito in a taped radio broadcast admitted, "The war situation has developed not necessarily to Japan's advantage." The most destructive war in human history was finally over.

The extensive and detailed plans for an amphibious Allied invasion of Japan would not be needed. Operation Downfall, in which an initial landing on the southern Japanese island of Kyūshū (Operation Olympic) was to be followed by a landing on Honshū near Tokyo (Operation Coronet), would never happen.

Instead, on September 2, 1945, the documents confirming Japan's surrender were signed on board the USS *Missouri* in Tokyo Bay. General

Douglas MacArthur and Fleet Admiral Chester Nimitz were present beneath Commodore Perry's pennant, which had been flown out from the naval museum in Annapolis. Gunrooms aboard the *"Mighty Mo"* were prepared to fire on the imperial palace in the event of any trickery.

MacArthur presided over the occupation that followed. The emperor of Japan was the only head of state from the Tripartite Pact who would survive the war. MacArthur, keen to have a strong ally in the region, instead of concentrating on revenge on Japan, focused on alleviating the massive suffering the Japanese people had faced in the latter stages of the war and on the swift reconstruction of Japan and its economy.

US forces remain stationed in Japan to this day, and Japan is one of our closest allies with numerous and strong military links. Joint exercises are, for instance, conducted by the US and Japan's Self-Defense Forces with a view to potential regional challenges, such as an unpredictable North Korea.

JORDAN

OFFICIALLY, THE COUNTRY IS NAMED the Hashemite Kingdom of Jordan. Jordan has traditionally been seen as one of the more pro-Western Arab countries through the long years of the Cold War and the even longer years of the Arab-Israeli conflict. Obviously, times have existed when Jordan and the West have had very different views on a situation, but still the links are long-standing.

We first started giving military aid to Jordan in 1957. In that year, we also sent formidable forces into the Eastern Mediterranean to show our support for the king of Jordan, Hussein. Hussein was faced with a major political crisis in April 1957, as he dismissed his cabinet, faced large demonstrations, and imposed martial law. The American naval forces sent included two carrier battle groups, a battleship, two cruisers, twenty-four destroyers, the Marine Amphibious Ready Group, and submarines. Wow. We weren't taking it lightly.

And the next year, in 1958, when the king felt threatened by a coup in neighboring Iraq and the British sent paratroopers, we sent ships again.

In 1970, things got even more tense. Jordan was host to large numbers of Palestinian refugees and PLO fighters. In September, bitter fighting broke out as Hussein launched his Jordanian forces against Palestinian targets. As fighting raged, the Syrians sent forces into Jordan on the side of the Palestinians. US ships and marines were ready to intervene to protect American interests, and the 82nd Airborne Division in Germany was told to prepare to move in and take Amman Airport. However, as the crisis began to subside and a peace deal was finally signed, the intervention was called off. Still, that September and October, USAF C-130 aircraft did fly relief supplies and equipment into Jordan in Operation Fig Hill to help deal with the crisis.

In recent decades, despite occasional disagreements at times, for instance, over Iraq, Jordan has become a key US partner in the Middle East, particularly in the search for a peace deal to end completely the Arab-Israeli conflict but also, more recently, for example, on the present crisis in Syria.

We have given huge amounts of military aid to Jordan. A US-Jordanian Joint Military Commission was set up in 1974, and over the years, thousands of Jordanian military personnel have been trained in the United States. US and Jordanian forces regularly work alongside each other in training exercises, and the United States supported the building of the King Abdullah II Center for Special Operations Training. Jordan has helped train Iraqi and Afghan government forces and has sent military hospitals and medical personnel to Iraq and Afghanistan.

The Syrian crisis has inevitably focused US attention on Jordan, as well, because of its key location next to Syria and because Jordan plays host to large numbers of Syrian refugees. Attempts have been made to play down the US military presence in Jordan during the crisis, but hundreds of troops have been located there, sometimes staying behind after planned exercises, and many of them based near the Syrian border. The troops are there to help prevent any threat to Jordan and to help with refugees but presumably also offer the US government some ability to react to future developments in the complex and somewhat unpredictable Syrian crisis. It has also been speculated that US forces in Jordan have been helping train Syrian rebels.

KAZAKHSTAN

KAZAKHSTAN IS A BIG COUNTRY, the ninth largest in the world. It has a long and interesting history and was the scene of a truly epoch-making event on April 12, 1961.

Perhaps the time we took the most interest in it was during the Cold War when it was part of the Soviet Union. At the time, Kazakhstan was home to some vital Soviet strategic facilities, in particular places like the nuclear weapons site at Semipalatinsk, the ballistic missile range at Sary Shagan, and the space launch area at Baikonur. Yep, it was from Kazakhstan on April 12, 1961, that Yuri Gagarin was launched in *Vostok 1* to become the first man to achieve an orbital spaceflight.

We wanted photos of all the strategic sites, and U-2s and SR-71s flew over Kazakh territory to get them.

We also have some strategic interests in independent Kazakhstan, for instance, because of oil and its key location in a vital area, and we have signed assorted agreements on military cooperation with the Kazakhs.

A small number of Kazakhs served with coalition forces in Iraq. They have also allowed us to send flights through their airspace to support operations in Afghanistan. American troops have taken part on Kazakh soil in the Steppe Eagle exercises, and Kazakhstan takes part in our Caspian Guard Initiative to improve security in the Caspian Sea area. The Arizona National Guard is partnered with Kazakhstan. The US Department of Defense also organizes counter-narcotics operations in Kazakhstan.

KENYA

KENYA IS AN EAST AFRICAN COUNTRY NOTED FOR ITS WILDLIFE, safaris, and excellent coffee. Barack Obama's ancestry forges the most recent direct link between the US military's current commander-in-chief and Kenya.

Humans have lived in what is now Kenya for millions of years, though Americans have been in the area only comparatively recently!

American privateers and buccaneers did, however, sail the Indian Ocean in search of plunder in the period before the American Revolution, and not far away, Zanzibar had extensive American trading connections in the early nineteenth century. During World War I, Americans were caught up in the fighting in this region when some of them joined the Twenty-fifth (Frontiersmen) Battalion of the Royal Fusiliers in the British Army. The battalion disembarked at Mombasa, the main port of Kenya, in 1915 and was deployed in what is now Tanzania and in Kenya.

During World War II, we set up an air transport base at Nairobi, now the capital of Kenya, though Allied advances in North Africa in 1942 and 1943 eventually reduced its importance.

Kenya gained its independence from Britain in December 1963 and was soon recognized by the United States in 1964.

Mombasa has long been a port of call for the USN. For instance, in 1976, after the Israeli raid on Entebbe in neighboring Uganda had been launched with Kenyan assistance, the USN conducted various maneuvers to demonstrate US support for Kenya and prevent any Ugandan retaliation, including two US frigates calling in at Mombasa. In 1982 alone, more than thirty thousand US sailors made port-of-call stops in Mombasa driving up sales of beer and T-shirts.

And in recent times, Kenya has become a vital area for us in the fight against Somali piracy and the fight against Islamist extremists.

In September 2008, in one of the more lengthy piracy incidents, the MV *Faina*, a Ukrainian merchant ship, was bound for Mombasa. It was seized by Somali pirates. In the hold, thirty-three Russian T-72 tanks and other weaponry were found. The ship was part of an effort by the Kenyan government to supply arms to the militias in South Sudan. USN vessels surrounded the ship, and hostage negotiations dragged on for weeks. About four months later, a $3.2 million ransom was paid, and the ship and its crew proceeded to Kenya. Its cargo eventually made its way to South Sudan. In 2009, Captain Phillips's ship, the *Maersk Alabama* finally ended up in Mombasa after his dramatic rescue by the USN. The USN has taken suspected pirates to Mombasa for trial there.

Kenya came to the forefront of our conflict with Islamist extremists in 1998 when the US embassy in Nairobi was bombed by al-Qaeda killing over two hundred people. A similar attack was made in Tanzania at the same time. In response, US military personnel were rushed into Kenya to help deal with the emergency situation.

Camp Simba, where USN Seabee engineers have helped build an air strip, was established at Manda Bay on the Kenyan coast in 2004. The exact nature of what goes on there is a matter of some debate, but military officials happily accept that Seabees are located there and US military personnel are engaged in work with the Kenyan armed forces and in humanitarian work. Manda Bay is situated not far south of the Somali border, and there is speculation about US Special Forces being stationed there.

Today, a wide variety of links between the US military and the Kenyan military exist, and Kenyan forces have become key partners in the fight against Islamist extremists in Somalia.

In September 2013, a terrorist attack at a mall in Nairobi claimed the lives of over seventy people. The terrorist group al-Shabaab claimed responsibility. USN SEALs were later deployed to Somalia in an unsuccessful attempt to capture or kill an al-Shabaab leader.

KIRIBATI

FEW PEOPLE HAVE HEARD OF KIRIBATI, and fewer know that seaweed is an important export from the country. A lot of people will, however, have heard of Tarawa.

Kiribati is an island nation in the Pacific consisting of a large number of islands and groups of islands. Before World War II, it was an area of major British influence.

We did, however, have a claim on some of the islands. On Enderbury Island, for instance, an American company mined guano in the nineteenth century. Under the Guano Islands Act of 1856, it and a number of other islands in the area could be claimed. In 1938, FDR, thinking they might be in a strategic location, declared Enderbury and nearby Kanton Island under US jurisdiction. The British, though, weren't so keen on the idea, and eventually a compromise was reached where the two islands came under joint jurisdiction.

Then came the war. And the Japanese. Some of the more remote islands in what is now Kiribati escaped Japanese invasion. Some of them didn't. The USCGC *Taney* (now in Baltimore's inner harbor) evacuated Enderbury, but the Japanese never came to it. Banaba, or Ocean Island, though, was seized by the Japanese in 1942 and wasn't liberated by our troops until 1945.

With some of the other islands, it was a very different story. One of the major island groups in Kiribati is the Gilbert Islands, and two of the names connected to this group will be familiar to many Americans, Makin and, in particular, Tarawa.

The Japanese took both very early in the war, in December 1941. But in August 1942, 221 US marines, under the command of Colonel Carlson, landed from submarines on Makin (Butaritari) in an attempt to divert Japanese attention from Guadalcanal and seize intelligence. The raiders dealt with most Japanese resistance on land, though they faced enemy air attacks, and re-embarkation proved a challenge.

In September 1943, US air raids hit both Makin and Tarawa, and then on November 20, US troops stormed ashore on Makin and Tarawa. On Makin, the troops landed on Red Beach and Yellow Beach. Fighting was fierce, but within a few days, our troops had taken control. On Tarawa, the marines headed for Red Beach 1, Red Beach 2, and Red Beach 3. Heavy and determined Japanese resistance, effective Japanese strongpoints, and problems with boats and reefs meant heavy casualties among the landing force, but eventually the marines managed to get ashore and push inland.

On November 21, bitter fighting continued as Green Beach was taken and reinforcements landed there. Early in the morning of November 23, a massive Japanese counterattack hit US lines but was fought off with artillery support leaving hundreds of Japanese dead. Eventually, after more fighting, the Japanese defenders were split up into pockets and virtually wiped out.

Subsequent operations involved landings on other nearby islands. To add to all the US losses in the actual landings, heavy US casualties were suffered when the aircraft carrier *Liscombe Bay* was torpedoed.

After the battle, assorted US facilities were constructed, including the development of the Japanese airbase on Tarawa as Hawkins Field.

The post-war period saw some US military involvement in the area. For instance, we had a missile tracking station on Kanton Island at one stage. And in the 1960s, we exploded nuclear bombs on Christmas Island, Kiritmati.

Kiribati became independent in 1979, and we and the British relinquished joint control of Enderbury and Kanton Islands and acknowledged control by Kiribati over some other islands, although we still have Baker Island and Howland Island and a few other tiny territories.

US military personnel have taken part in humanitarian operations in independent Kiribati.

KOSOVO

WE WERE INVOLVED IN THIS AREA MILITARILY during World War II, but it was in the 1990s that we started taking a bit more military interest in Kosovo. Well, a lot of military interest actually.

Tension between ethnic Albanians and ethnic Serbs had long existed, and in 1997, the Kosovo Liberation Army started a guerrilla war against Serb control of Kosovo. As the guerrilla campaign spread, so did heavy-handed and ruthless measures by Milosevic's forces, leading to the deaths of many civilians as well as guerrillas. After a failed attempt at a ceasefire in late 1998, the Rambouillet Conference was assembled, out of which came the Rambouillet Accords demanding a NATO presence in Kosovo to supervise a peace deal. When Milosevic rejected the accords, the bombing campaign started.

It lasted from March 24 to June 11, and US aircraft and cruise missiles played a crucial role hitting targets in Serbia, Kosovo, and Montenegro. As time advanced and Milosevic showed no sign of giving up and with the US ground forces of Task Force Hawk building up near Kosovo's border, preparations were also made for the possibility of a ground offensive. In Kosovo itself, Milosevic's forces stepped up a campaign of ethnic cleansing, and the Kosovo Liberation Army, or KLA, attempted to resist. Plenty of people have speculated about assistance by Western Special Forces to the KLA, but it's hard to find out full details of what happened.

Finally on June 3, Milosevic gave in and agreed to withdraw his forces from Kosovo and allow NATO forces to enter. The United States was allocated control of MNB-East (multi-national brigade sector east). On June 11, a small US advance party of twenty vehicles and fifty-five personnel moved in, and this was rapidly followed by many more US troops, including most of Task Force Hawk, and a contingent from the First Infantry Division that had been flown from Germany to Macedonia for entry into Kosovo. More US troops were soon to follow, and two initial camp locations would turn into Camp Bondsteel and Camp Monteith.

The NATO forces were welcomed by the ethnic Albanians as liberators, but many ethnic Serbs fled through fear of ethnic Albanian violence in the period during and after NATO's arrival.

US forces have been in Kosovo long, long after the departure of Serb forces. The Iowa National Guard is partnered with Kosovo.

Kosovo declared independence on February 17, 2008, and the US recognized it as an independent state the next day. However, not all countries have recognized Kosovo's independence, so it is not, for instance, a UN member state.

KUWAIT

Kuwait is a small oil-rich (very oil-rich) nation on the northeastern corner of the Persian Gulf that has borders with Iraq and Saudi Arabia. The Al-Sabah family has ruled since 1938. From 1899 until 1961, it was a British protectorate. The United States recognized it as an independent nation in 1961.

Iraq has a long-standing claim to Kuwait and traditionally saw as part of its territory. Almost as soon as Kuwait was independent, Iraq made threatening moves against it. British troops had to rush in once again until things settled down.

American oil companies established trading links with Kuwait and other Gulf states early on, and after Britain's retreat from empire, the United States eventually took over the British position as the chief protector of Kuwait.

Our first major military action in support of Kuwait took place during the long, bitter Iran-Iraq War. Fearing that revolutionary Iran's influence might spread in the Gulf, Kuwait was, despite Iraq's claims on Kuwait, supportive of the Iraqi war effort. Iran, angered by this and by Iraqi attacks on its oil industry, started to target oil tankers linked to places it regarded as supportive of Saddam. Kuwait requested American protection for its tankers, and to protect vital oil supplies to the world, we gave it. Operation Earnest Will starting in the summer of 1987 involved reflagging Kuwaiti ships with the American flag and then the USN escorting them through waters where they were vulnerable to Iranian attack. The mission came to an end after the war did in the summer of 1988.

However, this is not the main operation people tend to think about in association with American military operations and Kuwait.

Saddam Hussein decided to do something about Iraq's long-standing claims to Kuwait and launched his invasion of Kuwait on August 2, 1990. Saddam had, however, seriously miscalculated America's intentions and capabilities. Only six days later, President George H. W. Bush announced the deployment of US troops to Saudi Arabia to preempt further Iraqi aggression. Eventually, over half a million US troops were deployed to the Middle East.

Operation Desert Shield was to be a multi-lateral coalition force deployment with the armed forces of thirty-four different nations. The fall of the Berlin Wall and the end of the Cold War had made multi-lateral action possible. Saddam's invasion of Kuwait was viewed as a direct challenge to the central mandate of the United Nations. Shortly after Saddam's invasion, the UN Security Council, in a series of resolutions, condemned Iraq, issued trade embargoes, demanded an immediate withdrawal from Kuwait, and authorized the use of "all necessary means" to liberate that country. Saddam, however, ignored the UN threats.

An intensive six-week air campaign began on January 17, 1991, targeting vital Iraqi infrastructure and military forces both inside Iraq and in Kuwait itself. Despite firing Scuds at Saudi Arabia and Israel in an attempt to drag Israel into the conflict, Iraq had little answer to the onslaught from cruise missiles, stealth aircraft, B-52s, and a wide range of other aircraft. Even before the ground war began, Iraq's ability to resist had been seriously weakened.

The ground assault, Operation Desert Storm, began on February 24, 1991, and lasted only about one hundred hours. Much of the actual combat took place in Iraq as a massive allied thrust penetrated Iraqi territory to the west of Kuwait and then swung round towards Kuwait from that direction. The campaign was a complete mismatch. The American main battle tank, the M1 Abrams, destroyed over two thousand Iraqi tanks without a single Abrams destroyed by enemy fire.

Dire predictions of massive coalition casualties at the hands of the "elite" Republican Guard in the end proved unfounded. A total of 482 coalition deaths were reported in the First Gulf War, most of them due to accidents or friendly fire. By contrast, over twenty-five thousand Iraqis were also killed in the course of the campaign, many on the "highway of death" as they attempted to retreat to Iraq. Iraq's chemical weapons were never used.

A cease fire was agreed to in April of 1991. Coalition forces agreed to permit Saddam use of helicopters allegedly for humanitarian purposes. Uprisings against Saddam's regime in Kurdistan and elsewhere, which might have toppled the regime, were brutally repressed by Saddam's helicopter gunships.

The Kuwaiti government and Al-Sabah family were restored to power. The Kingdom of Saudi Arabia largely financed the entire liberation of Kuwait (paying thirty-six billion dollars out of the sixty-billion-dollar total cost).

In 1993, Saddam was accused of authorizing an assassination attempt on President George H. W. Bush while he visited Kuwait. Accordingly, in June 1993, President Clinton ordered a cruise missile strike on Baghdad.

When we invaded Iraq in 2003, Kuwait was where most of the invasion force assembled, and when the last US forces left Iraq almost nine years later, they crossed the border into Kuwait, the gate was closed behind them, and US and Kuwaiti forces shook hands and posed for photos.

Kuwait today remains a major non-NATO ally of the United States and a supporter of the global war on terror. We continue to have close military links with the country. For instance, Kuwait will host the major US multilateral exercise Eagle Resolve in 2015.

KYRGYZSTAN

TAJIKISTAN IS SITUATED TO THE NORTH OF AFGHANISTAN, and beyond that is the large (but comparatively little-known in the West) country of Kyrgyzstan.

The name Kyrgyz seems to derive from a word meaning forty, and the sun on the Kyrgyz flag has forty rays. Both are supposed to refer to forty clans that were important in the early history of the region.

Among its other claims to fame, Kyrgyzstan has the unusual distinction of having had both Russian and US military bases on its soil.

Our Manas Air Base, close to the Kyrgyz capital in Bishkek, opened for business in December 2001, supporting air operations in Afghanistan to the south. Combat aircraft, tankers, and transports have all been based here, and it has become a major transit point for soldiers entering and leaving Afghanistan.

However, the base has at times proved controversial in the area, and our operations at Manas ended in 2014.

The US Department of Defense also currently organizes counter-narcotics operations in Kyrgyzstan, and the Montana National Guard is partnered with Kyrgyzstan.

LAOS

LAOS, NAMED IN THE PAST "THE COUNTRY OF A MILLION ELEPHANTS," is a landlocked nation in Southeast Asia. That is to say, the Laotians have no ocean.

Laos was a French protectorate from 1893, along with Vietnam and Cambodia. During World War II, the Japanese eventually took control, and the United States first got involved militarily there. For instance, in September 1945, the OSS Raven Mission was sent from Kunming to Vientiane to search out Japanese POW camps and gather intelligence on the situation in the area. The mission found 143 internees near Vientiane.

The Kingdom of Laos gained its independence in 1953, but a rough road lay ahead. Civil war broke out almost immediately between the Laotian government, supported by France, and the Communist Pathet Lao, supported by North Vietnam.

And as French power in the area came to an end, we stepped in to support the forces opposing the Communists. President Dwight Eisenhower feared that Laos might be one of the falling dominos in Southeast Asia. His administration provided about three hundred million dollars in assistance to the Laotian government.

A complex three-sided battle for power among Laotian Communists, neutralists, and rightists would follow, with the United States and its allies and Communist powers intervening in the country.

Laos shares a long border with Vietnam. During the Vietnam War, the Ho Chi Minh Trail ran through Laotian territory. It was by means of this trail that the VC in South Vietnam were resupplied from the north.

Beginning in 1960, the United States launched a covert war to interdict the Ho Chi Minh Trail. The CIA supported the Hmong with money, arms, and supplies in a war against the Pathet Lao. Visiting US congressional delegations were entertained by CIA officers at the White Rose nightclub in Vientiane.

By April 1961, under the Kennedy administration, about 430 military advisors were operating in Laos.

Two linked wars were basically being fought side by side in Laos, one for control of Laos itself, much of the fighting being focused on the strategic Plain of Jars, and another over the Ho Chi Minh Trail.

CIA officers acted as forward observers for the B-52 strikes that pounded the head of Ho Chi Minh Trail. American bombing turned Laos into the per-capita most heavily bombed nation on the planet. Unexploded bombs are still being removed from Laos today.

In February 1971, the United States supported an invasion of Laos by about fifteen thousand ARVN forces with air and artillery support. However, the South Vietnamese forces encountered five battle-hardened North Vietnamese divisions that routed them, chasing them across the border again.

After both Saigon and Phnom Penh had fallen to the Communists in 1975, later the same year, the Pathet Lao entered Vientiane and took over the country.

After the Communist seizure of power in 1975, the Hmong people who had supported American geopolitical interests were persecuted. Many fled across the Mekong River to Thailand. Some forty-five thousand may have perished during the journey.

Successive waves of immigration have brought many Hmong to the United States. Today, over a quarter million Hmong people are resident in the United States.

The US military has recently been involved in some humanitarian work in Laos.

LATVIA

L ATVIA IS THE MIDDLE ONE OF THE THREE BALTIC STATES, with Lithuania to the south and Estonia to the north. Latvia's currency until 2104 was the lats. It would be much easier if everyone's currency sounded a bit like his or her country, like France and the old francs, but then again, we'd have to swap the dollar for an "americ" or "usa."

The area that now forms the modern state of Latvia had a fairly lively history during the medieval period, with a lot of jostling for power in the area by Germans, Poles, Russians, Swedes, and the locals. The duchy of Courland had an interesting history, including forming now little-known colonies in the Caribbean and on the African coast.

Finally by 1795, the whole area had become part of the Russian Empire. Latvia as a nation struggled to be born in the turmoil that followed the end of the Great War and declared its independence on November 18, 1918. Latvian forces fought the Germans (Battle of Wenden) and later the Russians.

US General Sherwood Cheney was a key member of the Allied Commission that organized the removal of German troops from Latvia and Lithuania in 1919.

We also had USN forces in Latvian waters during this period to protect US interests and assist with US aid, relief, and medical efforts in the area. For instance, the American destroyer, the USS *Evans*, under Commander F. H. Sadler, was at Liepāja, Latvia, in July 1919. And in September 1920, we unintentionally made a landing on Latvian rocks: The USS *Pittsburgh* ran aground near Liepāja, and in Antwerp, the USS *Frederick* had to rapidly disembark members of the US Olympic team it was carrying to the games there and race to Latvia to assist the *Pittsburgh*.

The USG recognized Latvia on July 28, 1922.

In 1931, George Kennan would become the third secretary at the US embassy in Riga where he became fluent in Russian. The Baltic republics became a haven for White Russians fleeing the Soviets, and Kennan may have absorbed some of the White Russian attitudes towards Lenin's Soviet experiment. He would later (in 1946) go on to become the author of the famous "long telegram" that warned that at the "bottom of the Kremlin's neurotic view of world affairs is the traditional and instinctive Russian sense of insecurity." He became the intellectual architect for America's policy of Cold War containment.

The Molotov/Ribbentrop agreement of 1939 carved up Europe into spheres of Soviet/Nazi influence. The Baltic states fell into the Soviet sphere. Latvia's fate was sealed. On June 17, 1940, the Red Army invaded Latvia, which offered no resistance. The United States refused to recognize the incorporation of Latvia into the Soviet Union. After Hitler's invasion of the Soviet Union in the summer of 1941, Latvia was occupied by the Nazis. Latvians were drafted into fighting on both sides during World War II. Tragically, Latvia's Jewish population of about seventy-five thousand was sent by the Nazis to the concentration camps.

After the war, Latvia was dominated by the Soviet Union. As in the other Baltic states, a local resistance movement, the Forest Brothers, operated for some time against the Soviets, and the CIA made some attempts to assist this process, but in the end, resistance was crushed.

After the collapse of Communism, Latvia regained its independence from the Soviet Union in 1991.

Since that time, the United States has developed close military links with Latvia. The country, for instance, joined NATO in 2004 with the other Baltic states. Latvia contingents have fought alongside American troops in Kosovo, Iraq, and Afghanistan. American and Latvian troops have trained alongside each other and cooperated on a variety of projects. The Michigan National Guard is partnered with Latvia.

LEBANON

L EBANON, ON THE SHORES OF THE EASTERN MEDITERRANEAN, is an ancient land with much history and much beauty. It was home to that well-known sea-faring people, the Phoenicians, who ventured beyond the Pillars of Hercules. Some have even suggested they crossed the Atlantic long before the Vikings. Lebanon has seen many, many (and add a few more to that) invaders pass through.

In 1867, Mark Twain led an "invading" army of American tourists to Lebanon and the Holy Land. He praised "the beautiful city of Beirut, with its bright, new houses nestled among a wilderness of green shrubbery spread abroad over an upland that sloped gently down to the sea; and also at the mountains of Lebanon that environ it."

The British invaded Vichy-Lebanon in 1941 with Operation Exporter. After World War II, Lebanon gained its independence, and power was shared among its different religious groups. For a time, it became known as the "Switzerland of the East" with major bank headquarters and a cosmopolitan flair.

The United States first intervened in Lebanon in July 1958 at the request of President Camille Chamoun. Radical Iraqi nationalists had overthrown a monarchy that had received support from Britain. The American-friendly monarchies in Jordan and Saudi Arabia felt threatened. President Dwight Eisenhower responded by ordering three marine battalions of the 6th Fleet ashore. Three US aircraft carriers (*Essex, Saratoga*, and *Wasp*) were deployed off the Lebanese coast. There was no fighting, and no casualties were taken. The marines withdrew four months later.

A brutal, complex, and confusing multi-sided civil war, in which the alliances and enemies changed regularly, tore Lebanon apart from 1975 to 1990. We got sucked into it. The situation was so complex and went on for so long that this can only be a summary of some of the events.

Twice in 1976, the US 6th Fleet went in to evacuate civilians from Lebanon.

The Israeli Defence Force, equipped with among other things US-made weaponry, invaded Lebanon in 1982 in an attempt to push the PLO forces away from the Israeli border and end their ability to threaten Israel. After some sharp but short fighting, the Israeli eventually penned much of the PLO's fighting force inside a part of Beirut and laid siege to them there. In the end, a deal was arranged whereby the Palestinian fighters would be evacuated to Tunisia, and President Ronald Reagan sent in hundreds of marines to help see that the evacuation went smoothly.

By the end of September 1982, with the Palestinians gone, marines were working with the multinational force in Lebanon to try to restore the Lebanese government's control of the chaotic country. Not all the Lebanese wanted our troops there. On April 18, 1983, suicide bombers blew up the US embassy in Beirut.

On September 19, 1983, USN ships found themselves firing 338 rounds in support of the Lebanese Army that was trying to defend Souk el Gharb. The next month, on October 23, 1983, a suicide truck-bomb loaded with TNT attacked the US Marine barracks, and 241 US and fifty-eight French servicemen were killed. Then on December 4, 1983, two USN aircraft based on the *Hancock* were shot down by Syrian antiaircraft batteries operating in Lebanon. One pilot was killed, and another, Robert Goodman Jr., was captured and held in a Syrian prison. The Reverend Jesse Jackson subsequently visited Damascus and secured his release from the Assad government. The Goodman incident lent more urgency to the development of our unmanned drone program

Reagan ordered the withdrawal of US forces from Lebanon on February 7, 1984. And from February 8 to 14, the USN fired parting shots at Syrian military positions located in the Bekaa Valley.

On September 20, 1984, a bomb exploded outside the American embassy annex in East Beirut killing twenty-three people.

The withdrawal did not end the danger to Americans in Lebanon. In 1985, the carrier *Enterprise* was sent to the Eastern Mediterranean because staff from the US embassy in Beirut needed to be evacuated to Cyprus by helicopter.

In the late 1980s, the hostage crisis in Lebanon saw USN ships sent to the area on a number of occasions.

And in 1989, once again, Americans were evacuated, and our training of the Lebanese military was suspended. In 1990, though, with the end of the civil war, the US ambassador returned, and the US embassy reopened in 1991. The same year, we also started selling weapons again to the Lebanese army, and in 1993, we started training them again.

In April 1996, Israel launched Operation Grapes of Wrath against Hezbollah in Lebanon, and along with France, America co-chaired the Israel-Lebanon Monitoring Group set up to implement the understanding that ended the fighting.

In 2006, US forces were once again headed to Lebanon to evacuate US citizens who wanted to avoid the possibility of being involved in fighting between Hezbollah and Israel. And after the 2006 war, we increased support for the Lebanese Armed Forces and other internal security forces and, in October 2008, signed a military cooperation agreement that established the US-Lebanese Joint Military Commission. Recent aid has included spares for Huey helicopters to improve the readiness of the Lebanese helicopter fleet, boats and a forty-two-meter coastal security craft for the navy, and for the army, hundreds of Humvees and a wide range of other equipment, including M113 armored personnel carriers, mortars, and anti-tank weapons.

Security concerns about what's going on in Lebanon for a long time focused on the south of the country and the border with Israel. They now have shifted to the north of the country and the border with Syria as the vicious civil war tears apart the neighboring country and threatens to ignite ethnic and religious tensions in Lebanon.

LESOTHO

L ESOTHO IS A SMALL LANDLOCKED COUNTRY, and this is going to be a small chapter. Lesotho is located in southern Africa, or to be more precise, it's located within the country of South Africa, one nation totally surrounded by another.

We haven't had that much military involvement with Lesotho. In 2011, the planning for AFRICOM-sponsored multinational communications exercise Africa Endeavor took place in Maseru, the capital of Lesotho, and members of the Lesotho military took part in Africa Endeavor in Douala, Cameroon, in 2012.

LIBERIA

S ADDAM HUSSEIN WASN'T THE ONLY DICTATOR TOPPLED by President George W. Bush in 2003. Elsewhere in the world and receiving considerably less attention in the West, something else was going on.

Today, few Americans know much about Liberia. Yet for much of US and Liberian history, Liberia has been a little slice of America in Africa.

Benedict Arnold letter. My ancestor, Captain Van Rensselaer, was invading Canada in 1776 under the command of Benedict Arnold. He was "anxious to go home" to New York. (*Photograph by Karim Merie.*)

John Paul Jones spiking the guns statue, Whitehaven, UK. John Paul Jones (1747–1792) spiked the guns in his raid on Whitehaven in the early morning hours of April 23, 1778. One British collier was burnt. (*Author's photograph.*)

John Paul Jones pub sign, Whitehaven, UK. In 1999, the town of Whitehaven officially pardoned John Paul Jones, "Father of the US Navy," for his 1778 raid on their town. (*Author's photograph.*)

The majority of the crew joined Victory from other ships of the fleet during 1803, a further 64 volunteered and 27 were newly'pressed men'. Twenty-two different nationalities were represented on board; these were:

English	515	Irish	88
Scottish	67	Welsh	30
African	1	American	22
Brazilian	1	Canadian	2
Danish	2	Dutch	7
French	4	German	2
Indian	2	Jamaican	1
Maltese	6	Norwegian	2
Portuguese	1	Swedish	4
Swiss	2	West Indian	4
Unknown	48		
	Total 820		

HMS *Victory* sign, Portsmouth, UK. Twenty-two Americans served on board the HMS *Victory* with Admiral Nelson at the Battle of Trafalgar on October 21, 1805. (*Author's photograph.*)

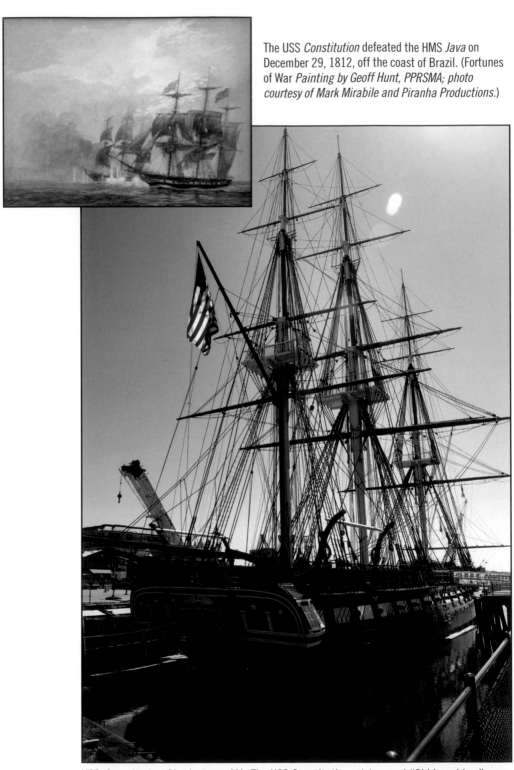

The USS *Constitution* defeated the HMS *Java* on December 29, 1812, off the coast of Brazil. (Fortunes of War *Painting by Geoff Hunt, PPRSMA; photo courtesy of Mark Mirabile and Piranha Productions.*)

USS *Constitution*, Charlestown, MA. The USS Constitution, nicknamed "Old Ironsides," was a 44-gun frigate that won three sea battles against the Royal Navy during the War of 1812. (*Photo courtesy of Chris Moran.*)

William Walker plaque, Nashville, TN. William Walker (1824–1860), the "grey-eyed man of destiny," led American invasions of Mexico, Nicaragua, and Honduras. (*Photo courtesy of Ladonna Parker.*)

RIGHT: Commodore Matthew Perry statue, Newport, RI. Commodore Matthew Perry (1794–1858) prised open the Japanese oyster with two visits to Tokyo Bay in 1853 and 1854. (*Photo courtesy of Sam Jernigan.*)

FAR RIGHT: John Monaghan statue, Spokane, WA. Ensign John Monaghan (1873–1899) of the USN was killed on April 1, 1899, in the Battle of Vailele in Samoa. (*Photo courtesy of Visit Spokane—Mark Baker.*)

107th Regiment statue, Central Park, NYC. American doughboys of the American Expeditionary Forces in World War I from the 107th Regiment. (*Author's photograph.*)

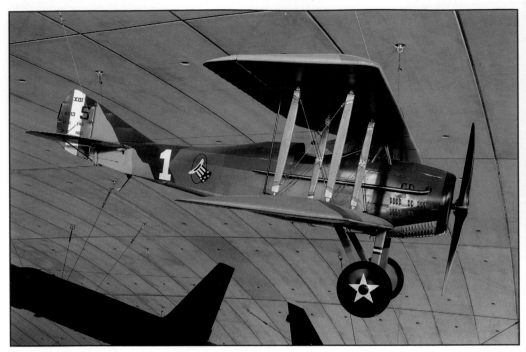

Spad S.XIII, American Air Museum, IWM Duxford, UK. Eddie Rickenbacker (1890–1973), the leading American fighter ace of World War I, scored twenty-six aerial victories. This is a replica of Eddie Rickenbacker's Spad S.XIII from World War I. (*Photograph by Karim Merie.*)

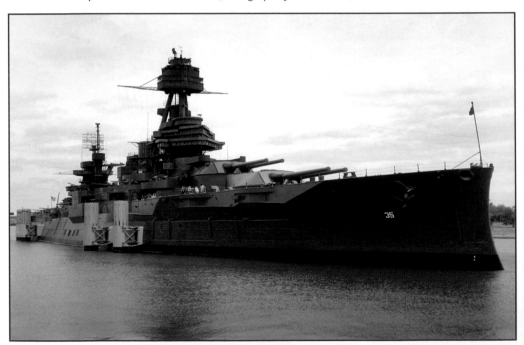

Battleship *Texas* BB-35, Battleship *Texas* State Historical Site, Texas Parks & Wildlife Department, La Porte, TX. The *Texas*, the only dreadnought battleship afloat today, was launched in 1912. The ship provided convoy escort in World War I and shore bombardment at Normandy on June 6, 1944, in World War II. (*Photo courtesy of James Hooper.*)

Queen Marie of Romania, Goldendale, WA. Queen Marie of Romania (1875–1938), granddaughter of Queen Victoria, was the Soldier Queen of Romania in World War I. She visited the United States in 1926. (*Printed with permission from Maryhill Museum of Art.*)

US Naval Monument, Brest, France. Built to commemorate the service of the USN in World War I, the monument was destroyed by the Germans on July 4, 1941, and rebuilt in 1958. (*Author's photograph.*)

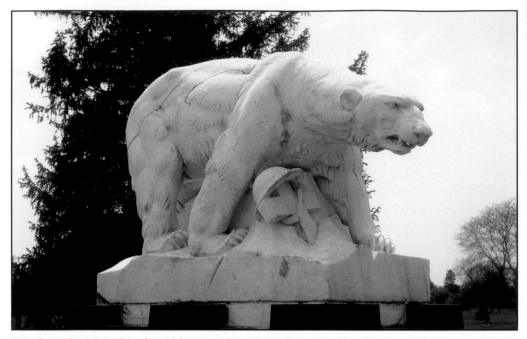

Polar Bear Memorial, White Chapel Cemetery, Troy, MI. The Polar Bear Expedition invaded and occupied parts of Northern Russia from 1918 to 1919. (*Photo courtesy of Vicki Aiello.*)

Statue of American Eagle squadrons, Grosvenor Square, London, UK. This statue commemorates Americans who joined the RAF and fought in the Battle of Britain in World War II. (*Photograph by Karim Merie.*)

FDR statue, Grosvenor Square, London, UK. Franklin Delano Roosevelt (1882–1945) was president of the United States for most of World War II. (*Photograph by Karim Merie.*)

USS *Pamapanito*, San Francisco Maritime National Park Association, Fisherman's Wharf, San Francisco, CA. The USS *Pampanito* (SS-383), launched in 1943, sank Japanese merchant ships in World War II. (*Author's photograph.*)

Jimmy Doolittle bust, American Air Museum, IWM Duxford, UK. On April 18, 1942, Jimmy Doolittle (1896–1993) led sixteen B-25s in a bombing raid on Tokyo, Japan, from the USS *Hornet*. (*Photograph by Karim Merie.*)

North American TB-25J "Mitchell" bomber, RAF Museum, Hendon, UK. (*Photo courtesy of Vincent Driano.*)

Dwight David Eisenhower statue, Grosvenor Square, London, UK. "Ike" (1890–1969) planned Operation Overlord, the cross-channel invasion of Nazi-occupied Europe, from his offices at 20 Grosvenor Square. It would be the most famous American invasion of all time. (*Author's photograph.*)

Willys MB Jeep, West Point Museum, United States Military Academy. Over six hundred thousand Jeeps were produced by the "Arsenal of Democracy" in World War II. (*Author's photograph.*)

P-51 Mustang, RAF Museum, Hendon, UK. The iconic P-51 Mustang could escort Allied bombers all the way to Berlin. (*Photo courtesy of Vincent Driano.*)

Tommy Hitchcock's grave, Cambridge-American Cemetery, Cambridgeshire, UK. Tommy Hitchcock joined the Lafayette Escadrille in WWI, played polo, and championed the introduction of Rolls Royce engines into the P-51 Mustang. (*Photograph by Karim Merie.*)

Douglas C-47 Skytrain, American Air Museum, IWM Duxford, UK. This Douglas C-47 Skytrain transport plane was painted with the D-Day stripes to avoid friendly fire that had plagued the invasion of Sicily in 1943. (*Photograph by Karim Merie.*)

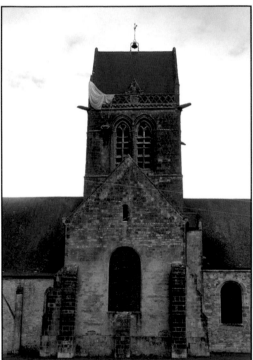

Private John Steele, Ste. Mère-Église, France. Private John Steele (1912–1969) of the 82nd Airborne landed on the steeple of the church at Ste. Mere-Eglise in Normandy on June 6, 1944. (*Author's photograph.*)

Stained glass window of the Virgin Mary and US paratroopers, Church of St. Mary, Ste. Mère-Église, France. (*Author's photograph.*)

George Patton statue, West Point, NY. General George S. Patton Jr. (1885–1945), "Old Blood and Guts," studied the Koran prior to his 1942 invasion of North Africa and helped to rescue the Lipizzaner stallions in Austria. (*Author's photograph.*)

Bust of General Anthony McAuliffe, Bastogne, Belgium. When asked to surrender by the Germans at the siege of Bastogne in December 1944, General McAuliffe famously replied, "Nuts." (*Author's photograph.*)

M4 Sherman, Musée Airborne, Ste. Mère-Église, France. Nearly fifty thousand M4 Sherman tanks were produced by a variety of American companies during World War II. (*Author's photograph.*)

The Spirit of American Youth Rising from the Waves, Normandy American Cemetery and Memorial, Colleville-sur-Mer, France. (*Author's photograph.*)

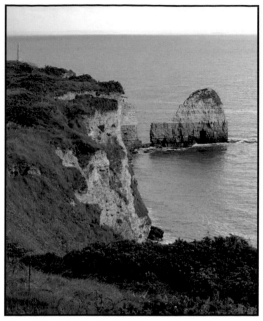

The cliffs of Pointe du Hoc, France. The US Army Rangers scaled these cliffs on June 6, 1944, to take out the German guns that threatened the Allied landing zones. (*Author's photograph.*)

ABOVE: A Thai violinist playing "Colonel Bogey's March" on the Bridge on the River Kwai, Kanchanaburi, Thailand. Over three hundred American POWs died building the Burma Railway. (*Author's photograph.*)

LEFT: Statue of Douglas MacArthur, United States Military Academy, West Point. Douglas MacArthur (1880–1964) returned to the Philippines, occupied Japan, and masterminded the landings at Inchon during the Korean War. "There is no substitute for victory." (*Author's photograph.*)

Battle of Huế, Vietnam. The bullet-riddled walls of the imperial city of Huế bear witness to the site of a major battle between the US Marines and North Vietnamese during the Tet Offensive and the location of a Communist massacre that claimed over three thousand civilian lives in 1968. (*Photo courtesy of Bernie Podurgiel.*)

SR-71, American Air Museum, IWM Duxford, UK. The SR-71 "Blackbird" spy plane, introduced in 1964, flew above Mach 3 at over eighty thousand feet. (*Photograph by Karim Merie.*)

Major Jack Coughlin (USAF, Ret.), who later flew "jingle runs" with a C-130 in Vietnam, standing in front of his T-38 Talon trainer. (*Photo courtesy of Major Jack Coughlin.*)

Statue of Ronald Reagan, Grosvenor Square, London. President Reagan (1911–2004) armed the Mujahideen in Afghanistan, armed the Contras in Nicaragua, and authorized Operation Urgent Fury, which invaded the island of Grenada in 1983. (*Photograph by Karim Merie.*)

Statue of the two Bushes, George W. Bush Library, SMU, Dallas, TX. President George H. W. Bush liberated Kuwait in 1991, and President George W. Bush led invasions of Afghanistan in 2001 and of Iraq and Liberia in 2003. (*Photo courtesy of Vincent Driano.*)

A-10 "Warthog," American Air Museum, IWM Duxford, UK. The A-10 "Warthog" was an effective tank destroyer in both Gulf Wars. (*Author's photograph.*)

National September 11 Memorial & Museum, New York, NY. Today, the 9/11 memorial in Lower Manhattan is a popular site for enlistment and re-enlistment ceremonies for the US military. (*Author's photograph.*)

American eagle over the US embassy, Grosvenor Square, London. (*Photograph by Karim Merie.*)

Liberia was founded by freed slaves who began returning to Africa in the 1820s under the auspices of the American Colonization Society. The first ship to head there had eighty-six settlers on board and was called the *Mayflower of Liberia*. Monrovia, their capital, was named after the fifth US president, James Monroe. The name Liberia means "land of the free," and the Liberian flag is similar to the US flag but with one big white star instead of fifty and only eleven stripes instead of thirteen. For much if its history, Americo-Liberians (Liberians descended from settlers that originally came from America) have played a leading political role.

And for much Liberia's history, the US military has played a leading role there as well.

In fact, the USN played a key role in founding the first Liberian settlement. In 1821, the USS *Crocodile* went looking for suitable land for the colony, and eventually, the USN helped get hold of a stretch of the mainland where the colony would grow.

In November 1843, Matthew Perry (the one later of Japan fame, not the one later of Chandler Bing fame) led another of many US military visits to Liberia as he came ashore with seventy-five sailors and marines in whaleboats at Monrovia in search of information about the murder of two American ship captains. Following that, he then cruised up and down the Liberian coast, showing the US flag to the non–Americo-Liberian locals, landing to talk and accompanied by marines who occasionally had to return fire.

In 1847, Liberia declared independence with a constitution based on the US Constitution and a first president, Joseph Jenkins Roberts, who'd been born in Norfolk, Virginia.

Independence did not mean the end of close connections with the United States. Close links with the USN, for instance, continued. Monrovia became something of a base for the navy's anti-slaving patrols. Not only did they intercept slavers in the area, but they also brought some of the slaves that they freed to live in Liberia.

However, the process of settling Americans in Liberia in some ways replicated the colonial process where white Europeans created colonies in Africa, and it produced some of the same results. The cultural differences between the Americo-Liberians and the indigenous Africans of the area and the political power of the Americo-Liberians over the indigenous Africans caused friction and conflict.

The USG regularly sent the USN to Liberia when tensions led to violence. For instance, in 1876 tensions between the Liberian government and the Grebo peoples erupted into war, and President Ulysses S. Grant sent the USS *Alaska* to help end the war. Again, in 1910, when there was war between the Liberian government and the Grebo people, President William H. Taft sent the USS *Birmingham*.

In 1912, we took over training the Liberian Frontier Force sending black American officers to take charge.

In 1915, the Liberian government got into another war with indigenous people, this time with the Kru, and President Woodrow Wilson sent the USS *Chester* with guns and ammunition for the government.

Liberia eventually declared war on Germany during World War I a few months after we did.

And Liberia was to play a key role in our war effort in World War II. In 1942, we signed a Defense Pact with Liberia, under which we'd get bases and the vital strategic rubber we needed for the war effort and Liberia would get more infrastructure.

We developed the Pan American airbase for transatlantic flights at Roberts Field, and it became a key stop in the air-ferry route that led from Brazil across the Atlantic to Africa and then on to the Middle East and beyond. After the war, it became a major international airport for Liberia. We also developed dock facilities at Monrovia and built roads. Thousands of American military personnel were based in Liberia at the time.

In the decades after World War II, American influence on the Liberian army remained strong, For instance, in 1951, an American military mission was established in Liberia to help train the Liberian military. In the late 1960s, the Liberian chief of staff was Lieutenant General George T. Washington.

In 1980, however, things changed when Master Sergeant Samuel Doe launched a coup and killed President William Tolbert. Doe was from the Krahn people, and his coup marked the end of 133 years of Americo-Liberian domination of Liberia.

Doe managed to remain friends with the United States through the 1980s because of shared strategic interests, but towards the end of the decade, the Cold War was ending, and inside Liberia, things were starting to fall apart. Ahead lay almost a decade and a half of instability and brutal civil war that would tear the old Liberia apart and even suck in neighboring countries.

The Liberian civil war of 1989–1996 was started by a rebellion led by Charles Taylor against the government of Samuel Doe. This conflict claimed the lives of more than two hundred thousand Liberians, including Doe, and saw horrific atrocities.

During this war, US forces were sent in a number of times to protect US citizens and interests. In 1990, an assault ship, USS *Saipan*, was sent to Liberia, and US marines were sent ashore to help evacuate 330 US citizens and others. In 1996, the USS *Guam* was dispatched to assist in the evacuation of forty-nine US citizens and other foreign nationals from the US embassy in Monrovia.

In September 1996, a peace deal was patched up among assorted militias, and in 1997, Charles Taylor won elections. But the instability did not stop.

For instance, in September 1998, fighting broke out between fighters loyal to Roosevelt Johnson and some of Taylor's forces. President Clinton again sent troops to Monrovia to protect US citizens from the political instability in Liberia.

In 1999, the civil war resumed, bringing again atrocities and large-scale killing. Finally in 2003, the Special Court for Sierra Leone issued an arrest warrant for Taylor over activities in neighboring Sierra Leone, and the US Congress also decided to offer a two-million-dollar bounty for Taylor's arrest. In June, President George W. Bush sent more troops to reinforce the US embassy in Monrovia, and in August, the UN Security Council authorized the dispatch of a multi-national force to Liberia. We sent in Joint Task Force Liberia, the USS *Iwo Jima*, and the Iwo Jima Amphibious Ready Group with the 26th Marine Expeditionary Unit. On August 14, marines stormed ashore to capture Roberts International Airport (which saw so much US activity during World War II) and the Freeport of Monrovia. Nigerian forces were also airlifted into Monrovia. Charles Taylor was forced into exile where he remains to this day. In 2012, Taylor was convicted of multiple war crimes in The Hague.

Since 2005, the US military has done extensive work in Liberia with the aim of totally reforming and reconstructing the Armed Forces of Liberia. Recently, the USAF transported Liberian peacekeepers to Mali. The Michigan National Guard is partnered with Liberia.

LIBYA

IT'S NOT GOING TO COME AS NEWS TO MANY AMERICANS that we've been at war in Libya, but not everyone will know what a long history of conflict in the country we have.

In 1801, Tripoli (now capital of Libya; then, with its surrounding territory, a sort of state on its own) became the first nation to declare war on the United States, although obviously (after the Revolution and the failed British attempt to crush it) not the first to make war on it. Yussef Karamanli, pasha, of Tripoli, had his minions chop down the flagpole at the US consulate in Tripoli. Not the most subtle method of expressing your displeasure with another country, but one bound to get noticed.

As covered elsewhere in this book (see "Algeria," "Morocco," and "Tunisia"), we had a bit of a pirate problem at the time—or actually quite a lot of a pirate problem. And we weren't alone. Barbary pirates operating from the North African coast had taken over one million European slaves from the sixteenth to the nineteenth century. And between 1785 and 1815, more than six hundred American citizens were captured and enslaved.

We had tried to solve the problem by paying the Barbary States not to seize our ships and our sailors, but finally, Thomas Jefferson had grown weary of paying tribute. Hence the chopped down flagpole. In reply, Jefferson dispatched elements of the tiny USN (six ships in total in 1803) to North Africa to fight the First Barbary War.

In one of the first actions of the war, the USS *Enterprise* (with Lieutenant Sterrett in command, not Captain Kirk) defeated a Tripolitan corsair, not very imaginatively named *Tripoli*.

Things didn't go that smoothly for us early in the war, though. On October 31, 1803, the 36-gun frigate, USS *Philadelphia*, commanded by William Bainbridge, ran aground just off the shore of Tripoli. The frigate and its entire crew of 307 men were captured by the pasha. He put his first ransom demand for the return of the crew at $1.69 million, which was an enormous amount at the time; in fact it was more than the entire United States' military budget then.

US honor was rescued, and the pasha was prevented from using our own ship against us, however, by what we would now call a daring commando night raid on February 16, 1804, in which Lieutenant Decatur and a small band of marines on board a captured Tripolitan boat crept into the harbor and set light to the *Philadelphia*.

Now Jefferson sent William Eaton, a former sergeant in the Continental Army, to go on a secret mission to the Barbary Coast. Eaton had also had diplomatic experience serving as the US consul in Tunis. The dispatch of Eaton represented the first occasion in which the US government attempted to overthrow a foreign government by covert means. It would not, of course, be the last time.

One of the most famous incidents in the history of the USMC took place in Libya in 1805. William Eaton led a group of eight marines and a party of mercenaries on a 520-mile march through the desert from Alexandria in Egypt to Derna in Libya. It was at the battle of Derna on April 27, 1805, that Eaton led his men against the pasha's forces in a siege that finally culminated with an assault. Eaton personally led a bayonet charge against a larger foe with Lieutenant Presley O'Bannon by his side. This was the first time the fifteen stars and stripes of the US flag were raised on a foreign shore. It was here that the US Marines famously earned a victory against the pasha on "the shores of Tripoli."

The pasha of Tripoli was now beginning to feel the heat, and not just because a Libyan summer was approaching. With a US land attack on Tripoli now possible, a peace was agreed. After all that, though, Eaton's heroics at Derna were somewhat undercut by a diplomatic deal being done by Tobias Lear who authorized the payment of sixty thousand dollars in ransom for the liberation of the *Philadelphia*'s crew.

The Second Barbary War (see "Algeria") was mainly against Algiers, but in 1815, Decatur, was once again in Tripolitan waters, this time using a show of force to secure a favorable deal from the Tripolitans.

In the century and a half after the Second Barbary War, Libya had plenty of dramatic history going on, but not much of it was to do with us. After the Italo-Turkish war of 1911–1912, for instance, the Italians took over. Then in 1940, Mussolini attempted, very unwisely and very unsuccessfully, to use Libya as a springboard for an invasion of British-controlled Egypt. His forces had to be rescued by Rommel and the Afrika Korps. But in 1942, British and Commonwealth forces, partially equipped by American lend-lease tanks, defeated Rommel's Germans and the Italians at the battle of El Alamein. Axis forces in North Africa surrendered in late 1942.

After the war, Libya came under British and French control for a while, and then it became an independent kingdom.

It seems in some ways hard to believe, after the recent decades of tension between the United States and Libya, but for a long time towards the end of World War II and for many years after, there was a part of Libya that was once a "little America." In 1943, US bombers started operating out of a previously Italian airfield, then called Mellaha Air Base. In 1945, it became known by the name which many Americans still know, Wheelus. The airbase became a hugely important facility for our air force before America finally withdrew from the base in 1970.

It was a time when other major changes were also happening in Libya. In 1969, Muammar Gaddafi came onto the international scene, leading a successful coup against King Idris. Gaddafi is one of those characters who, as they say, needs no introduction. Most Americans will be very well aware of him, so we'll only give some brief examples of our long history of trouble with a man President Ronald Reagan called the "mad dog of the Middle East."

The Gulf of Sidra, claimed by Libya at the time as theirs but regarded by America as largely international waters, was a recurrent source of tension. In an incident on August 19, 1981, a Soviet-built Su-22 fired on USN F-14 Tomcats. Two Su-22s were subsequently shot down. In March 1986, US and Libyan aircraft and ships confronted each other in the Gulf of Sidra again, which resulted in the eventual destruction of a number of Libyan patrol craft. And two more Libyan aircraft were shot down over the Gulf of Sidra in 1989.

The 1986 bombing of a Berlin discotheque killed two US servicemen, was blamed by the USG on Gaddafi, and led to Operation El Dorado Canyon. Eighteen US Air Force F-111 bombers took off from RAF Lakenheath in Suffolk, England, with orders to attack three targets near Tripoli. On April 15, just ten days after the disco bombing, the bombers were to hit a place called Sidi Bilal where Libyan commandos trained, the military part of the Tripoli airport, and the el-Azzizaya barracks. According to a poll taken in the aftermath, 77 percent of the American people approved of the strike on Libya.

In 2011, as first demonstrations and then a rebellion broke out against Gaddafi, the United States and its NATO allies, plus a few other countries, intervened mainly from the air, but with some covert activity on the ground, against Gaddafi's forces.

Winston Churchill once said, "Dictators ride to and fro on tigers from which they dare not dismount. And the tigers are getting hungry." On October 20, 2011, Gaddafi was killed by rebel militiamen in Libya, devoured by the hungry tigers he had been riding for so long.

Violence and anarchy continue to plague Libya at the time of writing. On September 11, 2012, four Americans, including ambassador Christopher Stevens, were killed in an attack on the US consulate in Benghazi, Libya.

In October 2013, a commando raid captured Nazih Abdul-Hamed al-Ruqai in Tripoli.

The United States has been for some time trying to help the Libyan government build a professional army, and in March 2014, small detachments of US troops were sent to Libya to assist with plans for training Libyan soldiers in Bulgaria.

But with the central government still struggling to impose its authority on some parts of the country, in March 2014, USN SEALs were dispatched to the Mediterranean to seize the oil tanker *Morning Glory* that had loaded oil from a port in Eastern Libya and was outside government control. Sailors from the USS *Stout* then went aboard to help take the tanker to a government-controlled Libyan port.

LIECHTENSTEIN

NO, NOT THE POP ARTIST, Roy, this Liechtenstein is the country with its capital Vaduz.

It's a tiny European state, sandwiched between Switzerland and Austria, and OK, we haven't exactly had major military involvement with it, but a few interesting stories are still worth mentioning.

In World War I, though we weren't at war with Liechtenstein, the Allies did blockade it because it was regarded as being too close both geographically and politically to our enemies. For instance, a number of men from Liechtenstein volunteered for the Austrian army. Then, during the Paris Peace Conference in 1919, little Liechtenstein went as far as issuing an ultimatum to the Allied powers. They wanted involvement with the League of Nations negotiations started by President Woodrow Wilson, or they would cut off communications to us. This doesn't at first seem like a massive threat, but at that time, one major route between Paris and Vienna ran through Liechtenstein, so it was a little more serious than it first seemed. Liechtenstein was, in the end considered for League of Nations membership in 1920. And rejected. Some of those opposing its membership raised concerns about its size, how independent it was, and the fact it had no army.

Liechtenstein stayed neutral during World War II and escaped the wounds of war, though the Liechtenstein City Palace in Vienna, which is owned by the Liechtenstein royal family, wasn't quite so lucky. It was hit by a falling American bomber during an air raid. American bombers certainly flew on occasion in the vicinity of Liechtenstein and possibly over it.

However, as with Switzerland, Liechtenstein did see a certain amount of espionage activity linked to America's OSS. Some of this was focused on Vaduz, which was seen as a convenient meeting place with comparatively easy access to the large neutral country of Switzerland and to Austria, then part of Hitler's Reich. In 1945, as part of Operation

Sunrise, negotiations that led to the surrender of German forces in Italy, it is recorded that OSS representatives were dispatched to Buchs on the Swiss/Liechtenstein border.

In the last days of the war, tiny Liechtenstein saw a certain amount of drama, as hundreds of members of the Russian Liberation Army, which had at times fought alongside the Germans, marched into Liechtenstein and allowed themselves to be interned there, rather than be captured by the Allies and face being sent to Russia and Stalin's revenge.

And at almost the same time, US troops occupied territory around the borders of Liechtenstein, including setting up base at Feldkirch, just a couple of miles from the Liechtenstein border. In the chaos of the period, it seems hard to believe that at some stage American troops did not cross the border, even if unintentionally. The Swiss Army has demonstrated on more than one occasion how easy it is to get confused about tiny Liechtenstein's borders. In the most recent incident, in 2007, about 170 soldiers managed to wander across the unmarked border and penetrate over a mile into Liechtenstein before they realized their mistake and returned to Swiss soil.

At least one GI crossed into Liechtenstein in 1945 in uniform, though he did it intentionally because he was visiting his family. Konrad Sele had left Liechtenstein for Los Angeles in 1929. When he returned in 1945 as an American soldier, his German-speaking had fallen somewhat out of use, and his sister had some trouble communicating with him.

LITHUANIA

LITHUANIA IS THE MOST SOUTHERN OF THE THREE BALTIC STATES with its capital at Vilnius, an ancient and historic city (incidentally the target of Teutonic Knight Crusaders in the fourteenth century).

And the fictional Captain Marko Aleksandrovich Ramius, played by Sean Connery in the film *Hunt for Red October*, was Lithuanian.

On February 16, 1918, while World War I was still raging, the Council of Lithuania declared an independent Lithuania. In the aftermath of World War I, US Brigadier General Sherwood Cheney, as part of an inter-Allied Commission, helped remove German troops from Lithuania. The United States recognized Lithuania officially in 1922.

We also had a certain amount of involvement in the Klaipėda crisis of 1923. Klaipėda, or in German, Memel, is now a key port in Lithuania, but at the end of World War I, it had a significant German population, and it had been placed under League of Nations mandate while it was decided who should control it. Lithuania was anxious to secure this vital port, and Lithuanians in the Klaipėda region eventually rebelled and seized control. Lithuanian Americans assisted this process, and US diplomat Norman Davis eventually chaired a three-member international commission that awarded control of Klaipėda to Lithuania.

On June 15, 1940, the Red Army invaded Lithuania. The Wehrmacht would invade and occupy Lithuania from the summer of 1941 until its "liberation" by the Soviets in 1944. Lithuanians served in both armies in the war, and nearly two hundred thousand Lithuanian Jews were liquidated by the Nazis.

During the German occupation, Stalag Luft 6 was located in Heydekrug (now Silute), Lithuania. Over two thousand American USAAF airmen were imprisoned there during the war. Several were killed in Lithuania while trying to escape.

From 1944 to 1953, a partisan group called the Forest Brothers fought a bitter guerilla war in all three Baltic states against their Soviet occupiers. Thousands of Lithuanians were killed, and many more were deported to Siberia. The Forest Brothers received a small amount of covert aid from the CIA as well as MI6 and Swedish intelligence. In 1950, for example, a Lithuania named Juozas Lukša, who had already fought both Germans and Soviets, was trained by the CIA in West Germany and parachuted by C-47 into Lithuania. He was eventually captured and killed in 1951.

On March 11, 1990, Lithuania became the first republic to break away from the former Soviet Union.

Our closest military links with Lithuania have been in recent years. Lithuania joined NATO in 2004, along with her Baltic sister states. Lithuanian forces have served alongside American and Western forces in Iraq and Afghanistan. There have been regular visits by the US military— for instance, in 2009 the USS *Mount Whitney*, flagship of the US 6th Fleet, paid a call on Klaipeda in Lithuania. And we have offered Lithuania military assistance in a number of different areas, for instance, recently advising them on the development of their airpower capabilities. The Pennsylvania National Guard is partnered with Lithuania.

During the Crimea crisis in 2014, US fighter jets were dispatched to Lithuania to send a message to Russia, and US troops were sent there to take part in NATO exercises.

LUXEMBOURG

NOT EXACTLY AMONG THE BIGGEST AND BEST-KNOWN COUNTRIES in the world (except in the financial world where this little country is big), but yes, we've invaded it.

The motto of the grand duchy of Luxembourg, one of the tiniest countries in the world, is, *"Mir wëlle bleiwe wat mir sinn,"* or "We want to remain what we are." They seem to have done this remarkably well because it's one of those European micro-states, like Andorra, Monaco, Liechtenstein, and San Marino, that has managed to last until the present day without being permanently swallowed up by any of their much, much larger neighbors.

In World War I, Luxembourg was occupied by the Germans. With the Germans withdrawing rapidly towards the end of the war, the US 33rd Infantry Division ended up, on November 11, 1918, at Stenay, about twenty-five miles from the Luxembourg border. But it did enter Luxembourg after the war, and for instance, in March 1919, the division headquarters were to be found at Diekirch in Luxembourg.

Hitler invaded tiny neutral Luxembourg in the spring of 1940 as part of his campaign against France.

On September 10, 1944, the US 5th Armored Division liberated Luxembourg City (not surprisingly the capital of the country Luxembourg) from German control. However, this wasn't exactly the end of the battle. Hitler chose to launch his counterattack, the Battle of the Bulge, through the northern part of Luxembourgish territory in December 1944, meaning parts of Luxembourg had to be liberated all over again. The area around Wiltz, for instance, saw very heavy fighting. And American forces were in the Diekirch area again. It was the scene on the night of January 18, 1845, of the famous crossing of the River Sauer by the US 5th Infantry Division.

Not all Americans were having such a rough time in Luxembourg, though. On December 17, 1944, Ernest Hemingway arrived in Luxembourg as a war correspondent for *Collier's* magazine and was put up in the old mill of Abbé Nicolas Didier. While there, he found the Abbé's wine cellar, drained several bottles, and proceeded to urinate into them, subsequently giving them the label of Schloss Hemingstein. However, one night in the darkness, he grabbed a bottle, only to find himself having to rapidly spit out, yep, a mouthful his own Schloss Hemingstein.

On December 9, 1945, General George Patton was involved in an automobile accident whose injuries eventually killed him. Feeling that it was appropriate for soldiers to rest on the fields where they fell, Patton had insisted his body should not be returned to the United States. He also insisted that his nineteen-year-old military chauffeur not be punished on account of the accident. General Patton, the commander of US Third Army, is buried amongst over five thousand other American military personnel in Luxembourg.

Luxembourg today is an active NATO member and longstanding ally of the United States. Interestingly, despite the fact Luxembourg is tiny and therefore has tiny military forces, NATO's AWACS fleet is registered in Luxembourg.

MACEDONIA

A Balkan country that's a little bigger than Vermont, Macedonia is partnered with the Vermont National Guard.

Allied forces did advance into what is now the modern country of Macedonia in the final campaign of World War I, but our troops were busy elsewhere.

In World War II, however, we had more to do with the area militarily. The USAAF bombed assorted targets in the area. For instance, on October 18, 1943, US bombers attacked railway targets in and around Skopje, now Macedonia's capital. And again on January 24, 1944, B-24s from the Fifteenth Air Force, escorted by P-38 Lightnings, bombed targets in and around Skopje, including the airfield. But we were also flying in supplies and personnel to the partisans then operating in the area. This could be a difficult job. Even apart from the threat from German forces, other problems could arise. For instance, in late 1944, on one airstrip near Skopje, twenty oxen were needed to pull a C-47 out of a bomb crater.

From 1944 onwards, the area was part of Tito's Communist Yugoslavia, so for a long time, our military links with the area were few and far between. However, on July 26, 1963, an earthquake flattened much of Skopje killing thousands. The USAF rushed to help, flying in whole field hospitals and other emergency supplies.

In 1991, the break-up of Yugoslavia started, and soon Macedonia was to emerge as an independent country. But in a region where several countries were torn apart by war, the new country of Macedonia faced some major challenges, and we tried to help the new country survive them. In 1993, President Clinton sent 350 troops to assist the UN Protection Force there and help maintain stability. And more US troops arrived in 1994. Camp Able Sentry was established near Skopje Airport. And even though its UN function ceased in 1999, Camp Able Sentry stayed because another international crisis had erupted nearby. When the Kosovo crisis erupted between NATO and Serbia in 1999, Macedonia allowed NATO to conduct some activity from Macedonia.

And trouble was about to erupt in Macedonia as well. After the Albanian rebellion against Serbia in Kosovo, a rebellion broke out in 2001 among Macedonia's Albanian minority. A compromise was reached a few months later with the Ohrid Agreement, and NATO moved in to enforce the deal first with the Task Force Essential Harvest collecting weapons and then Amber Fox and Allied Harmony. US forces played a part, for instance, in providing air transport.

In recent years, the United States and Macedonian militaries have developed close links, and Macedonia has sent troops to Iraq and Afghanistan.

MADAGASCAR

IT'S THE FOURTH LARGEST ISLAND IN THE WORLD (and, yes, a number of popular cartoon movies featured the name Madagascar), but the island also has a fascinating history, heritage, and culture.

Our earliest armed connection with Madagascar comes from even before the United States existed. In the late seventeenth and early eighteenth centuries, Madagascar was a key port of call for assorted American pirates and privateers, including John Halsey and William May, operating in the Indian Ocean. Thomas Tew, a pirate from Rhode Island, had close links to Madagascar and a base there. He is even said to have had a son with a local princess, a son who went on to create a kingdom on the island. And American pirate Nathaniel North lost his ship near Sainte-Marie Island off Madagascar when he was cornered by four British warships.

In the nineteenth century, we still took a certain amount of interest in Madagascar, as assorted Western powers competed for influence over the island. In the 1860s, for instance, we signed a trade agreement with

Queen Rasoherina, and at one stage, the USS *Juniata* was dispatched from our Pacific squadron to Madagascar to reconnoiter French moves on the island. In 1884, USN Lieutenant Mason A. Shufeldt marched across western Madagascar, across parts nobody from Europe or America had visited, with a small army of locals and soldiers, fighting off assorted attacks until he reached the sea. In 1887, the USS *Alliance* arrived at Madagascar investigating suggestions American-flagged ships had been transporting slaves from East Africa to Madagascar and other islands.

It was the French who ultimately became the Western power dominating the island, which meant that in 1942, with Vichy France in control of Madagascar, strategically located near vital Allied supply routes, the Allies had a problem. The result was the British invasion of Madagascar in that year, Operation Ironclad. Now we didn't play much of a role in that, at least not openly, but it is interesting to note that almost as soon as the invasion was complete and successful, we sent in people to start shipping graphite from Madagascar to America as a crucial component of the project to create eventually an atomic bomb. The first nuclear chain reacting pile was built towards the end of 1942 and used four hundred tons of graphite. The second was built in the spring of 1943 with the first graphite shipment from Madagascar. Some have even suggested the acquisition of this graphite was at least one of the motives for the invasion in the first place.

We did have a NASA tracking station on the island until the 1970s, but then the friendship between the US and Madagascar governments went through a bad period, and among other measures, Madagascar closed the tracking station.

In 2007, the USS *Normandy* became the first USN ship to visit Madagascar since 1972, and the dock-landing ship USS *Ashland* followed that up with another visit the year after. However, in 2009, a change of government that the United States considers a military coup d'état occurred.

MALAWI

MALAWI IS A LITTLE COUNTRY IN CENTRAL AFRICA with a big, big lake. The lake, called, not surprisingly, Lake Malawi, takes up about a fifth of the country. It had one-party rule from 1966 through 1994. Malawi is best known to many Americans as the source of several Madonna adoptions.

Malawi's not been an area of major US military involvement, but we have had a few links.

For instance, Medreach 2011 was an exercise to help the US and Malawian military cooperate on medical and humanitarian matters. We've also built a transit base at Malawi Armed Forces College in Salima that's capable of taking an entire battalion as the US military trains them in peacekeeping technique. For, example we trained Malawian peacekeepers for their mission in Ivory Coast, and Malawian peacekeepers have served recently in the Democratic Republic of the Congo and helped defeat the M23 rebel group that had destabilized a large area of the country.

MALAYSIA

THE AMAZING LAND OF MALAYSIA has not been one of the areas where we've been most involved militarily, but an American diplomat did run part of it for a while.

Claude Lee Moses was appointed consul general in Brunei in 1864. And at that stage, the sultan of Brunei controlled significantly more territory than he does now, including a big chunk of north Borneo, which C. L. Moses proceeded to lease from him. However, things didn't quite go to plan for Moses on the commercial front, and the sultan leased the lands to someone else. Eventually, after a couple of others taking up the lease, a Briton took control there, and eventually the area became firmly within the British sphere of influence.

We have had military involvement there as well. For instance, during World War II when it was occupied by the Japanese, we flew many missions against targets connected with the Japanese war machine there. For example, in October 1944, fifteen B-24s mined the inner approaches to Penang. And on March 10, 1945, twenty-four B-29s of the Twentieth Air Force bombed the marshalling yards at Kuala Lumpur, now the capital of Malaysia.

In 1963, border tensions mounted between Malaysia and Indonesia. The British helped the Malaysians resist pressure from their neighbors, but we took some measures during the crisis as well.

Over the years, the United States has developed extensive links with the Malaysian military, including training and many exchanges, joint exercises, and visits. For instance, in June 2013, US marines and sailors conducted amphibious assault training with Malaysian forces at Batu Beach, Pahang, in Malaysia. Malaysia and the United States have cooperated extensively in the war against terror. And Malaysia sent a small number of military personnel, including doctors and paramedics, to Afghanistan.

Recently, US ships and planes have helped search for Malaysia Airlines' Flight 370 that was lost in March 2014.

THE MALDIVES

THE MALDIVES IS A NATION OF CORAL ATOLLS in the Indian Ocean containing some superbly beautiful islands. The Maldives also has the lowest elevation of any nation on earth, six feet or less above sea level. It's situated south of India and west of Sri Lanka.

We made regular use of the British airbase on Gan Island and at one stage after the British temporarily abandoned it in March 1945. American B-25s that used it occasionally seem to have had it much to themselves. At one time in the 1960s, there was even discussion of the USAF and USN making more permanent use of the facilities, but in 1971, we started work on our major base at Diego Garcia a few hundred miles away.

We also had an army air force weather detachment based in the Maldives during World War II.

And American ships have regularly called in on the Maldives. It's possible some of the colonial-era American pirates and privateers active in the Indian Ocean in the pre-1776 period may have visited here, and certainly the USN has been a regular visitor. For instance, the USS *Momsen*, the USS *Russell*, the USS *Dubuque*, and the USS *Higgins* have all visited the Maldives. Obviously a popular venue.

We have also conducted some training of Maldivian forces and conducted exercises with them. For instance, in 2012 American boots returned to Gan, as US marines trained with marines of the Maldivian National Defence Force in Exercise Coconut Grove.

There has recently been speculation over a possible Status of Forces Agreement between the United States and the Maldives and a possible expansion of US military involvement in the islands, but very little is definite.

MALI

A LARGE LANDLOCKED AFRICAN COUNTRY that's been linked to some mighty African empires (Ghana, Malinké, and Songhai), Mali has also been a bit in the news in recent years. And, yes, we've been involved.

In the period after 9/11 and as fears began to grow about extremist Islamist activity in the area, US Special Forces started training Malian troops as part of the War on Terror. Special Forces Training Teams from Special Operations Command Europe were at one stage located at Bamako, Gao, and Timbuktu helping train Malian troops to protect the country's borders against any attempted incursions.

However, by 2012, despite US assistance with training, the Malian government was facing major problems in the north of the country. Simmering discontent among the Tuaregs there, which had already resulted in conflict, led to the outbreak of fresh rebellion in January 2012 with Tuareg rebels fighting for an independent state they call Azawad. Some of those fighting were Tuaregs who had fought for Gaddafi in Libya and after his death had headed for Mali, battle-hardened and well-armed.

The situation became more complex with extreme Islamist groups, including Ansar Dine and al-Qaeda in the Maghreb operating increasingly openly and expanding their influence.

Then suddenly in March 2012, the crisis became even worse. A coup in Bamako, the capital, led to chaos and the virtual collapse of the Malian army's resistance to the opposing forces in the north. They seized their opportunity and started advancing south taking major cities, like Gao and Timbuktu. In a short time, the Malian government lost control of virtually the entire northern half of the country, and in the following months, as fighting broke out between the Tuareg rebel movement and extreme Islamists, the extreme Islamists took control.

In January 2013, Islamist forces lurched forward, taking Konna only about four hundred miles from Bamako. In response, France, the former colonial power in the country, rapidly launched a major international intervention to prevent the fall of Bamako and counter the Islamist assault. The United States played a significant role in it. For instance, we shared intelligence with the French. USAF C-17s flew into Mali hundreds of French troops and hundreds of tons of equipment. And the USAF flew in contingents from other countries willing to assist in the international effort and flew a large number of refueling missions, with KC-135 Stratotankers of the 100th Air Refueling Wing operating out of RAF Mildenhall in the UK to help French fighter aircraft in their sorties supporting French ground troops.

The international effort forced the Islamists to retreat and rapidly pushed them out of large areas and a number of major towns and cities that they had previously held.

MALTA

NESTLING IN THE MEDITERRANEAN, Malta is almost as close to Africa as it is to Europe. Naturally, Malta's people share links with people on the African mainland to the south, yet it's long been linked to Europe and is now part of the EU. The biggest island of the group is, not surprisingly, called Malta. The second largest is called Gozo, which sounds a bit like one of the Marx Brothers but obviously isn't.

Malta has a key strategic location at the center of the Mediterranean. Look at that map again, and you'll see that it's slap bang in the middle of the sea channel that runs between Sicily and Africa. The only way between the Western Med and the Eastern Med runs past Malta. Good for Malta from a trade point of view; often a liability for foreign powers wanting to turn up and conquer it.

Largely due to this outstandingly attractive strategic location, Malta has had a long, fascinating, and often bloody military history, including involvement in the Punic Wars between Carthage and Rome (sitting where it is between North Africa and Sicily, it could hardly avoid involvement, really), the Great Siege of Malta (not so great for the besieging Ottoman Turks who lost or even for the defending Knights Hospitaller who won, but at a cost), and a visit from Napoleon (the French took control briefly, and then the Maltese with British help chucked them out).

We've not had that much to do with Malta's long and fascinating history, but we have had a little. Ships from Teddy Roosevelt's Great White Fleet called in here in 1909, and during World War I, Valetta, Malta's main city, was something of a base for American subchasers operating in the Mediterranean and escorting convoys in the area.

But it was the Second World War that was to bring one of Malta's most distinguished historical periods, and it's also perhaps the era when we've had most to do militarily with this small and beautiful island nation.

Once again, it was Malta's strategic location between Sicily and Africa that put it in the firing line. This time it wasn't the Romans and Carthaginians who were the key players; it was the Italians and Germans on one side and the Brits and Commonwealth, with some American help, on the other. With World War II raging across North Africa and with Rommel's eyes fixed on the largely British-controlled Middle East, Malta sat astride some pretty vital supply lines. It controlled the British sea route into the Eastern Med, and at the same time, it was in the part of the Med the Germans and Italians needed to send supplies to their men fighting the Brits in North Africa. And with Malta only about sixty miles from the Italian island of Sicily but a lot, lot further from Britain, Malta was highly vulnerable to air attack.

The Axis siege of Malta lasted from Mussolini's declaration of war on June 10, 1940, until Italy surrendered and joined the allies in the summer of 1943. During this time, Malta was subjected to the most intense and prolonged bombing of any part of the planet during the Second World War, and we provided vital assistance to Malta's brave defenders. For instance, in April and again in May of 1942, the USS *Wasp* ferried Spitfires and their pilots. Winston Churchill himself rang up the captain of the USS *Wasp* and said, "Many thanks to you all for your timely help. Who said a Wasp couldn't sting twice?" Not a bad joke considering how much pressure the British prime minister was under at the time.

Also the SS *Ohio* was an American-built (though English crewed) ship that was part of the critical convoy called Operation Pedestal and has been called "the tanker that saved Malta." Hit by numerous bombs and torpedoes, it barely managed to reach Valletta Harbor delivering her precious cargo of aviation fuel. Other American ships, including the SS *Santa Elisa*, also took part, along with their American crews in the campaign to supply Malta.

And flying in the defense of Malta was one Art Roscoe, a twenty-one-year old Californian. He had longed to fly but had slight astigmatism in one eye and was turned down by the US military. So instead he joined one of the American Eagle squadrons of the RAF and was trained as a Spitfire pilot in Essex. Transferred to Malta, he became a decorated RAF ace. He was shot down by cannon fire from an ME-109 in October 1942 but managed to survive the crash and the war.

After the siege of Malta lifted in 1943, there was a flood of American troops and officers into Malta. Italy had failed to beat the defenders of Malta; now it was time to strike at Italy. In June of 1943, General Eisenhower, commander-in-chief of Allied Forces North Africa, planned Operation

Husky, the invasion of Sicily, from his headquarters in the Lascaris War Rooms, an amazing underground complex in Valetta.

FDR paid two visits to the plucky island once in December of 1943 and again for the Malta Conference with Churchill in February 1945. On December 7, 1943, the second anniversary of Pearl Harbor, while in Malta, FDR declared:

> *In the name of the people of the United States of America, I salute the Island of Malta, its people and defenders, who, in the cause of freedom and justice and decency throughout the world, have rendered valorous service far above and beyond the call of duty.*
>
> *Under repeated fire from the skies, Malta stood alone, but unafraid in the center of the sea, one tiny bright flame in the darkness—a beacon of hope for the clearer days which have come.*
>
> *Malta's bright story of human fortitude and courage will be read by posterity with wonder and with gratitude through all the ages.*
>
> *What was done in this Island maintains the highest traditions of gallant men and women who from the beginning of time have lived and died to preserve civilization for all mankind.*

Malta became independent on September 21, 1964, and the Royal Navy base was withdrawn in 1979. Today, Malta is a member of the European Union. USN ships often visit and Maltese military personnel have taken part alongside US military personnel in training exercises.

MARSHALL ISLANDS

THE MARSHALL ISLANDS ARE NAMED AFTER BRITISH EXPLORER John Marshall, who turned up there in 1799. The Germans took colonial control of the islands and the people who lived there in 1885 but lost the islands to the Japanese in World War I when Japan was on the Allied side.

On February 1, 1944, as part of the island-hopping campaign, US troops landed on Kwajalein Atoll in the Marshalls. Their arrival had been preceded by a devastating bombardment from sea and air that included fourteen-inch shells and B-24 Liberators. The result was a pockmarked lunar landscape. One person who saw it suggested it looked as if the whole island had been taken up to twenty thousand feet and then dropped. Resistance was, despite this, still sometimes fierce, but within a few days, Kwajalein had been taken.

Other islands were next. Eniwetok Island was invaded on February 19 and had been taken by the twenty-first. Parry Island was captured on February 22.

However, our forces didn't take all the Marshalls at this point. Japanese forces remained in control of Jaluit, Wotje, and Maloelap until September 1945.

In the areas we did take in early 1944, however, we rapidly set about building naval and airbases.

After World War II, the United States took administrative control of the Marshall Islands as part of the Trust Territory of the Pacific Islands. And parts of the Marshalls were to become even more famous, in particular Bikini and Eniwetok Atolls, with those nuclear explosions.

In 1986, the Marshall Islands became independent under a Compact of Free Association with the United States. Under the compact, the United States is responsible for the defense of the islands. The United States has use of the US Army Kwajalein Atoll missile range. Many Marshallese have volunteered for the US military. Operation Christmas Drop where the USAF delivers food, supplies, and toys around the holidays (see "Micronesia"), has also visited the Marshall Islands, as has Pacific Partnership.

MAURITANIA

NO, NOT THE *LUSITANIA*'S SISTER SHIP (that was the *Mauretania* with an *e*); Mauritania is the African country situated to the north of Senegal and to the west of Mali.

During World War II, we had an airbase in Mauritania. The USAAF Air Transport Command used Atar Airport as a link in various supply routes, particularly in the period after Operation Torch, the American and British invasion of North Africa.

In 1960, we were the first nation to recognize Mauritania's independence from France, and in more recent times, we have had additional, if somewhat limited, military involvement there.

For instance, on June 8, 2003, there was a coup attempt in Mauritania, and on June 9, President George W. Bush announced he had sent about thirty combat-equipped US troops to Mauritania to help protect the embassy in Nouakchott, the capital, and to evacuate American citizens.

The rise of jihadist groups in the region has added to the strategic importance of Mauritania and increased its attractions for anyone interested in counterterrorism operations and surveillance. For instance, in 2004, US forces were once again at Atar. This time they were US Special Forces training Mauritanian troops as part of the War on Terror.

There have been official military encounters of other types in recent years, for example, when the HSV-2 *Swift* visited Nouakchott in 2009 for discussions with the Mauritanian navy.

MAURITIUS

AN ISLAND NATION IN THE INDIAN OCEAN, Mauritius has some really beautiful places to visit, and we had a consulate there as early as 1794.

Not surprising, considering its location, USN ships have often called in and continue to do so. For instance, a comparatively early visit was one by the USS *Dolphin* in the winter of 1848–49. After being hit by bad weather on its passage around the Cape of Good Hope, it had to spend a month in Mauritius being repaired before resuming its journey. As much more recent examples, the guided-missile frigate *Samuel B. Roberts* paid a goodwill visit (no repairs needed) to Mauritius in 2011, and the guided-missile destroyer USS *McFaul* paid a visit in 2012.

US military aircraft have also visited the island. For instance, in January 1980, after a devastating cyclone had hit the island, a USAF C-141 of the 86th Military Airlift Squadron was rushed to Mauritius with emergency supplies for the islanders.

In 1991, the Mauritian government agreed to participate in the US International Military Education and Training Program, so Mauritian officers could get US training. And in recent years, the United States has seen Mauritius as an important partner in tackling Indian Ocean piracy. So, for instance, in August 2011, sailors from East African coast guards and navies and from the United States could all be found in Mauritius training aboard two Mauritian coast guard vessels.

Mauritius claims sovereignty over the Chagos Islands, including Diego Garcia, on which we have a huge military base.

MEXICO

AH, MEXICO, A LAND SO CLOSELY LINKED to the United States by history, by geography, and by people.

Most Americans know that US troops have seen action on Mexican soil, but there are many less well-known facts about our military involvements with our southern neighbor.

After gaining its independence from Spain in 1821, Mexico was a sprawling nation, twice as large as it is today, stretching from its present borders up through the western third of what is now the United States. Mexican administration of these sparsely populated lands was often weak, unstable, and vulnerable.

The Comanche had often been allies of the Spanish colonial authorities against the Apaches, and these links had been profitable for the Comanche. The newly established Mexican authorities didn't have the money to keep paying the Comanche, who, under pressure from tribes and settlers from the East, saw opportunity in the weakness of the Mexican authorities. The Comanche launched a long series of raids into Mexican territory in search of livestock and captives. In 1852, they even got as far south as the Mexican state of Jalisco, south of Baja California. And they weren't alone in challenging the recent Mexican nation.

In 1836, the Texas Revolution broke out as Mexican authorities and settlers from the United States struggled for control of the area. Notable during this contest was Mexico's Napoleon, General Antonio de Padua María Severino López de Santa Anna y Pérez de Lebrón, better known as Santa Anna. Born of European descent in Veracruz, he was first a Spanish Nationalist, then a revolutionary, a general, a dictator, and eleven-time president of Mexico. He led the siege of the Alamo, attacking and offering no quarter; he also ordered the massacre of Texan prisoners at Goliad. Ultimately, Santa Anna was defeated by Sam Houston at the brief but decisive battle of San Jacinto. The American government and its military did not directly participate in the Texas Revolution, though many of its leaders were American (e.g., Jim Bowie, Davy Crockett, William Travis, and Sam Houston).

We played a very minor part in the Pastry War (NOT a Monty Python sketch!) between Mexico and France, which broke out in 1839. Monsieur Remontel, a French pastry cook, claimed that his shop in Mexico had been looted and wrecked. The French government, which was also pretty unhappy with Mexico over some multi-million-dollar loans, sent in some warships. A brief war ensued. In the chaos surrounding the war, the US schooner *Woodbury* was sent to protect US ships from Mexican privateers, but it ended up colliding with a French warship and had to put into Veracruz for repairs.

In 1845, just prior to James Polk's inauguration, President John Tyler annexed Texas to form the twenty-eighth state in the Union. And this set the stage for the Mexican-American War of 1846–48.

In 1845, Polk dispatched John Slidell as minister-designate to Mexico City to purchase Mexican territory in the West for the sum of twenty-five million dollars. He was rebuffed. So Polk, not about to take a rebuff for an answer, dispatched Zachary Taylor, a Whig general, with an army of about thirty-five hundred men to Fort Brown, Texas, on the Rio Grande near the Gulf coast.

Polk's order to Taylor of January 13, 1846, indicated that the United States was not intending to go to war with Mexico but, if Mexico declared war or acted hostilely, then operations should not be limited to the defensive. Thus the president of the United States delegated to a field commander the decision as to whether a state of war existed between Mexico and the United States.

The Thornton skirmish was the spark that ignited the powder. On April 25, 1846, a reconnaissance patrol led by Captain Thornton ran into and was defeated by a Mexican force of two thousand men near Brownsville, Texas.

It might seem surprising, but the Mexican-American War was the costliest war for the United States in terms of percentage of casualties versus participants — 13,768 died out of the 104,556 that served. Many of these casualties were due to sickness and disease as the Americans won nearly every engagement of the war and occupied Mexico City. At the Mexico City National Cemetery, you will find the graves of 750 unknown Americans who perished in the Mexican-American War and are buried in a common grave.

The war was by no means popular with everybody, and it produced a vigorous anti-war movement. Henry David Thoreau refused to pay taxes and spent a night in jail over his opposition to the war. The Whig politician Henry Clay, whose son Lieutenant Colonel Henry Clay Jr. was killed at the battle of Buena Vista (an American victory), led the political opposition to the war calling it "needless, wicked and wrong." The Illinois congressman Abraham Lincoln would follow his political icon Henry Clay ("my beau ideal of a statesman") in opposition to "Polk's War."

Rio Grande to raid settlements in Texas and US troops would cross into Mexico in pursuit of them. Porfirio Diaz, who became president in 1876, attempted to modernize Mexico and to police its borders. He also opened up Mexico to foreign investment with Americans taking control of some key assets. Ulysses S. Grant, the reluctant warrior of the Mexican-American War, became the first president of the Mexican Southern Railroad.

From 1891 through 1893, Catarino Garza, a Mexican national who had been married (then divorced) to a Texan and lived in Texas, ignited the Garza Revolution. A series of raids were launched from Texas into Coahaila, Mexico. The US Army and, especially, cavalry worked in conjunction with Mexican forces to fight and capture the rebels. Eventually in 1895, Garza was killed while storming a jail in another revolutionary uprising in Colombia.

In 1908, America's Great White Fleet called in at Magdalena Bay on its epic voyage around the world.

Then the Mexican Revolution began in 1910 with the deposition of Diaz and resulted in near anarchy in the country.

In September 1913, marines from the transport *Buffalo* briefly landed in Ciaris Estero to rescue US citizens.

Woodrow Wilson, even though he had denounced the interventionist policies of his Republican predecessors as "gunboat diplomacy," intervened multiple times in Mexico. In the fall of 1913, he is even recorded telling the secretary of the British ambassador to the United States: "I am going to teach the South American republics to elect good men!" It was hardly the most anti-interventionist of stances, and Wilson refused to recognize the Huerta regime in Mexico.

After the arrest and brief detention of a party of visiting USN seamen in Tampico, Wilson had his pretext. US warships, including the newly commissioned dreadnought *Texas*, were dispatched to shell Veracruz and occupy the port with US marines. American losses at Veracruz were seventeen killed and sixty-three wounded, while about 126 Mexicans were killed. Mexican newspapers denounced the American occupation of Veracruz as an "international crime."

Wilson intervened again in Mexico in 1916, this time to strike at Pancho Villa, a notorious bandit leader who had launched a series of raids along the US-Mexico border. Brigadier General John Pershing was sent to lead the Punitive Expedition from New Mexico into Chihuahua. Pershing was a tough veteran of Indian wars and the Moro uprising in the Philippines (see "Philippines"), who would later lead the American Expeditionary Forces in World War I. A young George S. Patton Jr., whose attractive sister Nita was dating the widower Pershing, was detailed to Pershing's staff.

Pancho Villa, as it turned out, proved to be somewhat elusive, but Patton, leading a small patrol, participated in a skirmish at San Miguelito in which three Villistas were killed. When about fifty Villistas approached the hacienda, Patton beat a hasty retreat with the three dead men strapped across his automobile hood. Patton was promoted to first lieutenant.

Among assorted other actions during this chaotic period was the Battle of Ambos Nogales on August 27, 1918. This dispute at a border post at Nogales led to American troops fighting their way into the Mexican border town, and subsequently, a permanent border barrier was erected at Nogales.

In the 1930s, FDR initiated the Good Neighbor Policy, which attempted to normalize links with Mexico and other Latin American nations. This policy bore fruit in World War II when Mexico, after Mexican ships were sunk by German U-boats, joined the Allied cause and fought alongside Americans against the Axis from 1942 to 1945. A Mexican expeditionary force even formed an air squadron, often known by its nickname, the Aztec Eagles, that was attached to the 58th Fighter Group of the USAAF, which saw action in Luzon in 1945.

Some military links continued during the period after World War II with, for instance, some Mexican officers receiving US counter-insurgency training.

And, of course, in recent years the United States has been actively helping Mexican police and military forces in their war on the drug cartels. The Merida Initiative, for security collaboration between the USG and Mexico in the drug war has cost over a billion dollars with mixed results.

MICRONESIA

THE FEDERATED STATES OF MICRONESIA, its proper title, consists of the states, or island groups, of Yap, Chuuk, Pohnpei, and Kosrae.

The islands had a complex experience of European colonialism. The Spanish took full control first. They then sold them to the Germans in the late nineteenth century, who didn't get to enjoy them very long because the Japanese, who were on the Allied side in the First World War, won them in that war and were the colonial power in the islands on December 7, 1941.

Chuuk is more familiar to many Americans as Truk, its name until 1990. Truk became a massive Japanese naval and airbase, heavily defended with coastal and anti-aircraft artillery. In some senses it could be regarded at the time as Japan's version of Pearl Harbor as it was a strategic target for us with similar results. On February 17, 1944, in Operation Hailstone, a massive US naval and air assault lasting three days devastated the Japanese base and sank large numbers of Japanese vessels. More air US air strikes hit Truk in April, and the area was isolated by US forces.

Finally on September 2, 1945, Lieutenant General Shunsaburo Mugikura, commander of the Thirty-first Army, boarded the USS *Portland*, Admiral Murray's flagship, and signed the surrender of his forces, including almost forty thousand men on Truk.

Yap was bombed on many occasions, and also on September 2, 1945, Lieutenant General Sadae Inoue surrendered his forces on Yap to Brigadier General Ford O. Rogers, island commander on Peleliu.

We did, however, take Ulithi Atoll near Yap before the end of the war. US troops landed there in September 1944 after the Japanese abandoned it, and it became a huge US naval base and staging base for other major operations. As such, it also became a major target for the Japanese, who launched a number of different attacks on it, including one by manned Kaiten torpedoes and another by kamikaze aircraft.

Kosrae, too, had a Japanese garrison and handed over control to the USS *Wyman* on September 8, 1945.

Pohnpei, or Ponape as it was formerly known, also had a Japanese garrison on it, and US forces occasionally shelled and bombed it. On September 11, 1945, Lieutenant General Watanabe also boarded the USS *Hyman* to enact the surrender of Ponape, and US troops took control the following day.

After the war, the four island groups became part of the United Nations Trust Territory of the Pacific Islands, administered by the United States. They became independent under a Compact of Free Association with the United States in 1986.

Links between the United States and the Federated States of Micronesia remain strong, and under the Compact of Free Association, we have defense responsibility for Micronesia. Many Micronesians have volunteered to serve in the US military. An opening ceremony in Guam on December 10, 2013, marked the beginning of the annual Operation Christmas Drop (supplies, food and toys dropped via parachute by the USAF), the sixty-second year that it's happened, as aircraft set off for drop locations in Micronesia.

MOLDOVA

Little Moldova is a country in Eastern Europe that's only a bit larger than Maryland. It's a country that's had a complicated history. For instance, in the twentieth century, the area was disputed between Romania and Russia with territory changing hands on a regular basis. Finally, in 1990, it became independent.

Moldova is in a sensitive position with Russia, which has given some assistance to Transnistria, an area on the eastern edge of Moldova, next to Ukraine, that has claimed independence from Moldova.

However, we have had a bit of military involvement in recent years. For instance, Moldova sent troops to serve with us in Iraq, and we've trained some of their officers. Moldova is partnered with North Carolina in the State Partnership Program, so National Guard members from North Carolina have been to Moldova for exercises. US Special Forces have trained in Moldova with Moldovan Special Forces. Moldova has participated in multinational exercises with us, and US military personnel have helped with restoration projects in the country. For example, the US Army Corps of Engineers renovated a fire station in Comrat, Moldova.

MONACO

A tiny European country, Monaco is widely known in the United States for, among other things, Monte Carlo and Grace Kelly, former actress and then princess of Monaco until her death in 1982.

In 1942, the Italians occupied Monaco, and in 1943, the Germans did. In 1944, our forces arrived to liberate the area. August 1944 saw mass Allied landings in southern France, and in late August, Monaco experienced a number of Allied air raids. Then at the beginning of September, La Turbie and Mont Agel were shelled from the sea, and on September 3, 1944, US paratroopers arrived in Monaco with jeeps and chewing gum.

Since then, US military forces have occasionally visited. For instance, in November 2012, the amphibious command ship USS *Whitney* visited Monte Carlo to take part in Monaco's National Day celebrations, and sailors from the ship and members of the US Naval Forces Europe Band marched through the streets.

MONGOLIA

MONGOLIANS HAVE QUITE A HISTORY as invaders themselves. Genghis Khan is well-known for his military activities, and in 1241, the empire of his son Ögedei Khan stretched as far as the gates of Vienna. That's a big empire.

Our forces probably didn't reach Mongolia in 1919, but they definitely came pretty close. American troops were deployed in Siberia and northern China, and we had decided to get the local railroad running properly. To help achieve this, American railroad professionals, including John F. Stevens and Colonel George H. Emerson, formerly general manager of the Great Northern Railway, were sent in and so were American troops. We soon had soldiers installed, among other places, in Harbin in northern China, about three hundred miles from the Mongolian border. In the chaos of the period, it's certainly possible that American troops ended up closer to Mongolia at some point, maybe even in it.

An American diplomat, Charles Eberhardt, did make it to Urga (now Ulaanbaatar, the capital of Mongolia) in 1920 and returned with a recommendation that we should establish a permanent diplomatic presence there, but this was not acted upon.

Soon after this, Communists took power in Mongolia, which did little to improve links with the United States. And it wasn't until the end of the 1980s, but really the beginning of the 1990s, that we began to establish closer ties, including military links, with Mongolia.

In 1991, for instance, the USAF flew emergency medical supplies into Mongolia after the collapse of the Soviet Union. And Mongolia sent small numbers of troops to serve in Iraq and Afghanistan. We have also teamed up with Mongolia to co-sponsor the Khaan Quest series of multinational peacekeeping exercises. The Alaska National Guard is partnered with Mongolia.

MONTENEGRO

A COUNTRY SITUATED ON THE EASTERN ADRIATIC COAST, Montenegro borders Croatia to the north and Albania to the south. Italy is across the sea to the west. Montenegro means "black mountain."

US ships operated in the Adriatic in World War I, but our main involvement in Montenegro in that period came at the end of the war. The 332nd Infantry Regiment had served alongside the Italians. In the period after the armistice, the Second Battalion was sent alongside Italian troops to occupy briefly parts of Montenegro, in particular at the strategic port city of Kotor, where US submarine chasers also ended up at this stage. The American troops, however, reluctantly found themselves in the middle of a confusing political storm (not for the last time in this part of the world) as Italians, Yugoslavs, and Montenegrins all competed for control of the area. The French were involved as well, and at one stage, a French general ordered American troops to suppress a Montenegrin rebellion, the Christmas Rebellion, which had been prompted by a decision to unite Montenegro with Yugoslavia. Our troops advanced, but the rebellion basically collapsed before they could get involved, probably much to the relief of the American commander.

Montenegro became part of Yugoslavia, so the next time we got involved militarily in the area was during World War II, helping the Yugoslav partisans. For example, our aircraft would fly in supplies to the partisans and take out wounded fighters and civilians. And we extensively bombed enemy targets in the area, including Podgorica, the capital of Montenegro and a key point on German transport routes, which was heavily bombed.

In 1979, the USAF returned to Podgorica (called Titograd under Tito), this time on a much more friendly mission. A devastating earthquake had hit the area, and US aircraft raced in with over one hundred tons of supplies.

However, during the 1999 air campaign against Milosevic, we had aircraft over Montenegro again, this time with rather less humanitarian intent. Forty-eight US aircraft destroyed much of the airbase.

Montenegro declared independence in 2006, and since then we've established a number of military links with the new country. For instance, the Maine Army National Guard has established a partnership with Montenegro's military, Montenegro has sent troops to Afghanistan, and Montenegro has taken part alongside the US military in assorted exercises, such as Immediate Response and Combined Endeavor.

MOROCCO

AH, Morocco, the name itself speaks of exotic destinations, of far-off lands with fascinating heritages and amazing histories. And the United States military has a place in that history.

We'll come to the invasion part in a bit, but first the diplomacy part because Morocco, after a slightly rocky start, has become one of our longest-standing allies.

Morocco was, in fact, the very first nation in the world formally to recognize an independent United States on December 20, 1777. A treaty of friendship between Morocco and the United States, the longest unbroken agreement in US history, was signed in 1786.

Sounds good. But then came the rocky start, linked to the Barbary pirates. We've dealt with these in a lot more detail in the Algeria and Libya chapters, so we'll just quickly point out here that, at the time the United States came into being, these pirates already had a long history of operating from the North African coast. That wasn't good for our merchant ships, and it wasn't good for US business. For instance, in just one encounter in 1784, the American ship *Betsy*, carrying salt from Cadiz in southwestern Spain and bound for Philadelphia, was seized by Moroccan pirates. Paying them off didn't work, so we sent in the navy. The emperor of Morocco at the time was having second thoughts about the 1786 treaty, less than twenty years after it was signed, but a show of force at Tangier from Commodore Edward Preble with assorted USN ships, including *Constitution* and *Nautilus*, persuaded the emperor to renew the treaty.

There was another slight hiccup in our long friendship with Morocco in 1842. The local US consul in Tangier, Thomas N. Carr, was unhappy because he had to house and feed two lions given to him by the sultan. Eventually, he was fired by Secretary Webster but then got himself detained by the local lieutenant-governor. Commodore Charles W. Morgan was sent in to rescue the ex-consul, get an apology, and get a twenty-one-gun salute for his flag.

Morocco saw turbulent times later in the nineteenth and early twentieth centuries as European powers battled to control it, with France ending up taking the lion's share (nothing to do with Thomas N. Carr and his pets).

Another minor crisis in the US-Moroccan friendship occurred in 1904. In what has become known as the Perdicaris Affair, an American-born businessman, Ion Perdicaris, was kidnapped and held for ransom by a Moroccan, Ahmed ibn-Muhammed Raisuli, who was seeking money and political influence. Teddy Roosevelt, in turn, sent a naval squadron to Morocco seeking, in the memorable words of secretary of state, John Hay, "Perdicaris alive, or Raisuli dead." We got Perdicaris alive, and actually, Raisuli got some of his demands.

In 1942, a hundred years after Commodore Morgan had turned up on the USS *Fairfield*, we were getting ready to invade Morocco seriously. The French authorities in Morocco had stayed loyal to the Vichy regime with its links to Hitler, and Morocco was going to be one of the prime targets of the American and British Operation Torch, our first major landing in the Mediterranean theatre.

Landings were to take place in Algeria and Morocco, and a mighty thirty-five-thousand-strong task force was sent direct from the United States to seize Morocco.

On November 8, 1942, US troops, under the command of General George "Blood and Guts" Patton, who studied the Koran on the voyage across the Atlantic, landed on three sites on the coast.

The United States, in invading Morocco, was attacking a nation with which it was not at war at the time—Vichy France was technically neutral. The point of Operation Torch invasions across North Africa was to strategically outflank Rommel's Africa Corps and the Italians in Libya who faced the British driving west from Egypt.

Despite hopes the Vichy troops would not put up much resistance, there were some fierce clashes. Nevertheless, compared to many later WWII operations in the Mediterranean, casualties were light, the fighting was brief, and the port city of Casablanca, a major target of Torch, eventually fell. About seventy-two hours' worth of fighting was sufficient to satisfy the demands of French honor.

The classic movie *Casablanca* was actually filmed in 1942 before the US capture of the city but had its world premiere in New York City on November 26, after it. If the timing of Torch had been different, so might movie history have been.

After the battle of Casablanca, the red carpet was rolled out for the surrendering French officers who had ruled Morocco. After negotiating the terms of surrender with the French, Patton, who was fluent in French, "held up his hand and told them there was one last formality to be completed." Worried looks were quickly replaced by smiles as champagne bottles were opened and Patton offered a toast to the renewal of France and America's age-old friendship.

Patton also turned out to be a surprisingly successful diplomat when he served as the putative viceroy of Morocco. He wrote to the sultan of Morocco assuring him they came as friends, not as conquerors, and did not intend to stay after the war. Patton frequently entertained the sultan (whom he referred to as Sa Majesté) and escorted him on inspection trips.

Casablanca was transformed into a vast supply depot for the American forces with troops enjoying its pleasure so much that it became known as the Ice-Cream Front.

In January 1943, occupied Casablanca would also be the site of one of the most important Allied conferences of the war, which took place following the British triumph at El Alamein in Egypt and during the German debacle at Stalingrad. The Casablanca Conference was a landmark in a number of ways. Churchill managed to get accepted his plan to invade Sicily and Italy later that year, rather than launching the cross-Channel invasion favored by Admiral King and others. Churchill also lobbied on behalf of Charles de Gaulle to be acknowledged as the leader of Free France, though FDR remained highly suspicious of de Gaulle. After a photo opportunity with de Gaulle, FDR announced the Allied war goal of unconditional surrender by Germany, Italy, and Japan.

In the period after World War II, Morocco gained its independence from France and Spain and became a Cold War ally of the United States. We maintained strong military links in the area. Nouasseur Air Base near Casablanca, for instance, was a Strategic Air Command base for most of the 1950s.

Our long tradition of friendly links with Morocco has continued, and Morocco and the United States have, for example, shared many military exercises, including, in 2013, Exercise African Lion 13. However, occasional political differences can still sometimes cause hiccups.

The Utah National Guard is partnered with Morocco.

MOZAMBIQUE

WE'VE NOT HAD A HUGE AMOUNT to do with Mozambique militarily. Indeed, one of the main approaches to Mozambique was a deliberate decision, after some debate, NOT to intervene there militarily.

American pirates in the pre-1776 period cruised the waters of the Mozambique Channel. Though, to be fair, they were largely interested in the bit of land to the east of the channel, that is Madagascar where a number had bases, than the bit of land to the west, Mozambique.

We haven't had much to do militarily with Mozambique because for a long time it was a Portuguese colony. During World War I, we didn't get involved in that part of the world. And in World War II, Portugal was neutral so we left its colonies alone.

In the 1960s, however, FRELIMO, the Mozambique Liberation Front, started a guerrilla war attempting to remove Mozambique from Portugal's control. And like other parts of the Portuguese empire, independence was to come to Mozambique after the 1974 leftist military coup in Portugal. By 1975, Mozambique was independent, and FRELIMO was in power in a one-party Marxist state. Shortly after that, though, a different guerrilla group, RENAMO, or Mozambican National Resistance, emerged, which in turn was dedicated to toppling FRELIMO. RENAMO was anti-Communist, and some in the US Senate argued that the United States should offer it some support, but eventually the US government rejected the idea.

The war between FRELIMO and RENAMO was a long and bitter one and only finally ended in 1992 with the Rome General Peace Accords. A UN mission, United Nations Operation in Mozambique, was sent in to oversee the peace and successfully prepare the way for general elections. Some Americans were involved with this mission, for instance, as helicopter pilots. The Cease-Fire Commission had US members, and the USG provided substantial financial support as well.

Since the war, Mozambique has turned into a something of a success story, though in 2014, there has been a small amount of renewed fighting.

In recent years, we've had assorted military links with Mozambique. For instance, a US task force with hundreds of reserve marines among its members, helped Mozambican troops train for peacekeeping operations abroad in Exercise Shared Accord 2010. In 2011, the USS *Samuel B. Roberts* paid a visit to Maputo. The same year, thirty-eight Mozambican soldiers completed a USN de-mining course in Maputo.

NAMIBIA

NAMIBIA IS AN AFRICAN COUNTRY with a long Atlantic coastline. However, it's located further south than the main area of operations for our Africa Squadron's anti-slavery patrols in the nineteenth century.

USN ships have occasionally called in more recently. For instance, the USNS *Private Jose F. Valdez*, a technical research ship with communications experts on board that used to cruise around Africa in the 1960s, called in at Walvis Bay.

However, as so often with countries around the world, one decisive point in Namibia's history involves our military personnel. In the late nineteenth century, Namibia became a German colony. However, in World War I, Allied troops, mainly from next-door South Africa, invaded and took over Namibia. So South Africa administered the territory under a League of Nations mandate between the wars, and even though after World War II the UN eventually revoked South Africa's mandate, the South Africans stayed on. This led to the rise of a guerrilla organization, SWAPO (South West Africa People's Organization) fighting for the withdrawal of the South Africans and freedom for Namibia. The whole thing then got tied up with the crisis in next-door Angola because of SWAPO bases there and because of South African intervention in the Angolan civil war.

Finally, a deal was done with major US involvement to get the Cubans out of Angola (see "Angola") and the South Africans out of Namibia, and a UN mission, UNTAG, the not very sexily named UN Transition Assistance Group, was sent in to, well, assist transition to independence. We provided some air transport into Namibia for the initial deployment of the military forces involved. For instance, an Australian advance party was flown in March 1989 by USAF C-5 Galaxy from RAAF (Royal Australian Air Force) Learmouth to Diego Garcia and then on to Windhoek, capital of Namibia. And three days later, the advance echelon of the Australians' 17 Construction Squadron, another key element of UNTAG, was flown by USAF C-5 Galaxy to Grootfontein in central Namibia.

In recent years, our military has had assorted links with Namibia. For instance, in 2009, members of the Namibia Defence Force visited Multinational Training Command in Grafenwoehr in Germany to learn how American soldiers and international partners train, and in 2012, HSV *Swift* called in at Walvis Bay, the first time a USN ship has visited Namibia since 1999. Oh, and Namibia was one of eleven nations taking part in the Seventh World Military Golf Championship at Naval Air Station Jacksonville in 2012 after the Sixth World Military Golf Championship had been held in, yep, Windhoek.

NAURU

NAURU IS A SMALL ISLAND COUNTRY in the massive Pacific Ocean (in fact, it's the world's smallest republic) with an almost equally small involvement by the United States.

This island had long been inhabited before Westerners turned up. The Germans took control in the 1880s; then Australian troops took it in World War I. The Japanese took it in World War II, and then in September 1945, the Australians took it back. Finally it became independent and self-governing in the 1960s.

During World War II, however, the Japanese presence on the phosphate-rich island and the runway that the Japanese built there were sources of major concern to the United States. There were fears that the Japanese on Nauru could affect the fighting in the Gilberts.

So from March 1943 through 1945, American aircraft repeatedly bombed Nauru and Japanese attempts to resupply the island. There's a famous photo of a B-24 Liberator over Nauru with smoke and dust and debris rising from the small island below. Inevitably, the bombing campaign came at a price. Japanese troops were killed, but so were some islanders. And US airmen died too. The *Coral Princess*, for instance, a B-24 from Makin Airfield that had already flown many combat missions, was hit by anti-aircraft fire over Nauru on June 19, 1944, and exploded. Parts of the wreckage are still to be found on the island.

On November 19, 1943, the USN joined in the bombardment as well, with the USS *Saratoga* and USS *Princeton* heavily shelling targets on the island.

NEPAL

A HIMALAYAN MOUNTAIN NATION on the northern rim of the Indian subcontinent, Nepal is home to Mount Everest, the roof of the world. Nepal was a kingdom for centuries until it became a republic in 2008. It shares a border with China and India.

Nepal's Gurkha soldiers, who have long served British interests and continue to do so, served in the Burma campaign against Japan. Gurkhas also served in the American-led occupation of Japan that followed the Second World War.

The United States first recognized the kingdom of Nepal in 1947.

In 1950, Tibet was invaded and occupied by Communist China. The CIA provided support and training for Tibetan guerrillas based in Nepal from this point until the camps were closed by the Nepalese army in 1974. President Nixon's rapprochement with China ultimately put an end to the covert program.

My (Chris Kelly's) friend Jim Whittaker launched a friendly "invasion" of Nepal when he became the first American to summit Everest in 1963. He was accompanied on this expedition by a Sherpa guide, Gombu. I had the honor to accompany both of them on a return to Everest base camp on the fortieth anniversary in the spring of 2003.

Nepalese soldiers have served alongside our own in Iraq, Haiti, and elsewhere. And Nepalese and US military personnel shared in exercises, for instance, in the Pacific Resilience Disaster Response Exercise and Exchange in Katmandu, Nepal, in September 2013.

NETHERLANDS

FRANK SINATRA MAY NEVER HAVE SUNG "New Amsterdam, New Amsterdam," but we still have a long history with the Dutch. (My [Chris Kelly's] maternal ancestors, the Van Rensselaers, came from the Netherlands to New Amsterdam.)

On November 18, 1776, the Dutch governor of their colony at St. Eustatius in the Caribbean responded to a salute from an American warship. It was the first official recognition of the United States in our history.

In 1780, the Netherlands joined with the French and Spanish governments in supporting the thirteen American colonies in the battle for independence against the British Crown. Britain declared war on the Netherlands in December of 1780, and the Anglo-Dutch War lasted until 1784. John Adams, later our second president, served as the US ambassador to the Dutch Republic where he helped to secure formal recognition of the United States in 1782. The Dutch helped to provide vital financial aid to the Continental armies.

The Netherlands managed to stay neutral during World War I but was not so fortunate in World War II when it was bombed, invaded, and occupied by the Nazis. A majority of the 140,000 Jews in the Netherlands, including the young Anne Frank, were tragically shipped to Nazi death camps.

US air crews saw extensive action in the skies over the Netherlands, either while attacking targets, like German airbases in the Netherlands, or while heading for or returning from targets in Germany.

After the D-Day landings of June 1944, the Germans began their revenge campaign of launching V-1 and V-2 rockets at London. After the collapse in France, the Germans used the Netherlands as a launching platform for the V-2 rocket campaign. This made the Allies anxious to invade the Netherlands and, perhaps, bring an early end to the war.

On September 13 and 14, 1944, American troops liberated Maastricht, the first Dutch city to be freed from the Nazis. From September 17 through 26, we and the British launched Operation Market Garden deep into the Netherlands in an attempt to punch a hole through to Germany by taking a number of vital strategic bridges in a row. General Bernard Law Montgomery's idea was to use airborne forces to seize the bridges and then make a heavy armored thrust through German lines to link up with the American and British paratroopers and glider forces.

The north-south road that ran from Eindhoven to Veghel to Njmegen to Arnhem was the key to Operation Market Garden. However, fierce German resistance all along this road rapidly led to it being called "Hell's Highway."

Our 101st Airborne and 82nd Airborne had significant successes in their missions, though at a price. In particular, a heroic attack by men of the 504th Parachute Infantry Regiment across the River Waal under heavy fire led, after heavy losses, to the capture of the crucial bridge at Nijmegen. Unfortunately, the success of the whole plan still relied on the capture of the bridge at Arnhem, and there things weren't to go quite so well.

Failure to get sufficient troops to the bridge quickly, communications problems, the unexpected presence of German tanks units in the area, and the delay of the armored force attempting to relieve them created a situation in which the British and Polish paratroopers sent to Arnhem, despite their heroism, could not win. Hopes that Market Garden could end the war by Christmas ultimately were tragically not fulfilled.

In October of 1944, the Timberwolves Division (104th Infantry Division), serving under Montgomery, liberated Zundert, Netherlands, and took control of the Vaart Canal defense. They drove forwards towards the Mark River on November 2 and shortly afterwards reached the Maas River on November 5.

Sadly, though, after the failure of Market Garden, the Allies were able to free only about a fifth of the country in 1944. In the area still held by the Germans, food supplies ended up being cut drastically due to a number of factors, including deliberate Nazi punitive actions, dislocation caused by war, and a harsh winter that arrived early. These all led to the infamous Hunger Winter of 1944–1945 in which something like sixteen thousand Dutch died of starvation. In 1945, with the war almost at an end, a deal was finally agreed with the German occupation forces to allow the British and us to fly food supplies, without being fired upon, to the desperate Dutch. The British had Operation Manna; we had Operation Chowhound, also a great name.

Finally on May 5, 1945, the Germans in the Netherland surrendered, and that is celebrated in the Netherlands as Liberation Day.

Today an American cemetery in the Netherlands near Maastricht, liberated by Americans all those decades ago, contains over eight thousand members of the American armed forces, a part of the cost of that liberation.

Since the war, we have maintained close military links with the Netherlands. For instance, the Netherlands became a founding member of NATO member in 1949. About three thousand Dutch soldiers served directly in the US 2nd Division in the Korean War. Dutch contingents have served alongside Americans in Iraq and Afghanistan.

Assorted US military units have been based in the Netherlands. During the Cold War, for example, the US III Corps had a forward headquarters at Tapijnkazerne, also near Maastricht, and for a long time there were major USAF facilities at Soesterberg near Utrecht. The US Army Garrison at Schinnen outside Maastricht, a base for US personnel at the Allied Joint Force Command at nearby Brunssum, is currently the only US Army installation in the country.

We should also make a quick mention here of two overseas territories of the Netherlands, Aruba and Curaçao. We've had military links with both. For instance, on Aruba, the USAAF established a base at Dakota Field and even helped fight off German submarines attempting to shell the oil refinery, and the US army set up coastal guns at Colorado Point. On Curaçao, we operated anti-submarine patrols from Hato Field, which is now Hato International Airport and still hosts a USAF Forward Operating Base.

NEW ZEALAND

THE BEAUTIFUL LAND OF NEW ZEALAND set the stage for J. R. R. Tolkien's works or, rather, for the recent movie versions of his *The Lord of the Rings* and *The Hobbit*. It's also a land with a history in which we've played a part.

American whalers began visiting the area around New Zealand even before 1800, but eventually Britain became the colonial power there, and for a long time, New Zealand was part of the British Empire. The first US consul to New Zealand was appointed in 1839.

From mid-1942 to mid-1944, hundreds of thousands of Americans in total were based in New Zealand. The first marines landed at Auckland on June 12, 1942, and two days later, marines started landing at Wellington as well. US troops were there to help protect New Zealand but also to use New Zealand as a staging post for operations further north. In the novel *Battle Cry*, much of it based on the author's experiences in World War II, Leon Uris tells of the battles fought by a group of marines. It also tells of their two visits to New Zealand, the first time training for Guadalcanal, the second resting and recovering before Tarawa. In August 1943, Eleanor Roosevelt arrived in New Zealand and visited some of the American forces there.

Usually links with the locals were friendly, sometimes very friendly. Almost fifteen hundred New Zealand women married American servicemen. But tensions could arise as well, as in the Battle of Manners Street, on April 3, 1943, when hundreds of Americans and New Zealanders ended up brawling in Wellington.

Gradually, however, as Allied forces began to advance and the fighting moved further away from New Zealand, the number of US troops in New Zealand started to decline. The 43rd Division departed from Auckland in the summer of 1944, and in October, our naval base there was closed.

But military links remained after the war. In 1951, Australia, New Zealand, and the United States were joined in the ANZUS security pact, and they cooperated in SEATO as well. New Zealand forces served alongside ours in Korea, and the country was one of the few friends of ours that sent troops to Vietnam. In more recent years, New Zealanders have served in the Gulf War and in Iraq and Afghanistan. New Zealand has also played an important role in a number of peacekeeping missions. New Zealand's decision to ban nuclear-powered and nuclear-armed warships from its waters did, however, cause tensions, though some recent announcements have suggested closer military ties again.

NICARAGUA

NICARAGUA LIES ON AN ISTHMUS just to the north of Panama in Central America, and Lake Nicaragua is the largest freshwater lake in Central America. The country occupies a crucial strategic position with coastlines on the Pacific and Atlantic Oceans, and the United States has had a long history of interventions there.

Nicaragua gained its independence from the Spanish Empire in 1821.

In 1848, gold was found at John Sutter's mill near Sacramento launching the California gold rush. Prospectors wanted to travel from east to west but were frustrated with the difficulties and pace of overland travel through an area where hostile Indians controlled much territory. The transcontinental railroad was not completed until 1869, and the Panama Canal did not open until 1914. So, in the meantime, taking a steamship from New York to Nicaragua and crossing it was among the most efficient and safest means of travel.

The American tycoon Cornelius Vanderbilt controlled the highly profitable Accessory Transit Company, which monopolized transportation across the rivers and lakes of Nicaragua. Vanderbilt's steamships would take passengers from New York to Greytown on the Atlantic coast and then cross Nicaragua via river, lake, and track arriving at San Juan del Sur on the Pacific coast. Another steamer would then bring these passengers up to San Francisco's Barbary Coast. Handy.

Nicaragua, therefore, occupied a valuable strategic and commercial position (or transit choke point) in the world at that time, and Vanderbilt wasn't the only American interested in it.

William Walker of Nashville, Tennessee, was a doctor, lawyer, journalist, and adventurer (quite a full **résumé**) who led a group of American filibusters to Nicaragua in 1856. Sam Houston, an American who had become the president of the Republic of Texas, was Walker's idol, and in spite of the neutrality acts of 1794 and 1818 that explicitly outlawed such activities, Walker and his filibusters sought to build a Central American empire.

On October 11, 1856, he and his supporters arrived in the paddlewheel steamer *La Virgen* at Granada, Nicaragua's capital. The next day, his forces captured the town and soon after established their own republic of Nicaragua. In June of 1856, Walker was elected president of Nicaragua, receiving over 68 percent of the vote in a four-way race. His government was recognized by President Franklin Pierce and received support from US ambassador John Wheeler. His supporters referred to him as the "grey-eyed man of destiny."

Though he was not ideologically pro-slavery, having opposed it while serving as a newspaper editor in New Orleans and San Francisco, Walker was convinced to espouse a pro-slavery policy for Nicaragua. In a bid for sectional support, he bowed to expedience allowing the establishment slavery in Nicaragua.

While Walker may have sullied his reputation with his compromise with slavery, his fatal mistake was in siding with Vanderbilt's commercial rivals, taking away Vanderbilt's transit charter. Vanderbilt dismissed Walker as a mere "tin sojer boy."

Many neighboring Central American states feared Walker's expansionist Nicaraguan republic. Honduras, El Salvador, Guatemala, and Costa Rica all received arms, supply, and money from Vanderbilt. The tycoon also worked behind the scenes to undermine Walker's support within the US government. Disease, hunger, and desertion plagued Walker's filibuster army, which was soon cut off from outside support in Rivas near the Pacific coast. Of the several thousand Americans who served with Walker in Central America, half are estimated to have died from wounds or disease. Commander Charles Davis, captain of the USS St. Mary's, finally arrived in February 1857 to negotiate Walker's surrender and to provide evacuation of his remaining filibusters to safety in America.

Indefatigable, Walker returned to Nicaragua seven months later with a second expedition of 270 filibusters aboard the side-wheeler steamer Fashion that had sailed from Mobile, Alabama. Walker's second attempt to establish the Republic of Nicaragua was, however, foiled by Commodore Hiram Paulding of the USN who landed a force near Greytown on Nicaragua's gulf coast that compelled Walker's second surrender. Paulding wrote that he considered Walkers' supporters to be "outlaws who had escaped from the vigilance of the government."

The Nicaraguan government moved swiftly to restore Vanderbilt's transit charter monopoly.

The Walker adventure (or misadventure) in Nicaragua represented a threefold US intervention in Nicaragua. First, there was Walker's overt attempt at empire building. Second, Vanderbilt's gold represented a covert intervention that financed the opposition of neighboring Central American states to oppose Walker, the democratically elected president of Nicaragua. Finally, the USN intervened twice in neutral Nicaraguan territory removing Walker and his followers from the country. In 1860, Walker, not a man to be easily deterred by anything, was killed by a Honduran firing squad while leading a third attempted invasion of Nicaragua (see "Honduras").

The Walker episode also set the tone for the future of links between the United States and Nicaragua. These would be characterized by American financial investment in Nicaragua, particularly in banana plantations and mining, as well as transportation, US interventions to safeguard these interests, political instability, and violent transitions of power.

Even before Walker, we had sent in the troops. For instance, in July 1854, we had already bombarded and destroyed much of Greytown (San Juan del Norte) over a variety of grievances. And more, much more was to come. USN vessels would land forces on numerous occasions over many American administrations. In 1894, for example, the USN cruiser *Columbia* landed troops at Bluefields, and in 1898, the USN gunboat *Alert* landed forces at San Juan del Sur. The USN Caribbean squadron had a duty to protect American lives and interests along the coasts of Central America.

And the interventions kept on happening. Major Smedley Butler, who would later become an outspoken critic of US overseas interventions, served in Nicaragua from 1909 to 1912. Rear Admiral William Kimball commanded a US expeditionary squadron of nine American warships that arrived at Corinto on the west coast of Nicaragua in December 1909. US forces fought on behalf of President Adolfo Diaz against rebel forces. The Battle of Coyotepe Hill was the sharpest engagement of the 1912 Nicaraguan expedition. Thirty-seven marines were killed or wounded in the campaign. In the end, a legation guard of one hundred marines was left in Managua as an expression of American power in Nicaragua.

In August of 1914, at the same time that World War I was breaking out in Europe, the United States and Nicaragua negotiated the Bryan-Chamorro Treaty. Nicaragua's independence was to be preserved, sort of, while the United States assumed substantial control over Nicaraguan finances.

And, in fact, the marine delegation was still there in 1925 when a Nicaraguan civil war broke out. Marines from the USS *Cleveland* were landed in Bluefields yet again to protect American lives and interests. In 1927, President Coolidge declared that the United States had a "special responsibility" in the Caribbean. In 1927, Henry Stimson, who would later become FDR's secretary of war, negotiated a peace settlement between the Nicaraguan government and the rebels. When told of the Central American habit of resorting to revolution as a remedy for electoral defeat, Stimson suggested that Nicaraguans "ought to play more football, baseball, etc." Stimson helped to negotiate the Tipitapa Accords that would eventually bring a measure of peace to Nicaragua. General Matthew Ridgway, who would later command US troops in World War II and the Korean War, earlier in his career helped to supervise free elections in Nicaragua.

However, a rebel officer named Augusto Sandino had remained skeptical about the independence of the Nicaraguan government from the United States and led a group of followers, called Sandinistas (sound familiar?) into the mountains to wage a guerilla campaign. On July 16, 1927, the Battle of Ocotal, which pitted US marines and national guard units against the Sandinistas, marks the first dive-bombing combat attack in history. One marine and three hundred Sandinistas were killed. Sandino used a depiction of a rebel decapitating a US marine with a machete on his official seal.

Finally, President Hoover ordered the withdrawal of US marines, which took place in January 1933. The year 1936 marked the beginning of the Somoza dynasty (Anastasio Somoza Garcia and, after his 1956 assassination, his sons) that was to rule Nicaragua until 1979. The United States assisted the Somoza regime in training its national guard forces, and links with us remained strong. FDR said of Somoza, "He may be an SOB, but he's our SOB." On December 8, 1941, immediately following the Pearl Harbor attack, Nicaragua joined the Allies in declaring war on Japan and Germany. Nicaragua did not contribute troops, though it did receive some lend-lease aid, and airbases were constructed in Corinto.

We had a long alliance with the Somozas, but in the 1970s, a civil war erupted in Nicaragua pitting the Somoza regime against rebel forces that included the Sandinistas. At least twenty-five thousand people were killed in the fighting and repression, including ABC reporter Bill Stewart, executed by the national guard before President Jimmy Carter cut off US military support to the Somoza government, and it finally collapsed. In 1979, Sandinista leader Daniel Ortega formed a provisional government, and in 1984, elections confirmed him in power.

However, the Sandinistas were developing increasing links with Cuba and other Communist countries ringing alarm bells in the White House. In spite of congressional opposition, the Reagan administration responded to the growing crisis in Central America by funneling support to the Contras, or Counter-revolutionaries, and the neighboring Honduran government. In defiance of international law, the CIA arranged in April 1984 the mining of Nicaraguan waters near the port of Corinto on the Pacific coast. Colonel Ollie North's "neat idea" to pay for illegal arms shipments to the

Contras with Iranian funds led to the Iran-Contra scandal that disrupted much of President Reagan's second term. A guerilla resistance movement also sprang up in Miskito territories.

Many Nicaraguans also fled into neighboring countries creating a refugee crisis throughout the region. In March of 1986, Sandinista forces invaded neighboring Honduras in pursuit of Contra forces who opposed the Sandinista regime.

Finally, after years of bitter conflict, in February 1989, the Tesoro Beach accords brought regional peace to Central America. The Contra forces agreed to disband, and Nicaragua agreed to hold free elections. Over thirty thousand lives were lost in the Sandinista/Contra conflict (or Nicaraguan Revolution).

On February 25, 1990, certified free and fair elections in Nicaragua drove the Sandinistas from office. However, in 2006, Daniel Ortega, leader of the Sandinistas, was returned to power in elections, and he is still president of Nicaragua.

The United States has left a complicated, ambivalent legacy in its long and tangled history of interventions in Nicaragua. Nicaraguans today celebrate every September 14 as one of their national days in commemoration of a Nicaraguan victory over General Walker's Yankee *filibusteros* at the San Jacinto ranch.

However, that is not the entire picture. For instance, in 2004, a contingent of Nicaraguan troops served alongside our troops in the American-led coalition's invasion of Iraq, and the US military has been involved in humanitarian projects in Nicaragua. Wisconsin has a State Partnership Program with Nicaragua, which included the Wisconsin Military Engagement Team's missions to Nicaragua.

NIGER

A LAND NAMED AFTER THE RIVER NIGER, Niger is the middle of the three big states in northern central Africa. Mali is situated to the west, and Chad is to the east.

Since the rise of al-Qaeda–linked jihads in the region, Niger has become a highly strategic location. Before the French-led intervention there, extreme Islamists had taken control of half of Mali and were threatening the south. Boko Haram (means "Western education is sinful") has been a major threat in Nigeria to the south, and the chaotic situation in Libya to the north has left the southern region of that country often only weakly controlled by the government in distant Tripoli.

It's hardly surprising, therefore, that we've been taking an increased military interest in the country recently. For instance, AFRICOM recommended placing unarmed, remotely piloted aircraft in Niger, and in February 2013, President Obama announced that the last of one hundred US military specialists had been sent to Niger in support of intelligence gathering and sharing operations in the region. Not surprising, they're mostly air force specialists, and they're based in the capital Niamey.

Niger saw a couple of serious terrorist attacks within its borders in 2013, including one on a vital uranium ore mine at Artit and one on military barracks at Agadez. The Niger foreign minister said in September 2013 that he would welcome the deployment of armed drones in the country.

The United States is also planning in 2014 to hold in Niger regional military maneuvers, called Operation Flintlock, and has been helping the Niger military with other support as well, such as supplying them with a couple of new planes and some trucks through US security cooperation programs.

NIGERIA

A LARGE AND IMPORTANT AFRICAN COUNTRY, Nigeria is home to many peoples and cultures. For instance, Nigeria has the largest number of Mormons in Africa, perhaps somewhere over one hundred thousand.

Our military forces first came into contact with Nigeria during the USN's anti-slaving operations in the region in the nineteenth century.

During World War II, we used Kano Airport in Nigeria and Maiduguri and Lagos as links on our air-ferry routes across Africa. Even though these bases were a long distance from the fighting, flying still had its risks, and the records include details of a number of American aircraft accidents and losses in Nigeria during the war.

During the long and bitter Biafra War, America was deeply involved in the humanitarian airlift to take food and supplies to starving civilians, supplying also a number of C-97 US Air National Guard transport aircraft and pilots. Among those who volunteered for the often dangerous missions was August Martin, a former Tuskegee airman who was killed in a plane crash.

The US and Nigerian governments haven't always been exactly best friends. For instance, in 1993, the United States imposed sanctions on Nigeria over human rights and other concerns. However, in recent years, the United States has been getting along much better with the Nigerian government, and a variety of military links have developed. For instance, in 2003, Nigerian forces took part alongside US forces in operations in Liberia to oust Charles Taylor and restore stability. Nigeria peacekeepers have also played a significant role in a number of conflict-hit areas, including Darfur and Mali. The US Air Force has helped fly Nigerian peacekeepers, and the US military has helped train them. Nigerian forces have also taken part in assorted exercises alongside US forces. The California National Guard is partnered with Nigeria.

The rise of extremist Islamist organization Boko Haram in Nigeria has been a major worry for the US military, and AFRICOM has been partnering with Nigerian forces to counter Boko Haram's attacks. In 2014, after the abduction of hundreds of girls by Boko Haram, we sent military personnel and aircraft to assist with finding and rescuing the girls.

NORTH KOREA

NORTH KOREA IS A LAND OF MYSTERY, a hermit kingdom whose intentions we struggle to understand.

Our first contact with what is now North Korea was not a happy one. In 1866, an American ship, the SS *General Sherman*, arrived off Korea and then proceeded to sail upriver to Pyongyang, now the capital of North Korea, in an attempt to start Western trade with Koreans. The Koreans were wary of Western traders, and a dispute arose that led to violence and the eventual burning of the SS *General Sherman*.

Our next major visit to North Korea was going to be pretty challenging as well.

To avoid too much repetition in this book, the beginning of the Korean War until the first liberation of Seoul is covered in the South Korea chapter.

After the liberation of Seoul by UN forces on September 26, 1950, the United Nations forces faced a strategic dilemma. Would they advance north of the thirty-eighth parallel and dispose of the regime that had started the conflict, or would they stop at the line that originally divided North and South Korea?

Two considerations—the discovery by the UN command that thousands of civilians in South Korea had been killed by the Communists between June and September of 1950 and the comparatively swift collapse of the North Korean Army after Inchon—were seized upon by those arguing in favor of crossing the thirty-eighth parallel. Ultimately, both the UN command and the Truman administration decided in favor of regime change in the North at this time.

As a result, United Nations forces swept north of the thirty-eighth parallel. On October 19, Pyongyang was captured, and Bob Hope even gave a USO performance for the troops in the North Korean capital!

United Nations forces drove north of the thirty-eighth parallel advancing towards the Chinese border. Kim Il Sung's northern regime was in a state of near total collapse when suddenly the situation changed entirely.

Mao, mindful that North Korea had recently been the jumping-off point for the Japanese invasion of Manchuria in the 1930s, was determined to intervene in Korea on a huge scale. In late October of 1950, massive Chinese formations began to cross the Yalu River into North Korea. In the end, over 1.3 million Chinese would fight in the war.

The Chinese forces had years of experience in battling the Japanese and the Chinese Nationalists. They employed human-wave tactics and specialized in night attack to avoid UN superiority in the air.

Among Mao's forces were recently-surrendered Nationalist Chinese. This later complicated the negotiations over prisoner exchanges as many who had fought on the Communist side had no desire to be repatriated to North Korea or the People's Republic.

The Chinese intervention was a hammer blow to the UN forces and totally changed the course of the war. During the Chosin Reservoir (December 1950) campaign, the commander of 1st Marine Division, O. P. Smith, famously remarked, "Gentlemen, we are not retreating. We are merely advancing in another direction."

The autumn also saw the first MiG-15s deployed in the country in support of the North Koreans and Chinese, challenging UN dominance of the skies.

The UN retreat continued through the bleak winter of 1950, and the Chinese tidal wave swept all in its path and threw the UN forces into chaos. Pyongyang was recaptured by the Communists on December 5, 1950, and Seoul was evacuated by UN troops on January 4, 1951. In desperation at the situation, Douglas MacArthur began to support drastic measures to stem the Chinese tide, including bombing the Yalu bridges across which the Chinese supply lines flowed, bombing targets of opportunity in Manchuria, taking Chiang Kai-shek up on his offer of deploying thousands of well-trained Nationalist Chinese troops to Korea, and even considering the use of atomic weapons. On April 5, 1951, MacArthur released a letter criticizing the Truman administration's policy of limited war. In response, President Harry Truman, who never cared much for "Dugout Doug," charged the supreme commander with blatant insubordination.

The wisdom, or otherwise, of Truman's dismissal of MacArthur on April 11, 1951, remains a matter of controversy to this day. Some argue that Truman occupied the firmer constitutional ground and that MacArthur's proposed escalation might have led to Russian retaliation, use of atomic weapons, and the start of World War III. Others point out that MacArthur's departure may have led to two unnecessary years of war; in January of 1952, even Truman himself was considering an ultimatum to the Soviet Union and China over their support for North Korea.

Before MacArthur's final removal, however, the Chinese onslaught had already been slowed and then halted. The Eighth Army under Matthew Ridgway, the commander of the 82nd Airborne in Operation Market Garden (see "Netherlands") began to push north again, and in March 5, 1951, Seoul changed hands for the third time as his forces advanced towards the thirty-eighth parallel. Nevertheless, a grinding war still lay ahead with no apparent end in sight.

Out of over 1,319,000 Americans who served during the three years of the "forgotten war" in Korea, about thirty-six thousand were killed — comparable to the fifty-eight thousand claimed by Vietnam over ten years. Over one million Koreans from the north, south, and all ideologies, including many civilians, were also killed in the war. Truman's ambition for a third presidential term was also a casualty of the war.

With a simple five-word speech, "I shall go to Korea," Dwight Eisenhower was catapulted to electoral victory in the fall of 1952. As president-elect, America's most distinguished soldier visited Korea in late November of 1952. Mark Clark, a West Point classmate of Eisenhower's, tried to argue that the war was winnable, but Ike was determined to gain a truce. Ike told Clark, "I have a mandate from the people to stop this fighting."

The Eisenhower administration launched a high-stakes poker game designed to resume the stalled peace talks at Panmunjom. A tactical nuclear device, designed to be used by artillery, was tried out in January 1953. In May of that year, Allen Dulles, the secretary of state, visited Prime Minister

Nehru of India and asked that a warning be conveyed to the Chinese: If a truce were not agreed to, bombing north of the Yalu would commence. The talks resumed and made rapid progress.

Finally, the Korean War ended with an armistice signed on July 27, 1953, which basically restored the antebellum status quo. But the truce has not been an unbroken one. Regular incidents have occurred, including in 1968 when North Koreans boarded and captured the USS *Pueblo*. The *Pueblo* remains today the only USN vessel in enemy hands.

And today, it is Kim Jong-un, the grandson of Kim Il Sung from the Korean War, who presides over secretive North Korea and keeps the rest of the world guessing about what he's going to do next.

NORWAY

L EIF ERICSON, WHO WAS OF NORWEGIAN DESCENT, may have launched the first European incursion into North America sometime around the year 1000 AD. We returned the favor nearly a thousand years later during World War II.

Norway had remained neutral in World War I. But not in World War II.

The Nazis invaded Norway in April 1940 and occupied it for the remainder of the war in Europe. Haakon VII, king of Norway, fled with a government in exile to England. The king and his government landed in Rotherhithe on the Thames in southeast London—the same spot the *Mayflower* left from with the Pilgrims in 1620. King Haakon VII would worship with his family at St. Olav's Church in Rotherhithe and would also give wartime broadcasts to the Norwegian people from this church.

In Norway, with German support, Vidkun Quisling formed a collaborationist government.

Not surprisingly, since we weren't actually in the war at the time, we didn't have anything much to do with the fighting in Norway in 1940. However, two incidents do stand out.

On April 21, 1940, Captain Robert Moffat Losey, serving as US military attaché in Norway, while trying to ensure the safe evacuation to Sweden of American diplomats, was killed by Luftwaffe bombs.

And in the summer of 1940, President Franklin Roosevelt sent a troopship, the USS *American Legion*, on a special mission to Petsamo in what was then northern Finland (it's now, after border changes, in Russia). Its main mission was to evacuate Crown Princess Martha of Norway, plus hundreds of other assorted civilians, including one Dane then called Børge Rosenbaum. This it successfully did, being the last neutral ship out of Petsamo. On arrival in the United States, Princess Martha went on to become close (very, very close, some suggest) to President Roosevelt while Børge Rosenbaum went on to become Victor Borge. However, it wasn't just people that the USS *American Legion* rescued from Petsamo that day; it also carried away something that would make a huge contribution to the US war effort. Taken on board at Petsamo was a Swedish-made 40 mm twin-mount Bofors anti-aircraft gun. In America, the USN would adopt the type, order its domestic production, and fit it on its ships.

After the launch of Operation Barbarossa, the Nazi invasion of the Soviet Union, the Axis occupation of Norway became a particular thorn in the Allies' side as Norwegian air and sea bases were used to prey on the arctic convoys that were bringing lend-lease supplies to the Soviet Union. Film star Douglas Fairbanks Junior was a naval lieutenant aboard the USS *Wichita* in the summer of 1942 and witnessed the disastrous PQ 17 convoy that was almost wiped out by German attacks. Plenty of supplies did, however, get through on convoys.

In addition, the German presence in Norway helped assure the transportation of vital Swedish iron ore for use in building the Wehrmacht war machine. Consequently, Churchill repeatedly advocated Operation Anvil, a projected Allied invasion of Norway, to address these concerns. Eisenhower and others in the Allied staff, however, believed that Operation Anvil would be a distraction from the cross-channel invasion of France through Normandy; they prevailed in Allied strategy sessions.

As a result, most of the opposition to German forces in Norway came from brave Norwegians in the resistance. But not all of it.

We conducted assorted air operations over occupied Norway. For example, we were part of the campaign to prevent a Nazi atomic bomb. The Germans were attempting to make heavy water for their nascent nuclear program and using a hydroelectric plant in Vermork, Norway, to do so. In 1943, this plant was hit by a 143-plane raid of USAAF B-17s that did extensive damage.

But not all US operations in Norway during World War II were to be in the air. On March 24, 1945, a squadron of B-24 Liberators launched Operation RYPE (Norwegian for "grouse") dropping a team of specially trained OSS forces near Jarlsbad in central Norway. The thirty-six-man group immediately linked up with Norwegian resistance forces. The 99th

Battalion, who were proficient skiers and demolition experts, managed to destroy the Tangen bridge near Jorstad. On May 12, 1945, they took over Steinkjer from German forces. Major William Colby, who was later appointed head of the CIA by President Nixon, was the leader of the OSS team in Norway.

On June 10, 1945, the 99th Infantry Battalion would form the honor guard for Crown Prince Olaf's triumphant parade through Trondheim.

Norway was a founding member of NATO in 1949. Norway's strategic location on the northern approaches to the Soviet Union made it an important area for bases for the USAAF and USN during the Cold War.

Even after the end of the Cold War, tensions could still occur in the area. For example, on January 25, 1995, Norway launched a rocket to gather scientific data on the Northern Lights near Svalbard. The launch had not been publicly disclosed in advance, and its trajectory was near Russian territory, which caused a minor crisis with the Russians who briefly panicked, fearing that it was a US submarine-launched missile. Thus, Norwegian scientists nearly started World War III after the Cold War had ended.

And we still have strong military links with Norway. For instance, the USAF's 501st Combat Support Wing remains based in Stavanger to this day. Norway is a NATO member. The Norwegians sent troops to fight alongside our own in the coalition forces in Afghanistan, and Norwegian jets played a major role in the operations in Libya in 2011.

OMAN

ONE OF THE MANY INTERESTING FACTS ABOUT OMAN is how long we've had links with the country. We tend to think of US interest in the Gulf and Arabian peninsula as a comparatively recent phenomenon, but actually as early as 1833, we signed a Treaty of Friendship and Navigation with Muscat (the capital of Oman) when diplomat Edmund Roberts turned up on the sloop of war USS *Peacock*. At the time, the sultan of Oman also ruled Zanzibar (see "Tanzania") and was interested in us as a possible counterbalance to the expansion of British influence.

As the nineteenth century wore on, however, British influence did increase in Muscat. And it was during World War II that we started to take a renewed interest in the country. For instance, America requested and received permission for USAAF planes to use facilities in the country.

British influence in Oman remained strong for a considerable time after World War II (and the countries still have strong links), but in 1980, we signed an agreement on US access to assorted Omani military facilities, airbases, and naval bases, and we then started work on the facilities there.

One of the main airbases we have used in Oman is Thumrait Air Base. US aircraft, for instance, operated out of Thumrait during Operations Desert Shield and Desert Storm, and US refueling aircraft have used the base as well.

Omani troops served with the Gulf War coalition during Desert Storm, and Oman has become a strong US partner in the war against terror.

PAKISTAN

ONE OF THE MOST DRAMATIC American invasions and one of the shortest in our history took place in Pakistan in 2011.

Pakistan occupies a strategically significant location, separating the Middle East from the rest of Asia beyond and separating Central Asia from access to the sea. In the nineteenth century, the British and the Russians fought the Great Game for control of the subcontinent over the mountain passes of its northwest frontier. In a 1947 interview, Mohammed Ali Jinnah, the founder of modern Pakistan, said, "America needs Pakistan more than Pakistan needs America. Pakistan is the pivot of the world, as we are placed … the frontier on which the future position of the world revolves … Russia is not so very far away."

We first got militarily involved with the area in World War II precisely because of this strategic location. US aircraft that had been ferried across from Africa and the Middle East needed to pass through it so they could reach airbases in India and China. It was also a location where supplies could be landed from the sea. So among other facilities, we established a major presence at the airport at Karachi, Pakistan's major city and major port.

However, it is since World War II that we have taken most military interest in the area.

In 1947, as the British Raj came to an end, Muslim-majority Pakistan and East Pakistan (now Bangladesh) were separated from India.

As Cold War tensions developed, Pakistan's conservative military elite and strong Muslim identity were increasingly seen by the United States as a bulwark against Communism. In 1954, the United States signed an arms agreement with Pakistan. Pakistan shared concern about the encroachments of the nearby Soviet Union. The United States sought assurances that the weapons would not be used against India, with which Pakistan had longstanding disputes.

Pakistan granted the United States the right to build an airbase at Budaber, near Peshawar, Pakistan. U-2 spy planes operated from there, and a major NSA listening post was developed. On May 1, 1960 (Communist May Day), Francis Gary Powers, flying a U-2 surveillance plane at seventy thousand feet over the Soviet Union, was shot down; his plane, headed for Norway, had taken off from Budaber.

In 1959, METO (Middle East Treaty Organization) was formed allying the United States with Pakistan, Iran, and Turkey. Pakistan was a founding member of the Southeast Asia Treaty Organization in 1954 but withdrew in 1973, precipitated by what it perceived as insufficient support for its conflict with India over Bangladesh.

In one of those little-known links, Sardar, the horse Pakistan gave to Jackie Kennedy, was the riderless horse used at JFK's funeral in 1963.

In 1965, we suspended military assistance to Pakistan (as well as India) during that year's war between the two countries, and arms sales weren't started again until 1975.

Prior to his historic trip to China, President Nixon, had, however, come to regard Pakistan as "a valuable channel to China," and he developed something of a personal friendship with President Yahya. In spite of the evidence of massive human rights violations, the United States supported Pakistan in its efforts to retain its hold on East Pakistan. In 1971, however, East Pakistan separated from West Pakistan and became independent Bangladesh. During the crisis, Nixon deployed the USN carrier *Enterprise* into the Bay of Bengal (see "India").

After the Soviet Union invaded neighboring Afghanistan in December 1979, Pakistan became a major conduit of arms supplies to the mujahideen resistance. In 1981, the United States agreed to a $3.2 billion military and economic assistance program to Pakistan.

Many Americans tend to think of the mujahideen struggle against the Soviets in Afghanistan as "Charlie Wilson's War." Wilson was a Texas congressman who lobbied for arms shipments to the mujahideen that were funneled through Pakistan's intelligence service, the ISI. But the conflict could also be considered "Zia-ul-Haq's (president of Pakistan) War,"

"William Casey's (CIA head) War," or even "Ronald Reagan's War." Prior to becoming president, Reagan had said, "My idea of American policy towards the Soviet Union is simple: We win and they lose." In order to avoid US casualties and create deniability, billions of dollars' worth of support were funneled through Pakistan's ISI. The Saudis matched the American financial contribution.

After Zia-ul-Haq met Reagan on a visit to Washington, the president noted in his diary that the two leaders got along well, that Zia-ul-Haq had given his word Pakistan wasn't building a nuclear bomb, and that the Pakistani were dedicated to helping Afghanistan and stopping what the Soviets were up to. And the Soviets were indeed stopped in Afghanistan, though at a terrible cost to the Afghan people and at the cost of giving a boost to jihadi radicalism.

Close ties between the CIA and the ISI dissolved in the 1990s as the United States lost interest in Afghanistan after the Soviet withdrawal. On other levels, too, the implosion of the Soviet Union seemed to make Pakistan a less important American ally, and the nuclear question was about to re-emerge big time.

In 1990, we again suspended military assistance to Pakistan over concerns about Pakistan's nuclear program. In May 1998, India demonstrated its nuclear capability by exploding nuclear bombs underground, and in response, Pakistan did the same.

However, we were about to focus on the region again even more intently and for reasons even more compelling than Pakistan's and India's nuclear weapons programs.

As warlords fought for control of Afghanistan after the Soviet withdrawal and the eventual collapse of the Afghan regime they had supported, the 1990s saw the rise in Afghanistan of the Taliban, an organization with strong links across the border in Pakistan, and alongside the Taliban was rising another new force.

On August 20, 1998, after the embassy bombings in Kenya and Tanzania, President Clinton launched a cruise missile strike on Osama bin Laden's camp at Khost in Eastern Afghanistan. The USN fired missiles over Pakistani territory alerting that government prior to the strike. Osama bin Laden managed to evacuate the camp prior to the arrival of about seventy missiles, which killed about twenty people.

General Mahmud Ahmed, the head of the Pakistani ISI, happened to be in Washington at the time of the 9/11 terrorist attacks. Summoned to a meeting the next day with Richard Armitage, the deputy secretary of state, Ahmed pledged his country's unwavering support to the new war on terror, despite the fact that Pakistan had been one of only three countries to recognize the Taliban regime in Afghanistan.

The Pakistani government did, indeed, prove useful in the fight against terror, and the United States supplied extensive financial assistance. In 2004, with Afghanistan now the US government's priority, not Pakistan's nuclear weapons, President George W. Bush declared Pakistan a Major Non-NATO Ally. However, as fighting increased in Afghanistan, US concerns about Taliban links inside Pakistan, particularly in the border areas of the country, only very loosely controlled by Pakistan's central government, grew, and the use of drones to attack targets began.

During the 2008 election campaign, Senator Obama staked out a surprisingly aggressive position: "If we have actionable intelligence about high-value targets and President Musharraf won't act, we will." After being elected president, Obama would have an opportunity to follow through on those words.

The use of drones to attack targets within Pakistan increased dramatically and became a regular occurrence creating in many senses a new form of war. But in 2011, the biggest target of all in the War against Terror was about to present itself, and it wouldn't be a drone that was sent in.

On May 1, 2011, four US helicopters flew from Jalalabad in Afghanistan to Abbottabad, Pakistan, on a mission aimed at Osama bin Laden. In spite of the crash of one stealth Black Hawk into the compound, Operation Neptune Spear was a near total success. Two Black Hawk helicopters carried USN SEALs to Osama's secret compound. Two CH-47s carried extra fuel and additional forces. The SEALs relayed the code signal "Geronimo" back to the White House confirming that Osama bin Laden had been positively identified. Osama bin Laden, three other males, and one female were killed; there were no SEAL casualties.

The intelligence-gathering phase of this mission had required about ten years with several "enhanced interrogation" sessions along the way. The action phase of this invasion of Pakistan and the subsequent withdrawal lasted about four hours. No Pakistani military or civilians were killed in the raid.

Osama's body was identified with DNA methods and transported to the USS Carl Vinson. The burial was at sea in the north Arabian Ocean. Soon after the death of Osama was announced a crowd thronged around the White House chanting "USA, USA ..."

One of the MC-130E Combat Talon I planes that had been used when President Jimmy Carter ordered the disastrous Operation Eagle Claw to free American hostages in Iran was used to ferry SEAL Team Six to Kentucky for a congratulatory visit with President Obama. Navy SEAL Team Six received a Presidential Unit Citation—the highest unit award in the US military. President Obama credited the "countless intelligence and counterterrorism professionals" who had labored for over a decade in three US administrations to achieve this result.

The urgent need to bring justice to the author of the 9/11 attacks had outweighed considerations about the violations of Pakistan's sovereignty and our links with that country.

But the death of Osama did not mean the end of the drone war in Pakistan. In October of 2011, secretary of state Hillary Clinton, on a visit to Islamabad, warned Pakistan that the United States would continue to take unilateral action against terrorists, and drone strikes continued.

Currently Pakistan's problems with the Taliban are unresolved. The Pakistani government was attempting to hold negotiations with the Pakistani Taliban, and subsequently, a lull occurred in drone strikes. However, as we go to press, US drone strikes in Pakistan have been resumed by the Obama administration.

PALAU

THE NAME OF ONE OF THE PALAU ISLANDS in the Pacific will be more familiar to many Americans than others: Peleliu.

In the nineteenth century, the Spanish were in colonial control of the Palau Islands and the people who lived there until they sold the islands to Germany in 1899. The Japanese, who were on the Allied side in the First World War, won them in that war, which meant Japan was the colonial power in the islands on December 7, 1941.

On September 15, after underwater demolition teams had tackled beach obstructions, and after bombing and bombardment of Peleliu, the 1st Marine Division stormed ashore. The initial landings faced heavy resistance, but the marines battled forward and, by the end of the day, held a beachhead. On the next day, they advanced further and managed to capture the airfield on Peleliu. Bitter fighting for Japanese fortifications on "The Point" followed, and our men faced a number of desperate Japanese counterattacks. But even though the fighting had been tough so far, the worst was yet to come. Our forces had to try to take a north-south ridge running along the island, one that the Japanese had heavily fortified. Bitter fighting followed on Bloody Nose Ridge, and the Japanese tried to reinforce their troops by sea at night. By September 26, the Japanese defenders were finally surrounded, but the fighting continued. In late September and increasingly in October, troops from the 81st Division took up the burden of the fighting. It wasn't until November that fighting ceased. American forces suffered huge casualties, but the Japanese lost even more.

Meanwhile on September 17, the 81st Division landed on nearby Angaur Island. Other nearby islands, including Ngesebus Island, were also captured by our forces.

The end of the bitter battle for Peleliu and nearby islands did not, however, mean the end of the war in the Palau Islands. Some of them, notably Koror and Babeldoab (or Babelthuap), remained occupied by the Japanese, and more intermittent action, particularly bombing raids against them, took place.

After the war, the Palau Islands were under US control as part of the Trust Territory of the Pacific Islands. In 1994, after an extended dispute over the signing of the Compact of Free Association with the United States, both parties signed it, and Palau became independent, and the United States took responsibility for the defense of Palau.

Many Palauan citizens have volunteered for service in the US military. The USN visits, and US military and Palauan security forces have trained alongside each other. Palau has benefited from Operation Christmas Drop (see "Micronesia").

PANAMA

JOHN QUINCY ADAMS, OUR SIXTH PRESIDENT, recognized the strategic importance of Panama in the 1820s and even helped to set up an isthmian canal company. Though, obviously, a lot of time was yet to pass and a lot of Frenchmen were going to be disappointed before a Panama Canal was finally built.

However, even without a canal, people were using the isthmus to travel between the Atlantic and Pacific Oceans. With the finding of gold in California, for instance, many Americans crossed overland through Panama on their way to and from the gold fields (see "Nicaragua" for a more detailed explanation about why such a roundabout route made sense).

And, as an indication of our major interest in the strategic isthmus, in 1846, we signed with Colombia, which was then the national power in Panama, the Mallarino-Bidlack Treaty. We got free travel for our citizens across the isthmus, and in return, we guaranteed the neutrality of the area and Colombian sovereignty over it. Our strategic interest in the isthmus, and the deeply divided nature of politics in Panama for much of the nineteenth century were going to keep our military very busy over the coming decades.

Almost as soon as the ink on the treaty was dry, in 1847, New York businessmen started the Panama Railroad Company. The Panama Railway, financed by Americans, was opened in 1855.

And already, by 1856, our troops were being deployed in Panama. In that year, the Watermelon War broke out, though it was really more of a Watermelon Riot, which was triggered by an intoxicated American railroad traveler who took a slice of watermelon from a Panamanian fruit merchant and refused payment. Fifteen Americans were killed in Panama City, and we sent our troops in to restore order and protect American citizens.

In 1860, the USS *Saint Mary's*, a twenty-two-gun sloop of war, sent sailors and marines ashore in order to protect the Panama Railway from insurgents.

Our troops were deployed again in 1865, this time to protect Americans during a revolution.

In 1873, more of the same, really, as local groups clashed and American troops moved in to protect Americans.

And all the while, people had been thinking about the possibility of a canal between the Atlantic and the Pacific. After the US Civil War, the United States tried twice (1867 and 1884) to build a canal through Nicaragua (see "Nicaragua").

In 1880, Frenchman de Lesseps, who had tackled the Suez Canal, began building a Panama canal. By 1889, however, the venture was out of money, and construction stopped with the canal incomplete.

Meanwhile, in 1885, Pedro Prestan led a revolt in Panama, which formed part of Colombia at the time. The rebels burned the American consulate in Colon and destroyed considerable property. A force of six USN warships and the full East Coast complement of US marines (about two thousand) were dispatched to Panama where the Colombians requested their intervention against the rebels. A derby-wearing Prestan was hanged in front of a large crowd.

In 1901, we sent in troops once again to keep transport flowing and protect American property, and it was about now that America also began a serious push to build a Panama canal. Soon after, the US government began to think it would be easier to build such a canal through an independent Panama, rather than continuing to deal with the Colombian government.

Consequently, in 1903 when Panama revolted against Colombia, this time the United States, led by Teddy Roosevelt, sided with the Panamanian rebels. TR dispatched two USN ships (*Nashville* and *Dixie*) in support of the rebels. A battalion of marines commanded by Major John Lejenue landed at Colon. A bribe of eight thousand dollars was paid to the Colombian commander to hasten his exit from Panama. TR would later (in 1911) claim, "I took the Canal Zone." Surely it was Teddy Roosevelt who provided the inspiration for the palindrome, "a man, a plan, a canal, Panama." The US government recognized the new Panamanian nation and negotiated a treaty to control the Canal Zone. The treaty gave the United States extensive rights in the Canal Zone that extended about five miles on either side of the canal and some rights in Panama outside the Canal Zone and was to be a source of some tension between Panama and the United States in the years ahead.

And the years ahead were also to see more deployments of US troops.

For instance, in 1918, US marines were sent to Chiriqui Province to quell local disturbances.

In 1925, US troops were used, at the request of the Panamanian government, to disperse a mob of rent rioters

The outbreak of the Second World War in 1939 and rising tensions around the world only increased the strategic importance of the canal. Matters were complicated by the fact that, for the early part of the war, Panama was ruled by the fascist-leaning Arias. However, he was handily toppled in October 1941, before Pearl Harbor. After the Japanese attack on Pearl Harbor, fears of subversion or a Japanese naval strike intensified, and indeed, both Germans and Japanese developed plans to attack the canal. In response, we organized a deal with the Panamanian government to allow us to occupy additional sites to protect the canal.

In 1977, the Torrijos-Carter Treaty was signed that provided for the return of the Panama Canal Zone to Panama in 1999. That, however, isn't quite the end of this chapter.

In 1983, Manuel Noriega, a cocaine kingpin, became the president of Panama. He had also been the CIA's man in Panama from the 1960s until 1988 when he was indicted in Florida. President Reagan and George H. W. Bush had tried to dislodge him by covert means and failed. It would take an invasion to remove this former American friend from power in Panama.

On December 16, 1989, an off-duty US marine was shot and killed at a Panamanian Defence Forces roadblock. A line had been crossed.

In December 1989, only a month after the Berlin Wall fell, President George H. W. Bush launched Operation Just Cause to drive Manuel Noriega from power. A force of twenty-five thousand troops overwhelmed the Noriega's Panamanian Defence Force. Twenty-three Americans were killed in the fighting. The Panamanian strongman sought refuge in the Vatican embassy where US soldiers blasted him with rock 'n' roll hits, such as "The End" by the Doors, "Welcome to the Jungle" by Guns 'n' Roses, and "All I Want Is You" by U-2, among others. Noriega was extradited to Miami where he was convicted of drug trafficking, racketeering, and money laundering.

In more recent years, we have maintained assorted military links with Panama, for instance, taking part in joint exercises. US warships still travel through the Panama Canal. The Missouri National Guard is partnered with Panama.

PAPUA NEW GUINEA

PAPUA NEW GUINEA IS THE EASTERN HALF of the enormous island of New Guinea, just north of Australia, plus some additional islands. Errol Flynn, before his discovery by Hollywood, lived on the island for five years between the world wars, trying to make his fortune raising tobacco and mining.

The western half of New Guinea is now part of Indonesia but used to be Dutch East Guinea. Papua New Guinea also has a colonial past. North of the island's central mountains used to be German New Guinea, while south of it was Papua controlled by Australia. In World War I, the Australians invaded and occupied German New Guinea so that all the east of the island was under Australian administration. Its principal islands, which used to be called the very Germanic New Pomerania and New Mecklenburg are now, the very much less Germanic New Britain and New Ireland.

And the area was to see a lot more action in World War II. In January 1942, less than two months after the attack on Pearl Harbor, Japanese troops took Rabaul, the capital of former German New Guinea, and landed at Buna on the north coast. One of their ultimate targets was Port Moresby on the southern coast of the island, just a few hundred miles across the sea from Australia. In the Battle of the Coral Sea, our navy prevented a Japanese attempt to take Port Moresby from the sea, so the Japanese decided to take it by land instead. They advanced over the Kokoda Trail through the mountains of the Owen Stanley Range towards Port Moresby. Bitter fighting followed as Australians fought desperately to prevent their homeland from the advancing Japanese. Finally, the Japanese were forced to retreat, and a combined Australian and American offensive was launched against some of the Japanese bases in the north of the island. The fighting was intense, and casualties were heavy. The US 32nd Infantry Division had a particularly rough time, and the 41st Infantry Division suffered as well. Eventually, it was an Allied victory, and Buna was captured, but many Japanese still remained in the area.

The Japanese lost again in the Battle of Milne Bay in September 1942 when they launched an attack on an Australian base there. And in March 1943, in the Battle of the Bismarck Sea, the USN did severe damage to a Japanese attempt to bring thousands of reinforcements to their base at Lae.

In April of 1943, Magic (US decryption of Japanese wartime codes) revealed that Admiral Yamamoto would be flying from Rabaul to Bougainville over New Guinea. On April 18, 1943, USAAF P-38 Lightning aircraft from Henderson Field in the Solomons were ordered to intercept and shoot down his aircraft. His charred corpse was later found in the jungle near Buin showing evidence of being hit by 50-caliber bullets. His body was returned to Japan and given a state funeral on June 5, 1943.

Operation Vengeance marked the first time that a US president authorized an assassination in wartime. Both FDR and the Japanese admiral were alumni of Harvard University.

Douglas MacArthur was focused on the Philippines, but before he could return there, he had to smash Japanese resistance in key places like Lae. The push for Lae began. On June 30, the First Battalion of the 162nd Infantry landed at and captured Nassau Bay, forty miles from Lae. As American forces advanced along the coast, Australian forces advanced from Wau in a pincer movement.

On September 5, ninety-six C-47s with two hundred fighters and bombers escorting them ferried the US 503rd Parachute Regiment to the Nadzab airfield near Lae. Our men rapidly took the airfield, and Australian troops were soon flown into it. By mid-September 1943, the town had fallen to Allied forces.

In December 1943, US troops landed on the island of New Britain. More landings on islands and New Guinea itself followed, and on April

22, 1944, the US I Corps landed in Hollandia on the western side of the island. MacArthur now had a platform from which to launch his liberation of the Philippines.

However, pockets of Japanese resistance in the jungles of New Guinea and on assorted smaller islands lasted until the war's conclusion.

Papua New Guinea gained its independence in 1975.

In recent decades, Papua New Guinea has faced assorted challenges, for instance, the fighting on Bougainville in the 1990s. The United States had some minor involvement in the Bougainville crisis, including certifying the collection of arms on Bougainville.

Our military has also had some links with the country. For instance, USN vessels, such as the USS *Cleveland*, have visited Papua New Guinea and provided medical and humanitarian assistance. US forces, through PACOM, have given some training to the Papua New Guinea Defence Force and have held small-scale exercises with it.

PARAGUAY

PARAGUAY IS ABOUT THE SIZE OF CALIFORNIA with its capital at Asunción. Spanish is a major language, but over 90 percent of people speak and understand the local language, Guarani.

In 1855, the USS *Water Witch*, a steam-powered side-wheel gunboat captained by Thomas Jefferson Page of Virginia, was cruising along the coast of Paraguay. His mission was to chart the course of the Rio de la Plata. The US ship was fired upon by guns in a Paraguayan coastal fort in what was labeled an "unprovoked, unwarrantable and dastardly attack." One crewmember, the helmsman (Samuel Chaney), was killed. In 1858, the Paraguayan expedition, made up of nineteen ships in the USN, arrived at Asunción to demand an apology from the Paraguayan government. This was received, compensation was paid, and a bi-lateral commercial treaty was negotiated.

In 1886, Elisabeth Nietzsche, the sister of the philosopher, helped to found a "racially pure" colony in Paraguay, which was called Nueva Germania. The colony was a failure, but German influence in Paraguay persisted. Paraguay formed the first Nazi party in South America in 1932, which was the last to dissolve in 1946. However, as World War II progressed, Paraguay gradually became closer to the Allies with, for instance, a US

Military Aviation Mission and US Army Mission being established there in 1943. Paraguay eventually joined the United States in the Allied cause, though only three months prior to V-E Day.

The dictator Alfredo Stroessner, whose father was originally from Bavaria, was president of Paraguay from 1954 to 1989. He already had links with the US military having graduated from a general staff course at Fort Leavenworth, and in 1953, he was invited to tour assorted military facilities in the United States. After he took power in a coup, his regime received over a hundred million dollars' worth of USG support. The United States assisted with counter-insurgency training and supplied trucks, planes, artillery, and small arms. Stroessner enjoyed close links with LBJ and even offered to send Paraguayan troops to Vietnam. In 1968, he went on a formal visit to Washington.

The Carter era, however, saw Washington distancing itself from Stroessner, and in the 1980s, the US ambassador was several times threatened with expulsion over criticism of press censorship. Finally, Stroessner was toppled in a coup in 1989. In 1996, the United States helped prevent another military coup in Paraguay.

In recent years, US troops have taken part alongside Paraguay in both bilateral and multilateral exercises, and the presence of US troops for exercises inside Paraguay in 2005 led to speculation about the possible creation of a US base there. The Massachusetts National Guard is partnered with Paraguay.

PERU

PERU IS THE LAND OF (AMONG MANY OTHER THINGS) THE INCAS and home to the amazing city of Machu Picchu.

We had a little bit of involvement with Peru early on, but not that much. For instance, in 1813, a US frigate captured a Peruvian privateer off Chile, and in the same year, the same US ship helped recapture another American ship off Callao in Peru.

In 1835 and 1836, the USMC landed on several occasions in Peru to protect US lives and property in Callao and Lima during revolutionary conflict there. USN ships would occasionally call in at Callao after that, and sometimes others were extremely glad they did. In 1873, marines from a USN ship rushed to help put out a fire on an Italian merchant ship in the harbor there.

Interestingly, the French had quite a lot of military influence in Peru at the end of the nineteenth century and in the early twentieth century, but after World War I, we began to take more of an interest. For instance, in the 1920s, the USN helped construct a naval academy in Peru.

During World War II, links expanded. We sent lend-lease equipment to Peru, and a US military mission began operations there. And we even operated an airbase at Talara, Peru, from 1942 to 1944 (we used the base after that until 1947 for communications training). Peru declared war on the Axis powers late in the war.

After World War II, the Cold War was a factor throughout South America, and our Military Assistance Advisory Group organized a program of military aid to help keep Peru closer to the United States than to the Communist powers. In 1965, when guerrilla groups emerged in mountainous territory, US aid and advisors helped the Peruvians rapidly crush them. The Tuna War (see "Ecuador") also caused tensions with neighboring states.

In the 1970s, by contrast, with a left-wing government in power, significant amounts of Soviet military assistance flowed in.

Then in the 1980s with the rise of the Shining Path (Sendero Luminoso) and the beginning in Peru of the war against illegal narcotics, US military links with Peru were reinvigorated. For instance, in September 1989, President George H. W. Bush sent US Special Forces to Peru to help train government troops for operations against illegal drug producers and traffickers. The United States also dispatched AWACS and Orion planes to fly over significant parts of Peru and established two radar stations in Peru to track aircraft used in connection with illicit drugs. Political disagreements between US and Peruvian governments, however, sometimes affected such programs.

The battle against illicit narcotics has continued to be a priority for the United States in Peru, and the US and Peruvian militaries have regularly cooperated on activities, such as training and exercises. The West Virginia National Guard is partnered with Peru.

PHILIPPINES

THE PHILIPPINES DERIVES ITS NAME FROM KING PHILIP II of Spain, and the Spanish controlled the island-country for hundreds of years. Then we came along.

The United States has had a long and complex involvement with the Philippines that has included multiple American invasions.

Early on the morning of May 1, 1898, Admiral George Dewey turned to his captain and said, "You may fire when you are ready, Gridley." The USN sent the Spanish Navy's Asian fleet to the shallow bottom of Manila Bay that day in the Spanish-American War.

A rebel who had fought the Spanish for Philippine independence from Spain, Emilio Aguinaldo was brought by the Americans from Hong Kong back to the Philippines in an attempt to enlist the help of the Philippines' freedom fighters against Spain.

US and Filipino forces fought side by side against the Spanish, and on June 12, 1898, they proclaimed Filipino independence. It was not to last.

By the peace deal that ended the Spanish-American War, the Spanish handed control of the Philippines not to the Filipinos but to the United States.

In a 1903 interview, President William McKinley offered this explanation of his rationale for taking control of the Philippines:

> I would like to say just a word about the Philippine business. I have been criticized a good deal about the Philippines, but don't deserve it. The truth is I didn't want the Philippines, and when they came to us, as a gift from the gods, I did not know what to do with them. When the Spanish War broke out Dewey was at Hong Kong, and I ordered him to go to Manila and to capture or destroy the Spanish fleet, and he had to; because, if defeated, he had no place to refit on that side of the globe, and if the Dons were victorious they would likely cross the Pacific and ravage our Oregon and California coasts. And so he had to destroy the Spanish fleet, and did it! But that was as far as I thought then.
>
> When I next realized that the Philippines had dropped into our laps I confess I did not know what to do with them.

I sought counsel from all sides—Democrats as well as Republicans—but got little help. I thought first we would take only Manila; then Luzon; then other islands perhaps also. I walked the floor of the White House night after night until midnight; and I am not ashamed to tell you, gentlemen, that I went down on my knees and prayed [to] Almighty God for light and guidance more than one night. And one night late it came to me this way—I don't know how it was, but it came: (1) That we could not give them back to Spain—that would be cowardly and dishonorable; (2) that we could not turn them over to France and Germany— our commercial rivals in the Orient—that would be bad business and discreditable; (3) that we could not leave them to themselves—they were unfit for self-government—and they would soon have anarchy and misrule over there worse than Spain's was; and (4) that there was nothing left for us to do but to take them all, and to educate the Filipinos, and uplift and civilize and Christianize them, and by God's grace do the very best we could by them, as our fellow-men for whom Christ also died. And then I went to bed, and went to sleep, and slept soundly, and the next morning I sent for the chief engineer of the War Department [our map-maker], and I told him to put the Philippines on the map of the United States [pointing to a large map on the wall of his office], and there they are, and there they will stay while I am President!

After a period of increasing tension between US forces and Filipino forces, the situation erupted into outright war.

In the initial phase of the war, the Filipinos attempted to fight US forces in a conventional war. However, it rapidly became apparent that it was a hugely unequal fight, and the Filipino forces dispersed in an attempt to wage a guerilla war that required over 120,000 US soldiers to tackle it over years. There were 4,324 US casualties in the war, most on account of disease. More than twenty thousand Filipino fighters were killed, and perhaps as many as two hundred thousand civilians died through violence, disease, or starvation.

This war was often brutal. The Americans were said to be civilizing the Filipinos "with a Krag"—a .30-caliber Krag-Jorgensen five-shot magazine rifle. The war featured American machine guns, heavy artillery, and naval bombardments against Filipino troops, some of them armed with little more than spears and bolo knives. This war also saw the first use of water boarding by American troops.

This, however, only represents a part of what the Philippine-American War was about. The Philippines was by no means a homogenous people at the time but, instead, a mass of varying tribal loyalties. The war's greatest significance for the Filipinos was that, even in defeat, it helped to bind their many diverse islands together and create a national Philippines identity.

The Americans decisively won the Philippine-American war in the space of three years with a combination of extensive force, guile, and some enemy disarray.

Major General Arthur MacArthur, a US Civil War veteran, helped implement the pacification of the islands earning him hostility among the Filipinos. His son, Douglas MacArthur, would atone for the crimes of the father and redeem America in Filipino eyes.

In 1908, America's Great White Fleet called in at Manila on its epic voyage around the world.

The United States introduced a wide number of reforms into the Philippines, and in 1935, under the Tydings-McDuffie Act, the Philippines became a self-government commonwealth with future full independence from the United States envisaged.

However, Japanese bombers began hitting airbases in the Philippines on December 8, 1941, and immediately destroyed half the American air forces on the ground. An invasion followed later that month, and the Americans fell back to the island fortress of Corregidor. Over one hundred thousand Americans were made prisoners of the Japanese for the duration of the war while MacArthur escaped via PT boat to Australia vowing, "I shall return." Many Americans and their Filipino allies were killed in the Bataan Death March.

The Japanese occupiers compelled a Filipino puppet government to declare war on the United States.

In October 1944, MacArthur made good on his promise wading ashore with a force of 160,000 US troops at Leyte. In spite of opposition from the USN, which preferred a more direct island-hopping strategy, MacArthur had secured the support of FDR for his return to the Philippines. Manila was nearly completely destroyed in the battle with 60 percent of the housing demolished by bombing, shelling, or fire.

After the surrender of Japanese General Yamashita, however, problems persisted in the Philippines. On July 4, 1946, the independent Philippine Republic was proclaimed, but American influence was still strong. The

Huks, who had resisted the Japanese, turned their attention against the Philippine government.

Major General Edward Lansdale, a former Madison Avenue professional who had worked with the OSS in World War II, helped lead a successful counter-insurgency against guerillas in the Philippines during the Cold War.

In 1989, US fighter planes helped the Aquino government defeat a coup attempt.

For decades after the war, the Philippines were home to large numbers of US service personnel. Many Filippinos also served in the US military. Clark Air Base and the US naval facilities at Subic Bay were particularly important US bases. Both closed in 1992, but we still have military links with the Philippines. For instance, under the 1999 Visiting Forces Agreement, US military personnel on a rotational basis have assisted the Philippines military in developing their expertise, among other things, for the fight against Islamist rebels. The Guam and Hawaii National Guards are partnered with the Philippines.

POLAND

POLAND MAY BE A LONG WAY FROM THE UNITED STATES, but a shared experience of fighting for freedom (as well as Polish immigration into the United States) has created many close links between the two nations.

Poles fought for the American cause right from our founding.

Tadeusz Kościuszko (1746-1817) fought for America's independence from Britain in the American Revolution and then went on to fight for his homeland's independence from Russia. He directed the fortification of West Point and rose to become a brigadier general in the Continental Army. A statue of Kościuszko stands atop the US Military Academy at West Point today.

Another Pole, Casimir Pulaski (1745-1779), also rose to the rank of brigadier general in the Continental Army and fought against both the Russians in Poland and the British in America. At the battle of Brandywine on September 11, 1777, he even helped save General George Washington from near certain capture. Pulaski died from wounds received at the Battle of Savannah. For his efforts and for his bravery, he has often been called the "father of the American cavalry."

Kosciuszko, Pulaski, and the other Poles who fought on our side in the Revolution were major factors in giving Poland a good reputation in the United States. When, in November 1830, the Poles rose against up against Russia, there was plenty of support in the United States for the Poles. For instance, a young soldier in the US Army wrote this letter to his commanding officer in 1831:

> *Having no longer any ties which can bind me to my native country—no prospects—nor any friends—I intend by the first opportunity to proceed to Paris with the view of obtaining, thro' the interest of the Marquis de La Fayette, an appointment (if possible) in the Polish Army. In the event of the interference of France in behalf of Poland this may easily be effected—at all events it will be my only feasible plan of procedure.*

The author of this letter was Edgar Allan Poe (who, in the end, never did make it to the fight in Poland).

A Georgian, Dr. Paul Fitzsimmons, though, did join the Polish Army in the 1830-31 war against Russia where he served as a field surgeon.

It was all in vain, though. Russian forces crushed the Poles, and despite further armed resistance and continued sympathy in the United States, it would take until 1918 for an independent Poland once again to emerge. That it did so and received international recognition was to a certain extent due to President Woodrow Wilson who championed the cause of the Poles. His thirteenth point (of his famous Fourteen) specified an independent Polish state.

In the turbulent period after World War I, our forces played an occasional role in Poland. For instance, the USS *Pittsburgh*'s first visit to Estonia ended prematurely when USN Secretary Daniels instead sent it to Danzig, now the Polish port of Gdansk, to protect US citizens there.

And the efforts of Tadeusz Kościuszko in our Revolution against Britain were still being appreciated. American volunteer pilots, including Cedric E. Fauntleroy, joined the 7th Air Escadrille to fight the Russians in the Polish-Soviet War, and in reference to Kościuszko, the squadron became known as the Kościuszko Squadron.

But the Polish people's fight for freedom was far from finished. When Hitler invaded Poland on September 1, 1939, followed by Stalin's invasion from the east on September 18, the United States, not yet part of World War II, remained a neutral observer.

For Poland, the war was a tragedy of almost unimaginable proportions. Suffering six years of war and occupation from 1939 to 1945, Poland lost over six million people in World War II representing over 16 percent of its total 1939 population.

Once we were in the war, we did make some efforts to help the Polish resistance. For instance, the OSS supplied arms and equipment from August until October of 1944 in support of the Warsaw revolt, and the USAAF dropped some supplies from the air. But the revolt was doomed. Stalin ordered a pause in the advance of the Red Army to allow the Nazis to crush the rebellion, thus eradicating a source of potential opposition to Stalin's plans for Communist domination of post-war Poland.

We also attacked German targets in what is now Poland. For instance, on two occasions, B-17s attacked a Focke-Wulf plant at what is now Malbork in Poland, and the USAAF bombed Stettin, which is, after border changes, now Szczecin in Poland.

The Cold War years saw assorted US covert operations inside Poland, including a fiasco when the CIA attempted to aid the Freedom and Independence Movement, known as WIN, in the early 1950s. And we spent hundreds of millions of dollars sponsoring an "airborne" invasion of Eastern bloc countries via radio wave with the Radio Free Europe.

When the Solidarity trade union was formed in 1980, it received strong support from the American government. President Ronald Reagan, a former union leader himself (the Screen Actors Guild), developed a strong personal friendship with both Lech Wałęsa and the Polish pope, John Paul II.

Since the collapse of Communism in 1989, strong bilateral military links have formed between Poland and the United States. Poland joined NATO in 1999, and Poland sent large contingents to the wars in Iraq and Afghanistan. The Illinois National Guard is partnered with Poland. Today, we even have a small permanent military presence stationed on Polish soil at Lask Air Base, although there have also been much agonizing and arguing over US plans for a missile defense system based on Polish soil.

NATO air power in Poland was increased during the Crimean crisis of 2014, and US troops were sent there on exercise.

PORTUGAL

PORTUGAL HAS SOME LOVELY BEACHES AND A LONG HISTORY of exploring the world, and at one stage, it had a major empire.

In 1786, when John Adams was ambassador to the Court of St. James, he invited Thomas Jefferson over from France to London to assist in negotiating a treaty with Portugal. We wanted Portuguese assistance in dealing with the Barbary pirates. Adams and Jefferson got a deal, but unfortunately, the Portuguese minister who agreed to it didn't have authority to do so. In the end, the deal was off, although they did help us out for a time by preventing pirate ships from Algiers exiting into the Atlantic and threatening our merchant ships there.

In 1791, Portugal officially recognized the fledgling American republic.

Obviously USN ships have sailed the waters off Portugal and sometimes fought in them. For instance, in February 1815, the US frigate *Constitution* captured the British ship *Susannah* off Lisbon.

Over the centuries, USN ships have frequently called in at Portuguese ports. For instance, in 1904, four US battleships, USS *Alabama*, USS *Kearsarge*, USS *Maine*, and USS *Iowa* paid a special visit to Lisbon to mark the entrance of the infante (prince of Portugal) into Portuguese naval school.

In World War I, Portugal, like the United States, was neutral at first but later joined the Allies in fighting the Central Powers. Portuguese troops arrived at the Western Front in 1917, the same year as the American Expeditionary Forces.

In World War II, despite being a long-standing British ally, Portugal remained neutral. Consequently, Lisbon became a hotbed for espionage intrigue during the war. The Japanese alone are said to have had two hundred agents based in the city. "Wild Bill" Donovan set up OSS stations in Lisbon, and the OSS in Portugal managed to infiltrate the Japanese embassy stealing some low-grade Japanese naval traffic from the trash. General Marshall mistakenly feared that OSS activities in Lisbon might have compromised our Magic decryptions. These allegations were later raised as one of the arguments for disbanding the OSS after the war.

But our closest military involvement with Portugal during World War II, and indeed after it, wasn't on the mainland of Portugal; it was on the Azores, strategically located Portuguese islands in the Atlantic.

In May of 1941, prior to Pearl Harbor, FDR had ordered the War Department to create War Plan Gray, a plan for US invasion of the Azores. The president feared that the Germans might try to take control of these Atlantic islands to attack Allied shipping. In the end, it was never implemented.

By 1943, Portugal had granted the US basing rights in the Azores. Over two thousand US planes stopped at Lajes Airbase over the course of the war. And US Naval blimps flew ASW air patrols in neighboring waters from Port Lyautey during the war. Meanwhile in the seas off the Azores, the USN was hunting U-boats too.

Portugal became a founding member of NATO in 1949 and remains one today. There are various links between the US military and the Portuguese military, including joint exercises, aviation training, many port visits, and assorted agreements. Portugal sent national guards to Iraq for a time and troops to Afghanistan.

Lajes Airbase, though it has recently been downsized, remains home to the 65th Air Base Wing to this day.

In January 1980, following an earthquake on Terceira Island where Lajes is situated and responding to a request for help from the Portuguese government, USAF C-141s flew in hundreds of tents and blankets.

QATAR

OIL WAS DISCOVERED IN QATAR IN THE 1930S, and the country is now one the wealthiest in the world. It was part of a British sphere of influence until 1971.

With the decline of British influence in Qatar, US influence increased. The United States opened an embassy in Doha in 1973. US interest in Qatar was inevitably boosted by the fall of America's ally, the shah of Iran in 1979 and the conflict with Saddam over Kuwait.

The war to liberate Kuwait was a key milestone in the developing friendship between the United States and Qatar. For instance, Qatar sent troops to join the coalition forces with a battalion involved in the fighting at Khafji, and it helped in other senses as well, for instance, hosting US aircraft and their crews.

After the 1991 Gulf War, many US bases in Saudi Arabia were repositioned to Qatar. Qatar is the high-tech home to US Central Command (CENTCOM). The strategy for Operation Iraqi Freedom and Operation Enduring Freedom (Afghanistan) was formulated largely from Qatar.

The United States operates major facilities in Qatar at Camp As Sayliyah and Al Udeid Air Base.

On October 15, 2007, a Patriot missile based in Qatar was accidently fired in a training exercise. The missile landed in the backyard of the Qatari minister of defense. Oops! Fortunately, no one was injured.

Forces from Qatar joined the United States and NATO in 2011 in operations to remove Gaddafi from power in Libya.

In 2013, we signed a new Defense Cooperation agreement to continue joint training and exercises with Qatar, such as Exercise Eagle Resolve 13, which was conducted at various locations in Qatar, Bahrain, and the UAE in April and May 2013.

REPUBLIC OF THE CONGO

THIS IS THE OTHER CONGO COUNTRY, distinct from the Democratic Republic of the Congo (formerly called Zaire; see "Democratic Republic of the Congo"). The Republic of Congo's capital is Brazzaville.

It used to be a French colony. Because it was one of the earliest French territories to support the Free French instead of the pro-German Vichy French government in France, after the 1940 German invasion of France, Brazzaville was from 1940-1943 a sort of capital of the Free French.

We've had much less military involvement with the Republic of the Congo than with the Democratic Republic of the Congo. However, we have had a little.

For instance, in 1993, a USAF C-5 Galaxy flew into Brazzaville with heavy equipment for Belgian paratroopers preparing for a possible rescue mission in next-door Zaire, and in March 1997, US troops were sent to Brazzaville in preparation for an evacuation from Zaire.

Then, in June 1997 when fighting broke out in Brazzaville itself, the USAF flew in with a team of communications and security experts and flew out with civilians, thirty of whom were Americans, and a dog. The operations commander reported later that nobody had asked the nationality of the dog.

In July 2012, as AFRICOM commander General Carter F. Ham visited Brazzaville and met president of the Republic of the Congo, Denis Sassou-N'Guesso.

ROMANIA

A MONG OTHER INTERESTING FACTS ABOUT ROMANIA, you can find Transylvania there, legendary home of vampires and actual birthplace of Vlad Dracul, who also had the not very cuddly nickname Vlad the Impaler. Also Romanian, unlike the languages of the East European nations that surround it, is descended from Latin, the language of the Romans.

The United States formally recognized Romania in 1880 with the appointment of New Yorker Eugene Schuyler as ambassador. My (Chris Kelly's) maternal great-grandfather, Thomas Tileston Wells, served as the American consul general to Romania for about twenty years around the beginning of the twentieth century. My grandmother, Georgina Wells (1902-1997), had visited Romania twenty-one times by her twenty-first birthday, becoming acquainted with Romania's Queen Marie, a granddaughter of Queen Victoria and daughter of Prince Alfred, brother of the future King Edward VII.

During World War I, Romania, like us, initially remained neutral but later, influenced by Queen Marie, joined the Allied side. As a result, most of Romania ended up being occupied by enemy troops in the ensuing conflict. However, Queen Marie, with the assistance of her friend the American dance pioneer Loie Fuller, got hold of a major American loan that helped the Romanians to resist.

When the Russian Revolution took Russia out of the war, Romania found it could not fight on alone, and it was forced to seek peace with the enemy. It only re-entered the war (on the Allied side) on November 10, a day before the armistice.

After the Allied victory in 1919, Romania received some compensation for all its suffering. Thanks largely, once again, to the energetic efforts of Queen Marie, a woman to some extent in her grandmother's mold, Romania acquired large tracts of territory that had previously been part of the Austro-Hungarian and Russian Empires.

In 1926, this soldier queen made a triumphant visit to the United States facilitated by Thomas Tileston Wells. Despite having played such a significant role in World War I, she was not, however, to play any part in World War II. She died in 1938.

In 1939, Romania again initially tried to remain neutral. Marshal Antonescu, however, led a fascist coup in 1940, and this time, Romania ended up on the German side. Romanian forces participated in Operation Barbarossa, the invasion of the Soviet Union in 1941, and Romanian oil fields were a vital strategic resource to the Axis.

On June 5, 1942, the US Congress unanimously authorized a declaration of war against Romania. It wasn't long before we were targeting Romania militarily. For instance, USAAF B-24 bombers based out of Egypt began bombing the Ploeşti oil fields in 1942, and Bucharest was bombed beginning in April 1944.

Romania, however, was not going to hang on for ultimate defeat and devastating destruction as Germany did. On August 23, 1944, with Soviet tanks streaming towards Bucharest, King Michael of Romania, in coordination with Romanian opposition politicians and Communists, staged a successful coup, switching sides, and declared war on Germany.

The OSS staged Operation Bughouse a week later arriving in Bucharest to assess damage to the Ploeşti refineries and to gather intelligence. Two former college professors managed to locate forty intact mailbags full of German military documents at a Luftwaffe headquarters. Even more important, OSS members also helped to retrieve some 1,350 downed Allied airmen in Romania.

The Romanian volte-face did not, however, prevent the Red Army from moving into Romania. At first, OSS agents were able to hand out free cigarettes to Russian soldiers in exchange for information. The OSS soon learned that millions of tons of grain were being shipped back to Russia, and factory and refinery equipment was stripped and sent back to the Soviet Union on rail cars. They also found out that thousands of Romanian soldiers and Romanians of German descent were being shipped eastward for incarceration.

The Soviets were, inevitably, uncomfortable with OSS scrutiny and soon forced the American teams out of the country. The Iron Curtain had descended over Romania.

In 1946, a newly formed CIA attempted to help form an underground resistance to the Soviet occupiers. The former Romanian foreign minister and other colleagues were smuggled out of Romania to Austria. Soviet intelligence services, however, immediately cracked down on the covert operations.

Hundreds of thousands of Romanians were imprisoned during the Communist era. Nicolae Ceauşescu attempted to steer a more independent course for Romania within the Warsaw Pact, for instance, condemning the Soviet crackdown in Prague in 1968. Because of that and despite the brutality of his regime, Ceauşescu was at times popular with some Western governments.

In November 1989, free passage was allowed through the Berlin Wall, and its demolition started almost immediately. In December 1989, the Romanian revolution erupted. On Christmas Day 1989, Ceauşescu and his wife, Elena, were executed by firing squad. And a few days later, two C-130s flew into Bucharest bringing medical supplies to help those wounded in the fighting.

Since the revolution, close military links have developed between the United States and Romania. All four US service branches have conducted exercises within Romania. The Romanian contingent deployed to Iraq was among the last to leave that country. And we have an anti-missile base now under construction in southern Romania. The Alabama National Guard is partnered with Romania.

Romania has been a NATO member since 2004.

Romanian forces remain in Afghanistan as of this writing, and the United States will utilize bases in Eastern Romania to facilitate a gradual withdrawal from Afghanistan.

RUSSIA

A NYBODY WHO LIVED THROUGH THE COLD WAR is so used to the idea of the Soviet Union as a heavily defended superpower, bristling with nukes, and probably prepared to use them if ever invaded that the idea we've ever invaded Russia can seem hard to believe, and yet we have.

Russia and the United States of America have had, in a few senses, slightly parallel historical trajectories. Manifest destiny drove the Americans from the original thirteen colonies across a continent to the Pacific; the tsar charted an expansionist course east to Siberia and south to the edge of the subcontinent. Lincoln issued the Emancipation Proclamation in 1863, while Alexander II issued the Emancipation Reform of 1861 that freed the serfs. Convulsed by revolution, tsarist Russia dropped out of the Allied camp in World War I, even as Woodrow Wilson led America into war. Both nations joined in the war against Hitler. From 1945 to roughly 1989, the two superpowers, the United States and the Soviet Union, competed for power and influence throughout the world in the Cold War.

Soon after the American Revolution, military contact began between the United States and Russia. For instance, John Paul Jones, well-known as the Father of the United States Navy, after his distinguished service in our armed forces, became a rear admiral in the Russian Navy of Empress Catherine II.

In the early and mid-nineteenth century, we carried out a sort of peaceful invasion of what was then Russian territory. Tsarist Russia occupied much territory that now forms parts of the United States, including Alaska. Secretary of state William Seward negotiated the purchase of Alaska from the Russians for the sum of $7.2 million in 1867. Political opponents decried the move as "Seward's Folly," though it's hard to imagine the United States without Alaska today. The distinctive onion-domed Russian Orthodox churches remain today a highlight in Alaskan cities such as Sitka. Less well-known is that Russia claimed areas on the Pacific coast as far south as places like Fort Ross, California. Not surprisingly, this became a source of some tension with the US government as it expanded control westwards. In 1841, the Russians agreed to sell Fort Ross to American rancher John Sutter for thirty thousand dollars, though the Mexican-American War delayed the final deal.

During the Crimean War, many Americans sympathized with Russia in its battle against Britain, France, and Turkey, and we even sent some minor assistance to the Russians.

Occasional contacts between the USN and Russia continued throughout the nineteenth and early twentieth century. A diplomatic squabble, for instance, saw the USS *Prometheus* arrive in Kronstadt, St. Petersburg's port, in 1809 to calm the situation down. On the other hand, in 1866, we sent the monitor USS *Miantonomoh* (rather slowly) as far as Kronstadt to thank the Russians for supporting the Union side during our Civil War and to congratulate the Tsar Alexander II (who emancipated the serfs) on luckily escaping a recent assassination. It was not the last, and one tsar can have only so much luck. In 1867, a Pole tried to kill him during the World's Fair. In 1879, a student fired five shots from a revolver at him but missed. In 1879, a radical revolutionary group blew up the railway but didn't get the tsar. Then in 1880, other revolutionaries blew up his dining room, and killed eleven people but not the tsar who was late for dinner. They tried yet again in 1881, and this time they meant business. The revolutionaries sent three attackers with bombs. The first one blew up his carriage, but the tsar escaped. Then just as everyone was thinking he'd gotten away with it again, the second bomber struck and blew his legs off, fatally wounding him. And we think our presidents have had a tough time with assassinations!

During the war of 1877-1878 between Russia and Turkey, we even supplied the Russians with naval ships and weapons.

President Teddy Roosevelt helped to broker a peace between Russia and Japan with the Treaty of Portsmouth that ended the Russo-Japanese War of 1904-05. TR won a Noble prize for his efforts.

However, in the period leading up to the First World War, tensions were rising between the Russians and us over anti-Semitic actions in Russia.

There wasn't much crossover between Russia and the United States during the First World War. By the time we entered the war in April 1917, the tsar had abdicated, and Russia was in the grip of revolution. It would only be a few more months until the tsar was killed and Russia was basically forced out of the war. Nevertheless, we did manage to send some war material and loans to Russia. Soon, however, it became obvious the new Russia wasn't going to be much of an ally to us. Indeed, it soon became clear that we and Bolshevik Russia were about to become not allies at all, but the opposite.

Promising "bread for the people, land to the peasant and peace to all peoples," Lenin led the Bolshevik Revolution that toppled the tsar and ignited a civil war across Russia. After Lenin signed the Treaty of Brest-Litovsk and dropped out of the Triple Entente by making peace with the Kaiser's Germany, some of Russia's former allies felt betrayed, and some of them felt inclined to do something about it. Winston Churchill spoke about trying to "strangle the Bolshevik baby in its cradle."

Our president wasn't entirely happy about the situation either. In 1918, Woodrow Wilson ordered American forces to form part of the Allied North Russia Expeditionary Force that was being readied to support the White forces that were battling the Bolshevik Red forces in Russia. American sailors first landed in Murmansk from the USS *Olympia* on June 8, 1918.

Wilson had, for one of the few times in our history, granted authority to allow American troops to serve under foreign leadership. In November of 1918, just as the war in Europe was coming to a close, British Major General Edmund Ironside took over command of our force, what became known as the Polar Bear Expedition—great name, but not such a great outcome. In his diary, Ironside expressed doubts about his mission comparing the advance into Russia to sticking your hand into a huge sticky pudding.

Eventually, about five thousand American troops served in Northern Russia alongside British, Canadian, Australian, and White Russian forces. Some of them would not return to America. On the Dvina front on September 16, 1918, Private Philip Sokol from Pittsburgh was the first American to be killed in combat in the Russian campaign.

After initial success, stiffening Bolshevik resistance rapidly put the intervention forces in an increasingly desperate situation. Throughout the bitter Russian winter of 1918, General Ironside had to order his forces to retreat into a smaller and smaller area until ultimately they would be fighting just to survive.

Nevertheless, as in almost all wars, there were occasional brief, happier interludes. Godfrey Anderson was a Michigan farm boy who served in the 337th Field Hospital Unit in the Polar Bear Expedition. He describes a Christmas dinner in Shenkursk that featured fricassee of rabbit and chocolate layer cake. A balalaika orchestra and a dozen or so Russian girls were invited to attend and dance with the troops. On occasions, fraternization could lead to more; Private Joseph Chinzi of the 339th Supply Company married a Russian bride in Archangel.

A further eight thousand American soldiers were sent to Vladivostok, along with a variety of other Allied troops, including Japanese. US General Graves had more modest, and perhaps more realistic, ambitions than some of the other Allied generals in Siberia, and our troops ended up protecting the Trans-Siberian railroad from Bolshevik raids. Nevertheless, the intervention in Siberia proved ultimately as pointless as the intervention in Northern Russia, as chaos and conspiracy weakened the White Forces and the Red Forces advanced.

Wilson feared that the presence of American troops in Russia after World War I had ended could impede settlement of the Versailles Peace Treaty where he sought the creation of the League of Nations. The war to end all wars was finished. The Americans wanted all their boys to come home, and there was a growing feeling in the United States that the Russian intervention was a disaster that had failed to achieve anything very positive. Eventually, we did pull our boys out.

Today, though you can find a polar bear sculpture in a Detroit cemetery, the Allied North Russia Expedition is largely forgotten in the United States. In Russia, a visitor to Archangel will find several memorials of Russian resistance to the expedition.

Obviously, after all this, things weren't hugely friendly between Russia and the United States, and as late as 1959, on a visit to the United States, Nikita Khrushchev decided he needed to bring up the subject.

Finally, in 1933, we recognized the Soviet Union. There are few things to make you feel better about a former enemy than finding yourself fighting a new enemy with your former enemy on your side, especially for a fight on the scale of a world war.

On June 22, as Adolf Hitler launched his panzers into the Soviet Union, Russia suddenly found itself at war with Germany. President Franklin Roosevelt, already sympathetic to the Allied cause, started the process of aiding Russia. Shortly after December 7, 1941, Hitler declared war on us, and we suddenly found ourselves allied with Russia, and the process speeded up. Lend-Lease supplies, including thousands of aircraft and tanks and hundreds of thousands of trucks and even thirteen million pairs of boots, were sent to Russia playing a vital role in helping the Red Army destroy the German Army on the Eastern Front.

And there was occasional cooperation on the combat front as well. In Operation Frantic, US bombers based in Britain and Italy used Soviet airbases to land and refuel after bombing missions. (Since the Soviet airbases involved were in what is now Ukraine, we'll deal with this a bit more, in that chapter.)

As World War II ended and the Cold War began, friendly military cooperation came to an end. In the decades after 1945, there were to be assorted US operations in and over Russian territory and in Russian waters, but such covert activities are largely beyond the remit of this book. We'll just mention here Gary Powers, shot down in his U-2 near Sverdlovsk in Russia on May 1, 1960. The SR-71 Blackbird spyplane, which could fly at speeds over Mach 3.0 at 80,000 feet, was a significant improvement over the U-2.

Since the end of the Cold War, relations have often been more friendly between the Russians and us. On May 9, 2010, for instance, a friendly invasion by American troops occurred in Russia. The 2nd Battalion of the 18th Infantry Regiment and a naval band participated in the Victory Day parade in Moscow to mark the sixty-fifth anniversary of the end of World War II.

The crisis over Crimea in 2014 has, however, caused major problems between Russia and the United States.

RWANDA

MOST AMERICANS WILL BE AWARE OF PART OF RWANDA'S HISTORY, the very worst part of it. The genocide of 1994 is one of the most shocking and horrifying events of the post-World War II era.

In recent years we have had some military involvement in this small central African nation, for example, helping with training for peacekeeping.

Fortunately, Rwanda has been for some time in a situation where it can send peacekeepers to other countries, rather than need other countries to send peacekeepers to Rwanda. For instance, we have trained Rwanda peacekeepers headed to Darfur as part of UNAMID, the Unites Nations Mission in Darfur, and helped with transport flying supplies from Kigali, the capital of Rwanda, to Darfur for the Rwandan peacekeepers there.

SAMOA

THE SOUTH PACIFIC SAMOAN ISLANDS are divided into two groups, each a separate country, American Samoa and the Independent State of Samoa, or more commonly, just Samoa. Until 1997, Samoa was called Western Samoa, a term some still use.

Naturally we have strong connections with American Samoa, but we've actually also had quite a lot of military involvement with the Independent State of Samoa.

As early as February 1841, marines from the USS *Peacock* landed on the island of Upolu and burned three villages there after the death of an American sailor. But it was later in the nineteenth century that we managed to get even more seriously involved.

In 1888, the First Samoan Civil War was raging with local factions fighting each other but Western powers, including us, playing a role as well. Since we had an interest in and interests on the islands, we sent ashore marines to Apia to protect American lives and property. Things were already tense between us and the Germans (one of the other Western powers involved) when shelling had damaged American-owned property, and in 1889, we could have ended up in armed conflict with Germany, long before World War I. The Germans had sent warships, SMS *Adler*, SMS *Olga*, and SMS *Eber* to Apia Harbor, and we had USS *Nipsic*, USS *Vandalia*, and

USS *Trenton* there. The British, the third Western power involved, had sent HMS *Calliope*. The German and US ships were in a tense stand-off for months until finally the weather decided matters. A devastating cyclone hit on March 15, sinking four of the US and German ships and forcing the remaining two onto the beach. Only HMS *Calliope* was left afloat. By the time it was all over, nobody could really be bothered to fight, and they didn't have anything much left to fight with.

However, that was not to be the end of the nineteenth century superpower dispute over Samoa. By 1899, fighting between local factions was raging once again, with the United States and Britain throwing their weight behind Prince Tanu and with the Germans supporting his opponent, Mata'afa losefo. British and US naval forces, including the USS *Philadelphia*, shelled Apia in March 1899, and then US and British marines and sailors along with Tanu's followers pursued Mata'afa losefo's forces. What followed was the Battle of Vailele, in which the American, British, and Tanu's party were ambushed by large numbers of attackers. Our men fought bravely, but their commander and three other Americans were killed (including Ensign John Monaghan, a graduate of Gonzaga University and the US Naval Academy who was later commemorated with a statue in Spokane, Washington), and the attacking party had to withdraw. Shortly afterwards, a peace deal was reached, which split Samoa into German and American areas while Britain got territory elsewhere. The American part became American Samoa, and the German portion was captured by New Zealand forces at the beginning of World War I, long before we entered the war.

During World War II, in addition to having forces in American Samoa, we had marines based in the other part of Samoa, as well as built an airfield and seaplane base there. The country became independent as Western Samoa in 1962.

The US military has been involved in humanitarian projects there. And in 2013, the amphibious dock-landing USS *Pearl Harbor* visited Apia for Pacific Partnership 2013.

SAN MARINO

A TINY EUROPEAN COUNTRY OF JUST TWENTY-FOUR SQUARE MILES, San Marino is situated just inland from Italy's Adriatic coast near Rimini. Yes, it's well-known for its stamps, but it also has a fascinating history (and we've played a part in that).

For a start, it claims to be the world's oldest republic, dating from 301 AD, when Saint Marinus (as in San Marino) turned up from what's now a Croatian island and settled there. Since in 301 Italy was still very much part of the Roman Empire, it's a slightly curious foundation date, but anyway, there is a genuine and genuinely long tradition of San Marino being a republic at least since the Middle Ages.

To protect itself, San Marino has its own Crossbowman Corps, and even today, the San Marino Crossbow Confederation continues this proud tradition.

The nineteenth century saw a few interesting historical links between San Marino and the United States. In 1849, on one of Garibaldi's early (and unsuccessful) forays into Italy, the Italian patriot found himself forced to retreat with his men into Sammarinese territory to avoid the pursuing Austrian forces. Commanding a rearguard operation against the enemy was Colonel Hugh Forbes. He was an Englishman, but he was later to play a very significant part in US history when he was recruited as a military expert by John Brown, keen to fight slavery in the South.

Not long after, in 1861, San Marino wrote to Abraham Lincoln offering him honorary Sammarinese citizenship. Lincoln, in May 1861, with plenty else on his mind, still took the time to write warmly to San Marino to accept the offer and to comment on the two countries' shared experience of being republics. Lincoln's reply asserted that "government founded on republican principles is capable of being so administered as to be secure and enduring."

However, it's the twentieth century that brought military involvement with San Marino. The country remained neutral in World War II. However, the major Italian port and communications hub of Rimini is situated just a few miles to the northeast of San Marino, and targets there were repeatedly attacked by Allied bombers. Since many of them, which included Americans, were coming from bases in Algeria or Tunisia, it seems likely that US bomber crews must on some occasions have flown through Sammarinese airspace, even if unintentionally. Then on June 26, 1944, in a tragic accident, Allied bombers accidentally bombed San Marino.

However, the land war was getting gradually closer to San Marino's borders as Allied Forces advanced up Italy. With British and Commonwealth forces poised to take Rimini in Operation Olive, in early September, German forces moved into San Marino. The subsequent battle for San Marino was short but sharp, and by September 21, Allied forces were mopping up the last German soldiers in San Marino. That same day, the first American soldiers also entered San Marino. Alfred

Connor Bowman was an American officer who was there to help ensure that the people of San Marino were fed during the coming winter. He rapidly brought thirteen trucks loaded with supplies into the small country. It seems appropriate that the first American into liberated San Marino, the land of the crossbowman, was a Bowman himself.

And today, the United States and San Marino remain friendly with each other.

SAO TOME AND PRINCIPE

ÃO TOMÉ AND PRÍNCIPE IS A COUNTRY THAT CONSISTS basically of two big islands and some little ones. The two big islands, not surprisingly, São Tomé and Príncipe, are situated in the Gulf of Guinea, sort of south of Nigeria and west of Gabon.

It's a country that a lot of Americans have not heard of, but the USN has spent quite a lot of operational time in the seas around the islands.

The slave trade gave reason for our navy to spend much time in the area in the nineteenth century. As mentioned elsewhere, our Africa Squadron was tasked with intercepting slaving ships and deterring them. Principe, or Prince's Island, as we tended to know it then, was a key point on our navy's patrol routes. Prince's Island regularly appears in accounts of the Africa Squadron's operations, and São Tomé (or St. Thomas, as we called it then) also sometimes gets a mention. For instance, on September 29, 1857, the USS *Cumberland* spotted a suspicious-looking ship, the *Pearl*, off the coast of São Tomé. It was battle stations on the *Cumberland*, and Lieutenant Greene boarded the *Pearl*, only to let her go when he found her papers in order. The Africa Squadron hadn't freed any slaves this time, but it wasn't always so unlucky.

Today, Voice of America broadcasts to a large part of Africa from a relay transmitter located on São Tomé, and we have been involved in a number of projects in the country. For instance, the USN has helped the São Tomé and Príncipe Coast Guard install a new surface surveillance system, and the crew of the USCG Cutter *Dallas* helped train coast guard personnel from São Tomé and Príncipe.

SAUDI ARABIA

SAUDI ARABIA SEEMS TO HAVE BEEN IN THE AMERICAN NEWS quite A LOT over the last couple of decades.

During World War I, Lawrence of Arabia was active in part of what is now Saudi Arabia, working with the leaders of the Great Arab Revolt to attack Ottoman troops and drive them from the area. A character made famous in more recent times by Peter O'Toole in the Hollywood epic, Lawrence, although British, was made famous by an American, Lowell Thomas. Along with cameraman Harry Chase, Thomas, as an American journalist, turned up in the Middle East to meet Lawrence and film him. When Thomas got back to America, he turned Lawrence into one of the first war-media superstars, giving lectures accompanied by films at Madison Square Gardens and then around the world.

The United States began diplomatic relations with Saudi Arabia in 1933. That same year, the California Arabian Standard Oil Company (later ARAMCO) was formed to develop Saudi oil resources.

During World War II, Saudi Arabia remained technically neutral but also supplied Allied forces with masses of critical petroleum products. This fact did not escape the notice of the other side.

Mussolini's Italy joined the Axis side in 1940, and on October 19 of that year, four Italian bombers (Regia Aeronautica) took off from the island of Rhodes and attacked Saudi oil facilities in Dhahran (see "Bahrain").

Mussolini's air attack on the Saudi oil fields was a kind of Axis version of Doolittle's Raid. Doolittle's Raiders launched their B-25 bombers from the decks of the *Hornet* to attack Japan. Mussolini's Regia Aeronautica took off from an unsinkable "carrier," the Isle of Rhodes. Doolittle's fliers did not conform to the traditional bombing structure of take-off, fly to target, release bombs, and return; instead, after bombing Tokyo, most flew to China. The Italian bomber pilots bombed oil refineries in Saudi Arabia and Bahrain and then flew on to airfields in Italian East Africa (Eritrea)—the longest bombing run in aviation history at the time and one that exposed Saudi Arabia's military vulnerability.

The Doolittle Raid's physical impact on Japan was minimal, but its psychological impact was enormous; the Midway campaign was launched in order to extend Japan's defensive perimeters and prevent another American attack on the home islands. The Italian raid on Saudi Arabian oil refineries did little damage, but its psychological impact on the kingdom and its future links with America were significant.

World War II saw the real beginning of our military involvement with Saudi Arabia. For instance, the Saudi Kingdom allowed us to operate an air transport facility at Jeddah as part of a network that stretched across Africa and the Middle East. And Saudi Arabia permitted the construction of a US air field near Dhahran, which it operated from 1945 to 1962. Saudi Arabia, though neutral, also received about twelve million dollars in lend-lease, mostly in silver dollars.

In 1945, FDR, on his way back from the Yalta Conference, travelled on the USS *Quincy* to the Great Bitter Lake on the Suez Canal. He was there to meet three important regional leaders—Emperor Haile Selassie of Ethiopia, King Farouk of Egypt, and King Abdul Aziz ibn Saud of Saudi Arabia. On Valentine's Day 1945, a goat was slaughtered and eaten on board the ship to celebrate the kingdom's new links with America. The American military would protect the Saudi kingdom, while their oil would help fuel the tanks, planes, and ships of the US military. The broad outlines of America's pact with Saudi Arabia, despite profound differences between our two nations, have now lasted seventy years through many tumultuous times.

During their discussions, the Saudi king warned President Franklin Roosevelt that the Arabs would fight if Jewish settlements in what was then the British-controlled Palestine Mandate expanded. Thus, the creation of Israel in 1948 with American support put strains on our links with Saudi Arabia, particularly during the Arab-Israeli Wars of the Cold War era.

However, America and Saudi Arabia still had shared interests. For instance, during the Yemen Civil War, royalist, conservative Saudi Arabia clashed with Nasser's revolutionary, Communist-supported Egypt, and each ended up supporting a different side in the war. JFK threw US support behind the Saudis. USAF planes were mobilized to deter Nasser's Egypt from further action against Saudi Arabia.

Relations between the United States and Saudi Arabia reached a low point after the 1973 Arab-Israeli War, but eventually the relationship stabilized again. The Iranian revolution created a new power feared by both Saudi Arabia and the United States, and in the 1980s, America and Saudi Arabia found themselves jointly immersed in arming and helping the Afghan mujahideen fight the Soviets in Afghanistan and the Afghan regime they supported.

During the Iran-Iraq War, Saudi Arabia backed Iraq. On June 5, 1984, a US AWACS plane detected an Iranian fighter approaching Saudi's offshore oil facilities in the Gulf. Saudi aircraft intercepted the Iranian plane and shot it down.

However, when we really went to war in Saudi Arabia, it wasn't Iran that was the problem. Instead, it was Iraq. In August of 1990, Saddam Hussein's Iraqi Army invaded Kuwait and threatened Saudi Arabia (see "Kuwait"). President H. W. Bush led an international coalition that responded with Operation Desert Shield. In late January of 1991, Saddam Hussein ordered Iraqi forces to attack across the Saudi border. Saudi and Qatari troops, aided by US marines, artillery, and airpower, fought the Battle of Khafji. The Iraqi forces were repulsed at a cost of twenty-six American lives and eighteen Saudis.

American airpower based in Saudi played a decisive role in the First Gulf War. A-10 Warthogs, championed by the maverick USAF Colonel John Boyd, flew missions from Saudi bases destroying over nine hundred Iraqi tanks.

In the course of the First Gulf War, over half a million US troops were deployed to Saudi Arabia. Many stayed after Iraq was expelled from Kuwait in Operation Desert Storm. For instance, thousands of US troops stayed on to help enforce the no-fly zone over neighboring Iraq in Operation Southern Watch. The Saudi king and government supported the American alliance, but many in the Arab street were troubled. To some, of course, this represented an American occupation of the Muslim holy land and was one of the grievances behind Osama bin Laden's attack on 9/11. Indeed, fifteen of the nineteen hijackers in the 9/11 attack and their mastermind were Saudi nationals.

Attacks on US personnel took place in Saudi territory too. For instance, in 1996, a huge truck bomb destroyed part of the Khobar Towers complex and killed nineteen US servicemen. And in 2004, the US consulate in Jeddah was attacked.

The USAF operated Prince Sultan Air Force Base from 1990 until 2003. It was equipped with air conditioning and all amenities, including Baskin-Robbins and Burger King franchises, although female personnel were expected to wear an abaya when going off base.

Most American military personnel left Saudi Arabia in 2003. Small numbers are still based there, some of them apparently connected with the campaign of drone strikes in Yemen.

Saudi Arabia remains a significant ally of the United States. The two countries share, interests in oil and nervousness about Iran. Military links continue to be strong. For instance, the United States has been actively training Saudi defense forces from 1953 to the present, and the

Saudi military has purchased large quantities of weaponry and military equipment from American manufacturers, including aircraft, armored vehicles, and air defense weapons.

In 2011, the corpse of Osama bin Laden, a Saudi national, was offered for burial to Saudi Arabia, which declined in favor of burial at sea.

SENEGAL

IN THE FOURTEENTH TO SIXTEENTH CENTURIES, Senegal was home of the Jolof Empire.

Its location on West Africa's coast meant it was involved in the slave trade, and the USN's anti-slavery squadron patrolled the seas off Senegal in the nineteenth century. Gorée, for instance, in Senegal was a significant slaving port, and in 2013, President Obama paid an emotional visit to the island.

The area eventually became a French colony, and when we entered the Second World War, it was under French control and out of bounds to us. However, Operation Torch, our invasion with the British of Morocco and Algeria, changed all that. The Free French took control of the area, and we were free to fly planes there. This was important since previously our trans-Atlantic route for ferrying cargo and aircraft to the Middle East had had to go via a route further south; now we could use a shorter one. We first used an existing French airbase at Eknes Field, but then in 1944, we opened Mallard Field, which is the international airport of Dakar, Senegal's capital.

Senegal became independent from France in 1960, and in the decades since then, we've had a certain amount of military involvement with this country.

The United States has occasionally used Dakar airport. For instance, in 1996, the USAF flew in and out of Dakar evacuating Americans from Liberia. The US military has also trained Senegalese troops for peacekeeping missions under its Africa Contingency Operations Training and Assistance program, and the United States has recently been upgrading the peacekeeping operations training center at Dodji in Senegal. And American troops participate in exercises in Senegal. For example, in 2013, the USMC conducted amphibious landings in Senegal. The Vermont National Guard is partnered with Senegal.

SERBIA

MANY AMERICANS WILL BE AWARE that the United States bombed Serbia when Milosevic was in power there, but we have a long and much less well-known history of involvement with Serbia in wartime.

The Germans invaded Yugoslavia (of which Serbia was then a part) and occupied it in 1941. In reaction to that, two resistance movements emerged in Yugoslavia to fight the Germans—the Royalist Chetniks under Mihailovic and the Communist Partisans under Tito.

We were involved with helping both groups in Serbia sending supplies and OSS teams to help them. Colonel Richard Weil Jr. was sent to Tito's headquarters to assess him. Weil decided that Tito was both nationalist and Communist but more nationalist than Communist and emerged with a letter of greeting to Franklin Roosevelt. Both Partisans and Chetniks helped save American airmen shot down over Serbia, and in a major success, hundreds of airmen were successfully airlifted out in US planes from an airstrip at the Chetnik headquarters at Pranjani in 1944. Many US aircraft in the air over Serbia during the war were destined for crucial targets elsewhere, such as the oil fields at Ploeşti in Romania, but we also hit targets within Serbia. Belgrade, for instance, was bombed heavily on a number of occasions.

Partisans and Chetniks not only fought the Germans, however; they also fought each other.

This was a side war of less concern to the UK and US governments than fighting the Germans. In the end, the UK government decided that Tito's Partisans were more effective in their attacks on the Germans. The British committed themselves to the Partisans and abandoned Mihailovic and the Chetniks. The American government was less clearly decided about the matter but went along with their key allies in the end. After the war, Mihailovic was accused of treason by the new Communist government and shot. President Harry Truman posthumously awarded him the Legion of Merit for saving American airmen.

American airmen were in action again over Serbia not that long ago. After an ultimatum to Milosevic over Kosovo was rejected (see "Kosovo"), NATO's bombing campaign commenced on March 24, 1999. US aircraft and cruise missiles played a key role attacking many sites in Serbia, including again, many in Belgrade. In the end, on June 3, Milosevic agreed to withdraw his forces from Kosovo and allow NATO troops in.

The conflict in Serbia witnessed the first substantial use of Predator drones by the CIA to monitor Serbian troop movements allowing President Clinton a live feed in the White House.

Since the conflict about Kosovo, the USG and Serbia have established some military links. For instance, the Ohio National Guard is partnered with Serbia in the National Guard State Partnership Program.

SEYCHELLES

AN ISLAND NATION IN THE INDIAN OCEAN, Seychelles has some stunningly beautiful scenery. Prince William and Kate Middleton spent their honeymoon in the Seychelles.

And we've had US military personnel visiting there and based there as well.

The US Air Force built a tracking station on Mahé in 1963. It only finally closed down in 1996.

In 1976, Seychelles became fully independent from Britain, and then in 1977, France-Albert René, a socialist, came to power in Seychelles though a coup. Assorted alleged attempts to topple René followed. It's hard to know what the United States and the CIA may have known about any of these plans. Then in 1993, multi-party elections were held, which the involved parties and international observers accepted as free and fair. René won them, as well as elections in 1998 and 2001.

The USN has been a regular visitor to the Seychelles in recent years. For instance, the USS *Bainbridge* and the USS *Carter Hall* both visited in 2013, and the Seychelles Coast Guard has trained with USN personnel.

The United States has flown drones from bases in Seychelles intermittently since 2009.

SIERRA LEONE

YES, THE SIERRA, OR "MOUNTAIN RANGE," OF THE LION, Sierra Leone received its name from early Portuguese explorers.

It was, however, the British who in the late eighteenth century started a settlement there on the African coast for various groups, including freed slaves (some of them loyalists from America fleeing the American Revolution). So, it was, effectively, a British (and American) version of our Liberia. Or, since, the settlement in Sierra Leone started before the one in Liberia, Liberia is our version of what was happening in Sierra Leone.

Our navy's anti-slaving patrols operated in the vicinity in the nineteenth century.

Eventually, the whole area became a British colony until independence in 1961.

By 1991, with a vicious civil war raging in neighboring Liberia, a group called the Revolutionary United Front (RUF) launched their own rebellion in Sierra Leone. A decade of war and instability followed.

In 1992, after a coup, President Clinton sent in US planes to rescue Americans and others. In Operation Silver Anvil, US Special Forces flew into Sierra Leone and evacuated hundreds.

After another coup in 1997, the RUF and those who'd mounted the coup took Freetown, the capital of Sierra Leone. This time, Clinton sent in the USS *Kearsarge* Amphibious Ready Group, which evacuated thousands of Americans and others, and troops from ECOMOG went in to recapture Freetown for the government.

The Lome Peace Accord was signed in 1999, but it didn't stop the war, and in 2000, the RUF were once again advancing on Freetown. Once again, international forces went in to resist them. This time Clinton sent in a navy patrol craft to be ready to help evacuate Americans and a C-17 aircraft to fly supplies to the international forces.

Finally, decisive action by British troops defeated the RUF, and the war was officially declared finished in January 2002.

In recent years, we've developed more links with Sierra Leone's military. For instance, in 2013, a US-trained battalion deployed to Somalia as part of AMISOM, the African Union Mission in Somalia.

SINGAPORE

WE HAD A CONSULATE IN SINGAPORE IN 1836, long before it became the independent country it is today.

Of course, for much of the nineteenth and twentieth centuries, this great city was controlled by Britain, and its loss to the Japanese on February 15, 1942, was almost the same kind of shock to Britons as the attack on Pearl Harbor was to us Americans.

The recapture of Singapore was more of a British priority than an American one, but we did play a major role bombing and mining targets in and around Singapore. For instance, in one attack on February 1, 1945, eighty-eight Superfortresses, each carrying at least four one-thousand-pound bombs, were in the air over Singapore. Sixty-seven of these bombed the primary target, the Admiralty IX Floating Dry Dock at the navy yard, damaging it severely and setting light to a large ship inside it. The remaining twenty-one B-29s bombed a different part of the naval base causing extensive destruction. One B-29 was lost to Japanese fighters, and another was badly damaged.

In recent years, we have developed close military links with Singapore. American and Singaporean troops conduct an annual bilateral military exercise, and Singaporean troops served in Afghanistan. American naval and air units have made use of Sembawang base, and, for instance, a logistical support group for the US 7th Fleet is based at Sembawang. This is the same base our B-29s were bombing on that February day all those decades ago during World War II. Our navy also uses Singapore's newer naval base at Changi, and the USAF has made extensive use of Paya Lebar Air Base, which is, for example, home to the air operations of the 497th Combat Training Squadron.

SLOVAKIA

S LOVAKIA CONTAINS THE SITE OF THE FAMOUS Napoleonic battle of Austerlitz, which was fought in December 1805. Austerlitz was renamed "Slavkov" after the period of "de-Germanification" of Slovakia that followed World War II.

As covered in the chapter on the Czech Republic, Americans played a significant role in the establishment of an independent Czechoslovakia after World War I. American volunteers joined Czechoslovak units that fought alongside the Allies in the war and helped gain sympathy for the cause of Czechoslovakia. President Woodrow Wilson's support for granting autonomy to the people who had previously been part of the Austro-Hungarian Empire was key as well.

In 1993, as Yugoslavia was tearing itself apart to the south, the state of Czechoslovakia split peacefully into its two constituent parts, a Czech state and a Slovak state. Peacefully, but not without controversy, for instance, over the decision to split the country without a referendum in Slovakia.

However, this was not the first time since the formation of Czechoslovakia that Slovakia had been separated from the Czech part of the country. After the debacle of the Munich Agreement in 1938, in March 1939, the Slovak Republic declared independence, and on the next day the Germans occupied the rest of Czechoslovakia. The government of the new Slovak Republic was, however, very much under German influence and became an ally of Germany, sending troops to fight alongside the Germans in their invasions of Poland and the Soviet Union. On December 13, 1941 (two days after Germany), Slovakia declared war on the United States.

And as our bombing campaign across Europe got going, facilities inside the Slovak Republic that were important for the Axis war effort were on our list of potential targets. For instance, on June 16, 1944, our bombers attacked the Apollo Oil Refinery in Bratislava.

Soon, Americans were to be involved in fighting also on the ground in Slovakia.

As the Red Army pushed west in 1944, local resistance to the Germans and their collaborators increased and, on August 29, 1944, began the Slovak National Uprising as Slovak troops and partisans tried to liberate their country. Early September saw a number of successes for the rebels, and we and the Russians tried to send help. Later in September, we sent in an OSS team to liaise with the rebels, and on October 17, B-17s with a fighter escort landed at Tri Duby airbase to offload supplies and more OSS men and pick up escaped American air crew.

However, the Soviet advance in the east stalled, and German vicious counterattacks in October eventually largely crushed the rebels.

A tragic fate awaited the OSS members. They headed for the mountains and were awaiting an OSS supply drop on Christmas Day when they were betrayed and captured by the Germans. Only two Americans escaped to the Russian lines. Others were taken to Mauthausen Concentration Camp, brutally tortured, and then executed.

On April 4, 1945, the Red Army entered Bratislava, and post-war Czechoslovakia became part of the Soviet sphere of influence.

During the 1968 Soviet invasion of Czechoslovakian territory, the United States, preoccupied with the Vietnam War, did not intervene. Americans did, however, cheer on the Czechoslovak hockey team in its famous victory over the Soviets at the 1968 Winter Olympics in Grenoble, France.

Slovakia joined NATO in 2004. Slovakia criticized the United States over its 2003 invasion of Iraq but sent troops to Afghanistan as part of the Allied coalition. And in recent years, the US and Slovak military have teamed up to conduct assorted training operations and exercises. The Indiana National Guard is partnered with Slovakia.

SLOVENIA

SLOVENIA, WITH ITS CAPITAL AT LJUBLJANA, contains the northernmost point of what used to be Yugoslavia and roughly has Italy to its west, Austria to its north, Hungary to its east, and Croatia to its south.

During World War I, it was all part of the Austro-Hungarian Empire, but the war would change that. For much of the war, Italians had faced the Austro-Hungarians in the area of the River Isonzo, and some vicious fighting had already taken place in the region of what is now the Slovenian frontier. One of the battles, a huge disaster for the Italians, took place in 1917 near Caporetto, the Italian name for the Slovenian town of Kobarid. Caporetto features in *Farewell to Arms* by Hemingway, who served as an ambulance driver on the Italian front and was wounded by mortar fire.

In October 1918, American troops of the 332nd Infantry Regiment were part of the Vittorio-Veneto Offensive and, in the last days of the war, found themselves advancing eastwards towards what is now the Slovenian-Italian border. By the time the Austro-Hungarian Empire disintegrated, Slovenia had already broken away to become part of the state of Slovenes, Croats, and Serbs, which later joined with Serbia and other territory, and eventually all became Yugoslavia. But in the chaotic period after the armistice, before the Allied powers had decided exactly how the Austro-Hungarian empire should be split up and what new states and new borders should be internationally recognized, American forces were either in Slovenia or certainly very close to it, for instance, near Gorizia and at Rijeka.

Something remarkably similar was to happen at the end of the Second World War when American forces again advanced into Slovenia. The war had seen assorted US activity over and in Slovenia. For instance, on March 9, 1945, 15th Air Force bombers with fighter escorts bombed the marshalling yard in the Slovenian capital, Ljubljana. And on the ground, the OSS carried out vital activity. In November 1943, an OSS team was parachuted into partisan-held territory near Ljubljana and set itself up so that in 1944 in the vital period around D-Day it could report on German troop movements up from the Balkans.

However, in the last weeks of the war, US ground forces once again found themselves advancing on the Italian front towards Slovenia. And this time they went right into what is now the country. Unlike in 1918, where Italy had been a victorious Allied power and Slovenia had been part of the defeated Austro-Hungarian power, Italy had abandoned Germany in 1943 after being invaded by the Allies, whereas Tito's Yugoslav partisans had fought for a long time on the victorious Allied side. Once again, the border between Italy and its neighbor was disputed. While the details were being worked out, the entre border region was split in two by the Morgan Line, which left a portion of what's now Slovenia under American and British administration. The line was supposed to ease potential tension, but it did not succeed entirely. US reinforcements were rushed to the area, and two US planes were shot down.

In 1991, Slovenia became independent, and a very short war followed before the action moved to the much longer and more devastating wars in Croatia and Bosnia. Since then, assorted military links between the United States and Slovenia have developed. Slovenia became a member of NATO in 2004 and has sent troops to Afghanistan. The Colorado National Guard is partnered with Slovenia.

SOLOMON ISLANDS

A LTHOUGH MANY AMERICANS MAY BE UNFAMILIAR with the Solomon Islands, most will recognize the name of one of the islands, one of the biggest names in American military history—Guadalcanal.

The Solomon Islands are an island nation in the South Pacific. Different islands within the nation have different histories. Britain ended up being the main Western colonial power in the history of the Solomons, but on its Sikaiana Atoll, some inhabitants reckon they have been American since the nineteenth century. According to one view, Sikaiana is part of the Malaita Province of the Solomon Islands. But Hawaii was offered sovereignty over Sikaiana in 1856 and to some extent accepted it. Some, therefore, argue that when Hawaii became part of the United States, so did Sikaiana. However, the United States doesn't accept this.

Yankee whalers fished the waters off the Solomon Islands in the nineteenth century. Jack London visited with his famous boat, the *Snark*, in 1907.

However, it was during World War II that we were to have the most extensive involvement with the Solomons. Soon after Pearl Harbor, Japanese forces occupied some of the Solomon Islands as part of an eventual plan to interdict shipping lanes from the United States to the eastern coast of Australia. Something had to be done about it, and a start had to be made on recovering territory from the Japanese. In the summer of 1942, it was.

The marines stormed ashore on August 7, 1942. After fierce fighting, they took Tulagi and some other small islands. On Guadalcanal, they encountered little opposition at first and soon took control of the island's vital airfield, which our forces would call Henderson Field. However, things were soon going to change.

The fighting raged at sea, in the air, and on the land.

At sea, ferocious battles took place near Savo Island, and the waters around it and Guadalcanal are known as "Ironbottom Sound" due to the number of ships and sailors that are entombed beneath its waves. USN and cruise ships in the area still observe silence while cruising these waters. Japanese and US carrier forces also clashed in the Battle of the Eastern Solomons.

In the air, Japanese fighters and bombers flying from Rabaul clashed with US aircraft based at Henderson. The Cactus Air Force, commanded by Admiral John McCain Sr., was the name given to the mainly marine aviators who defended the airspace over Guadalcanal with obsolete Wildcat fighters.

On land, fighting raged on Guadalcanal as the Japanese began to bring in reinforcements in an attempt to retake the island. The so-called Tokyo Express saw Japanese troops rushed to the island on fast warships, and on occasions, US and Japanese warships clashed as the Japanese tried to land troops and supplies and to bombard US positions on Guadalcanal.

Ferocious battles followed as the Japanese desperately tried to retake the airfield and our forces desperately tried to stop them. Eventually, however, the Japanese command concluded that it was going to be impossible to retake the island and it would be necessary to evacuate what remained of their forces on the island.

By the time the Japanese finally withdrew from Guadalcanal in February 1943, ending a bitter campaign fought in a sometimes difficult environment, more than seven thousand Americans and twenty-one thousand Japanese were dead.

After the Japanese withdrawal, we developed extensive air, sea, and land facilities in the area.

The P-38 Lightning fighters that shot down Yamamoto in April 1943 (see "Papua New Guinea") were based on Henderson Field.

In August 1943, JFK's motor torpedo boat, PT-109, was cut in half by a Japanese destroyer, and members of the crew had to hide on assorted islands in the Solomons until they could be saved in an epic rescue with the help of brave Solomon Islanders. Part of PT-109 was finally located in the waters of the Solomon Islands in 2002.

All in all, the Solomons saw large numbers of US troops, equipment, and infrastructure during the war, and strong links were established.

After the war, British colonial administration resumed, but the capital was transferred from Tulagi to Honiara because of US military infrastructure there. The Solomon Islands became independent in 1978.

Starting in 1998, assorted internal conflicts and disputes erupted, sometimes turning violent, and resulted in the deployment in the Solomon Islands of an international force led by Australia and New Zealand in 2003.

We have had a little recent military involvement with the Solomon Islands. For instance, we've provided training to Solomon Islands Border Protection Force and carried out small-scale exercises with them. We've also helped national security officials with some military training.

The USNS *Stockham* was sent in with helicopter support to help after an earthquake and tsunami in 2007.

SOMALIA

DAVID BOWIE'S SUPERMODEL WIFE, Iman, was born in Somalia. Our forces have seen plenty of action, both inside Somalia and against Somalis in the seas off the country.

Somalia's strategic position in the Horn of Africa, right next to assorted major sea routes, has guaranteed our long-standing interest in the place.

Our first major involvement in Somalia happened in the context of the Cold War. In 1977, war broke out in the area as Somali dictator Siad Barre attempted to reclaim territory occupied by ethnic Somalis in the Ogaden and seize other bits of land. At the time, both he and the Ethiopian government were linked to the Soviet Union. The Somalis made big advances at first, but eventually, the Soviet Union and Cuba decided to support Ethiopia in the war, not Somalia, and their intervention in the conflict eventually helped the Ethiopians repel Barre's forces. Looking round for a new sponsor, Barre picked the United States.

During the 1980s, assorted militias and guerrillas, some of them clan-based, sprang up to challenge Barre's dictatorial rule. By 1990, the Somali economy was in deep crisis, and in 1991, Barre's government was toppled. The total collapse of Somalia was about to start, and we were about to get dragged deeply into the area.

For a start, we wanted to get our diplomats out. On January 1, 1991, the attempt to topple Barre turned into a confused and chaotic battle for control of Mogadishu. We launched Operation Eastern Exit, aptly named since it pretty much involved an exit eastwards. Marines, SEALs, and CH-53 and C-46 helicopters successfully rescued our diplomats and diplomats from other nations and took them to USN ships waiting offshore. Interestingly, some of the diplomats rescued were Russian.

So we were out of Somalia, but pretty soon we would return. As Somalia collapsed into violent chaos, people began to starve, and UN relief operations in the country were at risk. The United Nations Security Council decided the disaster in Somalia represented a threat to international peace, and in late 1992, American troops entered Somalia as part of Operation Restore Hope. On December 9, marines from USS *Tripoli*, USS *Juneau*, and USS *Rushmore* hit the beach at Mogadishu while other marines took the airport and port. We also went on to occupy other targets in Somalia, including the important port of Kismayo.

Ultimately, Operation Restore Hope did, in fact, restore hope … for a while, and the security and food situation in Somalia improved greatly. By May 1993, we were beginning to withdraw some forces.

However, in June of that year, things took a big turn for the worse as the forces of militia leader Mohammed Farrah Aidid attacked Pakistani UN troops and killed twenty-four of them. The UN Security Council consequently demanded Aidid be stopped, and our forces went in to do that. The scene was set for Black Hawk Down.

In early October 1993, eighteen Americans were killed in our ill-fated attempt to capture leaders of Aidid's militia in Mogadishu. Helicopters were shot down, and American and UN rescue forces battled to reach the crash sites and any Americans still alive (as depicted in the movie, *Black Hawk Down*). However, many more Somalis were also killed. A few days after the disaster, President Clinton announced that American troops would withdraw from Somalia no later than March 31, 1994. In fact, they were gone, by March 3.

But this wasn't to be the end of our involvement in Somalia, not at all. For a start, there were other international and UN forces still in Somalia, and when they finally withdrew in March 1995, we sent in troops to help get them out safely.

And then 9/11 took place, and what happened at the Twin Towers would change what happened in Somalia as well.

Among the forces competing for control of Somalia, Islamists started playing a more major role, and by 2006, the Islamic Courts Union (ICU) had taken control of much of Southern Somalia and imposed their own version of shari'a. However, we, along with Ethiopia, the African Union, and much of the international community, were giving support to the Transitional Federal Government (TFG) against the ICU, and in December 2006, TFG and Ethiopian forces entered Mogadishu driving the ICU out.

In January 2007, ICU forces found themselves trapped in Ras Kamboni, a Somali town near the Kenyan border, between Kenyan Army forces to the south and TFG and Ethiopian forces advancing from the north. Though the details of exactly what happened still remain controversial, at least one American AC-130 gunship was involved at the time in operations in and around Ras Kamboni against Islamist targets.

In addition to clan militias and the ICU, however, we were also getting involved with another opponent in Somalia and, more important, off Somalia's shores. By about 2008, Somali piracy was becoming a major problem, and our forces have become deeply involved in the international effort to combat it and keep safe the important but vulnerable sea routes.

In 2009, Somalia pirates captured the US-flagged *Maersk Alabama* — the first American vessel to be captured by pirates in some two hundred years. Captain Richard Philips, of Underhill, Vermont, was held hostage as the pirates attempted to sail a boat back to Somalia. The USG acted decisively deploying the USS *Bainbridge* and two other ships in the rescue of Captain Philips from the clutches of the Somali pirates. He was rescued after USN SEALs shot three of the pirates and captured one, who is currently in prison in Indiana.

But the war against jihadis in Somalia goes on as well. In recent years, al-Shabaab has emerged as the leading Islamist force in Somalia, and even though a combination of Somali government forces and the Kenyan Army have dealt it heavy blows, it is still a powerful force and has increasingly developed international links with al-Qaeda and other jihadi groups.

On October 5, 2013, USN SEAL Team Six launched a raid into Barawe on the Somalia coast south of Mogadishu. They were trying to capture or kill Abdulkadir Mohamed Abdulkadir, a senior al-Shabaab leader. After an intense firefight, concerned about high potential civilian casualties, SEALs eventually withdrew, their covert mission uncompleted. Drone strikes have also been reported targeting al-Shabaab, and in 2014, it was reported US military advisors had been sent in.

SOUTH AFRICA

FOR A LONG TIME, SOUTH AFRICA WAS PART OF THE BRITISH EMPIRE, and then after it became independent, apartheid policies of successive governments ensured international military isolation, which in turn meant that South Africa developed its own extensive arms industry.

A few hundred Americans did fight on the side of the Boers in the Second Anglo-Boer War. One of them, John A. Hassell, who had served with the Vryheid Commando and been twice wounded, went on to form an entire American volunteer unit. Some Americans also fought on the British side in the Boer War.

South Africa fought on the same side as us in both world wars, and USN ships have, of course, called in at South African ports. During World War II, as well, Wonderboom Airport at Pretoria in South Africa was the terminus for a US air-ferry route across Africa.

During the Korean War, we supplied the South African Air Force's 2nd Squadron first with P-51 Mustangs and then with F-86 Sabres, and we gave their pilots conversion training in Japan.

In the years since the collapse of apartheid and the development of South Africa as a full democracy and important African power, a range of military links have been established. For instance, in 2000, three Pave Hawk helicopters operated from Hoedspruit Air Force Base in South Africa, helping with flood relief efforts in next-door Mozambique. In 2009, ships from the *Theodore Roosevelt* Carrier Strike Group paid a visit to Cape Town to boost such links. And Shared Accord 2013, a bilateral US military and South African Defense Forces exercise in South Africa, involved more than four thousand troops and included airborne operations, as well as a humanitarian aid project.

The New York National Guard is partnered with South Africa.

SOUTH KOREA

F ROM THE END OF WORLD WAR II IN 1945 until the liberation of Kuwait in 1991, one of the most decisive strategic moves made by the US military was at Inchon in the Korean War.

However, what a lot of people don't know is that we had made a rather less brilliant strategic move near Inchon almost eighty years earlier in our first intervention in Korea, one in which nine Medals of Honor were won for outstanding bravery.

In 1853, the same year that Commodore Matthew Perry first called on Japan, in a rather less well-known visit, the USS *South America* arrived for a brief stop at Pusan in what is now South Korea. Just as Japan opened up after Perry's visit, we were hoping Korea would do the same. However, the Koreans were wary, understandably, after seeing what Western involvement had been doing to China, and it wasn't going to be easy.

In 1871, a US naval force of five ships plus marines arrived off Inchon. The mission had several purposes. It was sent to ensure any shipwrecked American sailors would be cared for, to open up Korea for trade, and to try to find out what had happened to the SS *General Sherman* (see "North Korea"). This was an American ship that had disappeared on a previous attempt to start Western trade with Korea and had, unknown to the US naval force, been destroyed in a conflict with the locals. Various American attempts to find an explanation had all failed.

At first, the situation seemed peaceful, but then as matters proceeded, the American force was fired upon. We returned fire, and when no explanation or apology was forthcoming, we attacked the Korean forts on Ganghwa Island. The fighting was bitter, but in the end, we won the battle decisively and destroyed a number of the forts. What we did not win, however, was the trade deal we had hoped for. We had to wait until 1882 for that.

In 1888, American troops arrived in Seoul to protect American citizens during civil disturbances, and Korea, trapped between Russia, China, and Japan, was, according to an old Korean proverb, "a shrimp crushed between fighting whales."

After the Chinese-Japanese war of 1894–45 (during which American troops were sent to Seoul to protect American diplomats and citizens), Korea was removed from the Chinese sphere of influence. But then after the Russo-Japanese war of 1904–05 (during which, again, American marines were sent to protect American diplomats in Seoul), Korea came under Japanese dominance, and it basically became a Japanese colony by 1910.

In August 1945, Soviet forces advanced deep into northern Korea smashing aside Japanese resistance, and when Japan surrendered on August 15, Korea, like Germany, was divided into different zones of occupation. Korea was split along the famous thirty-eighth parallel.

US forces first "invaded" the area that became South Korea in the fall of 1945 just after V-J Day. In September 1945, an American landing party led by General Hodges arrived at Inchon where our ships had arrived all those decades previously, but they were there this time to supervise the Japanese surrender. As the Cold War set in, though, just as with Germany, the division of Korea became increasingly solid and long-term. A corrupt right-wing government led by Syngman Rhee soon led the new government of the Republic of Korea while a Communist government supported by Stalin prevailed in the north.

Kim Il Sung had sounded out Stalin and Mao for support in a Moscow meeting in the spring of 1950. Mao would support Kim with the return of ethnic Korean soldiers who had been fighting the Nationalists in China. Stalin supported the North Koreans with weapons and supplies. At 4:00 a.m. on the morning of June 25, 1950, a deafening artillery barrage broke out. The North Korean Army, equipped with T-34 tanks, began advancing south of the thirty-eighth parallel. The North supported their advance with an air force of some two hundred Yak-9 fighters providing close air support.

The North Koreans had achieved total strategic surprise just as the Japanese had at Pearl Harbor. The OSS had been disbanded by Harry Truman after World War II, and the CIA was too small and focused on Europe to identify the North Korean threat.

Memories of the "betrayal at Munich" were fresh in the minds of many Americans, and Truman was determined not to repeat the mistakes of the 1930s (see "Czech Republic"). Aggression would be resisted, and this time, due to a Soviet boycott of the Security Council, the United Nations voted unanimously by nine to zero to "furnish such assistance to the Republic of Korea as may be necessary to repel the armed attack and to restore peace and security in the area." Fifteen other nations would join the United States in contributing troops to defend South Korea.

Even from the start of the conflict, a divide appeared between the Truman administration who believed they were fighting a limited war, or "police action," to protect South Korea from aggression and their supreme American commander, Douglas MacArthur, who believed that the battle raging on the Korean peninsula was the opening round in a struggle to eradicate Communism from the region. Respected as a great hero from World War II who had liberated the Philippines and dealt with Japan, MacArthur, seemed simply irreplaceable.

Since the demobilization that followed World War II, total US military personnel strength had declined from over twelve million in 1945 to under one and a half million in 1950.

Seoul and a large part of South Korea were rapidly captured by the North Koreans, and harsh measures were taken against those perceived by the North Koreans to be a threat. In August of 1950, American and Republic of Korea forces were driven into the Pusan pocket of southeastern Korea.

One of the few areas of UN success was in the skies where UN forces took on and ultimately triumphed over the North Korean air force allowing UN air forces to concentrate on attacking North Korean ground forces and supply routes instead.

Something dramatic had to be done, and MacArthur was about to do it. Douglas MacArthur was the architect of the Inchon Landings. He advocated the landing of the 1st Marine Division, in spite of strenuous opposition from nearly all American officers, especially those in the USN. MacArthur countered the doubters with these words:

> *The very arguments you have made as to the impracticalities involved will tend to ensure for me the element of surprise. For the enemy commander will reason that no one would be so brash as to make such an attempt ... I can almost hear the ticking of the second hand of destiny. We must act now or we will die ... We shall land at Inchon, and I shall crush them.*

The US Marines would soon deliver all that MacArthur had promised. On September 15, 1950, the US 1st Marine Division landed at Inchon on the east coast of the peninsula, and North Korean resistance immediately began to crumble. On September 26, Seoul, the capital of South Korea, was liberated, and soon thereafter the strongman Syngman Rhee was re-established amid much fanfare.

On October 15, 1950, President Truman met with General MacArthur on Wake Island to bask in the glow of Inchon's military success. The war situation would soon change, however, dramatically. To avoid repetition in this book, the rest of the war, the story of our advance into North Korea, of the subsequent Chinese intervention that pushed Western forces some distance south of the thirty-eighth parallel again, and of the see-saw struggle after that can be found in the North Korea chapter.

An uneasy peace, with a significant number of violations, has reigned between North and South Korea since an armistice was signed on July 27, 1953. At the time of writing, over twenty-eight thousand US military remain stationed on the south side of the DMZ. Their main function is not so much to defend South Korean territory as to be a tripwire where American casualties resulting from a North Korean incursion would trigger a deeper military commitment from the United States.

South Korea has remained a steadfast ally of the United States, and a wide variety of long-standing military links exist. South Korea, for instance, was one of the few countries to send ground troops in support of our efforts in the Vietnam War.

SOUTH SUDAN

WHEN IT SPLIT FROM THE REST OF SUDAN IN 2011, South Sudan became both Africa's and the world's newest country. It hasn't had an easy life so far, though, with tribal violence and renewed border conflict with Sudan causing major problems for the new state.

During the long years of war between the main southern rebel group, the Sudan People's Liberation Army, or SPLA, and the Sudanese government in Khartoum, the American government showed some signs of support for the SPLA. The United States at the time was strongly opposed to the Khartoum government on other matters, but it remains unclear exactly what kind of aid it may have supplied the SPLA. In November 1999, for instance, the Clinton administration approved a policy of sending food aid to the SPLA, but in the face of opposition from, among others, some people within the State Department, it then cancelled the policy.

America played a key role in supporting the 2005 peace deal with Sudan that eventually led to the creation of South Sudan, and we've had a small bit of military involvement there as well. For instance, in 2012, the White House announced that five US military officers would be sent to South Sudan to help the UN Mission in South Sudan as it wrestles with the new state's problems. And we've had a military team based at Nzara in South Sudan to help the authorities deal with the notorious Lord's Resistance Army.

Heavy fighting broke out between two factions in South Sudan in December 2013 leading to a variety of actions by the US military. For instance, two USAF C-130s flew into Juba and evacuated 120 people, including diplomats and US citizens. Members of the East Africa Response Force, a team based in Djibouti, were used to increase the protection of US diplomatic facilities in Juba. When trying to evacuate US citizens from the town of Bor, scene of some of the worst violence, three US military personnel were wounded when their aircraft were fired upon.

SPAIN

FANTASTIC PLACE TO VISIT with loads and loads of amazing sights and history, Spain is a big country by European standards.

With Spain at the very western end of Europe (along with Portugal, of course) and the Spanish a major naval power for much of their history, it's hardly surprising that they played such a big role in the European exploration and settlement of both North and South America. The Brits, of course, were not far behind them, and with a long history of hostility between the two countries, there was bound to be trouble.

So interestingly, among the first Americans fighting in Spanish regions is one from before the Revolution on behalf of the Brits—although fighting may not be quite the right word since John Halsey, born in Boston, was a privateer, a sort of pirate with official government permission to be a pirate but only attacking enemy ships. In 1704, with Britain at war with the Spanish (or at least some of them since confusingly there were Spanish on both sides), Halsey arrived in the Spanish Canary Islands (popular holiday destination and part of Spain, even though they're stuck out in the Atlantic off the coast of Africa) and attacked assorted Spanish ships.

After all the wars between Spain and Britain, Spain was only too delighted when we rebelled against English rule, and the Spanish crown supplied the rebel colonies with food, ammunition, and intelligence during the American Revolution. King Charles III of Spain even sent livestock to George Washington's farm at Mount Vernon. Very friendly.

However, on October 21, 1805, Admiral Horatio Nelson led the Royal Navy to one of the most decisive victories in its history off the coast of Spain at the battle of Trafalgar. Twenty-two Americans served aboard Nelson's flagship, the *Victory*, with many more throughout his fleet. A percentage of these were, no doubt, pressed men, those forced to serve in the fleet. Serve, though, they did with honor and shared in the victor's prize money, as was their right.

In 1815, we again ventured into Spanish waters when, during the Second Barbary War, Commodore Stephen Decatur scored naval victories over Barbary pirates based in Algiers at Cape Gata and Cape Palos off the coast of Spain. On that occasion, even though we were in Spanish waters, we were actually fighting the Barbary pirates rather than the Spanish.

But things were getting distinctly less friendly between the United States and Spain. In 1818, Andrew Jackson led a successful invasion of Florida during the First Seminole War, and the Spanish ceded Florida to the United States in 1821, which is how Jacksonville, Florida, got its name.

In 1898, the United States, led by President William McKinley, went into a full-scale war with Spain. In the Spanish-American War, however, despite occasional plans for us to do things, like attack the Canary Islands (again), in the end, there was no actual fighting in Spain. Therefore, we cover that war in the Cuba and Philippines chapters.

In 1936, the Spanish Civil War, as sort of a pre-game warm up for World War II, broke out. It's a fascinating and important war and deserves to be better known. When General Franco mounted a right-wing military coup against the left-wing Spanish government, foreign volunteers flooded in from across the world to defend the republic, and among them were plenty of Americans. The Soviet Union supported the republic. Hitler and Mussolini supported Franco.

The best-known American unit sent to aid the floundering republic was the Abraham Lincoln Brigade, or Battalion, many of its volunteers being members of the Communist Party United States, but there was also a George Washington Battalion, later amalgamated with the Abraham Lincoln unit. The fighting was ferocious, and Americans were in the thick of it in bitter struggles battles, like the Battle of Jarama and the Brunete and Aragon offensives, with horrifying casualty rates to match. Something like eight hundred of the approximately twenty-eight hundred Americans who served in the Spanish Civil War were killed. Oliver Law was a US Army veteran, a Chicago taxicab driver, and a Communist party member; during the Spanish Civil War, he became the first African-American officer to lead an American military unit. Many US veterans of the Spanish Civil War would go on to serve in the OSS during World War II.

Ernest Hemingway and the woman who would later become his third wife, Martha Gellhorn, went to Spain to report on the war. Robert Capa, a friend of Hemingway's, took his famous dying soldier photograph in the Spanish Civil War.

Even Errol Flynn, a naturalized American citizen, went to Spain as a war correspondent. The Loyalist side attempted to recruit Errol to their side in the conflict and gave him a machine gun, but he decided that killing people for politics in somebody else's war wasn't really his cup of tea.

Not all our military involvement with the Spanish Civil War was unofficial, For instance, in August 1936, the destroyer USS *Kane* was sent to Bilbao in Spain to rescue American citizens. On the way into Bilbao, a three-engine monoplane dropped bombs within a hundred yards, and the ship's crew had to open fire three times to drive it away. *Kane* then joined up with USN Squadron 40-T under the command of Arthur P. Fairfield, which during its time in the area rescued hundreds of Americans and others from the war.

With German assistance, Franco eventually led the Nationalists to victory in the bitter civil war.

Spain officially remained neutral during World War II, though it did send the so-called Blue Division to fight alongside the Germans in Russia, and German U-boats were able to utilize the "neutral" ports of Spain to resupply. Amidst fears that Franco might still join the Axis cause "Wild Bill" Donovan, the head of the OSS, visited Madrid, and an OSS detachment was established in Spanish Morocco. The OSS made contact with the remnants of the Republican underground and exiled Spanish government to explore the possibility of subverting Franco's regime, but that was about as far as it got.

After the war, fascist Spain was a political pariah for a time, but today Spain is a constitutional monarchy and a member of NATO and the EU.

We have major bases in Spain. Rota, once a sleepy fishing village near Cadiz, has served as a US naval base from 1953 to the present. It is referred to as the "Gateway to the Med" for the US 6th Fleet and other NATO forces since it's very close to the straits that lead from the Atlantic to the Mediterranean. The USAF also maintains Morón Air Base in Andalucia.

SRI LANKA

A BEAUTIFUL ISLAND OFF THE SOUTHEAST COAST OF INDIA, Sri Lanka was known as Ceylon until 1972.

For a long time, Sri Lanka was part of the British Empire. In recent decades, it suffered a long-running civil war in the north of the island that only finally ended in May 2009.

The Great White Fleet, dispatched by Teddy Roosevelt for a circumnavigation of the world, arrived in Ceylon on December 13, 1909, and spent a week there.

In World War II, the Allied South-East Asia Command headquarters were based from April 1944 at Kandy in Ceylon, and our forces made use of both naval and air facilities on the island. For instance, the RAF airfield at China Bay in Ceylon was the base for one of the USAAF's most spectacular raids of the whole war. On the night of August 10/11, 1944, thirty-one B-29s of the 58th Very Heavy Bombardment Wing assembled at China Bay and took off on a vital mission to bomb an oil refinery in distant Palembang, Sumatra, and sow mines in a river there. When they completed the mission and returned to China Bay with the loss of one B-29 that ran out of fuel, they had completed the longest non-stop mission by USAAF combat aircraft in World War II, something like four thousand miles long. An OSS Maritime Unit based in Ceylon also launched infiltrations of Japanese-occupied Sumatra.

The Japanese launched air raids against Ceylon causing the loss of many lives, but there was no land action during the war there. However, the classic war movie, *Bridge on the River Kwai*, winner of seven academy awards, including best picture, was filmed in Ceylon, even though the events shown were supposed to be taking place in Thailand.

Ceylon became independent from Britain in 1948, and there have been limited US military connections with Sri Lanka since then. For instance, the USN has been a regular visitor to Sri Lankan ports in recent decades, in particular Colombo, the capital of Sri Lanka. And sometimes, our navy has gone for purposes other than official visits and exercises. In 1957, when devastating floods hit the island, President Dwight Eisenhower sent the aircraft carrier *Princeton* with twenty helicopters on board, a seaplane tender, and two destroyers to help relief effort. And the US military helped after the 2004 tsunami with US marines from the 9th Marine Expeditionary Support Battalion and sailors from the 7th Seabee Battalion providing engineering support on the island.

Some reports suggest recent US Special Forces' links to Sri Lanka.

ST. KITTS AND NEVIS

ST. KITTS IS A NICKNAME FOR ST. CHRISTOPHER, a former name for the island and still sometimes used. We haven't exactly had that much military involvement with the Caribbean islands of St. Kitts and Nevis, but we have had a bit.

When we were at war with Britain, American privateers captured assorted British ships in the area, or at least tried to.

And it wasn't just the British we fought in the area. In 1799, during the quasi-war with France, the US frigate *Constellation* clashed with the French 40-gun frigate *L'Insurgente* in a battle fought off Nevis and, after a bitter fight, eventually captured the French ship and took it into port. In July 1800, the US schooner *Enterprise*, enterprisingly captured a French privateer off Nevis. In October 1800, the US frigate *Merrimack* captured the French privateer brig *Phoenix* off St. Kitts.

However, since then, US military personnel have visited the islands on a much more friendly basis as shown in the photo of the USS *North Dakota* during exercises there in about 1922, and much more recently the USS *Monterey* and USS *Carney* have paid visits.

In recent years, personnel from St. Kitts and Nevis have taken part alongside US personnel in exercises such as Tradewinds 2011.

ST. LUCIA

A BEAUTIFUL CARIBBEAN ISLAND visited by many American tourists, St. Lucia has not had a huge involvement with us militarily.

In the colonial period, the island changed hands several times between the French (during the French Revolution, they even imported guillotines to the island) and British, and eventually it ended up as a British colony.

Armed Americans, however, occasionally paid some attention to the area during the period. In 1814, for instance, Captain Boyle on board the armed brig *Chasseur* came within range of the guns on St. Lucia in its attempt to take the transport ship *Lord Eldon* and hoisted the Yankee stripes. Ships from St. Lucia were also vulnerable to US privateers further afield.

Over the years, St. Lucia has seen many visits by US warships, but the period when we were most actively involved with the island militarily was World War II. As part of the Destroyers for Bases deal, we were given access, among other locations, to sites on St. Lucia, and airfield preparation began in early 1941. Beane Field, or Beane Air Force Base, for instance, was used by the US Air Force for transport aircraft and for flying anti–U-boat patrols in the surrounding seas. There was also a naval air station at Gros Islet Bay.

The closure of the two airbases was not the end of US forces in St. Lucia. For example, the US maintained a missile-tracking facility in St. Lucia.

St. Lucia became independent from Britain in 1979. In 1983, St. Lucia offered military and political support to the invasion of Grenada. Since then, we have developed assorted other links with St. Lucia on the security front, for instance, giving some training to the coast guard and the Special Services Unit and taking part together in exercises. In May 2013, Exercise Tradewinds 2013 saw the US Coast Guard Cutter *Oak* involved in a live fire exercise off the coast of St. Lucia.

ST. VINCENT AND THE GRENADINES

THE RECORDING ARTIST KEVIN LYTTLE is a Vincentian.

American ships were in action in the waters around St. Vincent and the Grenadines during our early conflicts with Britain. For example, during the War of 1812, the US privateer *Chasseur* under the famous Captain Thomas Boyle caused so many problems to the merchants of St. Vincent by effectively blockading the Caribbean island that they reputedly demanded of the Royal Navy's Admiral Durham do something about it. The British frigate *Barossa* was eventually sent.

Since then, US ships have visited the islands on a friendly basis. For example, in May and June 1902, after a volcanic eruption, the USS *Dixie* was put to work transporting emergency supplies to Martinique and St. Vincent.

St. Vincent and the Grenadines supported the American invasion of Grenada in 1983, and in recent years, the US military has worked with personnel from the islands in assorted humanitarian projects and training exercises. In 2012, the United States donated patrol boats and communications systems to the islands to help the fight against transnational organized crime.

SUDAN

SUDAN HAS BEEN IN THE NEWS IN RECENT YEARS because of Darfur, in which we have been involved, but we've played other parts in the country's long history.

Charles Chaillé-Long, for instance (mentioned in the Egypt chapter), was an American soldier from Maryland who had already fought in the Union Army at Gettysburg. In 1874, after the war in Egypt, he found himself appointed in Khartoum, now capital of Sudan, second in command of an Egyptian Army to a Brit, Charles George Gordon. As if the situation wasn't confusing enough from a nationality point of view, Gordon's nickname was "Chinese" Gordon because of his previous military activities in China.

However, it was in World War II that we first had serious military involvement in the Sudan. A number of airbases there became crucial in our transport and plane-ferrying links from the Atlantic, across Africa, to the Middle East, and beyond. We had personnel based at El Geneina, El Fasher, and Khartoum, and even though they were a long distance from the frontlines then, it could still be dangerous (crashes by American aircraft are recorded at all three bases).

Sudan has not had an easy time in the years since gaining independence in 1956. In particular, two civil wars and the conflict in Darfur have killed many thousands and done enormous damage to the country's people and economy. We went through a comparatively brief period in the 1980s of supplying equipment to the Sudanese military, but that stopped after a military coup in 1989.

However, in 1993, the US government designated Sudan as a state sponsor of terrorism, and in August 1998, after the bombings of the US embassies in Kenya and Tanzania that month, President Clinton ordered cruise missiles strikes on targets in Afghanistan and on the Al-Shifa factory in Sudan.

We played a big role in the 2005 peace agreement that led to the end of the north-south wars and the creation of an independent South Sudan in 2011 and tried to help bring an end to the tragedy in Darfur. Our military has had some involvement in that effort. For instance, since 2004, they have spent millions airlifting thousands of peacekeepers and their equipment to and from Darfur and many tens of millions training and equipping those forces.

SURINAME

SURINAME IS SITUATED ON THE NORTHEASTERN COAST of South America with Brazil to its south, Guyana to its west, and French Guiana to its east. With both Guyana and French Guiana in the area, it's not surprising that Suriname often used to be called Dutch Guiana (though that entity did include other areas).

Interestingly, in 1667, in a peace deal ending a war between England and the Dutch, the English kept New Amsterdam that they'd taken from the Dutch while the Dutch kept a bit of what territory that they'd taken from the English. The English had called it Willoughby Land. The Dutch renamed it Suriname. If history had been different, it might have been Willoughby Land with a seat at the UN.

Suriname became independent from Holland only in 1973 (and plenty of Dutch is still spoken there), so you might think we've never sent troops into the country. If so, then you'd be wrong. In 1940, the Netherland fell to the Nazis. The bauxite mines in Suriname were strategically vital, then supplying more than 60 percent of the needs of the US aluminum industry. So in late November 1941, with war in the Pacific just a few days distant, US forces moved into Suriname with the agreement of the Dutch government in exile.

At the same time, we also established an airbase at Zandery (now Zanderij) Airport, twenty-eight miles south of the capital, Paramaribo. This then became a major link in the chain of airbases sending lend-lease supplies and aircraft across the Atlantic. US planes also flew some anti-submarine missions from the base during the war, and the USN was involved in trying to counter the U-boat threat in the waters off Suriname.

We might have gotten militarily involved again with independent Suriname in the early 1980s. Dési Bouterse seized power in Suriname in 1980 in a military coup. Some in Washington feared that Bouterse would become a major Cuban ally, and discussions in CIA circles took place about the possibility of mounting armed action to remove him.

Suriname has seen a variety of political conflicts, controversies, and governments in the period since then. The United States has, on occasions, attempted to put pressure on Suriname's rulers, but it has also supplied training to Surinamese forces. Currently, Desi Bouterse is once again president.

The South Dakota National Guard is partnered with Suriname.

SWAZILAND

SWAZILAND IS SMALL SOUTHERN AFRICAN COUNTRY with which we haven't had much military involvement.

However, in recent years, AFRICOM has been involved in efforts to help improve Swaziland's military medical capabilities. For instance, in 2009 AFRICOM and the Umbutfo Swaziland Defence Force conducted a two-week medical exercise, Medflag 09. And again in 2013, US military health-care personnel visited Swaziland to observe and assess.

SWEDEN

YES, SWEDEN, THE LAND OF VIKINGS, Abba, and the *Girl with the Dragon Tattoo*.

Sweden has a long military tradition, including such major figures as Gustavus Adolphus, one of the best-known generals of the Thirty Years' War that devastated large parts of Europe in the seventeenth century. But Sweden has also been known for its sometimes strict neutrality. Sweden was a nation that stayed neutral in both world wars and the Cold War. So you might suppose the US military personnel have never set foot in Sweden during a war, but if you thought that, you would be mistaken.

During the American Revolution, many Swedes volunteered to fight on the patriot side against Great Britain. Swedish Count Axel von Fersen, for instance, served as an interpreter between George Washington and the French general Rochambeau. And Count von Fersen was present at the battle of Yorktown and became a founding member of the Society of the Cincinnati.

And even greater links between Sweden and the United States were to come. Something like one third of the total Swedish population emigrated to North America between 1820 and 1930. Sherwood "Shakey" Johnson, for example, was one of a huge number of Americans of Swedish descent. He served in the USN during World War II and founded Shakey's, the pizza restaurant chain, in his hometown of Sacramento, California. He had learned about pizza while cruising on a USN ship that called on Italian ports during the war.

In World War II, Sweden supplied iron ore to Germany, which helped build the Nazi war machine. Early in the war, Sweden also permitted the transit of a German division from Norway to Finland through Sweden prior to the launch of Operation Barbarossa.

We didn't attack Sweden. However, it wasn't long after our entry into the European war that American service personnel ended up there.

Dozens of American bombers that had been so badly damaged that they could not reach their bases in Britain preferred to land in neutral Sweden than in German-held territory. Having landed in Sweden, the planes and crews were supposed to be held for the war's duration, but a secret repatriation program returned some to Allied territory.

And eventually, our ground troops arrived in Sweden as well. On March 24, 1945, near the close of the war in Europe, the OSS launched Operation RYPE to infiltrate a battalion of skiing demolition agents into Norway (see "Norway"). A squadron of eight B-24 Liberators was flown from Scotland, but one went off course and dropped its agents by parachute in Sweden. With help from the Swedes, the crew eventually rejoined their unit of thirty-six men in Norway.

The OSS battalion, commanded by Major William Colby (future head of the CIA), attacked infrastructure targets in Norway. On one occasion, after blowing up a bridge in Norway, they were spotted by Luftwaffe aircraft and pursued by Wehrmacht forces. According to Colby's account, they skied non-stop over two days for forty miles and across the border into neutral Sweden. There they found Sugartop hill where they rested and dined on elk.

As the war progressed, neutral Sweden gave more evidence of it not always being as neutral as sometimes thought. For instance, starting in 1943, the Swedish authorities started training Danes and Norwegians as paramilitary units to take over in Denmark and Norway after a German surrender or withdrawal. These units were officially described as police, but these Danish police included an air unit equipped with Swedish SAAB fighter-bombers! And in early 1944 in an extensive program, British and Swedish weapons started being smuggled through Sweden to the Danish resistance. Thousands of pistols and millions of rounds of ammunition went into Denmark this way. In 1945, American planes flew supplies from the Swedish capital of Stockholm to some of these Norwegian "police" in liberated north Norway to help maintain order there.

After the war, Colby returned to Stockholm where he was the CIA station chief in the 1950s. There he worked on Operation Gladio, which sought to create stay-behind cadres that would resist Soviet occupiers in the event of a successful Russian invasion of Sweden. Fortunately, there was never to be such an invasion. There has been speculation, though, about how neutral Sweden really was during the Cold War.

Sweden has a contingent of about five hundred troops serving in Afghanistan alongside NATO members. The Swedish Air Force was also involved with the NATO-led action in Libya in 2011, sending eight fighter jets to the Mediterranean.

USN ships have been calling on Swedish ports for years. For instance, in 1911, the Second Battleship Division called on Stockholm on its way to Russia. And Sweden is a key participant in the Baltic Operations series of maritime exercises hosted in the Baltic by the USN.

SWITZERLAND

MOUNTAINOUS, PICTURESQUE SWITZERLAND has a long history of neutrality. So have we ever attacked any fondue-eating, yoghurt-slurping, and chocolate-devouring Swiss? Well, not intentionally, but unintentionally, yes.

During both world wars, Switzerland remained, of course, neutral. In World War I, despite one or two Allied plans to invade Switzerland, or at least invade enemy territory through Switzerland, we didn't really have that much to do with the country militarily, apart from a bit of espionage.

With its strategic location at the heart of Europe, Switzerland became famous along with the fondue, clocks, and knives for spies during both world wars. There can be few more famous American spymasters than Allen Dulles, and he spent time in Switzerland during both wars. In World War I, he operated out of Berne and ran spies in Austria-Hungary, the Balkans, and Eastern Europe. Also one night, he apparently hung up the phone after a conversation with a Russian revolutionary about to leave Switzerland and desperate to speak to an American diplomat. That revolutionary turned out to be Lenin, and his destination, Russia and the Bolshevik Revolution.

In World War II, Switzerland once again became a hotbed of espionage activity while the war raged all around the country. And once again, Allen Dulles appeared on the scene, this time heading up the OSS there. Germany was now his focus, and Dulles worked with many anti-Hitler Germans. While in Switzerland, he managed to gather intelligence on the Me 262 jet and the German rocket programs and help the Italians surrender.

Stalin, not a fan of capitalists anyway, denounced the Swiss as "swine" and urged US forces to attack from France. We didn't. Well, as mentioned above, not intentionally anyway.

The air war over Europe was wide-ranging, vicious, and often chaotic, fought by crews with, by today's standards, very limited navigational technology. Some mistakes were inevitable. In September 1944, for instance, US pilots invaded Swiss airspace sometimes as many as thirty times a day. In another example, a squadron of US P-47s shot up a train headed from Zurich to Basel assuming it was German. In one of the most tragic incidents, Americans inadvertently bombed the Swiss town of Schaffhausen, killing tens of civilians. To be fair, Swiss airspace was also violated by the Luftwaffe hundreds of times in the course of the war. After the war, the US government paid compensation to the Swiss.

Sometimes, however, Switzerland was the intended destination of our men. A number of Allied bomber crews, for instance, thinking their planes were too damaged to return home, preferred to avoid becoming POWs and landed deliberately in neutral Switzerland where their planes and crews would be impounded for the duration of the war. And Switzerland was, of course, a destination of choice for American POWs attempting to escape from German prisoner-of-war camps.

SYRIA

YES, WE DID COME VERY CLOSE TO BOMBING SYRIA in 2013, and we have been offering the Syrian rebels support, of sorts, but overall, we've had a lot less military involvement with Syria than we have had with many, many other countries.

Syria is an ancient land with a remarkable history, and its capital, Damascus, has been (and continues to be) the center of it. On visiting Syria in 1867, Mark Twain wrote about the Syrian capital:

> *Damascus dates back anterior to the days of Abraham,*
> *and is the oldest city in the world. It was founded by Uz,*
> *the grandson of Noah. "The early history of Damascus*
> *is shrouded in the mists of a hoary antiquity." Leave the*

*matters written of in the first eleven chapters on the Old
Testament out, and no recorded event has occurred in the
world but Damascus was in existence to receive the news
of it. Go back as far as you will not the vague past, there
was always a Damascus. In the writings of every century
for more than four thousand years, its name has been
mentioned and its praises sung. To Damascus, years are
only moments, decades are only flirting trifles of time. She
measures time, not by days and months and years, but by
the empires she has seen rise, and prosper and crumble to
ruin. She is a type of immortality.*

Lawrence of Arabia fought against the Turks in Syria in World War I, however, was basically outside our area of operations.

And in World War II, when Syria was for a time controlled by the Vichy French regime, it was captured by British and Commonwealth troops in the Summer of 1941, months before the attack on Pearl Harbor.

In 1948, US-made planes bombed assorted targets in Syria, including a number of raids on Damascus carried out by Dakotas and a B-17. But these were raids on Syrian targets by the Israeli Air Force. However, American-made planes operated by the Israeli military have hit targets inside Syria on a number of occasions, and other American-made equipment, for instance, tanks and artillery, have played a major role in Israeli advances into Syria and in Israeli operations against Syria. We have also supplied intelligence on Syria. And, of course, it's not just American military equipment that has helped Israel against Syria; many American volunteers have gone to fight with the Israeli armed forces as well.

It has been alleged that the CIA attempted to mount coups inside Syria, including a plan for one in 1957.

We clashed with the Syrians in Lebanon when we had forces there. US pilot Lt. Robert Goodman was held in Damascus for a time after being shot down on a mission against Syrian forces (another reason for unmanned drones), and we have maneuvered navy ships in the vicinity of Syria during times of tension in the region.

During the Gulf War, Syria was on the same side as us against Saddam. But that rapprochement was not to last for long.

Already by 2002, then undersecretary of state John R. Bolton was grouping Syria alongside the original "axis of evil." And when we moved into Iraq after the 2003 invasion, clashes occurred near the Syrian border as the insurgency developed there and the Syrians started to assist local insurgents against our forces. For instance, in 2004, a bitter battle took place between US forces and insurgents at Husaybah near the border. And on October 26, 2008, US helicopters and commandos were reported to have crossed the border into Syria to attack a purported al-Qaeda target in a village a few miles inside Syria.

As already mentioned, during the current Syrian crisis, we have sent support to the Syrian opposition, and we may yet have more extensive military involvement in the country before the current crisis is finished. We have been militarily involved with Syria but have not invaded it … so far.

TAJIKISTAN

TAJIKISTAN IS A COUNTRY IN CENTRAL ASIA. It is also, let's face it, a place many of us, apart from those who've been serving in Afghanistan, would struggle to find on a map. So it's hardly surprising that Tajikistan hasn't exactly been destination numero uno for US forces. If our forces have met Tajiks, it's tended to be in Afghanistan where they make up a significant portion of the population. However, that's not saying we haven't been to Tajikistan at all.

We have because Tajikistan occupies a key strategic location north of Afghanistan and west of China. In the nineteenth century, the whole area around it was the scene of the Great Game as Russia and the Brits battled for domination of the area. The Brits had their successes in the game, but Tajikistan was pretty much a slam dunk for the Russian Bear, and well before the final buzzer, the Russians were in control there.

Things got a bit rocky for the Russians around the time of the Russian Revolution as locals rose up, but ultimately Tajikistan was part of the Soviet Union for a long time, up until gaining independence in 1992, so obviously it was much off limits to our military, except for things like spy flights at that stage. A strong Russian military presence continues in Tajikistan to this day.

After Tajikistan's independence, things got very messy with a bloody civil war raging from then until 1997. In October 1992, a USAF C-141 Starlifter flew into Tajikistan to evacuate Americans and other nationals.

In the same period, the situation was pretty bad in Afghanistan to the south with civil war and the rise of the Taliban and al-Qaeda there. And that is where we come in.

As we started operations in Afghanistan after 9/11, the Tajiks offered us permission to use their airspace. We accepted, and US forces sometimes refueled in Dushanbe. We've also supplied equipment and training for Tajik counter-narcotics and counterterrorism operations. But there are also suggestions that our special forces have been sometimes playing a more active role in Tajikistan.

As with so much involving our special forces, the details are cloaked in secrecy, but, for instance, it's alleged that a small number of US Special Forces went into Tajikistan in an anti-Taliban operation in August 2001. And again, in September 2010, they are said to have been involved in a skirmish that left twenty militants dead.

Defense Secretary Donald Rumsfeld visited Tajikistan in 2001 in hopes of negotiating an American airbase in Kalyub in Tajikistan. Instead, the US government decided to build the airbase in Manus, Kyrgyzstan. The US government helped to pay for a bridge in Tajikistan as a goodwill gesture—more long-lasting than flowers or a box of chocolates.

The Virginia National Guard is partnered with Tajikistan.

TANZANIA

FOR SOME TIME IN THE NINETEENTH CENTURY, stories of a snow-capped peak in this part of Africa caused some disbelief in the West, but Kilimanjaro is over nineteen thousand feet high.

Tanzania is a country that includes the fascinating island of Zanzibar. In fact, the name Tanzania comes, in part, from Zanzibar, because like the country itself, the name Tanzania is a combination of Tanganyika and Zanzibar.

Zanzibar has long been a major trading center and port, and we took quite an early interest in it. In fact, a very early interest. Zanzibar was one place in Africa where, in the early nineteenth century, we had more influence than the British, the French, or the Portuguese. Zanzibar sent us vast quantities of ivory and animal skins, and we sent them cotton and guns. The sultan signed a Treaty of Amity and Commerce with us, and in 1837, we sent him a US consul, Richard Waters, four years before the first British consul and seven years before the first French consul. And in 1838, the USS *John Adams* dropped into Zanzibar for a visit. In 1844, the USS *Constitution* called in on its round-the-world cruise.

One thing the sultan may have hoped for from the United States was some protection from British efforts to close down the slave trade. Indeed, not every US diplomat in Zanzibar was hugely keen on stopping the slave trade. But as time passed and attitudes in the United States changed, so eventually did those among US diplomats in Zanzibar. The USS *Yantic* arrived at Zanzibar in January 1873 as part of efforts to pressure the sultan to abolish slavery.

On the mainland opposite Zanzibar, by the 1880s, the Germans were busy constructing their colony of German East Africa. With the arrival of the First World War a few decades later, the British got busy demolishing it, or at least occupying it. One unit involved in the little-known but often rather vicious war in East Africa during WW1 was the 25th (Frontiersmen) Battalion of the Royal Fusiliers. It was formed in 1915 from a fairly varied assortment of volunteers, including a famous hunter who'd hunted in Africa with Teddy Roosevelt in 1909 and, allegedly, a number of American cowboys.

A big chunk of what had been German East Africa became a British colony and then in 1961 gained independence as Tanganyika. In 1964, a revolution in Zanzibar forced the sultan to flee. The day after the revolution started, the USS *Manley* raced in to rescue American citizens, only to be met by armed revolutionaries because no prior permission had been granted. After a tense stand-off and negotiations, eventually the *Manley* was allowed to carry out its mission.

Tanganyika and Zanzibar united to form Tanzania the same year.

Under long-term ruler Julius Nyerere, Tanzania became very friendly with Communist China, which, with the Cold War still going, meant our military involvement with Tanzania was pretty minimal.

In 1998, terrorists bombed our embassy in Dar es Salaam, Tanzania, and US military personnel and security personnel were rushed to Tanzania to help deal with the aftermath of the attack and to help boost security.

In recent years, US military personnel have trained with members of the Tanzanian military, for instance on a military police exercise in 2011 and on a program to develop expertise in international peacekeeping. Our military have also carried out assorted humanitarian projects in the country. Recent news on Tanzanian troops serving with the UN mission that defeated the rebel M23 group show that it can be a tough mission. A number were killed and wounded while serving there.

THAILAND

AN ANCIENT MONARCHY that prides itself on never having been conquered by a foreign invader, Thailand, or Siam as it was formerly called, was the first Asian country to establish diplomatic links with the United States in 1833 when the USS *Peacock* arrived in the Gulf of Siam.

Following that, Townsend Harris of New York was the consul to Siam who negotiated the Harris Treaty with Siam in 1856. Harris, in a paragraph that in some ways sums up a key tenet of what American foreign policy has often aspired to, said:

> The United States does not hold any possessions in the East, nor does it desire any. The form of government forbids the holding of colonies. The United States therefore cannot be an object of jealousy to any Eastern Power. Peaceful commercial relations, which give as well as receive benefits, is what the President wishes to establish with Siam, and such is the object of my mission.

And on the subject of peaceful relations, allegedly Harris, while later serving as the American consul in Shimoda, had an affair with a Japanese geisha and may have been the model for Lieutenant Pinkerton in Puccini's *Madame Butterfly*.

Thailand was on the Allied side in World War I, but in World War II, the country faced a much more challenging situation. Hours after the attack on Pearl Harbor, Japanese troops began moving into Thailand. After a brief period of fighting, Premier Pibun decided to order the Thai Army to offer no further resistance. As a result, Japanese troops moved through Thailand to invade British-controlled Burma with their sights ultimately set on India.

Soon Thailand had agreed to an alliance with Imperial Japan. On January 25, 1942, Thailand declared war on the United States. There were, however, many Thais who sympathized with the Allied cause. The Thai ambassador to Washington, Seni Pramoj, refused to deliver the declaration to our government. Instead, he helped to start the Free Thai movement.

And as early as April 1942, the OSS began working with Thai dissidents to subvert the Pibun government. Efforts were also made to rescue downed Allied airmen from the Japanese and return them to China.

After the Japanese naval defeat at the Battle of Midway, seaborne supply of Japanese ground forces in Burma became problematic. The Japanese responded by using thousands of Allied prisoners and Asians to construct a railway line 258-miles long to link Kanchanaburi to the Japanese base camp in Thanbyuzayat in Burma. This was the infamous "Railway of Death" depicted in the classic film, *Bridge on the River Kwai*.

I (Chris Kelly) paid a visit to the bridge at Kanchanaburi in southern Thailand in 2012. A Thai violinist, who was playing the famous "Colonel Bogey's March," asked me to feel the outside of the bridge that is pockmarked with bullet holes made by strafing Allied fighters from World War II.

From 1942 onwards, we also launched a large number of bombing raids on targets within Thailand. For instance, on June 5, 1944, the very first combat mission of the epic B-29 Superfortress was a raid aimed at vital railway yards in Bangkok.

Finally, pro-Japanese Premier Pibun was ousted from the premiership in July 1944 by a coup led by forces that secretly began to take a more pro-Allied line. In January 1945, two OSS majors landed by seaplane in Thailand bringing with them gifts for Premier Pridi from FDR and "Wild Bill" Donovan—two gold cigarette lighters. Ultimately, however, Japan surrendered before the Allies could launch the full, planned invasion of Thailand.

In 1946, the current king of Thailand, who is the world's longest reigning monarch, came to the throne. Bhumibol Adulyadej was born in 1927 in Cambridge, Massachusetts, when his father was studying at Harvard.

In 1953, "Wild Bill" Donovan, the former head of the OSS, was appointed ambassador to Thailand by President Dwight Eisenhower in the 1950s. Eisenhower wanted someone experienced in intelligence operations in charge in Thailand to provide a launching pad for American covert operations to thwart Communist expansion in Southeast Asia.

In the post-war period, as the Cold War heated up and with the French fighting in Vietnam, Thailand became an increasingly close US ally.

Thai troops fought alongside us in the Korean War, and in 1955, Thailand was a founding member of SEATO, an alliance of non-Communist countries with its headquarters in Bangkok.

In May 1962, with the Soviets having decided to arm the Pathet Lao in nearby Laos, we sent the 3rd Marine Expeditionary Brigade to Thailand as a show of force. It withdrew after a couple of months.

During the Vietnam War, the alliance became even deeper. Thailand was one of the few countries to send troops to fight alongside us. And we made extensive use of Thai naval bases and particularly airbases, with the USAF, for instance, flying a high percentage of air strikes against North Vietnam from Thailand. Bangkok was also used as a popular R and R stop for the American military. The fictional Sherlock Holmes of Thailand, John Burdett's Sonchai Jitpleecheep, is the son of an American Vietnam veteran and a Thai prostitute.

Thailand has been designated a Major US Non-NATO Ally. Thailand sent hundreds of troops to help us in Iraq, and the Thai and US forces regularly share exercises. For example, the US military has made regular use of U-Tapao airfield as a re-fueling stop to support operations in Iraq and Afghanistan.

The Washington National Guard is partnered with Thailand.

TIMOR-LESTE (EAST TIMOR)

O NE OF THE WORLD'S NEWEST COUNTRIES and located just to the north of Australia, Timor-Leste came into being as an internationally recognized independent nation in 2002.

Before 1974, Timor-Leste had been a Portuguese colony. Portugal remained neutral in World War II, but in December 1941, after Pearl Harbor, Allied forces in West Timor, fearing a Japanese invasion and thinking that an enemy landing in Timor-Leste would outflank them, occupied Portuguese Timor-Leste. The expected Japanese invasion wasn't long in coming. In February 1942, the Japanese landed in both West Timor and Timor-Leste.

A bitter battle ensued lasting a year, until the last Allied units were forced to evacuate the island, and even then, local forces continued to resist the Japanese. Most of the Allied forces involved were British, Australian, and Dutch (West Timor was part of a Dutch colony and would become part of independent Indonesia), but we did have some involvement in the battle. For instance, the last Allied ground troops were evacuated from Timor-Leste by the American submarine USS *Gudgeon* on February 10, 1943. And in the air, American aircraft flew bombing missions against Japanese targets in Timor-Leste, for instance, in and around the capital, Dili, both before the Allied withdrawal and after.

After the Second World War, the Portuguese once more took control of Timor-Leste, until in 1974 a leftist military coup overthrew the government in Portugal, and the days of the Portuguese empire started coming to an end. In 1975, after the Portuguese withdrew, Indonesia invaded Timor-Leste in an attempt to unify it with West Timor, which was already part of Indonesia. What ensued was a long battle for freedom by Timor-Leste guerrillas, which came to an end only in 1999. As the Indonesian forces finally withdrew, the International Force for Timor-Leste, INTERFET, moved into the politically and militarily tense area to establish security. We played a significant role in INTERFET, for instance, providing aircraft and helicopter transport and sending in the USS *Mobile Bay*, USS *Belleau Wood*, and the USS *Peleliu* and a number of troops on the ground.

Today our military has assorted links with Timor-Leste, including involvement with some civilian projects and exercises with the Timor-Leste Defence Forces (TLDF). For instance, in October 2012, US marines took part with TLDF units in Exercise Crocodilo 2012.

TOGO

TOGO IS A LONG, THIN COUNTRY, sandwiched between Ghana to the west and Benin to the east.

A town in southeastern Togo, now called Aného, used to be called Little Popo. It was the first capital of Togo when the country was a German colony, and before that, it was a big slave market. Consequently, it received a certain amount of attention from our Africa Squadron as it tried to combat the slave trade in the nineteenth century. For instance, in 1848, Captain William C. Bolton took USS *Jamestown* and USS *Boxer* for a cruise along the coast there, and he had Little Popo on his list of potential places to investigate.

The French took control of what is now Togo in the First World War. It remained a French colony until 1960, and after that, under its long-term leader, General Gnassingbé Eyadéma, who had himself served in the French army in the Indo-China and Algeria wars, it was still an area of significant French influence.

In recent years, though, we have had some minor links with the Togolese military. For instance, in the summer of 2013, three US soldiers were sent to Lomé, the capital of Togo now, to help the Togolese military with techniques for deploying units and equipment. More broadly, we're involved with Togo in helping it develop the expertise necessary for multinational peace-support operations. Togo has supplied hundreds of troops to the French-led effort in Mali, to which we have also given political and logistical support.

TONGA

TONGA'S CURRENT KING, TOUPOU VI, is a graduate of the US Naval War College.

Tonga is located east of Australia and northeast of New Zealand, though its name means "south," understandable since for its Polynesian inhabitants it's the southernmost bit of central Polynesia. After British Captain Cook visited it, Tonga rather sweetly became known to the British as the Friendly Islands, Cook presumably being unaware that some of the locals were allegedly arguing over who should attack him.

We did take some interest in Tonga in the nineteenth century. For instance, in 1886, the USS *Mohican* turned up there, and on October 2, in Nuku'alofa, we signed a Treaty of Amity, Commerce and Navigation with the Kingdom of Tonga. The treaty allowed US warships to use Tongan harbors as coaling stations. When the local prime minister was toppled in a coup in 1890, he asked for US intervention, but we refused. Tonga, however, was soon to pass firmly into the British sphere of influence, and in 1920, Britain terminated the agreement "on behalf of the King of Tonga."

With the Second World War, though, our military returned to Tonga in force. Tonga declared war on Japan shortly after the attack on Pearl Harbor, and in 1942, US forces arrived in Tonga to help the tiny Tongan Defence Force resist any Japanese attack and to prepare bases to assist in the general Pacific war effort. We gave it the codename "Bleacher."

Tonga became fully independent from Britain in 1970, and since then, we've developed assorted military links with Tonga. For instance, we've supplied training to Tongan military personnel, and Tongan forces have served in Iraq and Afghanistan.

TRINIDAD AND TOBAGO

THE REPUBLIC OF TRINIDAD AND TOBAGO has a proud heritage, including, on the sports front, Hasely Crawford's gold medal in the 100 meter dash at the 1976 Montreal Olympics.

During the Revolutionary War and the War of 1812, American ships targeted assorted ships sailing from Trinidad and Tobago. For instance, in 1777, the American privateer, the *Oliver Cromwell* allegedly raided the coast of Tobago near Fort Milford, though apparently without much success. The American privateer *Jack's Favorite* (although presumably not Trinidad's favorite) returned to New York in July 1812 having captured the schooner *Rebecca*, which was taking sugar and molasses from Trinidad to Halifax. And in February 1814, the US frigate *Constitution* captured a number of ships off Trinidad.

During World War II, we took a major military interest in the islands. Under the Destroyers for Bases deal, Trinidad became the home of a number of US bases. For instance, we got a naval air station and a naval operating base. Perhaps most important, we got two major airbases, Waller Field and Edinburgh Field. Waller Field served two major purposes. Aircraft employed on anti-submarine operations were based there, and Waller was a key point on the transatlantic air-transport and air-ferry route connecting the United States to the Middle East and European combat zones on the other side of the ocean. President Franklin Roosevelt, for instance, passed through Waller en route to the Casablanca Conference in 1943. The air transport and ferry function, in fact, became so significant and demanded so much space that Edinburgh Field, later named Carlsen Field, took over responsibility for most of the anti-submarine operations. US blimps were based on Trinidad as well.

Both bases closed soon after the war, but that wasn't the end of US military personnel there. For example, we built a missile tracking site at Macqueripe Bay, Chaguaramas, on Trinidad during the Cold War.

Trinidad and Tobago became independent in 1962. In the period since then, we've had assorted training and exercise links with Trinidad and Tobago. For instance, in 2011 Trinidad and Tobago hosted the multinational disaster response exercise Allied Humanitarian Forces 2011 in cooperation with US SOUTHCOM. Trinidad and Tobago's fast patrol craft *Chaconia* took part along with US Coast Guardsmen in a simulated counter-drug operation during Tradewinds 2013.

The Delaware National Guard is partnered with Trinidad and Tobago.

TUNISIA

CATO THE ELDER, A ROMAN SENATOR, famously said, *"Carthago delenda est"*—"Carthage must be destroyed!" The mighty ancient city of Carthage was located in what is now Tunisia, not far from the current capital, Tunis. And Carthage eventually was destroyed by the Romans after three bitter wars, which featured among other things Hannibal and his elephants. Cato might have been slightly disappointed to know, however, that after his death, Carthage rose from the ashes and became one of the largest and richest cities of the Roman Empire.

As with other North African countries (see "Algeria" and "Libya"), parts of what is now Tunisia fell under the sway of the Barbary pirates. And as with other North African countries, we had to find a way of dealing with this fact. Our approach to the Barbary States incorporated a combination of stick and carrot, or more accurately carrot and then stick, since we started out paying the pirates of Tunis to leave our ships alone and to free our sailors when they didn't leave our ships alone, and then we ended up threatening them to leave our ships alone.

Thus, concerned about American shipping, President Thomas Jefferson sent warships to Tunis, and in February of 1803, Commodore Richard Morris arrived with three frigates. As soon as he disembarked from his ship, he was arrested by Bey Hamouda of Tunis who demanded payment of twenty-two thousand dollars. Commodore Morris, from a wealthy Vermont family, agreed to pay the tribute.

Then, for example, in 1815, during the Second Barbary War, Stephen Decatur with a large American squadron stopped in Tunis to demand forty-six thousand dollars in compensation for an American ship that had been captured the previous year. The bey of Tunis agreed to pay, and Decatur later boasted to the secretary of the navy that the terms of settlement had "been dictated at the mouths of our cannon."

Tunisia was incorporated into the French Empire later in the nineteenth century.

But by late 1942, it was we and the British who were about to invade it. Operation Torch was launched on November 8 with US and British landings in Vichy-French–controlled Morocco and Algeria in an attempt to attack Rommel's Afrika Korps from behind. In response to these landings, however, the Germans rushed men and tanks into Tunisia to try to hold it against US and British forces advancing from the west, and our boys were in for something of a shock.

In February of 1943, two veteran panzer divisions attacked the inexperienced American forces at Sidi-Bou-Zid and Kasserine Pass pushing rapidly forward against them. After the humiliation of Kasserine, British soldiers even briefly dismissed their American allies as being the Allied version of Italians, a reference to the commonly held belief among British troops that the Italians fighting against them were generally lower quality troops than the Germans also facing them.

However, this was soon to change. Eisenhower dismissed Lloyd Fredendall and put General George "Blood and Guts" Patton in command of II Corps in Tunisia. With fresh leadership, there was an almost immediate improvement in morale. On March 16, Patton told his staff, "Gentlemen, tomorrow we attack. If we are not victorious, let no one come back alive."

On April 3, Patton held a meeting in Gafsa with Air Marshal Sir Arthur Tedder to demand that his soldiers receive better air cover; they were interrupted by three Focke Wulf fighters that strafed the streets and headquarters. Tedder, dusting himself off, inquired how the Germans had managed to achieve this, to which Patton famously replied, "I'll be damned if I know, but if I could find the sonsabitches who flew those planes, I'd mail each one a medal."

With new leadership and growing experience, American performance rapidly improved. With vastly superior Allied numbers being brought to bear on the Axis forces, trapped and short of supplies in Tunisia, the battle there was going to end only one way. Von Arnim surrendered on May 12, 1943, and over 250,000 prisoners surrendered, about the same surrendered by Paulus's Sixth Army at Stalingrad, though the victory at Stalingrad seems to have gotten better press over the decades and remains much better known today.

The Allies now had a secure platform from which they could invade Italy and drive Mussolini out of the war. Churchill commented in his memoirs that one continent had, at that point, been redeemed.

FDR visited Tunis on November 20, 1943, dining with Eisenhower and Kay Summersby (Ike's chauffeur and very, very, close wartime companion). The president inspected the ruins of Carthage before flying off to meet Churchill in Cairo. No doubt, looking at the city that Cato the Elder had been so determined should be conquered, FDR reflected on what it meant to be a conqueror.

The Allies suffered just over seventy-six thousand casualties in the Tunisian campaign, of which over eighteen thousand were Americans.

Today at Carthage, where Romans and Carthaginians clashed over two thousand year ago, a visitor will also find a cemetery with the names of 3,724 Americans who fell in battle in North Africa.

In 1956, the United States was one of the first major powers in the world to recognize the independence of Tunisia from France.

Americans brought war of a different kind in 1976 to Tunisia again when George Lucas filmed parts of *Episode IV: A New Hope* in Tunisia. *Star Wars* would return to film parts of *Episodes I* and *II* in the Tunisian desert as well.

Since the Jasmine Spring swept aside President Ben Ali's repressive government in January 2011, the United States has supplied over $350 million in aid for that country.

Among other military links, the Wyoming National Guard is partnered with Tunisia.

TURKEY

TURKEY'S CAPITAL, ISTANBUL, was once Constantinople, the capital of Byzantium and the Eastern Roman Empire. Digging deeper into its past, Heinrich Schliemann found the ancient ruins of Troy in Turkey in the nineteenth century.

A Turkish-American trade treaty was signed in 1830. And Americans helped start the process of modernizing the Turkish navy, operating the Imperial Naval Arsenal on the Haliç. Two Americans, Charles Ross and Forster Rhodes, served as naval advisors to the sultan.

In 1849, the USN intervened in Smyrna (now Izmir) when an American was detained there. And in 1856, the navy returned to Smyrna for what has to be one of the navy's more unusual missions. Jefferson Davis wanted to form an experimental United States Army Camel Corps for service in territory recently acquired from Mexico. So the USS *Supply* was sent to Smyrna to get camels. And get camels it did and took them to Indianola, Texas.

In the later nineteenth century, the Ottoman Empire was described, perhaps by Tsar Nicholas I, as being "the sick man of Europe." Their once vast empire seemed to many observers to be in a protracted period of disintegration and decline.

In 1912, the First Balkan War broke out, which removed from Ottoman control most of what remained of its territory in Europe. And towards the end of that year, American troops were put on duty guarding the American legation in Istanbul.

Meanwhile, one North America deeply involved in the Balkan Wars was Rear Admiral Bucknam who continued the tradition of American links with the Ottoman Navy by heading it. Ransford D. Bucknam was born in Canada but had been working in America and, according to some sources, became an American citizen. He had arrived from Philadelphia on board a gunboat built for the Turks and stayed on to captain it for them. During the First Balkan War, he engineered a sortie through the Dardanelles by a Turkish cruiser, which sank a number of Greek ships and shelled coastal fortifications. He died in 1915.

In World War I, the Ottoman Empire was allied to the Central Powers. The United States, led by President Woodrow Wilson, declared war on the Ottoman Empire in April 1917, shortly after our declaration against Germany. US forces were not deployed against Turkey, although the American reporter Lowell Thomas launched his career by promoting Lawrence of Arabia's campaign against the Turks in the Middle East (see "Saudi Arabia").

American marines landed in Turkey shortly after the war. In 1919, during the Greek occupation of the city, marines from the USS *Arizona* were sent to guard the US consulate in Istanbul. And again in 1922, troops were landed in Smyrna (Izmir) to protect US citizens and property there.

Actually, we could have ended up running part of Turkey after World War I because there was discussion among the Allies about forming an American mandate in the area.

In 1923, Kemal Atatürk became the first president of the Republic of Turkey. He is widely regarded as the founder of the modern secular Turkish state.

Turkey remained neutral during most of World War II, and consequently, Istanbul became a hotbed of espionage intrigue. The OSS maintained an important base in neutral Istanbul during the Second World War as Axis and Allied espionage and diplomatic services all plotted to bring Turkey over to their side in the war. The question of chrome shipments to Germany was also vital with Germany wanting them to continue and the Allies keen to stopping them. In the end, Turkey joined the Allied side in February 1945 and became a founding member of the United Nations.

The Turkish ambassador to the United States, Mehmet Munir Ertegun, died suddenly in Washington, DC, near the war's end. A naval task force built around the USS *Missouri* was charged with returning the ashes of the ambassador to his home country. US authorities wished to send a message to Stalin to deter any aggressive moves against Turkey. The battleship was received with great pomp and circumstance by the Turks.

Mutual fear of the Soviet Union brought Turkey and the United States into a close partnership after the war, and that was reflected in extensive military links that have remained, with occasional hiccups, to the present. What follows will, therefore, be only a summary of some of the key elements in those links.

During the Korean War, a Turkish brigade served on the peninsula alongside American forces.

Turkey joined the NATO alliance in 1952 at the same time as Greece. And a formal defense treaty with us followed in 1959.

The Jupiter missiles, which may have been Khrushchev's strategic target in the first place, were removed from Turkey after the Cuban missile crisis in 1962.

The US military has made use of a range of facilities in Turkey. The most important is Incirlik Air Base, first used by the United States in 1951. It has long been a major US base and remains the home of the USAF 39th Air Wing with about five thousand personnel. It was a key base for operations during the crisis in Lebanon to the south of Turkey in 1958 (see "Lebanon"). The USN has made use of the major Turkish naval base at Aksaz. Turkey is also home to some key NATO headquarters.

Links between Turkey and the United States were strained in the 1970s due to the conflict in Cyprus and subsequent arms boycotts authorized by the US Congress but gradually recovered.

During the Gulf War, sorties were flown from Incirlik into Iraq. After the Gulf War, the base played a central role in efforts to help the Kurds in northern Iraq and in enforcing the no-fly zone over northern Iraq. In 2001, it again played a crucial role in facilitating air operations in Afghanistan. And 2001 was a big year for Incirlik in another sense. After *Ocean's Eleven*'s premiere in Los Angeles, George Clooney, Matt Damon, Andy Garcia, Brad Pitt, and Julia Roberts, with director Steven Soderbergh visited the base.

In 2003, the Turkish parliament, with grave concerns over the future of the Kurds, denied use of Turkish territory for the Allied campaign against Saddam's Iraq. Links between the United States and Turkey experienced something of a brief chill.

A battery of Patriot missiles is currently deployed in Turkey to defend against possible attacks from Syria, and Turkey and the United States have cooperated to help the Syrian opposition in its attempts to force Assad out of power in Syria. A flood of refugees has streamed across the border into Turkey fleeing the Syrian civil war.

Turkish troops have served in Afghanistan. Turkey has received billions of dollars of military aid from the United States, and its military has made use of a lot of American-designed equipment. Turkish forces regularly take part in military exercises alongside US personnel.

TURKMENISTAN

TURKMENISTAN IS NEXT DOOR TO AFGHANISTAN. The country's capital, Ashgabat, is a twin sister city of Albuquerque, New Mexico.

One of the Doolittle crews from 1942 eventually ended up in Ashgabat, then a Soviet city, after they had landed in the east of the USSR. They tried to persuade the Soviet authorities to let them go but, in the end after many months, gave up. Instead, they bribed a local smuggler to take them across the border to Iran, where they then contacted a British consul who arranged to get them across the border to British-controlled territory in what is now Pakistan.

During the Soviet era, some surveillance flights operated over Turkmenistan. For instance on September 10, 1957, a US flight that set off from Adana in Turkey flew over the Caspian coastline city that was then called Krasnovodsk and is now Türkmenbaşy in independent Turkmenistan.

Post-independence links seem to have been mainly small scale. For instance, at one stage, we gave the Turkmenistani border guards one or two patrol boats to help build a navy.

Turkmenistan has a policy of positive neutrality but has allowed humanitarian overflights and ground transport to deliver humanitarian aid in the Afghan crisis and refueling privileges for humanitarian flights.

TUVALU

AN ISLAND NATION LOCATED IN THE PACIFIC, Tuvalu lies between Hawaii and Australia.

Americans were some of the earliest Western visitors to the islands and to the people who lived there. For instance, in 1841, the United States

Exploring Expedition under Charles Wilkes called in. However, Germany and Britain were the main Western powers competing for control of the area, and in the end, the British won control of Tuvalu.

In 1892, the islands became a British protectorate. This meant that after the attack on Pearl Harbor, the people in control of the island were on the same side as us.

During World War II, Tuvalu was just a little beyond the reach of the Japanese. Even though they occupied nearby islands, including Nauru to its northwest, the Pacific being a big, big place made "nearby" too far.

Still, we sent men and military equipment to what is now Tuvalu to defend it from Japanese attack. Marines arrived in October 1942. But we didn't want just to defend the islands; we wanted also to use them as a base from which to attack the Japanese. Patrol torpedo boats (PTs) were based there; a seaplane ramp was built and airfields as well. On April 20, 1943, B-24 Liberators from Funafuti bombed Nauru. In response, the Japanese bombed Funafuti and did so again on a number of other occasions. The Funafuti airfield became the location for the headquarters of the USAAF VII Bomber Command. Tuvalu also became a staging post for operations as US forces began to push westwards onto Japanese-held islands, and as the war moved west, inevitably Tuvalu's strategic significance became less.

Tuvalu became independent from Britain in 1978, and in 1979, we recognized Tuvalu's possession of a number of islands we had previously claimed.

The Funafuti airfield is now Funafuti International Airport.

Today we have only minor military contact with Tuvalu. For instance, in 2009, Tuvalu had someone graduating from the Asia-Pacific Center for Security Studies' Comprehensive Security Responses to Terrorism Course in Honolulu.

UGANDA

LOCATED IN CENTRAL AFRICA, Uganda, home of the mighty Buganda Kingdom, is about the size of Oregon.

American soldier and explorer Charles Chaillé-Long was sent to Uganda by the Egyptians on a political mission in the late nineteenth century.

In 1976, the infamous Idi Amin was in power there, and the daring Israeli raid on Entebbe to free the hostages took place on the day of our bicentennial celebration, July 4. Following that, the USS *Ranger* Carrier

Battle Group (CVBG) was ordered to move into position to prevent any attempts by the Ugandan military to take revenge on Kenya for enabling the Israeli aircraft to access Uganda. And again the year after, when Amin placed restrictions on Americans in Uganda, another carrier battle group, this time the *Enterprise* CVBG was positioned off the Kenyan coast until Amin lifted travel restrictions.

Significantly, the Israeli raid on Entebbe became one of the US Special Forces' models for subsequent operations, such as the assassination of Osama bin Laden in 2011.

Amin was forced from power in 1979, and in 1986, Yoweri Museveni became president.

Military training that we were giving to the Uganda People's Defense Force was cut off in 2000 because of Ugandan activities in the neighboring Democratic Republic of the Congo, but some links were restarted in 2003.

Uganda has faced some major challenges during its history, and one of those has been the Lord's Resistance Army (LRA).

Beginning in 1986, the brutal, rebel LRA started operations in the north and east of Uganda frequently murdering and kidnapping civilians and causing huge numbers to flee. The war against the LRA has dragged on and on, though the LRA has been steadily ground down and forced into smaller and smaller areas.

In May 2010, President Obama signed into law the Lord's Resistance Disarmament and Northern Uganda Recovery Act. As a consequence, US Special Forces have deployed to Entebbe, near Uganda's capital, Kampala, to train Ugandan forces and assist them in the hunt for the Lord's Resistance Army, and in particular, for its leader, Joseph Kony, accused of multiple crimes. In March 2014, US Special Forces with US aircraft were again dispatched to assist in the hunt.

The US military has also developed other links with the Ugandan military.

For instance, the Uganda military has played the leading part in AMISOM in Somalia. Uganda has had thousands of troops fighting extreme Islamists in Somalia, and a significant number have been killed or wounded.

We've given a lot of help to Uganda with its peacekeeping role. For example, in October 2013, a Uganda People's Defense Force military police company was being trained at the Peace Support Operations Training Center at Singo, about an hour and a half north of Kampala, in counterterrorism operations directed at the extreme Islamists of al-Shabaab.

UKRAINE

A COUNTRY THAT'S BEEN IN THE NEWS quite a lot recently, Ukraine has Belarus to its north, Russia to its north and east, Moldova and Romania to its south, and Slovakia and Poland to its east. Its location among assorted competing power blocs ensured significant chunks of its territory were devastated in both world wars and the local conflicts that sprang out of them. And generally, Ukraine's history in the twentieth century includes plenty of tragedy. So far, the twenty-first century has not been nearly as tough for Ukraine as the previous century was, but major political disputes continue.

The first time we focused on a military crisis in Ukraine was during the Crimean War in the 1850s. Though the war was fought in a number of places, the prime area of battle was the Crimea in the south of Ukraine (then part of the Russian Empire) where British, French, and Turkish forces landed in an attempt to take the key Russian port of Sebastopol. Much of the US public sympathized with the Russians. Some Americans asked the Russians about the possibility of the Americans acting as privateers, and in Kentucky, three hundred riflemen volunteered to fight alongside the Russians. Nothing came of either of those ideas, but thirty-five American doctors did volunteer to go to Russia, and the majority of them actually worked in the Crimea. Captain George B. McLellan, later a general on the Union side in the Civil War, also led a US military delegation to Russia to study the fighting.

Americans were involved again in the area during the bitter fighting at the end of World War I. In particular, the American volunteer pilots of the Kościuszko Squadron (see "Poland") played a significant part in the fighting against Soviet forces on territory that is now part of Ukraine, for instance, in the defense of what was then called Lwów. Between the wars, Lwów was Polish but is now Lviv in Ukraine.

During World War II, a lot more American flyers arrived in Ukraine, but this time they were there on a more official basis. Under Operation Frantic, Stalin allowed the US Air Force to establish three bases in Ukraine, at Poltava Airfield, Myrhorod Airfield, and Pyriatyn Airfield, with the aim of enabling US bombers to reach targets deeper inside Nazi-held territory than they had previously been able to. The operation was marred by suspicion from some Soviet authorities, and Allied advances elsewhere reduced the value of the basic plan, but still, it's a fascinating example of US-Soviet cooperation during World War II.

Such military cooperation was, of course, soon to come to an end as World War II drew to a close and the Cold War started. And with the start of the Cold War, once again, some US eyes were focused on the possibility of involvement in Ukraine.

In the period after World War II, some in the CIA wanted to use Ukrainian nationalists against the Soviets. So, starting in 1949, the CIA began training Ukrainians in the West and then parachuting them into Ukraine. The first team took in a C-47 on September 5, 1949, and landed in the dark near Lviv. Unfortunately, the Soviets captured most of the Ukrainians sent in, sometimes forcing them to send fake messages to the CIA requesting more personnel and supplies be sent. After five years, the CIA finally gave up on the operation.

Assorted other Cold War covert and surveillance operations in and over Ukraine were to follow, and then in the aftermath of the collapse of the USSR, American planes returned openly to Ukraine. In October 1991, for instance, US Air Force aircraft airlifted 146 tons of medical and relief supplies into the capital, Kiev.

The United States has since developed a number of military links with the Ukrainian military. For instance, we've given training to Ukrainian personnel, and the Ukrainian military has joined in assorted exercises alongside US forces. USN ships have visited Ukraine, and Ukraine has helped with operations in Kosovo, Iraq, and Afghanistan. In 2008, the United States implemented the US-Ukraine Charter on Strategic Partnership. The California National Guard is partnered with Ukraine.

In February 2014, in a conflict that started over whether Ukraine should be closer to the EU and America or closer to Russia, mass demonstrations in Ukraine forced President Yanukovych out of power after he accepted a Russian deal. During the confused situation that then developed, extra US marines were sent to Kiev to help guard the US embassy there. Subsequently, Russian troops took control of Crimea, and pro-Russian fighters became active in parts of eastern Ukraine. In response, among other actions, the United States sought to reassure countries in the region that felt threatened. For instance, it sent F-15s to Lithuania and US troops to take part in exercises in neighboring countries, while at the same time launching a diplomatic campaign against the Russian move.

UNITED ARAB EMIRATES

BRITISH INFLUENCE WAS STRONG in the Persian Gulf area for a long time (and to a certain extent still remains strong), so our military links with the United Arab Emirates (UAE) prior to the 1980s and 1990s were somewhat limited.

However, during World War II, the USAAF did use the RAF base at Sharjah on air-transport routes.

We got closer to the UAE during the Tanker War element of the Iran-Iraq War and during the Gulf War to liberate Kuwait. And we've established military links on the ground, in the air, and at sea. For example, the UAE has bought huge amounts of US military equipment. It has worked closely with the United States on counterterrorism and sent personnel to help liberate Kuwait and to serve in Afghanistan. The UAE participates with CENTCOM in exercises such as Eagle Resolve.

US aircraft have operated out of a number of bases in the UAE. For example, US A-10 Thunderbolt aircraft operated out of Sharjah Airport during Operation Desert Shield and Storm, and we've had aircraft based at Al Dhafra. Aircraft from the base have aided US operations in both Iraq and Afghanistan.

Jebel Ali has port facilities that have been very useful to the USN, and the UAE has hosted a large number of USN ships.

UNITED KINGDOM

OUR SPECIAL RELATIONSHIP WITH BRITAIN endures to this day. The United Kingdom is our pugnacious mother country that has itself invaded or fought conflicts in nearly 90 percent of the world's countries.

After two world wars, we have a long record of fighting alongside the Brits, and today the UK is one of our firmest allies. But that doesn't mean we haven't fought them in the past, most notably during the American Revolution and the War of 1812. And even though most of the fighting took place in or around North America, not all of it did.

In fact, pretty much as soon as we'd declared independence from Britain, we set off to invade it. In April of 1778, Captain John Paul Jones, the founding father of the American navy, and the crew of the *Ranger*, an

18-gun sloop, arrived in Britain and, unlike many Americans today, they weren't there to visit Westminster Abbey or have a taste of fish and chips.

Jones selected the English fishing village of Whitehaven on the Irish Sea as his target; Whitehaven was Britain's third busiest seaport at that time. He would attempt to destroy its shipping and to kidnap the Earl of Selkirk. The harbor of Whitehaven was protected by two small forts. In the early hours of April 23, 1778, he and about forty volunteers from his crew scaled the fortress wall. They kicked in the door of the guardhouse. The sleeping guards surrendered without a shot. Jones's men proceeded to spike about thirty-six guns of the battery with nails driven into the cannon's touchholes. About half of his crew then broke into a local tavern and proceeded to get drunk. This caused a commotion and roused the local townspeople. Jones beat a hasty retreat and set fire to a merchant ship, a collier (that's a coal ship and nothing to do with Lassie) named *Thompson*.

Soon after, the *Ranger* sailed about twenty miles to enter the bay off St. Mary's Isle. Jones took about a dozen men armed with cutlasses and muskets to a Georgian manor house owned by the Fourth Earl of Selkirk. Jones soon discovered that the earl was not in residence and could not be kidnapped. Instead, he demanded the silver plate be delivered up. The loot was hauled back to the *Ranger*. Shortly after, the 18-gun *Ranger* fought and captured the 20-gun *Drake* of the Royal Navy in an action that Jones described as "warm, close and obstinate."

Jones's raid on Whitehaven had succeeded in bringing the American Revolution "home to their own doors," as he put it. The English press was incensed. The *London Public Advertiser* asked, "When such ravages are committed all along the coast, by one small privateer, what credit must it reflect on the First Lord of the Admiralty?" No one was killed or even injured in the Whitehaven raid, but insurance rates doubled. The Whitehaven raid lasted about two and a half hours and was an even shorter invasion than the assassination of Osama bin Laden in Pakistan in 2011. Jones had second thoughts about the silver he stole from the Earl of Selkirk and later returned most of the loot.

Herman Melville described John Paul Jones as "a mixture of gentleman and wolf." At a critical moment in his later sea battle with the *Serapis*, when called upon to surrender, Jones uttered the immortal words, "I have not yet begun to fight." Jones is buried with full honors at the US Naval Academy chapel in Annapolis.

In 1797, in pretty much the last major hostile invasion of British soil, an Irish-American, Colonel William Tate, led La Légion Noire ashore near Fishguard in Wales as part of revolutionary France's attempt to attack

Britain. It wasn't a huge success for Tate or his troops or revolutionary France. Three days after landing, they surrendered.

The United States would fight its last war with Britain in the War of 1812, which ran from 1812 to 1815. Canada was invaded, the American navy won its first major laurels, the White House was burned by the British, and Andrew Jackson led the Americans to victory at the Battle of New Orleans. There were assorted actions at sea, and USN sailors, like the crew of the USS *President* under Commodore Rodgers, once again cruised British waters, but there was to be nothing quite like the Whitehaven invasion of 1778.

The next American invasions of Britain were to be much friendlier all round. This little book isn't the place to cover in full depth the well-documented close friendship and military partnership that developed between the United States and the UK after the nineteenth century, playing a key role in winning two world wars. Instead, we'll just touch on a few stories from those years.

In December 1910, President William Taft sent twenty-six battleships of the Atlantic fleet to visit Portsmouth. Admiral William Sims of the USN gave a prophetic speech at London's Guildhall: "There is a strong blood-tie between our two peoples ... If the time ever comes when the British Empire is seriously menaced by an external enemy, it is my opinion that you may count upon every man, every dollar, and every drop of blood of your kindred across the seas."

World War I was the first war in which Americans joined the British and fought alongside as allies. Many doughboys transited through Britain on their way to the Western Front.

But it was in World War II that the friendship between the Brits and us became particularly close. Even prior to the attack on Pearl Harbor on December 7, 1941, many Americans volunteered to serve with the British forces in the war against Hitler. The American Eagle squadrons, made up of American pilots, served with distinction in the Battle of Britain in 1940. And on the home front, expatriate bankers, teachers, and others formed the 1st American Squadron of the Home Guard, ready to battle Hitler's panzers, if they ever landed in Britain

Meanwhile CBS correspondent Edward R. Murrow delivered live broadcast reports from London during the blitz that stimulated great sympathy for the besieged British people.

And after the Japanese attack, there was a flood of American military personnel to Britain as we prepared to fight and defeat Nazi tyranny.

Brave people from all the US services went to Britain to battle for victory over Hitler.

US troops were immediately dispatched to help garrison Northern Ireland.

Brave USN crews, for instance, defied the U-boats and escorted vital convoys across the Atlantic to ports in the UK, like Liverpool, Southampton, and Plymouth. The critical battle of the North Atlantic could not have been won without the assistance of the USN.

The USAAF used Britain as an unsinkable aircraft carrier from which to bomb Nazi Germany. Many thousands of American aircrew flew from Britain to face the perils of Luftwaffe fighters, anti-aircraft fire, and in general, flying long distances with, by today's standards, unsophisticated equipment. Among them was Jimmy Stewart, drafted by the US Army in 1940 and the first major American movie actor to serve in the war. He piloted over twenty combat missions in a B-24, bombing Axis targets while stationed at two RAF bases in Norfolk (Tibenham and Old Buckenham). He won two Distinguished Flying Crosses and the Croix de Guerre.

Dwight Eisenhower became the supreme Allied commander and planned for the invasion of occupied France from his offices at 20 Grosvenor Square in London (now a construction site). You can find a statue of Ike adorning Grosvenor Square today.

Like their counterparts stationed in other English-speaking countries during the war, the American soldiers in Britain squeezed in some fun. Famously "overpaid, oversexed, and over here," the young American soldiers, armed with Coca-Cola, chocolate, cigarettes, and nylon stockings, often proved very attractive. There were an estimated seventy thousand GI brides and nine thousand out-of-wedlock war babies born as a result of this friendly invasion.

Two months before D-Day, Tommy Hitchcock was killed while flying an experimental P-51 Mustang. Hitchcock, an accomplished polo player and former member of the Lafayette Escadrille in World War I, had championed the introduction of Rolls Royce engines into the iconic American fighter enabling it to escort bombers all the way to Berlin. He is buried at the Cambridge-American Cemetery.

And then there was D-Day. It was in Britain that the American contingent for Operation Overlord assembled and from Britain that they bravely landed on June 6, 1944, in one of the most dramatic military operations ever.

But all this bravery came at a heavy price. Visit the American Memorial Chapel in St. Paul's Cathedral, and you will find the Roll of

Honor, which lists over twenty-eight thousand American dead from World War II that served in Britain. A page from this book is turned every day. The American Battle Monuments Commission maintains two cemeteries in England, located in Brookwood and Cambridge.

On August 12, 1944, Lieutenant Joseph Kennedy Jr., the son of Ambassador Kennedy and older brother to JFK, was killed in Operation Aphrodite when the bomb his modified B-24 Liberator was towing exploded shortly after takeoff. He is memorialized on the wall of the missing at the Cambridge-American Cemetery.

In 1949, Britain became a founding member of NATO, and our long military partnership with Britain continues to this day. There are, for instance, still US military bases in Britain.

The latest major IRA campaign, the Provisional IRA Campaign, lasted from 1969 until the last ceasefire in 1997 and was mainly fought in Northern Ireland with occasional campaigns on the UK mainland. Support from some Americans, particularly financial, was a significant factor in assisting Irish Republican activity during this period.

Although the British Empire is gone, Britain still controls small territories (British Overseas Territories) around the world, and we've had major involvement with a few of them. For instance, with the Turks and Caicos Islands, American loyalists fleeing after the Revolution settled on the Caicos Islands.

And what about Bermuda? Famous for shorts and that triangle, but this British Overseas Territory is a site of assorted US military bases. And of another British territory, the Falkland Islands, scene of such controversy and Argentinian and British invasions in 1982? Yep, we've invaded them as well. In 1831, after three American ships had been seized in a dispute over seal hunting and fishing, the USS *Lexington* descended on the Falklands, seized seven prisoners, and charged them with piracy.

In 1999, the town of Whitehaven in Cumbria officially pardoned John Paul Jones and the Freedom of the Harbor was granted to the USN. In 2003, the USS *Leyte Gulf*, a missile cruiser, paid a friendly visit to Whitehaven.

URUGUAY

URUGUAY'S SOCCER TEAM won the first ever FIFA World Cup in 1930. And they won it again in 1950!

We recognized Uruguayan independence in 1836, but things didn't always run smoothly in Uruguay's early decades, and soon the United States found itself sending in the marines.

In November 1855, the US sloop *Germantown* landed marines in Montevideo to protect US property and interests while somebody was attempting a revolution.

And in January 1858, it was a similar situation, only this time it was the US frigate *St. Lawrence* landing the men.

Ten years later, in February 1868, we were there again, this time with six US warships landing marines and seamen in Montevideo.

In the late nineteenth century and early twentieth century, Uruguay had military links with a number of different countries, for instance, buying warships from, among others, Britain, Germany, and Italy.

Relations between the United States and Uruguay got a little friendlier during World War I. Uruguay didn't actually declare war on Germany, but it did break off links with the Germans in October 1917, one of only a few South American countries that did, and it then proceeded to lease to the United States Emergency Fleet Corporation for use during the war eight German vessels it had seized.

Things lapsed a little between the wars, but our military influence in the country began to rise again as in some other South American countries during World War II. Uruguay did not actually declare war on the Axis Powers until 1945, but it had already given some assistance to the Allies, including over convoys. In 1944, the cruiser USS *Memphis* and the destroyer USS *Somers*, plus Vice Admiral Jonas H. Ingram, arrived in Montevideo to express our support for Uruguay in a tense situation that had developed with Argentina. And later in 1944, we sent lend-lease arms to Uruguay. Responsibility for such things as US air transport to Montevideo, mapping, and watching out for Axis espionage in Uruguay in this period came under US Army Forces in the South Atlantic.

During the Cold War period, the United States was concerned about the activities of left-wing groups in Uruguay, and the full extent of US attempts to aid in crushing these is still a matter of much controversy. The 1960s saw the rise of the Tupamaro left-wing urban guerrillas and ruthless police attempts to combat them. This was followed from 1973 on by a military government that took its campaign against left-wings groups even further by committing a range of major human rights abuses.

In recent years, although we haven't been deeply militarily involved in Uruguay, we have had some links. For instance, we have provided military assistance to the Uruguayan military with equipment and training. The USN still visits Montevideo sometimes, and the Connecticut National Guard is partnered with Uruguay.

UZBEKISTAN

THE SECOND BIGGEST CITY IN UZBEKISTAN IS SAMARKAND, home of the mighty conqueror Timur, or Tamerlane. He was no slouch at invading, leading invasions of China, Russia, and India.

In the chaos after the Russian Revolution, we had an official representative, Roger Tredwell, operating in Tashkent (the capital of Uzbekistan) and the surrounding area. The Soviets used to accuse him of working with the British to try to topple Bolshevik power in the area, but he was really there to assess the political and commercial situation, particularly in respect of cotton, then of potential importance for the German war machine.

Uzbekistan has recently become of interest to the United States because of the usual matters, like energy sources and narcotics, and because of Afghanistan.

Our involvement in Afghanistan is the reason we had a major base in Uzbekistan. Between 2001 and 2005, we had a base at the Karshi-Khanabad Air Base, which acted as a major US support base for operations in Afghanistan. Eventually, however, US comments on Uzbek human rights matters led to a rift, and the Uzbeks forced the closure of the US base.

Nevertheless bilateral agreements were signed with the Uzbeks in 2012, which have started to help US policies in Afghanistan once again.

The Mississippi National Guard has been partnered with Uzbekistan since 2012.

VANUATU

AN ISLAND NATION IN THE SOUTH PACIFIC, Vanuatu used to be called the New Hebrides during the colonial period, at least by part of the colonial administration. The islands had a rather unusual colonial arrangement. They were ruled by both Britain and France in a condominium. Yep. With two different administrations. So they were also known as the Nouvelles Hébrides.

This could have caused a major problem after the German invasion of France in 1940, because the new Vichy authorities in France wanted the French administration on the Nouvelles-Hébrides to comply with their pro-German policies at a time when the British authorities on the New Hebrides were committed to fighting them (if any German military had turned up there). Fortunately, the French administration on the Nouvelles-Hébrides instead declared for the Free French.

The New Hebrides/Nouvelles-Hébrides were conveniently located for a number of key sites like Guadalcanal, so in 1942, we turned up and built on the island of Espiritu Santo various airstrips, a seaplane base, and assorted support facilities. In July 1942, B-17s flying from there attacked the Japanese trying to complete the airfield on Guadalcanal.

Another bomber base was added in 1943, and we built a major sea base there. Huge numbers of Americans passed through the island during the war. The Japanese would attack the island occasionally by sea or by air.

We also built airstrips and a naval operating base on nearby EfateIsland.

Vanuatu became independent and took its new, single name in 1980.

In recent years, the US military has had minor involvement with Vanuatu. Training links exist. And as part of Pacific Partnership 2011 to help with assorted humanitarian projects and actions, the amphibious transport dock ship USS *Cleveland* was the first USN vessel to visit Vanuatu since the period of the World War II bases.

VATICAN CITY

THE VATICAN CITY, A SMALL ENCLAVE WITHIN ROME that is home to the pope and the central administration of the Catholic Church, is an actual state. It's not a member of the UN, but it does have observer status there.

It's hard to say whether we've ever invaded the Vatican. We've never been at war with the Vatican, and during the Italian campaign, as President Franklin Roosevelt himself emphasized, Allied airmen had been specifically informed of the borders of the Vatican City and instructed to make sure none of their bombs fell within its borders. However, the pope owns a variety of sites in Italy, which are outside the borders of the Vatican City but have extraterritorial status. Some of these were a lot closer to the action than the Vatican itself. For instance, the pope specifically complained about Allied bombs falling in the vicinity of the papal summer residence at Castel Gandolfo and killing refugees there.

And, when American troops of the Fifth Army liberated Rome in June 1944, some of them ventured into the Vatican. A photograph, for instance, shows Fifth Army's Lieutenant General Mark Clark parked right outside the front of St. Peter's in a jeep with another jeep behind him and American soldiers in full uniform, including helmets. And just over a week after the capture of Rome, on June 12, after a number of instances of armed Allied vehicles entering St. Peter's Square inside the Vatican City, barricades were having to be put up across the end of the Bernini colonnade to prevent any further such occurrences. If it was any kind of invasion, though, it was an entirely friendly one. On June 12 alone, the pope is said to have received fifteen hundred Allied troops.

VENEZUELA

VENEZUELA WAS A SPANISH COLONY until it gained independence in 1811.
In 1812, in the Battle of La Guaira outside the Venezuelan port of La Guaira, the *Saratoga* under Captain Charles W. Wooster defeated the British ship *Rachel*. Although subsequently, HMS *Fawn* turned up and recaptured *Rachel*.

The Venezuelan crisis of 1902-03 was precipitated by Cipriano Castro's default on its debts to European creditors. The German and British Royal Navies collaborated to blockade Venezuelan ports. The Kaiser's warships sank Venezuelan gunboats and fired on her coastal forts.

Initially, some American officials expressed sympathy for the European actions. Vice President Teddy Roosevelt even said, "If any South American country misbehaves toward any European country, let the European country spank it."

After William McKinley's assassination, however, TR was sworn in as president on September 14, 1901, and in his new capacity, he began to see the Venezuelan debt crisis in a very different light. The rise of an imperial Germany was a potential threat to US interests. Around the turn of the century, the Kaiser's Hochseeflotte strategists had drawn up plans for a German invasion of the United States and a bombardment of New York City. The US naval attaché in Berlin learned in 1898 that the Monroe Doctrine was regarded as "gall and wormwood" in German circles.

There was also a small direct connection between Germany and Venezuela. Germans from Baden had founded a small colony in 1843 at Colonia Tovar in Venezuela.

TR began to champion the longstanding Monroe Doctrine, but he went much further by introducing the Roosevelt Corollary. This insisted not only that European nations should stay out of the Western hemisphere but also that the United States had a right to intervene in Central and South America to protect lives and property.

TR famously said, "Speak softly and carry a big stick." The USN was TR's biggest stick, and Admiral Dewey, the victor of the Battle of Manila Bay (see "Philippines") was his greatest naval commander.

In 1903, Teddy Roosevelt sent USN forces under the command of Dewey from their Caribbean base in Puerto Rico towards the coast of Venezuela. The crisis was resolved when the European nations changed their approach and the matter was referred for arbitration at the international court at The Hague. The court ruled in favor of preferred rights for the European powers.

During World War I, oil was discovered in Venezuela. The country remained neutral, though USN warships, such as the *Dubuque*, visited Venezuelan ports after the US entry into the war.

Venezuela remained neutral for most of World War II, though it did supply oil to the Allies and did declare war on Germany in February 1945. Venezuela also received lend-lease from the United States

We got a bit nervous about things in Venezuela in 1958. In January 1958, during a period of violence in Caracas, marines were sent on board the USS *Des Moines* to the waters off Venezuela to be ready to launch an evacuation if necessary. But it never actually happened.

And in May 1958, Vice President Nixon's motorcade was attacked by a crowd as it was travelling from the airport to Caracas. Assorted troops and vessels were put in place to be ready to intervene if necessary, but they weren't needed, and Nixon left Venezuela a couple of days later.

At times, Venezuela received substantial amounts of US military assistance, but the arrival of Hugo Chavez as president was going to change all that. Chavez served as president of Venezuela from 1999 until he died in 2013. Chavez aligned himself with Iran and was a fierce critic of US imperialism. After 9/11, Chavez disapproved of the Global War on Terrorism and repeatedly accused the United States of plotting to launch a coup or invasion of his country.

Terrible floods hit Venezuela at the end of 1999, and over a hundred US troops rushed to help relief efforts, but when the United States prepared to send two vessels with military engineers and equipment to help, Chavez objected, saying he didn't want US troops in the country.

In 2002, he accused the United States of being involved in the attempt by Pedro Carmona to topple him.

It is ironic to note that, in spite of Chavez's often fiery rhetoric, Venezuela may be a country where the US military never launched a major open intervention except in 1903 when TR supported Venezuelan sovereignty.

VIETNAM

AS WELL AS TRAGEDY, BRAVERY, HOPE, AND DISASTER, the story of America's military involvement in Vietnam is rich in irony.

Among other ironies, a war that ultimately led to the unification of Vietnam very nearly tore America apart. The American commitment to an Asian war was driven largely by European strategic concerns. In November 1963, the JFK administration agreed "not to thwart" a coup attempt against South Vietnam's President Diem that resulted in his brutal assassination in an armored personnel carrier in Saigon. A few weeks later, JFK himself would be assassinated in Dallas. During the Vietnam War, Americans would reach for the heavens in landing a man on the moon, but Americans would also plumb the depths of hell with the horrors of the My Lai massacre. It was a "living room war" that played out on color television and has been turned into countless films, although it may be best known for its haunting black-and-white still photographs.

Of course, Americans, and American military personnel had visited the region long before the 1960s. For instance, in 1832, Edmund Roberts, a US diplomat on board the USS *Peacock* arrived in Da Nang Bay in an attempt to a negotiate a trade deal with the emperor in Huế. Much talking at cross-purposes achieved little. In April 1836, Roberts returned, and the process was pretty much repeated, though it did not help negotiations that Roberts was extremely ill at the time and died soon afterwards. It was not a great start to our links with Vietnam.

And things weren't about to get much better. In 1845, the USS *Constitution* arrived at Da Nang. Some dispute exists about whether much actual firing took place, but Captain John Percival, believing a French bishop's life to be in danger, landed with marines to investigate and then took hostage local VIPs and seized a number of ships before finally releasing them and departing.

Increasingly through the nineteenth century, France became the colonial power in what is now Vietnam. By contrast, after initial difficulties, the United States began to become something of an inspiration for those in the area wanting freedom.

In 1919, a young Ho Chi Minh, or Nguyen Ai Quoc as he was then known, while working as a busboy at the Hotel Ritz in Paris and inspired by President Woodrow Wilson's vision of a world in which people would be granted freedom and self-determination, wrote a letter to try to interest the American delegation in his vision of greater freedom for the "Annamite people." A note still exists from an American official acknowledging receipt of his letter, but it is impossible now to tell who may have seen it. Certainly little, if anything, seems to have been done about it.

In 1940, France was conquered by Hitler and replaced with a Vichy government. Japan immediately seized on French weakness to expand their empire. On September 23 of 1940, the Japanese occupied the northern portion of Indochina. By July of 1941, Imperial Japanese forces would occupy the whole of Indochina. FDR demanded that Japan withdraw from China and Indochina; Japan responded with the attack on Pearl Harbor. On December 10, 1941, Japanese warplanes based on airbases in Indochina would sink the Royal Navy's battleships *Prince of Wales* and *Repulse* opening the door to the Japanese conquest of Singapore.

The Japanese occupation had devastating consequences for the Vietnamese people. In 1945 alone, a famine that swept through Japanese-occupied Indochina killed an estimated two million people—more than ALL the combat deaths on ALL sides in America's ten-year-long Vietnam War.

And we were supporting the cause of the Vietnamese. FDR believed that French colonial rule in Indochina was "rotten to the core." He even told Stalin at a 1943 conference that "after a hundred years of French rule in Indochina, the inhabitants are worse off than they had been before."

Near the end of the Second World War, an OSS team, code-named "Deer," parachuted into northern Vietnam to make contact with Ho Chi Minh and aid him in his struggle against the Japanese. We supplied arms, and OSS medics treated Ho Chi Minh for malaria and dysentery. A Deer team member, Henry Prunier of Worcester, Massachusetts, even instructed Vo Nguyen Giap on how to throw grenades. As we've already noted, our involvement with Vietnam has not been short of irony.

On September 2, 1945, Ho Chi Minh declared Vietnam's independence from France in quoting words familiar to Americans: "All men are created equal. They are endowed by their creator with certain unalienable Rights; among these are Life, Liberty and the pursuit of happiness ..." American P-38s flew above Hanoi that day in apparent celebration.

Ho Chi Minh went on to list a set of grievances with the French colonial administration that very much paralleled the colonists' objections to George III. Ho Chi Minh sought more OSS assistance and American recognition. However, due to Cold War politics, that would not be possible.

For all that, Ho Chi Minh was not George Washington. He was an ardent revolutionary and a dedicated Communist who looked to Moscow and Beijing for support.

In 1923, Ho Chi Minh had begun studying at the Stalin School in Moscow, which was also known as the Communist University of the Toilers of the East. He also became a disciple of Mao's theory of guerilla insurgency. During what the Vietnamese call the American War, the Soviet Union would supply billions of dollars' worth of military equipment and around three thousand military advisers and technicians to the radar and surface-to-air missile batteries. The Vietnamese would refer to the Russians as "Americans without dollars." From 1965 to 1970, more than three hundred thousand Chinese troops would assist with air defense, construction, and military training. North Vietnamese Air Force pilots would also receive training in the People's Republic of China.

The Soviet Union officially recognized Ho Chi Minh's government in February 1950. On receipt of this news, Dean Acheson, President Harry Truman's secretary of state, declared that this "should remove any illusions as to the 'nationalist' nature of Ho Chi Minh's aims, and reveal Ho in his true colors as the mortal enemy of native independence in Indochina."

It is also ironic, particularly given the subsequent lack of European support for America's commitment to the Vietnam conflict, that the American impulse to defend South Vietnam grew to some extent out of European strategic considerations. In the post-war years, the Soviet Union enjoyed an overwhelming superiority in conventional ground forces in Europe.

Given these realities, it was understandable that the United States felt compelled to support and cultivate its links with France, a major European ally, in spite of our many misgivings about the virtues of French colonialism.

For four years beginning in 1950, the United States would provide massive amounts of money to finance the French effort to maintain its control of Indochina. In 1954, the French were lured into battle at Dien Bien Phu, which one French official compared to a chamber pot (*vase de nuit*), with the beleaguered French at the bottom and the Viet Minh shooting from the rim above. The desperate French requested American air support. Dwight Eisenhower sent ten planes and two hundred mechanics—about half of what they had asked for.

The first American casualty of the Vietnam War took place at the grim siege of Dien Bien Phu. The great photo-journalist Robert Capa stepped on a landmine while covering the battle in 1954. Born in Budapest, Hungary, he is buried today in Amawalk, New York.

When the Joint Chiefs of Staff recommended the use of atomic weapons to aid the French forces trapped at Dien Bien Phu, Ike dismissed them out of hand. Nor would the overall commander who had been in charge of the D-Day landings sanction an escalation of conventional US ground forces in Vietnam.

However, things were about to change. JFK did not share Ike's compunctions about the use of ground forces in Vietnam. At his inaugural address in 1961, President Kennedy declared, "Let every nation know, whether it wishes us well or ill, that we shall pay any price, bear any burden, meet any hardship, support any friend, oppose any foe to assure the survival and the success of liberty." Few in the audience that day recognized that the price paid for liberty in Southeast Asia would be so very high. The number of US military advisers based in South Vietnam soared during JFK's administration from eight hundred in 1961 to over sixteen thousand by the end of 1963.

Colin Powell was one of the US advisers deployed by JFK, first arriving in Vietnam on Christmas Day in 1962. He would later win the Soldier's Medal for helping to rescue his commanding officer from a crashed helicopter. Later still, Powell would champion reforms in the US military and the "Powell Doctrine," which insisted upon overwhelming force and massive public support as preconditions for any use of military force—a direct departure from the gradualism of LBJ's strategic efforts in Vietnam.

LBJ almost immediately began to escalate US involvement in Vietnam. In August 2, 1964, the USS *Maddox* came under attack by North Vietnamese torpedo boats in the Gulf of Tonkin. The *Maddox*, which had been gathering intelligence at the time, sank one torpedo boat and was unharmed. Just a few days later, the US Congress passed the Tonkin Gulf Resolution that gave broad discretionary war powers to Johnson's administration.

From 1964 to 1968, LBJ dramatically escalated the US military presence deploying over five hundred thousand troops in Vietnam. American bombers struck North Vietnam while American ground forces fought a counterinsurgency against the Viet Cong in South Vietnam. General William Westmoreland was in command, but LBJ was in the driver's seat. LBJ, who with his team loved to micromanage the war, famously said, "Those boys can't hit an outhouse without my permission."

In spite of the bombing and declaration of free-fire zones, the Viet Cong guerilla war throughout South Vietnam continued while supplies flowed down the six-hundred-mile length of the Ho Chi Minh trail, which snaked through Cambodia and Laos.

The Vietnamese words for "country" and "water" happen to be exactly the same — "*nuoc*." Vietnam was, in many respects, an aquatic war. The American war in Vietnam began with a skirmish in the Gulf of Tonkin and ended with the suffering of the boat people. In between, a major riverine war was fought with river patrol boats and swift boats in an attempt to interdict the VC occupied Mekong delta.

In January of 1968, the North Vietnamese and the Viet Cong launched the Tet Offensive during the holiday, which marked the Vietnamese Lunar New Year. Eighty-four thousand troops launched simultaneous attacks across the country. The American embassy compound in Saigon was penetrated by a squad of VC commandos. US forces and their allies repulsed the attacks and launched punishing counterattacks, which claimed many enemy lives. The US Marines, for example, prevailed in the Battle of Huế.

On February 1, the execution of a VC prisoner by the South Vietnamese national police chief, Nguyen Ngoc Loan, was captured on film. The prisoner had recently killed one of Loan's best friends, but the footage and the black-and-white photograph was another propaganda victory for Hanoi.

In spite of Tet being a US military victory, it was also a shattering political defeat for the Johnson administration. In a historic departure, the ubiquity of television sets and the introduction of color television had brought the violence of Vietnam into most American homes with devastating political repercussions. The CBS news anchor Walter Cronkite declared that the United States was "mired in stalemate."

My father, Robert Kelly, a television broadcaster from Sacramento, went to Vietnam on a press junket sponsored by the US military in the late 1960s. He was particularly impressed with a tae kwan do demonstration put on by our South Korean allies. He would later send multiple local reporters and camera crews from KCRA TV to cover Vietnam.

In March of 1968, Westmoreland was relieved of command and replaced by Creighton Abrams. On March 31, LBJ stunned Americans with the announcement that he would halt the bombing campaign and suspend his own re-election bid.

On March 16 of 1968, Lieutenant William Calley ordered the slaughter of over one hundred unarmed women and children at My Lai. That same year, the Communists massacred civilians at Hue killing over three thousand and receiving far less media attention than My Lai.

In the fall of 1968, Richard Nixon, promising "peace with honor" in Vietnam and an end to the draft, was elected president. Nixon accelerated the process of Vietnamization—turning greater operational responsibility to the South Vietnamese army (ARVN). Nixon also recognized that the rate of US soldiers killed per year (peaking at 16,899 in 1968) was politically unsustainable. Nixon expanded the war in Cambodia and Laos to interdict supplies along the Ho Chi Minh Trail (for more, see "Cambodia" and "Laos"), but he also began significant drawdowns in US forces deployed in Vietnam.

Sometime between Tet and the final US withdrawal of forces in 1973, the US military very nearly reached its breaking point. There was a pronounced breakdown in morale and discipline. The number of reported fragging incidents (soldiers murdering fellow soldiers and especially officers, often with fragmentation grenades) peaked in 1971 at a rate of 333 per year. In 1969, about forty-five hundred sailors in the USN were discharged for drug use—thirty times more than in 1965.

On May 4, 1970, national guardsmen in Ohio fired on anti-war protestors at Kent State University killing four students. The anti-war movement exploded across the country.

Captain Jack Coughlin, a friend of mine (Chris Kelly's) is a retired USAF C-130 pilot who flew "jingle runs" from Taiwan to Saigon in the 1970s. On a jingle run, his plane would be loaded with three wooden pallets; each pallet contained ten million dollars in stacks of twenty-dollar bills. This was how the USG helped to fund the South Vietnamese government. Similar tactics would be employed much later in Afghanistan and Iraq.

In December of 1972, Nixon launched a "Christmas Bombing" offensive that shattered North Vietnamese antiaircraft defenses and may have forced Hanoi to reopen negotiations at the stalled Paris peace talks.

In 1973, Nixon made good on his pledge to end the draft, and the United States transitioned to an all-volunteer military. On March 29 of that year, the last US troops were withdrawn from the Republic of Vietnam. Also that year, the Watergate scandal ended with Nixon's historic resignation from the presidency. The scandal paralyzed the US government and made air support for Thieu's Saigon government an impossibility.

On April 30, 1975, Saigon finally fell as Operation Frequent Wind evacuated hundreds of Americans and just over four thousand Vietnamese to safety aboard US ships offshore. A much-anticipated bloodbath did not occur, but thousands were sent into re-education camps while many more attempted to flee Vietnam by boat. Tens of thousands of "boat people" died of exposure while attempting to flee Vietnam.

Today the names of 58,193 Americans who died while serving in Vietnam line the wall of the Vietnam Veterans memorial in Washington, DC. Our own casualty totals, however, were dwarfed by those of the Vietnamese people. Over two hundred thousand ARVN, about 1.1 million Communist troops (Viet Cong and People's Army of Vietnam), and about two million Vietnamese civilians were killed, all told about 3.3 million Vietnamese.

After the war was over, both sides claimed that it had been a noble effort. President Ronald Reagan dedicating the Vietnam memorial in Washington, DC, said, "We remember the devotion and gallantry with which all of them ennobled their nation as they became champions of a noble cause." General Giap, who had been taught to throw hand grenades by an American, said in the 1990s that, for his side, the war had been a noble sacrifice.

The Vietnam War left a devastating legacy of loss and injury both in the United States and in Vietnam, but in recent years, some links between the US military and Vietnam have restarted.

In 2003, the USS Vandegrift, a guided missile frigate, paid the first USN visit to Ho Chi Minh City (formerly Saigon) since 1975. A new era in links between America and Vietnam began that has included, for instance, humanitarian visits by US military personnel to Vietnam.

YEMEN

YEMEN LIES ON THE RED SEA and the Gulf of Aden. South Yemen gained its independence from Britain in 1967. North and South Yemen were united in 1990.

Some of our military personnel had already become acquainted with the area during World War II when our air force used the RAF base at Khormaksar in Yemen on air-ferry and transport routes.

During the 1960s, we had some peripheral military involvement in the area. For instance, during a civil war there in 1962, the USN boosted its presence in the Red Sea and established patrols to protect US interests and prevent the war spreading. During key months of fighting there in 1965, we had a naval presence keeping an eye on things. When North Yemen was fighting South Yemen in 1979, the *Constellation* Carrier Battle Group was ordered into the area. And during a civil war in South Yemen in 1986, USN vessels, including the USS *La Salle*, were present so they could launch an evacuation if necessary. In 1994, six USAF planes did evacuate hundreds of Americans and others from Yemen during yet another period of civil war.

However, with the appearance of al-Qaeda, we started taking a serious military interest in Yemen. Our involvement has become so extensive there over the years that we can give details only of a selection of incidents here.

In 1999, al-Qaeda planned an attack on a USN destroyer, *The Sullivans*, named after four Irish-American brothers who died on a ship in World War II. They planned to place a boat laden with explosives alongside. Their plans were foiled when the boat sank.

The USS *Cole*, a guided missile destroyer, was anchored in Aden's harbor in Yemen on October 12, 2000. A fiberglass fishing boat pulled up alongside and detonated killing seventeen and wounding more.

After the 9/11 attack, President Saleh visited Washington, DC, to lobby for a four-hundred-million-dollar aid package to combat terrorism near the Horn of Africa. Aware that Qaed Salim Sinan al-Harethi was behind the attack on the *Cole*, Saleh permitted deployment of US Special forces in Yemen in 2002. In November 2002, Al Harethi, whose cell phone had been tracked by the NSA, was killed by a missile fired at his Toyota Land Cruiser. Saleh was furious when news of the strike was leaked to the news media and forbade the use of Predator drones.

After the US embassy in Yemen was attacked on September 17, 2008, by Islamic terrorists and sixteen people were killed, General David Petraeus dramatically expanded the US presence in the country.

Actions were taken against suspected al-Qaeda with USN cruise missiles and bombs delivered by USMC *Harrier* jump jets. On December 17, 2009, several USN Tomahawk cruise missiles armed with cluster bombs hit a desert camp in Abyan. There were several civilian casualties.

On January 15, 2010, an air strike killed at least five al-Qaeda members in the mountains of Northern Yemen.

In May 2010, a missile strike killed Jaber al-Shabwani, who was the deputy governor of Ma'rib Province.

In May of 2011, the United States again authorized armed drones over Yemen that flew from bases in Djibouti and Ethiopia. An American citizen, Anwar al-Awlaki, was a cleric who preached violent jihad on YouTube and the Internet. On September 30, he was killed in Yemen. His sixteen-year-old son, Abdulrahman al Awlaki, born in Denver, went to Yemen looking for his father. On October 14, 2011, he was killed while sitting at a restaurant in Azzan.

Since the beginning of 2011, one source reckons at least eighty drone strikes have taken place.

In December of 2013, the Yemeni Parliament, concerned about who exactly is being killed by all the strikes and under what circumstances, passed a non-binding motion to ban drone strikes from its territory.

ZAMBIA

A N AMERICAN SCOUT AND WARRIOR, Frederick Russell Burnham, was one of the earliest Westerners to ride into what is now the African nation of Zambia, and in the process, he helped create the industry that is still a main part of Zambia's economy. Admittedly he was an American working for Britons at the time he rode into what's now Zambia, but he was still an American.

Frederick Russell Burnham had, to put it mildly, an unusual career. He was born on a Sioux reservation and experienced the Old West, getting sucked into the Pleasant Valley War and working as a tracker for the US military before heading for Africa. There, he got involved in the British drive into the African interior, seeing service in the First and Second

Matabele Wars. Somewhere in the middle of it all, he was sent on an exploration mission in what is now Zambia. While there, he saw locals wearing copper jewelry and evidence of copper deposits. The copper industry would later become massive in Zambia. Burnham went on to the Klondike Gold Rush, the Second Boer War, and to teach some of his tracking and scouting methods to Baden-Powell, the founder of the world scouting movement.

After Zambia became independent from Britain in 1964, Kenneth Kaunda was president from 1964 all the way through to 1991. Under Kaunda, Zambia eventually became a one-party state, and Kaunda adhered to a broadly left political stance. In terms of Cold War positioning, he became a leading member of the Non-Aligned Movement. As such, it was unlikely that Zambia under Kaunda was ever going to have major links with the US military.

However, in recent years, we have had more military involvement with Zambia. For instance, Zambia hosted Africa Endeavor 2013, AFRICOM's annual communications exercise, and we've helped the Zambian military develop their expertise in international peacekeeping missions. Oh, and Zambia was one of eleven nations taking part in the Seventh World Military Golf Championship at Naval Air Station Jacksonville in 2012.

ZIMBABWE

A COUNTRY IN SOUTHERN AFRICA, Zimbabwe is home to the impressive African archaeological site, Great Zimbabwe.

The British took colonial control of what is now Zimbabwe in the late nineteenth century, and until 1965, what was then called South Rhodesia and eventually just Rhodesia was administered by Britain. However, in 1965, the white minority inside Rhodesia, who basically controlled the country, declared a unilateral declaration of independence from Britain with the intention of avoiding majority, democratic rule.

Britain rejected the declaration and asked the UN to impose sanctions on the Rhodesian government, which it did, but Britain took no military action against the country. Our government supported the UK government's position and maintained the same approach, even as a bitter guerrilla war broke out and two organizations, ZAPU (Zimbabwe African People's Union) and Mugabe's ZANU (Zimbabwe African National

Union), that received support from other African countries and from Communist Bloc countries attempted to oust the Rhodesian government.

Some American individuals did, however, travel to Rhodesia to join the Rhodesian armed forces fighting the guerrillas, and some of them died there.

In 1976, Governor Ronald Reagan announced that if he were ever elected president he would consider sending a limited number of American troops to Rhodesia to help implement a peace deal. And in 1977, the US government (not Reagan's at that time) did help Britain come up with the Anglo-American proposals and, subsequently, British efforts to end the war, which eventually led to the Lancaster House peace agreement, the end of the war, and the international recognition of an independent Zimbabwe. A force from Britain was sent to supervise the ceasefire, and four American air force planes, a C-5 Galaxy and C-141 Starlifters, flew into Zimbabwe as part of the airlift to establish the mission.

However, early American hopes of close links with the new nation eventually faded, as the United States accused Mugabe of authoritarianism and human rights abuses. Consequently, any recent military links with Zimbabwe have been of a very, very minor nature.

However, in 2009, opposition leader Morgan Tsvangirai became prime minister in a unity government and met Barack Obama at the White House. In June 2012, eleven African defense attachés visited AFRICOM's headquarters in Stuttgart to find out more about how AFRICOM operates. One of those defense attachés was Zimbabwe's.

CONCLUSION

THE AMERICAN EAGLE, with arrows in one talon and an olive branch in the other, has spread its wings around the world. We have invaded or fought in nearly half the world and been militarily involved with almost all the rest.

Some around the world see us a high-tech global bully. Many nations in South and Central America perceive us as the "Colossus of the North." Others, on the other hand, remember that Americans have made countless sacrifices for other people's freedom. As we've seen in this book, the United States has made some mistakes, but it has also done many brave and good things.

One thing is not in doubt, though. The price of war is high. If you question this point, visit a cemetery and pay your respects to those who have sacrificed all for the sake of our liberty. Or pay a visit to a VA hospital full of wounded warriors. America has won many battles in many foreign lands, but the Duke of Wellington reminds us, "Nothing except a battle lost can be half as melancholy as a battle won."

The American Battle Monuments Commission's well-manicured graveyards help to mark the borders of what Jefferson described as the "Empire of Liberty."

The United States is an amazing country, and its history is an amazing story. Over the centuries, it has come to occupy a unique place in world history, and the world is different because of it.

In the twenty-first century, the United States will, no doubt, face major new challenges to its power and influence around the world, and it will face new demands to fight in the name of justice and freedom.

We can't know what the future will hold, and we can't predict how this and future generations of Americans will deal with that future, but we can know that they build on a solid foundation of bravery, daring, and sacrifice.

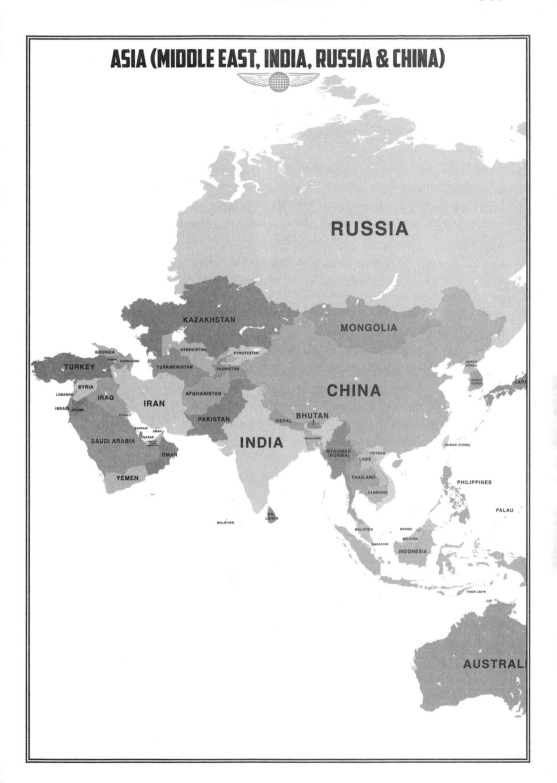

ASIA (MIDDLE EAST, INDIA, RUSSIA & CHINA)

RUSSIA

KAZAKHSTAN

MONGOLIA

GEORGIA

TURKEY

UZBEKISTAN

KYRGYZSTAN

AZERBAIJAN

NORTH KOREA

SYRIA

TURKMENISTAN

TAJIKISTAN

SOUTH KOREA

JAPAN

LEBANON

IRAQ

AFGHANISTAN

CHINA

ISRAEL JORDAN

KUWAIT

IRAN

PAKISTAN

NEPAL

BHUTAN

BAHRAIN

OMAN

QATAR

UNITED ARAB EMIRATES

SAUDI ARABIA

INDIA

BANGLADESH

TAIWAN (CHINA)

OMAN

MYANMAR (BURMA)

VIETNAM

LAOS

YEMEN

THAILAND

PHILIPPINES

CAMBODIA

PALAU

SRI LANKA

MALDIVES

MALAYSIA

BRUNEI

MALAYSIA

SINGAPORE

INDONESIA

TIMOR LESTE

AUSTRALI

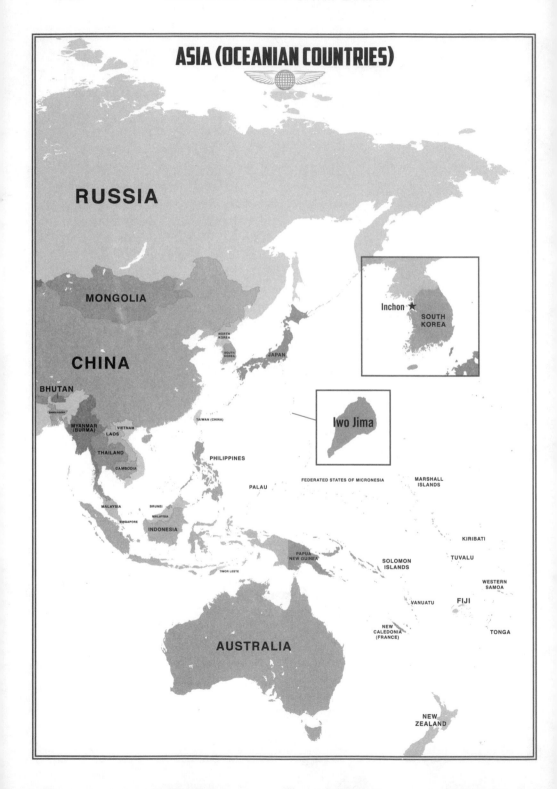

ASIA (OCEANIAN COUNTRIES)

RUSSIA

MONGOLIA

CHINA

BHUTAN

BANGLADESH

MYANMAR (BURMA)

LAOS

VIETNAM

THAILAND

CAMBODIA

NORTH KOREA

SOUTH KOREA

JAPAN

TAIWAN (CHINA)

PHILIPPINES

Inchon ★ SOUTH KOREA

Iwo Jima

FEDERATED STATES OF MICRONESIA

MARSHALL ISLANDS

PALAU

MALAYSIA

BRUNEI

MALAYSIA

SINGAPORE

INDONESIA

TIMOR LESTE

PAPUA NEW GUINEA

SOLOMON ISLANDS

KIRIBATI

TUVALU

WESTERN SAMOA

VANUATU

FIJI

NEW CALEDONIA (FRANCE)

TONGA

AUSTRALIA

NEW ZEALAND

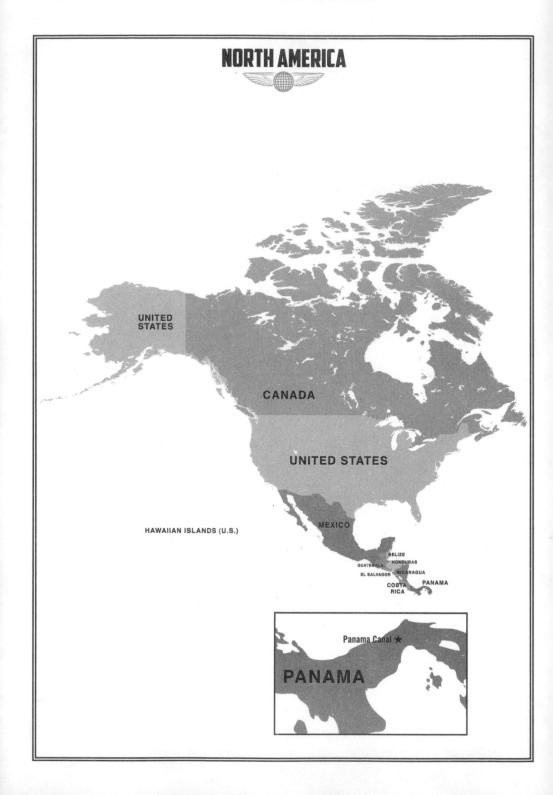

NORTH AMERICA

UNITED STATES

CANADA

UNITED STATES

HAWAIIAN ISLANDS (U.S.)

MEXICO

BELIZE
GUATEMALA   HONDURAS
EL SALVADOR   NICARAGUA
COSTA   PANAMA
RICA

Panama Canal ★

PANAMA

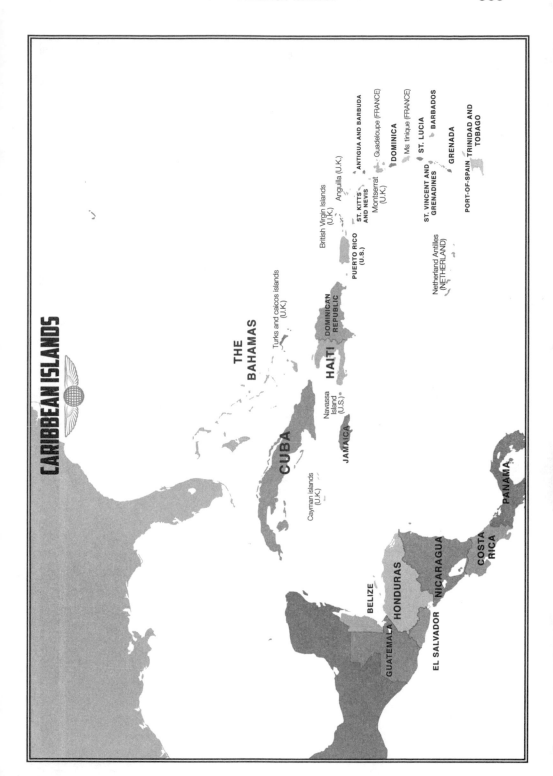

CARIBBEAN ISLANDS

THE BAHAMAS

Turks and calcos islands (U.K.)

CUBA

Cayman islands (U.K.)

JAMAICA

Navassa Island (U.S.)

HAITI

DOMINICAN REPUBLIC

British Virgin Islands (U.K.)

Anguilla (U.K.)

PUERTO RICO (U.S.)

ST. KITTS AND NEVIS

Montserrat (U.K.)

ANTIGUA AND BARBUDA

Guadeloupe (FRANCE)

DOMINICA

Ma tinique (FRANCE)

ST. LUCIA

BARBADOS

ST. VINCENT AND GRENADINES

GRENADA

Netherland Antilles (NETHERLAND)

PORT-OF-SPAIN TRINIDAD AND TOBAGO

BELIZE

GUATEMALA

HONDURAS

EL SALVADOR

NICARAGUA

COSTA RICA

PANAMA

SOUTH AMERICA

VENEZUELA

GUYANA

FRENCH GUIANA
(FRANCE)

SURINAME

COLOMBIA

ECUADOR

PERU

BRAZIL

BOLIVIA

PARAGUAY

URUGUAY

ARGENTINA

CHILE

SUMMARY OF INVASION AND MILITARY INVOLVEMENT BY COUNTRY

Country	Invaded or Fought In	Military Involvement
Afghanistan	Yes	Yes
Albania	Yes	Yes
Algeria	Yes	Yes
Andorra	No	No
Angola	No	Yes
Antigua and Barbuda	No	Yes
Argentina	No	Yes
Armenia	No	Yes
Australia	No	Yes
Austria	Yes	Yes
Azerbaijan	No	Yes
The Bahamas	Yes	Yes
Bahrain	No	Yes
Bangladesh	No	Yes
Barbados	No	Yes
Belarus	No	Yes
Belgium	Yes	Yes
Belize	No	Yes
Benin	No	Yes
Bhutan	No	No
Bolivia	No	Yes
Bosnia and Herzegovina	Yes	Yes
Botswana	No	Yes
Brazil	Yes	Yes
Brunei	Yes	Yes
Bulgaria	Yes	Yes
Burkina Faso	No	Yes
Burma	Yes	Yes
Burundi	No	Yes
Cambodia	Yes	Yes

Country	Invaded or Fought In	Military Involvement
Cameroon	No	Yes
Canada	Yes	Yes
Cape Verde/Cabo Verde	No	Yes
Central African Republic	No	Yes
Chad	No	Yes
Chile	No	Yes
China	Yes	Yes
Colombia	Yes	Yes
Comoros	Yes	Yes
Costa Rica	Yes	Yes
Croatia	Yes	Yes
Cuba	Yes	Yes
Cyprus	No	Yes
Czech Republic	Yes	Yes
Denmark	Yes	Yes
Djibouti	No	Yes
Dominica	No	Yes
Dominican Republic	Yes	Yes
Democratic Republic of the Congo	No	Yes
Ecuador	No	Yes
Egypt	Yes	Yes
El Salvador	No	Yes
Equatorial Guinea	No	Yes
Eritrea	No	Yes
Estonia	No	Yes
Ethiopia	No	Yes
Fiji	No	Yes
Finland	No	Yes
France	Yes	Yes
Gabon	No	Yes
The Gambia	No	Yes
Georgia	No	Yes
Germany	Yes	Yes
Ghana	No	Yes

Country	Invaded or Fought In	Military Involvement
Greece	Yes	Yes
Grenada	Yes	Yes
Guatemala	Yes	Yes
Guinea	No	Yes
Guinea-Bissau	No	Yes
Guyana	No	Yes
Haiti	Yes	Yes
Honduras	Yes	Yes
Hungary	Yes	Yes
Iceland	No	Yes
India	No	Yes
Indonesia	Yes	Yes
Iran	Yes	Yes
Iraq	Yes	Yes
Ireland	Yes	Yes
Israel	No	Yes
Italy	Yes	Yes
Ivory Coast	Yes	Yes
Jamaica	No	Yes
Japan	Yes	Yes
Jordan	No	Yes
Kazakhstan	No	Yes
Kenya	No	Yes
Kiribati	Yes	Yes
Kosovo	Yes	Yes
Kuwait	Yes	Yes
Kyrgyzstan	No	Yes
Laos	Yes	Yes
Latvia	No	Yes
Lebanon	Yes	Yes
Lesotho	No	Yes
Liberia	Yes	Yes
Libya	Yes	Yes
Liechtenstein	No	No

Country	Invaded or Fought In	Military Involvement
Lithuania	No	Yes
Luxembourg	Yes	Yes
Macedonia	Yes	Yes
Madagascar	No	Yes
Malawi	No	Yes
Malaysia	Yes	Yes
The Maldives	No	Yes
Mali	No	Yes
Malta	No	Yes
Marshall Islands	Yes	Yes
Mauritania	No	Yes
Mauritius	No	Yes
Mexico	Yes	Yes
Micronesia	Yes	Yes
Moldova	No	Yes
Monaco	Yes	Yes
Mongolia	No	Yes
Montenegro	Yes	Yes
Morocco	Yes	Yes
Mozambique	No	Yes
Namibia	No	Yes
Nauru	Yes	Yes
Nepal	No	Yes
Netherlands	Yes	Yes
New Zealand	No	Yes
Nicaragua	Yes	Yes
Niger	No	Yes
Nigeria	No	Yes
North Korea	Yes	Yes
Norway	Yes	Yes
Oman	No	Yes
Pakistan	Yes	Yes
Palau	Yes	Yes
Panama	Yes	Yes

Country	Invaded or Fought In	Military Involvement
Papua New Guinea	Yes	Yes
Paraguay	Yes	Yes
Peru	No	Yes
Philippines	Yes	Yes
Poland	Yes	Yes
Portugal	No	Yes
Qatar	No	Yes
Republic of the Congo	No	Yes
Romania	Yes	Yes
Russia	Yes	Yes
Rwanda	No	Yes
Samoa	Yes	Yes
San Marino	Yes	Yes
São Tomé and Príncipe	No	Yes
Saudi Arabia	No	Yes
Senegal	No	Yes
Serbia	Yes	Yes
Seychelles	No	Yes
Sierra Leone	No	Yes
Singapore	Yes	Yes
Slovakia	Yes	Yes
Slovenia	Yes	Yes
Solomon Islands	Yes	Yes
Somalia	Yes	Yes
South Africa	No	Yes
South Korea	Yes	Yes
South Sudan	No	Yes
Spain	No	Yes
Sri Lanka	No	Yes
St. Kitts Nevis	No	Yes
St. Lucia	No	Yes
St. Vincent and the Grenadines	No	Yes
Sudan	Yes	Yes
Suriname	No	Yes

Country	Invaded or Fought In	Military Involvement
Swaziland	No	Yes
Sweden	No	Yes
Switzerland	No	Yes
Syria	No	Yes
Tajikistan	No	Yes
Tanzania	No	Yes
Thailand	Yes	Yes
Timor-Leste (East Timor)	Yes	Yes
Togo	No	Yes
Tonga	No	Yes
Trinidad and Tobago	No	Yes
Tunisia	Yes	Yes
Turkey	No	Yes
Turkmenistan	No	Yes
Tuvalu	No	Yes
Uganda	No	Yes
Ukraine	No	Yes
United Arab Emirates	No	Yes
United Kingdom	Yes	Yes
Uruguay	No	Yes
Uzbekistan	No	Yes
Vanuatu	No	Yes
Vatican City	No	Yes
Venezuela	No	Yes
Vietnam	Yes	Yes
Yemen	Yes	Yes
Zambia	No	Yes
Zimbabwe	No	Yes
Subtotal invasions/ military involvement	84	191
Subtotal no invasions/ militaryinvolvement	110	3
Total countries	194	

GLOSSARY

ABDACOM: American British Dutch Australia Command in World War II

Abwehr: German military intelligence organization from 1921 to 1944

AEF: American Expeditionary Forces; deployed to Europe in World War I

AFRICOM: United States Africa Command

AMISOM: the African Union Mission in Somalia

ANZUS: Australia, New Zealand, United States Security Treaty

ARVN: South Vietnamese army

AWACS: Airborne Warning and Control System

BDF: Belize Defence Force

bluejacket: Enlisted sailor in the US Navy, typically used as part of a landing party

CENTCOM: United States Central Command

Cereus Network: Balkan spy ring based out of Istanbul, Turkey in World War II

CVBG: carrier battle group

DEA: Drug Enforcement Administration

DEFCON 3: Defense readiness condition three; USAF's level of alert, ready to mobilize in fifteen minutes

ECOMOG: Economic Community of West African States Monitoring Group

ELN: National Liberation Army, Colombia

EOKA: National Organisation of Cypriot Fighters

EUCOM: US European Command, in the US Department of Defense

EUF: European Union Force

FDR: Franklin Delano Roosevelt

FARC: Revolutionary Armed Forces of Colombia

Fenian: Brotherhood of Irish in the United States that supported Irish nationalism and independence from Great Britain

FIFA: Fédération Internationale de Football Association

filibuster: Derived from the Dutch vrijbuiter, or "freebooter"; one who forms part of an unauthorized military expedition

FMLN: Farabundo Marti National Liberation Front; guerilla group in El Salvador

FNLA: National Front for the Liberation of Angola

FRELIMO: Mozambique Liberation Front

Great White Fleet: Nickname for the USN battle fleet ordered by President TR to circumnavigate the globe and carried out between 1907 and 1909. Their hulls were painted white.

Hump: The flight path over the eastern Himalayas that was used by the Allies to resupply Nationalist China from India during World War II

HSV: high speed vessel

ICU: Islamic Courts Union of Somalia

IED: improvised explosive device

IFOR: Implementation Force; NATO-led peacekeeping force in Bosnia Herzegovina

INTERFET: International Force for Timor-Leste,

IRA: Irish Republican Army

ISIS: Islamic State in Iraq and the Levant

JFK: John Fitzgerald Kennedy

KLA: Kosovo Liberation Army

LBJ: Lyndon Baines Johnson

Lend-Lease Act: Passed in 1941, this provided massive aid to Allied countries engaged in fighting the Axis. For example, 13 million pairs of winter boots were supplied to the Soviet Union's Red Army in World War II.

LRA: Lord's Resistance Army

LSU: Louisiana State University

MI6: Military Intelligence, Section 6; the Secret Intelligence Service for the British government

Magic: US decryption of Japanese wartime codes

METO: Middle East Treaty Organization

MPLA: Popular Movement for the Liberation of Angola

MRAP: mine-resistant ambush-protected vehicle

NSA: National Security Agency

Neutrality Acts: Passed in 1794 and 1818, legislation that made it illegal for American citizens to fight in wars not backed by the US government

OAS: Organization of American States

Operation Christmas Drop: USAF training mission and humanitarian airlift that provides clothing, toys, and construction materials, as well as needed supplies in times of disasters, around the world

OSS: Office of Strategic Services, the forerunner to the CIA, also known as "Oh So Social" due to the number of Ivy Leaguers that served.

PACOM: United States Pacific Command based in Honolulu from 1947 to the present

philhellene: Lover of Greek culture

PLO: Palestine Liberation Organization

PT boat: patrol torpedo boat

RAAF: Royal Australian Air Force

RAF: Royal Air Force

RENAMO: Mozambican National Resistance

RUF: Revolutionary United Front

RYPE: "Grouse" in Norwegian; OSS operation in Nazi-occupied Norway in 1945.

Scud: Tactical ballistic missiles developed by the Soviet Union and exported to nations such as Iraq

SEATO: Southeast Asia Treaty Organization

SFOR: Stabilization Force; NATO-led peacekeeping force in Bosnia Herzegovina

SOE: Strategic Operations Executive of the UK; Churchill asked them to "set Europe ablaze."

SOUTHCOM: US Southern Command, in the US Department of Defense covering Central and South America

SPLA: Sudan People's Liberation Army

SS: Schutzstaffel; black-uniformed internal security force of Nazi Germany with absolute loyalty to Hitler

SS-Panzer: Hitler's personal body guard

subchaser: Small boats aimed at chasing submarines

SWAPO: South West Africa People's Organization

TR: Teddy Roosevelt

TFG: Transitional Federal Government (in Ethiopia)

TLDF: Timor-Leste Defence Forces

TSCTP: Trans-Sahara Counterterrorism Partnership

UAE: United Arab Emirates

Ultra decrypts: High-quality Allied intelligence project that decoded encrypted communications by the Axis powers during World War II; headquartered at Bletchley Park, London.

UNITA: National Union for the Total Independence of Angola

UNTAG: United Nations Transition Assistance Group, Namibia

USAAC: United States Army Air Corps, the forerunner of the USAAF, from 1926 until June 20, 1941

USAAF: United States Army Air Forces, the forerunner of the USAF, which was part of the US Army until the creation of the USAF in 1947.

USAF: United States Air Force

USCG: United States Coast Guard

USCGC: United States Coast Guard cutter

USG: United States government

USMC: United States Marine Corps

USN: United States Navy

USO: United Services Organisation that provides services and entertainment for US military forces

WMD: weapons of mass destruction

INDEX